CAMBRIDGE STUDIES IN MEDIEVAL LITERATURE

The Evolution of Arthurian Romance

This study is intended as a contribution to both reception history, examining the medieval response to Chrétien's poetry, and genre history, surveying the evolution of Arthurian verse romance in French. It describes the evolutionary changes taking place between Chrétien's *Erec et Enide* and Froissart's *Meliador*, the first and last examples of the genre, and is unique in placing Chrétien's work, not as the unequalled masterpieces of the whole of Arthurian literature but as the starting-point for the history of the genre, which can subsequently be traced over a period of two centuries in the French-speaking world. Beate Schmolke-Hasselmann's study was first published in German in 1985, but her radical argument that we need urgently to redraw the lines on the literary and linguistic map of medieval Britain and France is only now being made available in English.

Beate Schmolke-Hasselmann has published widely on Arthurian subjects, Tristan, hagiographic legends, courtly literature, iconography and Middle English lyrics. She is based in Germany.

CAMBRIDGE STUDIES IN MEDIEVAL LITERATURE

General editor
Alastair Minnis, University of York

Editorial board
Patric Boyde, University of Cambridge
John Burrow, University of Bristol
Rita Copeland, University of Minnesota
Alan Deyermond, University of London
Peter Dronke, University of Cambridge
Nigel Palmer, University of Oxford
Winthrop Wetherbee, Cornell University

This series of critical books seeks to cover the whole area of literature written in the major medieval languages – the main European vernaculars, and medieval Latin and Greek – during the period *c.* 1100–1500. Its chief aim is to publish and stimulate fresh scholarship and criticism on medieval literature, special emphasis being placed on understanding major works of poetry, prose and drama in relation to the contemporary culture and learning which fostered them.

Recent titles in the series

28 Charlotte Brewer *Editing 'Piers Plowman': The Evolution of the Text*
29 Walter Haug *Vernacular Literary Theory in the Middle Ages: The German Tradition in its European Context*
30 Sarah Spence *Texts and the Self in the Twelfth Century*
31 Edwin Craun *Lies, Slander and Obscenity in Medieval English Literature: Pastoral Rhetoric and the Deviant Speaker*
32 Patricia E. Grieve *'Floire and Blancheflor' and the European Romance*
33 Huw Pryce (ed.) *Literacy in Medieval Celtic Societies*
34 Mary Carruthers *The Craft of Thought: Meditation, Rhetoric, and the Making of Images, 400–1200*
35 Beate Schmolke-Hasselmann *The Evolution of Arthurian Romance: The Verse Tradition from Chrétien to Froissart*

A complete list of titles in the series can be found at the back of the book

The Evolution of Arthurian Romance

The Verse Tradition from Chrétien to Froissart

BEATE SCHMOLKE-HASSELMANN

Translated by Margaret and Roger Middleton

CAMBRIDGE
UNIVERSITY PRESS

CAMBRIDGE UNIVERSITY PRESS
Cambridge, New York, Melbourne, Madrid, Cape Town, Singapore, São Paulo

Cambridge University Press
The Edinburgh Building, Cambridge CB2 2RU, UK

Published in the United States of America by Cambridge University Press, New York

www.cambridge.org
Information on this title: www.cambridge.org/9780521411530

First published 1998
This digitally printed first paperback version 2006

A catalogue record for this publication is available from the British Library

ISBN-13 978-0-521-41153-0 hardback
ISBN-10 0-521-41153-X hardback

ISBN-13 978-0-521-02565-2 paperback
ISBN-10 0-521-02565-6 paperback

Originally published in German as *Der arturische Versroman von Chrestien bis Froissart*
by Max Niemeyer, Tübingen, 1980 and © Beate Schmolke-Hasselmann 1980.

Contents

Preface to the translation

BY ROGER MIDDLETON

Margaret did not readily talk about herself or her work, and the preface that she had prepared for her book was short in the extreme. Had she lived to see the task completed I think I should have persuaded her to be a little more expansive about some of the technicalities, but not about her own contribution. Her translation of the German is at the heart of the work, but it was by no means the whole of her effort. She was never content to deal simply with the words, she was always determined to understand the author's ideas and the subject to which they referred. She did not translate literally, but she had an intuitive way of grasping whole thoughts and expressing them in natural English. Yet at the same time she would also take great care to confirm the accuracy of the result.

She took immense care also with quotations and references. Except for the rare cases where items proved to be unobtainable, all quotations, whether from Old French texts or from modern scholars were checked in minute detail against their originals, and the text printed here is that of those sources. Bibliographical details were similarly confirmed, and every reference traced to its source to confirm its accuracy. Margaret simply took all this for granted.

Even during the few months of her final illness she continued the work of revision. The translation itself was finished by this time and had already been approved, but she still devoted herself to checking points of detail and searching for minute inconsistencies in her work and mine, such as between two occurrences of the same Old French quotation or between footnote and bibliography.

My own involvement in the project was progressive. At the beginning I had casually agreed to give moral support, including help with word processing on the computer and with matters concerning Old French literature where a knowledge of the subject might resolve some difficulty in translating the German, and eventually to read the finished text (as Margaret had always done for whatever I had written) simply to have a second opinion on the English as part of the final proof-reading. Not very onerous tasks, scarcely enough to warrant a mention in a preface let alone a place on the title page. My role soon changed, however, when it was decided to include translations of all Old French quotations and to provide camera-ready copy. Both these tasks clearly fell much more within my experience than Margaret's, and I was duly called upon to participate.

Ever anxious to diminish her own role it was Margaret who insisted that the book should appear as a joint production. Not, of course, in the sense that we had contributed in equal measure, but in the sense that each had contributed what was necessary. Our skills were exactly complementary, and the book depended upon their being brought together.

Sadly, in the end, Margaret did not see the work to its conclusion. She was taken ill in the middle of 1995 and died just after Christmas. She knew at that stage that she had done what was needed for the book to be completed, and however much it was the joint effort she thought it to be, it was in many other ways and will remain 'Margaret's book'.

The final division of labour was that Margaret translated everything that was in German or modern French, checked the quotations and references, and converted the original Bibliography to its present form. I translated the quotations from Old French (and the few examples of other languages), converted the German Index, extracted the Supplementary Bibliography from the fully documented footnotes of the Foreword supplied by Keith Busby, and converted Margaret's word processing to the finished camera-ready copy. That said, however, we both read each other's work and contributed accordingly.

In translating the Old French I have attempted to take account of any interpretation expressed or implied in the German. Consequently, where the Old French may be understood in more than one way the version given does not necessarily reflect my own preferences, but is chosen to be consistent with the commentary to which it gives rise. The danger of this is that the translation might appear to lend weight to an interpretation of the French that is open to discussion, but that cannot be helped. After all, authors must be allowed their own view of the text that they are discussing, and this must remain as true for a translation as for the original. On the same basis the quotations themselves are normally taken from the edition of the text used by Schmolke-Hasselmann so that the text before the reader is the same as that studied by the author. There are cases where someone writing today might prefer other editions, but we have not intervened except in the cases of *Beaudous* and *Fergus*. We have used the published edition for *Beaudous* in place of the unpublished dissertation, and we have used the modern edition of *Fergus*, mainly for the convenience of its sequential line numbering. The edition by Ernst Martin provided a dual system of reference by numbering the lines on each page separately and providing a running total at the head of the page, creating ample scope for error and confusion. Our use of a different edition occasionally creates a discrepancy between a quotation and the discussion connected with it; this is always duly noted when translating the Old French.

We have refrained as much as possible from adding translator's notes, but not all textual difficulties can be passed over in silence (especially in the case of *Hunbaut* where poet and scribe persistently stretch grammar and sense to their limits). Apart from these few instances closely connected with the Old French text there are also just one or two cases where we have felt it useful to introduce a note that provides some necessary piece of information not readily available elsewhere. All such interventions are placed within square brackets and marked as 'Translator's notes'. Some small additions supplied for the sake of clarity are simply placed within square brackets. These are almost exclusively the names of German poets whose works are likely to be less familiar to readers of this translation than of the original. Since we have translated all quotations from scholars not writing in English some of the bibliographical references take the form 'Translated from ...' as a reminder that the wording is ours not the original author's. All other minor interventions and corrections are made without comment.

The translation normally follows the structural divisions of its original very closely, but there are some cases where the paragraphing has been altered slightly and a few where subheadings have been avoided. The chapter numbering of Part Two conforms to the present publisher's practice of maintaining a continuous sequence throughout the book rather than numbering each part separately. The one systematic intervention on our part is the way in which we have treated the original footnotes. The first and most important change is that substantial notes, and particularly those that include extensive quotations in Old French verse, have been integrated into the text itself. Lengthy footnotes have been left as such only when their contents really are subsidiary to the main line of argument. The second change is that simple references to the line numbers of quotations are given after the quotation itself. Where it is clear from the immediate context (as it usually is) which text the quotation is from the line numbers are given without further indication. Only in cases where the text is not named in advance, or where more than one text has been mentioned, does the reference include a shortened title. In contrast to this simplification, references in the footnotes that remain have been expanded. The titles of Old French romances are now given in full rather in the form of one- or two-letter abbreviations, and references to modern scholarship are no longer reduced to author and date, but given in full on the first occasion and then subsequently with only minor abbreviation. The German system of numbering the footnotes consecutively throughout the volume has been replaced by the more usual English practice of numbering in a new sequence for each chapter.

Finally, our grateful thanks are due first of all to the Vinaver Trustees, especially to the successive chairmen Glyn Burgess and Geoff Bromiley who supervised the project through its various stages, and to all those amongst the trustees who read the different chapters and offered their valuable advice. It is also a pleasure to acknowledge our special debt to Keith Busby who has contributed the Foreword with all its wealth of bibliographical information. At Cambridge University Press our thanks go to Katharina Brett under whose auspices the project was begun and under whose guidance it progressed, and to her successors, Victoria Sellar and Ann Rex, who saw the work through its difficult final stages.

But to Margaret the last word. Her preface was quite simply: 'This translation has been produced at the instigation and with the support of the Vinaver Trust, to whom we are pleased to acknowledge our indebtedness. Since the aim is to make Dr Schmolke-Hasselmann's study accessible to students of Old French who are less conversant with German, we have translated not only the main body of the text but also any quotations from scholars not writing in English; there is an indication in the footnotes wherever such quotations are not in the original language. A translation has also been supplied for all quotations from the original medieval texts, while the quotations themselves have been checked against the appropriate editions, and we have taken the opportunity to correct a number of inaccurate references. At the end of the Bibliography a supplement has been added to include more recent editions of texts, translations and further studies which may be found useful but which were not available to the original study.'

Foreword

BY KEITH BUSBY

This book is a landmark in Arthurian scholarship. Regrettably, it has until now remained largely inaccessible to those without a reading knowledge of German. This has been doubly unfortunate, firstly because of the general importance of Beate Schmolke-Hasselmann's ideas for the understanding of the evolution of French Arthurian verse romance, and secondly because one of the book's central theses holds that much of what we have considered to be medieval French literature is in fact English literature in French. Although Anglicists have always been obliged to deal with the continental literature that provides Middle English with much of its foundations, Schmolke-Hasselmann goes a good deal further and plausibly argues that we urgently need to redraw some lines on the literary and linguistic map of Britain and France in the twelfth and thirteenth centuries. To define English and French literature in merely linguistic terms corresponds to modern preconceptions of ethnic and national identity and creates a highly distorted view of the medieval reality. These suggestions have not proved universally palatable, entailing as they do a radical revision of received views. It is in many ways remarkable that such received views have obtained for as long as they have, particularly since there has long been general agreement that the Norman invasion had profound cultural consequences for the British Isles. One of the stumbling blocks has probably been the assumption that texts written in continental French were written on the continent for continental audiences and that only those written in Anglo-Norman circulated in Britain. This is demonstrably not the case and manuscripts in various dialects circulated freely on both sides of the Channel. To put it somewhat bluntly, Anglicists will have to learn Old French if they are to understand fully the English literary culture of the period, and scholars of Old French will have to cede part of the French *patrimoine* to the insular descendants of the Normans.

As a chronological outline of the development of French Arthurian romance began to emerge from scholarship of the late nineteenth century, it gradually became clear that the verse romances written after Chrétien de Troyes owed much to his own works. Authors of such romances, whose period of composition extends from the end of the twelfth century through the late thirteenth (and into the second half of the fourteenth if one includes Froissart's 'anachronistic' *Meliador*), were by and large regarded as slavish and generally untalented imitators of Chrétien. Chrétien was taken to be the first and the best author of Arthurian verse romance, the decline of the genre setting in immediately after his death. This tiresome critical practice of odious comparison of the later romances with Chrétien has proved particularly obstinate, but Schmolke-Hasselmann's work finally provides us with a means of assessing them on their own terms. Drawing on and refining the work of earlier German scholars such as Erich Köhler and Hans Robert Jauß, Schmolke-Hasselmann examines the reception of Chrétien in the 'epigonal romances'. The concept of 'Epigonentum' is of particular importance, for it underlies the development of Schmolke-Hasselmann's arguments throughout the book. Epigones work within the tradition of the master, aware of his role in determining the nature of that tradition. They are equally aware that servile imitation is inadvisable as it will lead to their work being compared directly with accepted masterpieces of the genre. Indeed, there seems to have been a certain reluctance on the part of authors to follow in Chrétien's footsteps and invite the comparison, as witness the gap of a generation between his last romance and the regular production of other Arthurian romances in verse; this is what Schmolke-Hasselmann has called 'the Chrétien-complex'. If authors writing in Chrétien's wake managed to avoid disparaging comparison with their predecessor in the thirteenth century and have their work judged on its own merits, they have not been so fortunate in the twentieth. When the epigones do take up the challenge, it is as an act of creative reception, using and modifying the framework provided by Chrétien with a view to producing something to the taste of their particular audience or patrons. The Chrétien-epigones are generally neither slavish nor untalented imitators, as was assumed without any justification by earlier scholars. although this does not, of course, preclude the existence of bad epigones. However, this book does not aim to pass aesthetic value-judgements on the epigonal romances, but rather to provide a platform for and means of reading and understanding them in their historical, social and literary contexts. Schmolke-Hasselmann believes that Arthurian romance had a special, often political, significance for the highest social classes in Anglo-Angevin society. Furthermore, its audience seems to have been formed by a limited number of *aficionados* who knew Chrétien's works in great detail, presumably through listening to frequent performances, and interpreted the epigonal works as creative responses to them, as their authors probably intended. The evolution of verse romance is thus marked by both continuity and disruption, depending on the precise nature of the epigonal response.

Although Schmolke-Hasselmann's work (and I include her articles in French and English,[1] as well as German) is innovative, it is not isolated, and forms part of a general movement since the 1970s to re-evaluate the canon of Old French romance. A similar tendency can be noted in work on Middle High German romance, where scholarship has proliferated on what are now generally referred to as 'post-classical romances' ('nachklassiche Romane') written after Hartmann von Aue and Wolfram von Eschenbach.[2] The French and English articles have, to be sure, reached a somewhat wider audience than Schmolke-Hasselmann's work published in German, but they are either more specialized or summary, and do not present the kind of synthesis offered in the present book. In the rest of this Foreword, I will attempt to sketch the general state of scholarship on French Arthurian romance since 1980 (more or less) and to situate Schmolke-Hasselmann's work within it. It will sometimes be necessary to discuss earlier work, especially large projects whose publication extends over a number of years. The ground covered in this Foreword overlaps somewhat with that in an earlier article, where I discussed progress and trends in Arthurian scholarship during the period 1962–87, and where my view of work produced in the 1960s and 1970s can be found.[3] What is both significant and encouraging is that Schmolke-Hasselmann's work is indicative of only one of a number of directions currently being investigated in Arthurian scholarship. While some types of scholarship I discuss below may not seem directly, or on occasions even indirectly, related to the subject of this book, I believe the very diversity can be seen as part of the liberation of medieval literary scholarship from an exclusively—and oppressively—text-oriented approach.

[1] For example, 'King Arthur as Villain in the Thirteenth-century Romance *Yder*', *Reading Medieval Studies* 6 (1980), 31–43; 'Henri II Plantagenêt, roi d'Angleterre, et la genèse d'*Erec et Enide*', *Cahiers de civilisation médiévale* 24 (1981), 241–6; 'Le roman de *Fergus*: technique narrative et intention politique', in *An Arthurian Tapestry: essays in memory of Lewis Thorpe*, edited by Kenneth Varty (Glasgow, 1981), pp. 342–53; 'The Round Table: Ideal, Fiction, Reality', *Arthurian Literature* 2 (1983), 41–75.

[2] The first important study in this field predates the publication of the German version of this book by only three years: Christoph Cormeau, *'Wigalois' und 'Diu Crône': zwei Kapitel zur Gattungsgeschichte des nachklassichen Aventiureromans* (Munich, 1977).

[3] 'Medieval French Arthurian Literature: Recent Progress and Critical Trends', in *The Vitality of the Arthurian Legend: A Symposium*, edited by Mette Pors (Odense, 1988), pp. 45–70. I am also grateful to Garland Publishing, Inc., for permission to include in this Foreword material from the chapter on medieval French literature in *Medieval Arthurian Literature: A Guide to Recent Research*, edited by Norris J. Lacy (New York and London, 1996), pp. 121–209.

It is also worth pointing out here that a distinction has traditionally been made between verse romance on the one hand, and prose romance on the other, a distinction that makes sense and which is used by Schmolke-Hasselmann to keep her subject within manageable proportions. Verse romance exhibits certain 'generic' characteristics not shared by prose romance (and vice versa), and while it is true that verse romance, beginning in the 1160s, has the initial chronological priority over prose romance, which blossoms only in the first decades of the thirteenth century, the reception of Chrétien's verse romances as discussed by Schmolke-Hasselmann is taking place at precisely the same time that the prose romances are being written and disseminated in manuscripts. Many of the Chrétien manuscripts were produced at this time and some may even have been produced in workshops that also produced copies of Arthurian prose romances. I shall therefore include consideration of scholarship on Arthurian prose romance in the pages that follow where desirable. Indeed, it could be argued that we need another global study on the lines of Schmolke-Hasselmann's, this time dealing with the rise and reception of prose romance in the thirteenth century. Certainly, enough recent progress has been made in the study of prose romance to make this possible, if still something of a challenge.

Text-editions are, of course, an absolute prerequisite for scholars (unless they have permanent and easy access to large repositories of manuscripts), yet the practice of editing fell into disrepute in the 1960s and 1970s, coming to be regarded as the refuge of scholars with nothing to add to our understanding of the literature (it is probably true that Ph.D. students were often nudged in the direction of an edition *faute de mieux*). Editors would now respond that only by close examination of literature in its manuscript context can one fully comprehend the behaviour of the medieval text, and that all self-respecting medievalists should at least have dirtied their hands attempting an edition. One of the results of recent interest in literary theory has been a re-examination of medieval textuality and its consequences for the modern reader. Amongst other things, this has led to an apparently paradoxical surge in the production of text-editions of various persuasions and the renewal of the near-extinct art of editing. It is a curious, if understandable, fact that may speak volumes about scholarly methods and procedures that a new edition of a text often sparks a renewal of critical interest in it, this despite the accessibility in most major libraries of older, still serviceable, editions. At the time when Beate Schmolke-Hasselmann's book was published in Germany, there had been few recent editions of the texts she studies, and from that point of view alone, her work was unusual. In this sense, too, the production of editions constitutes a major stimulus to the progress of scholarship. If the publications of text-editions is a gauge of interest in a particular area of medieval scholarship, then Arthurian romance, prose and verse, may be said to be in a healthy enough state. There is here a symbiotic relationship at work between critics and text-editors: if new editions rekindle interest in texts, then innovative studies such as Schmolke-Hasselmann's may also suggest to editors that neglected romances are worth their attention. Thankfully, very few Old French Arthurian texts now remain inaccessible to the scholar; only substantial parts of the enormously long *Perceforest* and smaller sections of the Prose *Tristan* remain unpublished, and publication of even the last-mentioned is nearing completion. It needs to be restated here, however, that the extraordinary nature of the transmission and rewriting of the prose romances probably means that recourse will always have to be had to the manuscripts for certain purposes.

Recent editorial activity has been preceded and accompanied, as I have suggested, by much discussion of the principles of editing Old French texts in general and Chrétien's romances in particular. This discussion has in essence been the result of two stimuli, one the renewal of a long-standing polemic between 'interventionists' and 'non-interventionists', and the other, an apparent clash between traditional philologists and supporters of more radical 'modern' textual theories. Although viewpoints have varied in the first part of the debate, a consensus seems to have formed in that the 'best manuscript' method in its extreme formulation by Joseph Bédier, long tacitly accepted as the norm, is incapable of doing justice either to Chrétien de Troyes or to the rich manuscript transmission of his romances. Particularly noteworthy early contributions to the literature were by Tony Hunt and T. B. W. Reid,[4] who both criticize the best manuscript editions of Chrétien from theoretical and practical points of view. Brian Woledge's two volumes of textual commentary on *Yvain*[5] are also required reading for the editorial problem as the specific issues they raise are valid, *mutatis mutandis*, for Chrétien's entire *œuvre* and Old French literature in general. Mention ought to be made of a spirited exchange of views between David F. Hult, and Karl D. Uitti and Alfred Foulet,[6] in especial connection with the text of *Lancelot*. The more radical aspect of the controversy was catalysed in the last decade by attacks in both France and the United States on traditional philological practices; Chrétien's texts were often the focal point of heated

4 Tony Hunt, 'Chrestien de Troyes: The Textual Problem', *French Studies* 33 (1979), 257–71; T. B. W. Reid, 'Chrétien de Troyes and the Scribe Guiot', *Medium Ævum* 45 (1976), 1–19.

5 *Commentaire sur 'Yvain' ('Le chevalier au lion') de Chrétien de Troyes*, 2 vols (Geneva, 1986–8).

6 David F. Hult, 'Lancelot's Two Steps: A Problem in Textual Criticism', *Speculum* 61 (1986), 836–58, and 'Steps Forward and Steps Backward: More on Chrétien's *Lancelot*', *Speculum* 64 (1989), 307–16; Karl D. Uitti and Alfred Foulet, 'On Editing Chrétien de Troyes: Lancelot's Two Steps and Their Context', *Speculum* 63 (1988), 271–92.

debate.[7] It is particularly noteworthy how national traditions persist in such matters: British (and Italian) scholarship has long favoured various forms of the critical edition whereas it is still usually anathema in France or with scholars trained in the French manner; North American scholars have tended to show more sympathy with interventionism. Curiously, in Germany, where the philological tradition was born and where the first editions were produced, scholars are by and large no longer editing texts. Nevertheless, Schmolke-Hasselmann's book, like much modern scholarship, is built on the foundations of German philology and shares an awareness of the importance of the textual transmission of Arthurian romance. Her brief examination of the manuscripts in which the romances are preserved is sufficient witness to this.

Wace's *Brut* provided Chrétien with the example of an Arthurian text in Old French octosyllabic couplets, and its pseudo-chronicle framework was revitalized by the authors of the great prose cycles; it can therefore be seen to occupy an important place in the evolution of French romance. Moreover, in MS Paris, Bibliothèque Nationale fr. 1450, it actually provides a structure into which Chrétien's romances are inserted, furnishing evidence of one scribe's view of the genre: Chrétien's works are intercalated into the text of the *Brut* at the point where Wace talks of the Arthurian 'fables' told by the *jongleurs*, which deal with events which supposedly took place during the peaceful period of Arthur's reign.[8] One edition of the Arthurian section of the *Brut* has appeared recently, namely Emmanuèle Baumgartner and Ian Short's *La geste du roi Arthur*,[9] which presents the Arthurian part of the text from the hitherto unedited MS Durham, Cathedral Library C. iv. 27, an early Anglo-Norman copy written in a French close to that of Wace; the text of 4,458 lines is accompanied by a modern French prose translation and followed by a French prose translation of Geoffrey of Monmouth's *Historia Regum Britanniae* as edited from MS Bern, Burgerbibliothek 568 by Neil Wright.[10] This book is a major contribution to the study of Geoffrey and Wace and their role in the development of Arthurian literature. The relation between the versions of Geoffrey and Wace has been studied in a recent series of articles by Laurence Mathey-Maille and has put flesh

[7] See Bernard Cerquiglini, *Éloge de la variante: histoire critique de la philologie* (Paris, 1989) and some responses in *Towards a Synthesis?: Essays on the New Philology*, edited by Keith Busby (Amsterdam, 1993). The January 1990 issue of *Speculum* (vol. 65, no. 1) was devoted to 'The New Philology' and provoked not a little hostility on the part of some traditional scholars.

[8] See Lori Walters, 'Le rôle du scribe dans l'organisation des manuscrits des romans de Chrétien de Troyes', *Romania* 106 (1985), 303–25.

[9] *La geste du roi Arthur* (Paris, 1993).

[10] Geoffrey of Monmouth, *The Historia Regum Britanniae*, edited by Neil Wright (Cambridge, 1985).

on the bones of some old generalizations.[11] An assessment of Wace's achievement also provides an essential prerequisite for the study of Chrétien, since he seems to have been the latter's only immediate model for an Arthurian text in the vernacular. Study of Wace and the earlier evolution of Arthurian romance therefore also constitutes an essential preliminary to Schmolke-Hasselmann's book. That Chrétien and Wace are so different one from the other suggests that Chrétien chose very consciously to pursue another course, just as his epigones in turn made conscious decisions to strike out in other directions.

For many decades, there was a scandalous dearth of good editions of the romances of Chrétien de Troyes himself. This fact is all the more remarkable in the light of the general acceptance of Chrétien's crucial role in the evolution of the genre, so eloquently restated and newly argued in the present book by Beate Schmolke-Hasselmann. I have tried to articulate above some of the theoretical and practical problems involved in the text-editing debates, so suffice it here to say that scholars of Chrétien de Troyes have had recourse either to the 'critical' but often artificially reconstructed editions of Wendelin Foerster (and Alfons Hilka for *Perceval*) or to the 'best manuscript' editions of Mario Roques (Alexandre Micha for *Cligés* and Félix Lecoy for *Perceval*) based on Paris, BN fr. 794, the so-called 'copie de Guiot'; William Roach's edition of *Perceval* from BN fr. 12576 was also easily available and widely used. The availability and affordability of the Roques–Micha–Lecoy texts in the Classiques Français du Moyen Age led to their acceptance as the edition that most scholars had to hand, begging the question as to what extent economic factors and ease of use direct the course of scholarship. This easy and unquestioning acceptance of the CFMA editions was itself also rooted in a general unawareness of the nature of the medieval text and its manuscript transmission. As this situation changed and as scholars began to realize that slavish adherence to a base manuscript ran the risk of substituting one scribe, and only one, for the poet, in what may have amounted to a betrayal of the latter, efforts were undertaken to correct the lack. Editions of *Lancelot*, *Yvain*, *Erec et Enide*, and *Perceval* were all produced for the Garland Library of Medieval Literature.[12] These are somewhat more

[11] For example, 'Traduction et création: de *l'Historia Regum Britanniae* de Geoffroy de Monmouth au *Roman de Brut* de Wace', in *Ecriture et modes de pensée au Moyen Age (VIIIe–XVe siècles)*, edited by Dominique Boutet and Laurence Harf-Lancner (Paris, 1993), pp. 187–93, and 'De l'*Historia Regum Britanniae* de Geoffroy de Monmouth au *Roman de Brut* de Wace: traduction du texte latin et étude comparative', *Perspectives médiévales* 19 (1993), 92–5.

[12] *Lancelot*, by William W. Kibler (New York and London, 1981); *Yvain*, by William W. Kibler (New York and London, 1985); *Erec and Enide*, by Carleton W. Carroll (New York and London, 1987); *Perceval*, edited by Rupert T. Pickens and translated by William W. Kibler (New York and London, 1990).

interventionist, but still based on Guiot, and accompanied by facing English translations; they still exhibit a reluctance to confront the Guiot problem head on. It is perhaps symptomatic of the lesser attention paid to Chrétien's 'Byzantine' romance, *Cligés*, that it has not been the object of an edition in this series. Schmolke-Hasselmann shows in the present book that, of all Chrétien's romances, *Cligés* seems to have left the fewest intertextual traces in the thirteenth century. It is hardly mentioned in subsequent literature (although it was turned into Burgundian prose in the fifteenth century), and is not adapted into other languages. Its neglect by modern scholars is thus strangely in keeping with its medieval reception. The accessibility of editions of Chrétien, together with his position as one of the canonical authors of Old French literature, doubtless contributed to the plethora of studies of his works and the relative neglect of his epigones, a neglect redressed in this book.

A project initiated by members of the British Branch of the International Arthurian Society under the auspices of the Eugene Vinaver Memorial Trust has to date produced full critical editions of *Cligés* and of *Perceval*.[13] The Gregory–Luttrell *Cligés* is based on Guiot and my *Perceval* on BN fr. 12576, but both editions provide a generous amount of critical apparatus in an attempt not only to restore Chrétien's own words, where possible, but also to offer the reading of all individual manuscripts (within the limitations imposed by the format of the printed book). The presupposition of an authorial text is not at odds with modern views of *variance* as the prime characteristic of medieval literature, for the existence of the poet's text is a *sine qua non* for the development of any kind of textual transmission, however much variation it may show. Indeed, the specific case of Chrétien de Troyes and his relationship with his epigones illustrates exactly how important the figure of the poet can be for an understanding of literary dynamics in the Middle Ages: *Erec et Enide*, *Cligés*, *Lancelot*, *Yvain* and *Perceval* were clearly regarded by epigones as the work and words of the author, Chrétien de Troyes, and such a perspective had a radical influence on the way in which the genre evolved, as Beate Schmolke-Hasselmann shows here.

Although Foerster's editions were presented as parts of Chrétien's 'Sämtliche Werke' and those of Roques–Micha–Lecoy as 'Les romans de Chrétien de Troyes', there existed until 1994 no single-volume 'Œuvres complètes' of France's first and most important author of Arthurian romance. It is precisely the realization of Chrétien's status as the first French author to have bequeathed a sizeable corpus of extended narratives that led to the publication in the same year of two such enterprises. Post-modern claims concerning the death of the author

[13] Chrétien de Troyes, *Cligés*, edited by Stewart Gregory and Claude Luttrell (Cambridge, 1993); *Le Roman de Perceval ou Le Conte du Graal*, edited by Keith Busby (Tübingen, 1993).

seem to be exaggerated, and may even constitute in Chrétien's case a real hindrance to our appreciation of his legacy, as I have tried to suggest above; Chrétien as author is certainly central to many of the arguments in Beate Schmolke-Hasselmann's book. The series 'Lettres Gothiques', directed by Michel Zink and published by the Livre de Poche, included individual editions and French translations of all of Chrétien's romances, which were subsequently published in a single collected volume in the series 'Classiques Modernes'.[14] The romances were purposely based on manuscripts other than Guiot with a view to presenting a different text to the reading public. These editions, with their excellent introductions and modest apparatus, are valuable additions to our knowledge of the transmission of Chrétien's romances, and their very existence an indication of precisely how small a part of the textual evidence is actually available to scholars. The collective volume, which retains only a minimum of introductory material from the individual works, also includes an edition of Chrétien's lyrics by Marie-Claire Gérard-Zai and a translation by Olivier Collet which accompanies a reprint of C. de Boer's edition of *Philomena*; *Guillaume d'Angleterre* is not included. Since Schmolke-Hasselmann's focus is on the Arthurian romances, she does not consider the lyrics or *Philomena*; the attribution of *Guillaume d'Angleterre* to Chrétien is generally rejected nowadays.

The same year saw the appearance of a second 'Œuvres complètes', published under the general editorship of Daniel Poirion in the prestigious series 'Éditions de la Pléiade'.[15] The publication of this volume was accompanied in France by more media attention than Chrétien de Troyes had probably ever hitherto received. The romances are edited by an international team of scholars, including Peter F. Dembowski, Sylvie Lefèvre, Daniel Poirion, Karl D. Uitti, Philippe Walter and Anne Berthelot. The translations into modern French seem to be the centrepiece of this volume, with the Old French text (again based on the Guiot manuscript, but with some measure of intervention) in smaller print at the foot of the page. Paradoxically, perhaps, in the light of this, there is a substantial amount of critical and variant apparatus in the back of the book. This volume

[14] Chrétien de Troyes, *Romans*, suivis des *chansons*, avec, en appendice, *Philomena*, under the direction of Michel Zink, edited and translated by Olivier Collet, Jean-Marie Fritz, David F. Hult, Charles Méla and Marie-Claire Zai (Paris, 1994). The individual editions are: *Erec et Enide*, by Jean-Marie Fritz (1992), *Cligès*, by Charles Méla and Olivier Collet (1994), *Le Chevalier au Lion ou le roman d'Yvain*, by David Hult (1994), *Le Chevalier de la Charrette ou le roman de Lancelot*, by Charles Méla (1992) and *Le Conte du Graal ou le roman de Perceval*, by Charles Méla (1990).

[15] Chrétien de Troyes, *Œuvres complètes*, under the direction of Daniel Poirion, edited and translated by Anne Berthelot, Peter F. Dembowski, Sylvie Lefèvre, Daniel Poirion, Karl D. Uitti and Philippe Walter (Paris, 1994).

also includes Chrétien's lyrics, *Philomena* and the disputed *Guillaume d'Angleterre*. Critical reception of the Pléiade volume has not been uniformly positive. Chrétien's simultaneous appearance in the Livre de Poche and the Pléiade has provided him with entry into two quite different, but equally respectable, French literary institutions, and constitutes perhaps the latest episode in the extraordinary reception of his work, the first phase of which is the subject of this book.

Outside of these projects, other editions of Chrétien have appeared, the most notable of which is doubtless the *Lancelot* prepared by Karl D. Uitti and the late Alfred Foulet published in the Classiques Garnier series.[16] This is once more based on the Guiot manuscript, but with numerous interventions justified by the 'editorial grid' elaborated by the two scholars in a series of earlier articles; the text is accompanied by a translation into modern French. Also accompanied by modern French translations are editions in the Garnier-Flammarion series, but these all reprint earlier editions; their real significance is not scholarly, but lies in their apparent commercial viability at a time when the French paperback market would seem to be saturated by low-priced editions of Chrétien de Troyes.[17] The availability of texts of Chrétien's romances and a mass public at the end of the twentieth century stands in marked contrast to the medieval situation sketched by Beate Schmolke-Hasselmann, in which his works circulated in small numbers amongst a restricted audience of devotees. While numbers can be deceptive, it is clear that Chrétien's romances were not medieval best-sellers like the *Roman de la Rose*, which has survived in over two hundred manuscripts.

Chrétien de Troyes has not been the only author of verse romance to have benefited from renewed editorial activity and reflection, although his case is obviously the most prominent. In 1983 came the publication of Manessier's Continuation of *Perceval* and with it the completion of William Roach's monumental project to edit all of the sequels to Chrétien's last unfinished romance. The five volumes (1949–83) stand as a tribute to the memory and accomplishment of one of the great Old French scholars of our time.[18] Colette-Anne van Coolput-Storms has reprinted Roach's edition of manuscript *L* of the

[16] Chrétien de Troyes, *Le Chevalier de la Charrette (Lancelot)*, edited and translated by Alfred Foulet and Karl D. Uitti (Paris, 1989).

[17] Chrétien de Troyes, *Lancelot ou le chevalier de la charrette*, with notes and translation by Jean-Claude Aubailly (Paris, 1991); *Yvain ou Le Chevalier au Lion*, with notes and translation by Michel Rousse (Paris, 1990); *Erec et Enide*, with notes and translation by Michel Rousse (Paris, 1994).

[18] *The Continuations of the Old French 'Perceval' of Chrétien de Troyes*, vol. V, edited by William Roach (Philadelphia, 1983). On the project as a whole, see my 'William Roach's Continuations of *Perceval*', *Romance Philology* 41, 3 (February 1988), 298–309.

First Continuation, accompanied by a modern French translation, in the Lettres Gothiques. Schmolke-Hasselmann chose not to deal with the reception of Chrétien in the corpus of verse Continuations of *Perceval*, and it still awaits a thorough investigation. Nevertheless, a certain amount of recent scholarship (see below) on these texts does confirm the suspicion that the availability of a good edition is a spur to scholarship.

Of the epigonal romances that form the main subject of Schmolke-Hasselmann's book, a number have been recently re-edited: Guillaume le Clerc's *Fergus*, *Yder*, *Hunbaut*, Renaut de Beaujeu's *Le Bel Inconnu*, *L'Atre périlleux* and very recently, Girard d'Amiens's lengthy *Escanor*.[19] Because of their general overall quality and accessibility, these editions are likely to replace the pioneering work of scholars from the late nineteenth and early twentieth centuries. The nature of its textual transmission means that serious study of *Fergus* will probably require consultation of both Frescoln and the older edition of Ernst Martin. Some of the epigonal verse romances still stand in need of modern editions, however: *Les Merveilles de Rigomer*, *Claris et Laris* and *Li Chevaliers as deus espees (Mériadeuc)* foremost amongst them. Predictably, perhaps, these are amongst the latest and longest examples of the genre, which scholars long seem to have avoided. The publication of Schmolke-Hasselmann's book in English should stimulate a new reading of the re-edited romances and perhaps even lead to new editions of those in need of attention. Furthermore, realization that the composition of late romances such as *Les Merveilles de Rigomer* and *Claris et Laris*, which date from the third quarter of the thirteenth century, owe something to the rise of prose romance, opens up new perspectives, especially in the light of recent scholarship on the latter.

Some may be surprised not to find the Tristan romances or the Breton *lais* treated in Schmolke-Hasselmann's study, especially since these are traditionally regarded as Arthurian by many scholars. While there are undoubted similarities and shared generic characteristics, the Tristan romances originally evolved independently of the Arthurian tales, although the two worlds meet as early as Béroul's *Tristan*. It is certainly the authors of the Prose *Tristan* in the thirteenth century, however, who first fully exploit the similarities between the two legends and fully 'Arthurianize' the adventures of Tristan; this Arthurianization

[19] Guillaume le Clerc, *The Romance of Fergus*, edited by Wilson Frescoln (Philadelphia, 1983); *The Romance of Yder*, edited and translated by Alison Adams (Cambridge, 1983); *The Romance of Hunbaut*, edited by Margaret Winters (Leiden, 1984); Renaut de Bâgé, *Le Bel Inconnu*, edited by Karen Fresco and translated by Colleen P. Donagher (New York and London, 1992); *The Perilous Cemetery (L'Atre Périlleux)*, edited and translated by Nancy B. Black (New York and London, 1994); Girart d'Amiens, *Escanor*, edited by Richard Trachsler, 2 vols (Geneva, 1994).

is transferred into English when Malory uses the Prose *Tristan* as source for part of his Arthuriad and may be largely responsible for the perceived 'Arthuricity' of the Tristan material. As the Arthurian court 'claims' Erec, Yvain, Lancelot and Perceval as its own, so ultimately it assimilates the protagonists of an independent *matière*. Of the Breton *lais*, only Marie de France's *Lanval* (and possibly the Tristanian *Chèvrefeuille*) and the anonymous *Tyolet* and *Melion* can be considered truly Arthurian. For these reasons, amongst others, most of the *lais* are excluded from Schmolke-Hasselmann's corpus and treated only summarily here. Nonetheless, many of Schmolke-Hasselmann's conclusions with respect to the Arthurian verse corpus are susceptible of application to the Tristan texts. There is a reception history of early verse versions of the Tristan story, such as those by Béroul and Thomas, which passes through later verse texts (the *Folies*, Gerbert de Montreuil's *Tristan menestrel*) to the Prose *Tristan*, and which is in many respects comparable to the evolution of the Arthurian verse romances considered here.

Despite (or perhaps because of) their fragmentary nature and relative brevity, the *Tristan* romances in verse have been frequently re-edited in recent years.[20] Michael Benskin, Tony Hunt and Ian Short have just published a newly discovered fragment of Thomas's romance.[21] Of the Tristan romances in verse, Thomas's seems to have had the widest dissemination: the surviving fragments are from a number of separate manuscripts and he is mentioned by name by Gottfried von Straßburg. He may therefore be said to have left a legacy akin to Chrétien's, but on a much smaller scale. It is doubtless the unsatisfactory nature of the textual transmission of the verse Tristan romances that is responsible for the proliferation of editions: Béroul's corrupt text is a challenge to scholars desirous of proposing a series of satisfactory emendations. Two recent French collections were clearly produced with classroom use in mind.[22] There have been no major new critical editions of the *Lais* of Marie de France or of the anonymous *lais*.[23]

[20] Thomas of Britain, *Tristran*, edited and translated by Stewart Gregory (New York and London, 1991); *Le Roman de Tristan*, edited by Félix Lecoy (Paris, 1992); Béroul, *The Romance of Tristran*, edited and translated by Norris J. Lacy (New York and London, 1989); edited and translated by Stewart Gregory (Amsterdam, 1992); *Tristran et Iseut*, edited and translated by Herman Braet and Guy Raynaud de Lage (Leuven, 1989).

[21] 'Un nouveau fragment du *Tristan* de Thomas', *Romania* 113 (1992–1995), 289–319.

[22] *Tristan et Yseut: les Tristan en vers*, edited and translated by Jean-Charles Payen (Paris, 1974, revised edition, 1980); *Tristan et Iseut: les poèmes français, la saga norroise*, edited and translated by Daniel Lacroix and Philippe Walter (Paris, 1989).

[23] Alexandre Micha has re-edited the poems from MS London, British Library Harley 978 (Paris, 1994), and Laurence Harf-Lancner has reprinted Karl Warnke's 1925 text in the Lettres Gothiques (Paris, 1990); both editions are accompanied by translations into modern French. Micha has also

Arguably, the greatest progress in editing has been in the area of Old French prose romance, where an increasingly mature understanding of these works has both benefited from and stimulated editorial activity. One of the areas of Chrétien-reception not studied by Schmolke-Hasselmann in this book is, as I have mentioned, his legacy in prose romance. Chrétien was the first to tell the story of Lancelot and Guinevere, and part of the Prose *Lancelot* (often referred to as 'le conte de la charrette') is actually a retelling of his romance. But Chrétien's *Lancelot* has left more than a prose version of itself: the dissemination of the Lancelot story assumes extraordinary proportions with the composition of the Prose *Lancelot*, using as it does the Lancelot story as a frame for what is to become one of the most influential narratives in medieval literature. Until recently, scholars usually had recourse to the Sommer edition of the Prose *Lancelot* (part of *The Vulgate Version of the Arthurian Romances*, published between 1908 and 1916). In another *embarras de richesses*, there are now fine editions of both the non-cyclical and cyclical versions of the Prose *Lancelot*, by Elspeth Kennedy and by Alexandre Micha respectively.[24] Scholars will now be able to judge for themselves with confidence the question of priority of the versions of the *Lancelot*, which has figured so largely in the scholarship of recent decades. One particular topic for further research opened up by Schmolke-Hasselmann's book is the matter of the simultaneous and parallel development of verse and prose romance, for although the early verse epigones may pre-date the rise of prose romance, many, if not most, of them wrote at a time when prose was becoming the dominant form. The question of the intended public and social function of, say, the Vulgate Cycle, invites a thorough investigation along lines similar to those pursued by Schmolke-Hasselmann. Modern scholarship tends to draw a fairly straight division between verse and prose romances, but there are many points of contact, and even where these are lacking, the contrasts are instructive.

Chrétien's *Perceval* is ultimately the prime mover behind a complex genetic process which culminates in the writing of the *Queste del Saint Graal*, another part of the Vulgate Cycle (*Lancelot–Graal*). Although this text is radically different from Chrétien's Grail romance, it must be remembered, as in the case

---

reprinted Tobin's 1976 text of the anonymous *lais* (Paris, 1992). The various versions of the Horn/ Mantel test, often designated as *lais*, do not correspond to the usual definition of *lai breton*, although they are certainly Arthurian; there have been no recent re-editions.

[24] *Lancelot do Lac: The Non-Cyclic Old French Prose Romance*, edited by Elspeth Kennedy, 2 vols (Oxford, 1980); *Lancelot: roman en prose du XIIIe siècle*, edited by Alexandre Micha, 9 vols (Geneva, 1978–83). Kennedy's text has been reprinted with a modern French translation by François Mosès (Vol. I) and Marie-Luce Chênerie (Vol. II) in the Lettres Gothiques series, 2 vols (Paris, 1991).

of the *Lancelot*, that his is the first written rendition to have come down to us, and was in all probability the first 'literary' version of one of the fundamental myths of Western culture. The verse *Perceval* Continuations take one direction, noted above, and the sequence of prose Grail texts, another. The *Queste del Saint Graal* has been recently edited, with facsimile, from an Udine manuscript unknown to Pauphilet.[25] A lifetime of scholarship has gone into Fanni Bogdanow's edition of the partly reconstructed Post-Vulgate *Roman du Graal*, a work whose genesis is still more than a little obscure.[26] The *mise en prose* of the whole of Robert de Boron's trilogy from the Modena manuscript (*Joseph*, *Merlin* and *Perceval*) has been re-edited under the suggestive title of *Le Roman du Graal*,[27] and in what is likely to be the definitive edition, Richard O'Gorman has published both the verse and prose versions of Robert's *Joseph d'Arimathie*; the prose version of Robert's *Merlin* (together with the verse fragment) has also been re-edited.[28] The anonymous *Propheties de Merlin*, finally, has been re-edited from the Bodmer manuscript.[29] As different from the works of Chrétien and his epigones as they are, these romances are crucial to the whole picture not just because of the impetus provided by Chrétien, but also because they are being composed and copied in the same decades of the thirteenth century when the verse tradition was flourishing. Their very difference with respect to the latter constitutes in itself a form of reception, a conscious decision to do something different.

While there had always been Sommer's earlier edition of the Vulgate Cycle, those wishing to read the Prose *Tristan* had been more or less obliged to consult Löseth's long summary published in 1891. Renée Curtis's project to edit the romance from MS Carpentras 404 was completed in 1985.[30] While Curtis was convinced of the 'quality' of the text in the Carpentras manuscript, it is unfortunately fragmentary, and so although the edition of Carpentras 404 is complete, that of the romance itself is not. The manuscript tradition of the Prose *Tristan* is so complex that it is impossible to produce a critical edition akin to those that are conceivable for Chrétien's romances, and the second major Prose

[25] *La grant Queste del Saint Graal: La grande Ricerca del Santo Graal: Versione inedita della fine del XIII secolo del ms. Udine, Biblioteca Arcivescovile, 177*, edited and translated by A. Rosellini *et al.* (Udine, 1990).

[26] *SATF*, 4 vols (Paris, 1994).

[27] Robert de Boron, *Le roman du Graal: Manuscrit de Modène*, edited by Bernard Cerquiglini (Paris, 1981).

[28] Robert de Boron, *Joseph d'Arimathie*, edited by Richard F. O'Gorman (Toronto, 1995); Robert de Boron, *Merlin*, edited by Alexandre Micha (Geneva, 1979).

[29] *Les Prophesies de Merlin*, edited by Anne Berthelot (Cologny-Geneva, 1992).

[30] *Le roman de Tristan en prose*, edited by Renée Curtis, 3 vols (Munich, 1963; Leiden, 1976; Cambridge, 1985).

Tristan project is also in essence an edition of a single manuscript. Philippe Ménard has been directing a team of French scholars who have published to date eight volumes based on MS Vienna, ÖNB 2542. No doubt out of a desire to make as much of the romance as possible available to colleagues as quickly as possible, Ménard's vol. I begins where Curtis's vol. III ends. The imminent completion of this project will mark a major landmark in the accessibility of French Arthurian prose romance and help restore the reputation of a major work that has been largely misunderstood until the last two decades.[31] It is true of the Prose *Tristan* as of the other prose romances discussed above that much early scholarship was devoted to questions of genesis and transmission, of different versions, redactions and their interrelationship. While not all of these problems have been solved by the publication of new editions, the number and nature of the critical editions currently available reflect much more accurately the complex set of intertextual relations created by the continuous rewriting of the tales. Scholars are consequently now in a much better position to turn their attention to matters of meaning and structure, informed by a better awareness of medieval textuality. While Arthurian romance does continue to evolve, the corpus of texts is at its richest and most complex in the middle of the thirteenth century: Chrétien and his epigones, the *Perceval* Continuations, the Vulgate and Post-Vulgate *Lancelot–Graal* cycles and the Prose *Tristan*. It is precisely the state of the genre at this moment which is treated in Beate Schmolke-Hasselmann's book.

It is remarkable to note that many of these editions constitute what are in essence *editiones principes* (at the end of the twentieth century!). This is also true of the prose version of *Floriant et Florete* edited by Claude M. L. Lévy,[32] and of the monumental and still incomplete publication of the enormously long fourteenth-century prose romance *Perceforest* undertaken by Jane Taylor and Gilles Roussineau, a text hitherto accessible only in manuscript or incunabula.[33] André Giacchetti has provided an edition of *Ysaÿe le Triste*, a prose romance written at the very end of the fourteenth or beginning of the fifteenth century.[34] Together with the editions of Robert de Boron, of the Post-Vulgate Cycle and the Prose *Tristan*, these publications signify a notable expansion of the canon beyond the traditional confines of Chrétien and the *Lancelot–Graal*.

[31] *Le roman de Tristan en prose*, edited by Philippe Ménard *et al.*, 9 vols to date (Geneva, 1987–).

[32] *Le roman de Floriant et Florete, ou Le chevalier qui la nef maine*, edited by Claude M. L. Levy (Ottawa, 1983).

[33] *Le roman de Perceforest*, 1ère partie, edited by Jane H. M. Taylor (Geneva, 1979); 3ème partie, edited by Gilles Roussineau, 2 vols (Geneva, 1988–91); 4ème partie, edited by Gilles Roussineau, 2 vols (Geneva, 1987).

[34] *Ysaÿe le Triste: Roman arthurien du Moyen Age tardif*, edited by André Giacchetti (Rouen, 1989).

A number of important research tools specifically relating to French romance have appeared in recent years. As regards bibliographies, Douglas Kelly's volume on Chrétien de Troyes is to be followed by a supplement; David Shirt published a bibliographical guide to the Tristan poems; and Glyn S. Burgess has performed a similar service for Marie de France.[35] An excellent bibliography on the Prose *Tristan*, updating that in her 1975 thesis, has been provided by Emmanuèle Baumgartner.[36] While Schmolke-Hasselmann's book contains ample references up to 1980, it does not aim at exhaustivity, and a focused bibliography of the verse romances would render scholars a service. The only concordance of Chrétien's entire *œuvre* to date is that by Marie-Louise Ollier, although this is more properly a concordance of the scribe Guiot, being based on the CFMA editions; Gabriel Andrieu and Jacques Piolle had already produced a concordance of the Lecoy edition of *Perceval*. Pierre Kunstmann and Martin Dube have generated a concordance of the Vulgate *La Mort le roi Artu*, and Gérard Gonfroy of vol. I of Philippe Ménard's edition of the Prose *Tristan*.[37] More such work can be expected as progress is made with computerized databases and various types of 'word-crunching'. Karl D. Uitti has begun a project, known informally as 'the Princeton *Lancelot*', already available in partial form for consultation on the World Wide Web; Guy Jacquesson has also 'published' an electronic *Lancelot*.[38] Such work will eventually make all transcriptions of all manuscripts available for linguistic and stylistic analysis, and digitized scanned images of the manuscripts will accompany the transcriptions. This is likely to be the area in which most textual progress will be made over the next few decades.[39]

[35] Douglas Kelly, *Chrétien de Troyes: An Analytic Bibliography* (London, 1976); David J. Shirt, *The Old French Tristan Poems: A Bibliographical Guide* (London, 1980); Glyn S. Burgess, *Marie de France: An Analytical Bibliography* (London, 1977), Supplement no. 1 (London, 1986).

[36] Emmanuèle Baumgartner, *La harpe et l'épée: tradition et renouvellement dans le 'Tristan en prose'* (Paris, 1990), pp. 163–70.

[37] Marie-Louise Ollier, *Lexique et concordance de Chrétien de Troyes d'après la copie Guiot* (Montreal and Paris, 1986); Gabriel Andrieu and Jacques Piolle, *Perceval ou le Conte du Graal de Chrétien de Troyes: concordancier complet des formes graphiques occurrentes d'après l'édition de M. Félix Lecoy* (Aix-en-Provence, 1976); Pierre Kunstmann and Martin Dubé, *Concordance analytique de 'La mort le roi Artu'*, 2 vols, (Ottawa, 1982); Gérard Gonfroy, *Le roman de Tristan en prose: concordancier des formes graphiques occurrentes établi d'après l'édition de Ph. Ménard (t. I)* (Limoges, 1990).

[38] The Princeton *Lancelot* can be accessed on http://www.princeton.edu/~lancelot, and Jacquesson's on http://palissy.humana.univ-nantes.fr/CHARRETTE/Annexes/debut.

[39] The computer also promises much in the field of stemmatics, but the results to date have been somewhat disappointing. Cf. Anthonij Dees, 'Analyse par l'ordinateur de la tradition manuscrite du *Cligès* de Chrétien de Troyes', in *Actes du XVIIIe Congrès International de Linguistique et de Philologie Romanes, Université de Trèves (Trier) 1986*, edited by Dieter Kremer, vol. VI (Tübingen, 1988), pp. 62–75, and Margot van Mulken, *The Manuscript Tradition of the 'Perceval' of Chrétien de Troyes: A stemmatological and dialectological approach* (Amsterdam, 1993).

Its importance for further study in the area covered by Beate Schmolke-Hasselmann's book may reside in the opportunities it provides for testing and developing her conclusions concerning the reception of romance by detailed comparison of variant passages and by study of the manuscripts as artefacts with a specific historical and cultural context.

In the more properly critical domain, a number of major studies of Chrétien de Troyes have appeared in the last fifteen years. Jean Frappier's standard introduction to Chrétien was published in an English translation by Raymond J. Cormier in 1982.[40] Norris J. Lacy's *The Craft of Chrétien de Troyes* provides a fine analysis of the architectonics of the romances.[41] More traditional in their concern with such themes as chivalry, courtly love and religion are studies by Leslie Topsfield, Evelyn Mullally and Peter Noble, who concludes, not surprisingly, that Chrétien was a strong supporter of conjugal love, disapproving of adultery.[42] Beate Schmolke-Hasselmann considers both the structural and ethical aspects of post-Chrétien romance in her study and is indebted to what might be regarded as a kind of scholarship deriving from the work of Jean Frappier. But her emphasis lies elsewhere and one of the major merits of this book is that it suggests that the treatment of both structure and content by the epigones is far more than feeble imitation, and far more than mere decline which set in after the death of Chrétien. Katalin Halász acknowledges her debt to Paul Zumthor's *Poétique médiévale* and Erich Köhler's study of customs in an important study published in the same year as Schmolke-Hasselmann's book, in which she concentrates largely on *Erec et Enide* and *Yvain*, while Donald Maddox proposes a detailed and subtle post-Köhlerian reading of custom in Chrétien's *œuvre* as a whole; we see here the enormous influence of Köhler's *Ideal und Wirklichkeit in der höfischen Epik* (1956, published in French translation in 1974) which is also a major factor in the development of Schmolke-Hasselmann's views.[43] Studies such as those by Halász, Maddox and Schmolke-Hasselmann are excellent illustrations of the continuity of scholarship and how generations of scholars build on each other's work.

40 *Chrétien de Troyes: The Man and His Work* (Athens, Ohio, 1982).

41 *The Craft of Chrétien de Troyes: An Essay on Narrative Art* (Leiden, 1980).

42 Leslie Topsfield, *Chrétien de Troyes: A Study of the Arthurian Romances* (Cambridge, 1981); Evelyn Mullally, *The Artist at Work: Narrative Technique in Chrétien de Troyes, Transactions of the American Philosophical Society* 78, 4 (Philadelphia, 1988); Peter Noble, *Love and Marriage in Chrétien de Troyes* (Cardiff, 1982).

43 Katalin Halász, *Structures narratives chez Chrétien de Troyes* (Debrecen, 1980); Donald Maddox, *The Arthurian Romances of Chrétien de Troyes: Once and future fictions* (Cambridge, 1991); Erich Köhler, *L'aventure chevaleresque: idéal et réalité dans le roman courtois: études sur la forme des plus anciens poèmes d'Arthur et du Graal*, translated by Eliane Kaufholz (Paris, 1974).

Useful guides to the individual romances have been provided in the Grant and Cutler series 'Critical Guides to French Texts', although there is as yet no volume devoted to *Lancelot*.[44] Although introductory in nature, these studies nevertheless contain much that is of interest to the specialist reader of Chrétien; Burgess, Busby and Hunt in particular make use of Schmolke-Hasselmann's work, including *Der arthurische Versroman*, thereby providing a first, partial, introduction of her views to English-speaking students. Joan Grimbert's *'Yvain' dans le miroir* is a major study, which shows how the romance is predicated on what she calls an 'adversative structure', constantly challenging the audience to respond, creating ambiguity and questions as it proceeds.[45] Mention should further be made of Emmanuèle Baumgartner's perceptive monograph on *Lancelot* and *Yvain* which examines how these two romances echo each other and deal in different ways with some of the basic concerns of romance, such as love and adventure.[46] This particular study does for two of Chrétien's own romances what Schmolke-Hasselmann's book does for the genre as a whole, establishing a network of relationship and echoes, 'intratextually' within and between *Yvain* and *Lancelot* as parts of Chrétien's *œuvre*. In sum, while there is no real consensus concerning particular issues in Chrétien scholarship, it is fair to say that we have a much better grasp of the way his romances function with respect to their form and function than we did, say, only twenty years ago. While such a conclusion ought to be self-evident given the large amount of scholarship in existence, received views are particularly obdurate, and innovative scholarship takes time to become absorbed into the critical mainstream.

I have already said that Schmolke-Hasselmann's book was not isolated as an attempt to reassess the post-Chrétien verse romances, and critical concerns similar to her own inform my study of the figure of Gauvain, and the two-volume *The Legacy of Chrétien de Troyes*.[47] Numerous articles have also examined in detail the *Rezeptionsgeschichte* of Chrétien's *œuvre* in individual thirteenth-century works.[48] Claude Lachet has produced a thorough study of *Sone de Nansay*, a marginally Arthurian romance of 21,000 lines dated 1270–80, and even the 'last Arthurian romance', Froissart's *Meliador*, has been the centre

44 Glyn S. Burgess, *Erec et Enide* (1984); Lucie Polak, *Cligés* (1982); Tony Hunt, *Yvain* (1986); Keith Busby, *Perceval* (1993).

45 Joan Tasker Grimbert, *'Yvain' dans le miroir* (Amsterdam and Philadelphia, 1988).

46 Emmanuèle Baumgartner, *Chrétien de Troyes: Yvain, Lancelot, la charrette et le lion* (Paris, 1992).

47 Keith Busby, *Gauvain in Old French Literature* (Amsterdam, 1980); *The Legacy of Chrétien de Troyes*, edited by Norris J. Lacy, Douglas Kelly and Keith Busby, 2 vols (Amsterdam, 1987–8).

48 Particular items relating to specific topics not mentioned separately here can, of course, be located by consulting the annual *Bibliographical Bulletin of the International Arthurian Society* (*Bulletin Bibliographique de la Société Internationale Arthurienne*).

of some recent attention which seeks to situate it in its own time and as part of Froissart's *œuvre* as well as within the continuum of Arthurian romance.[49] *Meliador*, along with *Le Chevalier dou Papegau*, *Ysaÿe le triste* and *Perceforest*, is also studied in a major contribution to our understanding of Arthurian romance (verse and prose) in the fourteenth century by Jane Taylor; Taylor stresses the need for authors in this final phase of the evolution of the genre to integrate the *matière de Bretagne* into a pseudo-historical corpus and to devise the means of escaping from the straitjacket of tradition while at the same time using stock motifs, themes and topoi provided by the genre.[50] In many ways these studies extend chronologically the reach of Beate Schmolke-Hasselmann's book, demonstrating how later authors respond in yet more innovative ways, dictated by their own historical context and intended audiences, to the matter of Britain in French.

With the completion in 1983 of Roach's *Perceval* Continuations, the way was open for a minor surge in studies of these extraordinary texts. Corin Corley in particular has carried out detailed textual and philological work on the Second Continuation, defining its precise parameters and confirming its authorship by Wauchier de Denain, author of a prose version of the *Vies des Pères*. A thoroughly detailed exposition of these and other issues, followed by a glossary of the Second Continuation is contained in the published version of the author's dissertation.[51] A major study of Chrétien's *Perceval* and the First Continuation by Guy Vial, unfortunately incomplete, was seen through the press by Jean Rychner after the author's death. After a salvation-based reading of Chrétien's romance, Vial considers the divergences between the various redactions of the First Continuation; unfortunately, no version of a third part of Vial's planned book, a comparative study of Chrétien and the first continuator, was found amongst his papers.[52] Pierre Gallais's four-volume *thèse d'état* presents the results of a lifetime's study of the First Continuation.[53] From consideration of the

49 Claude Lachet, *Sone de Nansay et le roman d'aventures en vers au XIIIe siècle* (Paris, 1992); on *Meliador* see in particular Peter F. Dembowski, *Jean Froissart and His 'Meliador': Context, Craft, and Sense* (Lexington,, 1983).

50 Jane H. M. Taylor, 'The Fourteenth Century: Context, Text, and Intertext', in *The Legacy of Chrétien de Troyes* (above, note 47), I, 267–332.

51 Corin F. V. Corley, 'Réflexions sur les deux premières continuations de *Perceval*', *Romania* 103 (1982), 235–58; 'Wauchier de Denain et la deuxième continuation de *Perceval*', *Romania* 105 (1984), 351–9; *The Second Continuation of the Old French Perceval: A Critical and Lexicographical Study* (London, 1987).

52 Guy Vial, *Le Conte du Graal: sens et unité. La première continuation: textes et contenu* (Geneva, 1987).

53 *L'imaginaire d'un romancier français de la fin du XIIe siècle: Description raisonnée, comparée et commentée de la 'Continuation-Gauvain'*, 4 vols (Amsterdam, 1988–9).

quality of each manuscript copy to stylistic analysis, there is little that is not discussed; all study of the First Continuation must henceforth begin here. The late John L. Grigsby also investigated Chrétien's legacy and the reception of his aesthetic in the Continuations in two perceptive articles,[54] and Matilda T. Bruckner has written on the poetics of continuation from the same corpus.[55] Filippo Salmeri has published the only book-length study to date of Manessier's Continuation, concentrating on the religious symbolism and moral problems.[56] Schmolke-Hasselmann's book could function as a model for a much-needed comprehensive study of the Continuations as creative reception of Chrétien. The authors of the Continuations are in their own way epigones, emulating and elaborating the great project he began in the *Perceval*. Like the epigones who form the subject of Beate Schmolke-Hasselmann's book, they respond to, interpret, rewrite and eventually complete the words of the master. The Continuations contain many direct and indirect intertextual allusions to Chrétien's *Perceval* which indicate how his work was viewed and interpreted by their authors: verbatim quotations, episodes rewritten, loose narrative threads expanded and finally resolved, all owe their initial impetus to Chrétien's Grail romance.

The best recent introduction to the complex matter of the Tristan romances is now Emmanuèle Baumgartner's densely written *Tristan et Iseut: de la légende aux récits en vers*.[57] In some ways, this book, clearly written for a French student audience, deals with issues similar to those treated by Beate Schmolke-Hasselmann, namely intertextuality, reception history and audience response. Two more volumes in the Grant and Cutler Critical Guides series fulfil a similar function for Anglophones, although their approaches are somewhat more traditional than that of Baumgartner. Peter Noble has studied Béroul and the Berne *Folie* and Geoffrey Bromiley, Thomas and the Oxford *Folie*;[58] the pairings Béroul/*Folie* Berne and Thomas/*Folie* Oxford have long been a critical commonplace and correspond to the 'version commune/version courtoise' distinction. Also important is Merritt Blakeslee's *Love's Masks: Identity, Intertextuality, and Meaning in the Old French Tristan Poems*, a thorough

[54] John L. Grigsby, 'Heroes and their Destinies in the Continuations of Chrétien's *Perceval*', in *The Legacy of Chrétien de Troyes*, II, 41–53; 'Remnants of Chrétien's Aesthetics in the Early *Perceval* Continuations and the Incipient Triumph of Writing', *Romance Philology* 41, 4 (May 1988), 379–93.

[55] Matilda T. Bruckner, 'The Poetics of Continuation in Medieval French Romance: From Chrétien's *Conte du Graal* to the *Perceval* Continuations', *French Forum* 18 (1993), 133–49.

[56] Filippo Salmeri, *Manessier: modelli, simboli, scrittura* (Catania, 1984).

[57] *Tristan et Iseut: de la légende aux récits en vers* (Paris, 1987).

[58] Peter Noble, *Beroul's 'Tristan' and the 'Folie de Berne'* (London, 1982); Geoffrey Bromiley, *Thomas's 'Tristan' and the 'Folie Tristan d'Oxford'* (London, 1986).

examination of the central figure of Tristan in his manifold guises; central to Blakeslee's purpose is the elucidation of meaning generated by the process of continual rewriting of the story by a succession of authors.[59] Other studies devoted to the Tristan romances in general are discussed below as examples of mythological and psychoanalytical approaches to medieval romance.[60] The *Tristan menestrel* episode from Gerbert de Montreuil's Continuation of Chrétien's *Perceval* has been the object of studies by myself and by Jonna Kjær, of which the first in particular applies Schmolke-Hasselmann's intertextual methods to part of Gerbert's text.[61]

Interest in the epigonal verse romances, the Continuations of *Perceval* and the Tristan romances has been matched by the growth of critical studies of the prose romances, and has also been facilitated, as I have suggested, by the availability of more reliable editions. Until quite recently, only *La Queste del Saint Graal* and *La Mort le roi Artu* had been the object of much critical attention, thanks no doubt to the easily accessible editions of Pauphilet and Frappier, to the forbidding length of the Prose *Lancelot* and the Prose *Tristan*, and to the disconcerting complexity of their manuscript transmission. Four scholars have dominated the field: Elspeth Kennedy, Fanni Bogdanow (both pupils of Eugène Vinaver), Alexandre Micha and Emmanuèle Baumgartner. It is difficult to over-estimate the insights that their scholarship has provided into a complex, misunderstood and quite crucially important part of French Arthurian tradition. Firsthand knowledge of the manuscripts has led to considerable emphasis being placed on the roles of scribes and compilers in the genesis of the prose romances. Although scribal activity is particularly evident in the prose manuscripts, it is no less important in those of the verse texts, although it is by and large more discreet. The insights provided by study of prose manuscripts are an impetus to look again at codices containing the verse romances studied in this book. Kennedy's edition was followed by a major study of the Prose *Lancelot*, while Micha published studies of the *Lancelot* and Robert de Boron's *Merlin*.[62] Baumgartner's important thesis (1975) on the Prose *Tristan* was followed in 1990

[59] Merritt R. Blakeslee, *Love's Masks: Identity, Intertextuality, and Meaning in the Old French Tristan Poems* (Cambridge, 1989).

[60] See the studies by Philippe Walter and Jean-Charles Huchet (below, notes 94 and 93).

[61] Keith Busby, 'Der *Tristan menestrel* des Gerbert de Montreuil und seine Stellung in der altfranzösischen Artustradition', *Vox Romanica* 42 (1983), 144–56; Jonna Kjær, 'L'épisode de "Tristan ménestrel" dans la "Continuation de Perceval" par Gerbert de Montreuil (XIIIe siècle): essai d'interprétation', *Revue Romane* 25 (1990), 356–66.

[62] Elspeth Kennedy, *Lancelot and the Grail: A Study of the Prose 'Lancelot'* (Oxford, 1986); Alexandre Micha, *Essais sur le cycle du Lancelot–Graal* (Geneva, 1987); *Étude sur le 'Merlin' de Robert de Boron* (Geneva, 1980).

by another major study.[63] Colette-Anne van Coolput-Storms's study of the reception of the Grail romances in the Prose *Tristan* draws directly and indirectly on the work of these scholars at the same time that it reflects concerns about audience response and reception which inform the work of Beate Schmolke-Hasselmann.[64]

Emmanuèle Baumgartner has demonstrated the importance of the biblical paradigm in the construction and meaning of the prose romances. *L'arbre et le pain: essai sur 'La Queste del Saint Graal'* shows how romance is predicated on scriptural patterns, and paves the way for Michèle Szkilnik's *L'Archipel du Graal: Étude de l'Estoire del Saint Graal'* , an important study of one of the least well-known parts of the Vulgate Cycle.[65] Awareness of these same concerns informs E. Jane Burns's important study of the Vulgate which also stresses notions of writing, rewriting and the importance of the narrative voice of 'li contes'.[66] More specialized studies of narrative technique in the prose romances have examined the important device of 'entrelacement' in the prose romances. The state of scholarship in the prose romances is radically different to what it was a quarter of a century ago; vastly improved and more sophisticated, it has finally come of age. This progress is significant for the study of verse romance in two ways: it shows firstly how the Arthurian legend was capable of quite a different narrative articulation and secondly how that particular type of romance came to have a marked influence on later examples of the verse tradition.

Scholarship of the 1970s and 1980s on both prose and verse romance generally reflects the influence of notions of *mouvance* as developed by Paul Zumthor, according to which the medieval text is fundamentally unstable, moving in both space and time.[67] The practical consequence of this is that no two versions of the same text are identical and indeed frequently exhibit major differences. The Continuations of Chrétien's *Perceval* illustrate this point perfectly as do the various textual states of most of the prose romances, the Prose *Tristan* being a particularly clear case in point. With respect to the Chrétien and the epigonal verse romances, *mouvance* generally occurs on a smaller scale, generally restricted to a verbal and stylistic, rather than a narrative level. This is in Chrétien's case clearly related to his 'authorial' presence as well as the very fact that his romances are written in verse. Nevertheless, there are significant

63 *La harpe et l'épée: tradition et renouvellement dans le 'Tristan en prose'* (Paris, 1990).

64 *Aventures querant et le sens du monde: aspects de la réception productive des premiers romans du Graal cycliques dans le 'Tristan en prose'* (Louvain, 1986).

65 Baumgartner, *L'arbre et le pain: essai sur 'La Queste del Saint Graal'* (Paris, 1981); Szkilnik, *L'Archipel du Graal: Étude de l'Estoire del Saint Graal'* (Geneva, 1991).

66 *Arthurian Fictions: Rereading the Vulgate Cycle* (Columbus, 1985).

67 For example, in *Essai de poétique médiévale* (Paris, 1972).

omissions and interpolations in the text of *Perceval* which have somehow been displaced. The textual tradition of the epigonal romances is generally less complex, although once again, there are exceptions: the text of *Fergus* shows visible signs of *remaniement*, and one of the manuscripts of *L'Atre périlleux* has a longish episode absent in the other copy. Related to *mouvance* is the concept of *intertextuality* which views each individual work as part of a larger whole, the intertext; intertextual relationships can be either general or specific. The well-known links between Chrétien's *Lancelot* and *Yvain*, for example, may be viewed in an intertextual perspective, as can Chrétien's response to the Tristan legend, or the rewriting of Chrétien's *Lancelot* in the Vulgate or of his *œuvre* in the epigonal romances. The basic advantage of such an approach is that it frees scholars from the somewhat restrictive and vague notion of 'influence' of one text on another. Important work has been done in this area, for example, by Karl D. Uitti, Matilda T. Bruckner and Friedrich Wolfzettel.[68] Beate Schmolke-Hasselmann's book can be seen as owing much to the concept of intertextuality, as I have already suggested on a number of occasions, and although she does not address the idea specifically, it clearly underlies her discussions of reference, citation and allusion, and the underlying notions of audience response and a textual community.

The writing of romance is also conditioned by a rhetorical process governed by the 'rules' and prescriptions of the medieval arts of poetry, part of what could be viewed as the literary theory of the Middle Ages. This is an aspect of literary study not touched upon directly by Schmolke-Hasselmann, although her observations about epigonal responses to Chrétien are certainly susceptible of explanation in rhetorical terms as well. For example, what Schmolke-Hasselmann notes as, say, a rewriting of an episode from Chrétien in one of the epigonal romances might be seen as revealing use of one of the many techniques of *inventio*. No one has done more to sensitize us to the crucial role played by rhetoric than Douglas Kelly, much of whose work has been devoted to French Arthurian romance in both verse and prose. Kelly's work also shows that while in some respects Arthurian romance obeys its own rules, in others it is part of the mainstream of vernacular narrative fiction. Through a series of major articles to his landmark study on *The Art of Medieval French Romance*, Kelly has taken us beyond the simple search for examples of, say, the prescriptions of Geoffrey

[68] Uitti, 'Intertextuality in *Le Chevalier au lion*', *Dalhousie French Studies* 2 (1980), 3–13; Bruckner, 'Intertextuality', in *The Legacy of Chrétien de Troyes*, I, 223–65, and *Shaping Romance: Interpretation, Truth, and Closure in Twelfth-Century French Fictions* (Philadelphia, 1993); Wolfzettel, 'Zum Stand und Problem der Intertextualitätsforschung im Mittelalter (aus romanistischer Sicht)', in *Artusroman und Intertextualität* edited by Friedrich Wolfzettel (Gießen, 1990), pp. 1–17.

of Vinsauf's *Poetria Nova* in vernacular texts, and demonstrated how the precepts of Latin rhetoric lie at the very basis of romance structure and how they evolve in the twelfth and thirteenth centuries within the corpus of romances.[69] The reason this is so important is that Chrétien de Troyes and many of his successors were clearly trained in the great cathedral schools, Chrétien himself perhaps at Troyes, where the curriculum included in-depth study of the Latin arts of poetry. It would be difficult for such authors, writing in the vernacular, not to apply the precepts they had learned in the Latin context.

Although few would deny its importance, the relevance of the wider Latin cultural context for a better understanding of Chrétien de Troyes's work has received far less attention that might have been expected. Eugene Vance has explored the contribution of logic through the *trivium* to Chrétien's poetics in the transition from a Latinate culture to a vernacular one,[70] Jeanne A. Nightingale has also concentrated on Chrétien in a number of articles devoted to situating courtly romance within the broader tradition of mythographical discourse, particularly Macrobius and Ovid.[71] The implications of this type of approach have yet to be fully explored and assimilated by scholars. Since there is no *prima facie* reason for believing that Chrétien was any more learned than his epigones, reading of some of the post-Chrétien verse texts might also profit from consideration in the Latin context. Raoul de Houdenc, author of *Meraugis de Portlesguez* and possibly of *La Vengeance Raguidel*, for example, was the nephew of Peter the Chanter and his learned background practically assured. Such an approach would complement Beate Schmolke-Hasselmann's work.

An approach that has largely ceased to be practised in recent times is that developed by D. W. Robertson and others, known as the 'patristic-exegetical method', according to which medieval literature had to be read necessarily in the light of Augustinian doctrine to generate a meaning pertaining to the concept of *caritas*. While the 1970s produced a number of such studies on Chrétien, scholars have not by and large pursued this type of work; only Jacques Ribard has continued in this vein.[72] Instead, the undoubted messianic associations of the Arthurian hero and the possibilities of allegorical readings of Arthurian *aventure* have become integrated into other methods such as that which informs the studies of Baumgartner and Szkilnik mentioned above.

69 I mention here only Kelly's *magnum opus*, *The Art of Medieval French Romance* (Madison, 1992). The reader is referred to the standard bibliographies for further references.

70 *From Topic to Tale: Logic and Narrativity in The Middle Ages* (Minneapolis, 1987).

71 For example, in 'Chrétien de Troyes and the Mythographical Tradition: The Couple's Journey in *Erec et Enide* and Martianus' *De Nuptiis*', in *King Arthur Through the Ages*, edited by Valerie M. Lagorio and Mildred Leake Day (New York and London, 1990), I, 56–79.

72 For example, see his 'Ecriture symbolique et visée allégorique dans *Le Conte du Graal*', *Œuvres & critiques*, 5, 2 (1980–1), 103–9.

If patristic exegesis searches for a 'serious' moral message in literature, scholarship has become much more aware in recent years of the possibilities of ironic, parodic and burlesque intentions on the part of romance authors and the concomitant awareness on the part of their intended audiences. Suzanne Fleischman published a fine study of social parody in the Occitan romance of *Jaufré*,[73] but the major work on parody in romance is no doubt by Kathryn Gravdal, one chapter of which is devoted to Guillaume le Clerc's *Fergus* and its (parodic) relation to earlier tradition.[74] Although only one chapter is directly concerned with Arthurian romance, the method used and the use of 'interpretants' may provide a model for further study. One of my criticisms of Gravdal's book is that it fails to make use of Beate Schmolke-Hasselmann's, which covers much of the same ground.[75] The similarities in method between parts of Schmolke-Hasselmann's book and Gravdal's not only suggest shared views but also confirm the applicability of the former's methods to a wider corpus of medieval French literature. Apart from specific studies of parody, the acceptance on the part of scholars that it is widely present in Arthurian romance has meant that it is equally widely discussed. This recognition that medieval romance can contain parody, and even that parody may be the basic purpose of some works, marks a watershed in scholarship in my opinion. To be sure, Beate Schmolke-Hasselmann was not the first to treat the subject, but her work represents a certain maturation in this regard.

Whereas work on the rhetoric of romance and its Latin background has stressed the learned nature of the genre, some scholars have moved in the other direction and underlined the 'orality' of the genre. Recognition of orality in medieval narrative is not new, and Paul Zumthor's work has been seminal.[76] Joseph J. Duggan has considered such matters as improvisation, oral performance and memory in a pair of related articles,[77] but more provocative and radical has been the work of Evelyn B. Vitz on the Tristan romances and Chrétien. The octosyllabic rhyming couplet, the primary form of French Arthurian verse romance, is seen as a pre-literary medium, and while not all

73 '*Jaufre* or Chivalry Askew: Social Overtones of Parody in Arthurian Romance', *Viator* 12 (1981), 101–29.

74 *Vilain and Courtois: Transgressive Parody in French Literature of the Twelfth and Thirteenth Centuries* (Lincoln, Nebr., 1989).

75 See my review in *Zeitschrift für französische Sprache und Literatur* 103 (1993), 71–3.

76 See especially *La poésie et la voix dans la civilisation médiévale* (Paris, 1984) .

77 'Oral Performance of Romance in Medieval France', in *Continuations: Essays on Medieval French Literature and Language in Honor of John L. Grigsby*, edited by Norris J. Lacy and Gloria Torrini-Roblin (Birmingham, Ala., 1989), pp. 51–61; 'Performance and Transmission, Aural and Ocular Reception in the Twelfth- and Thirteenth-Century Vernacular Literature of France', *Romance Philology* 43, 1 (August 1989), 49–58.

verse romances were orally composed, some were, and a re-evaluation of the critically commonplace dichotomy 'oral–written' is urgently called for. Vitz's most controversial suggestion is that Chrétien de Troyes was a minstrel, not a *clerc*, and that he conceived his work as popular entertainment rather than as written literature. The view has not found wide acceptance.[78] Whether Chrétien and his epigones were minstrels or *clercs*, the physical situation of primary and secondary reception of romance is crucial both to Beate Schmolke-Hasselmann's book and to our understanding of medieval literature in general. Work performed orally and received aurally differs in many respects from that intended to be read silently by individuals. As well as determining the manner in which an author writes, it attributes to audiences both specialized knowledge of the genre and a retentive memory. In the last instance, it is this intimate situation which is conducive to the establishment of what might be called a complicitous relationship between author and audience. In Chrétien's case, his listeners are asked to admire his skill in composition and versification, and in the case of his epigones, they are expected to grasp the general and specific relationship of the romances to prior tradition.

A number of important studies of figures or types in Arthurian romance have appeared. Aileen Ann Macdonald has provided a useful treatment of the figure of Merlin in thirteenth-century prose romances (Robert de Boron, Vulgate and Post-Vulgate Cycles), considering his role as womanizer, kingmaker and prophet; the three central Merlin texts are interrelated and seen as products of collaboration between royal ladies, their court poets and the religious of the Fontevrist order.[79] It is interesting to note that Merlin scarcely appears in the verse romances of Chrétien de Troyes and his epigones which are the subject of this book: only in *Claris et Laris*, visibly written under influence of the prose romances, does he play a role of any significance. More all-encompassing is Marie-Luce Chênerie's study of the knight errant, which examines, in the traditional manner of a *thèse d'état*, all aspects of the presentation and role of the knight errant in the verse romance corpus. The book also constitutes a thorough description of, and guide to, the world of Arthurian romance (inhabitants, geography, spaces, sentiment, etc.) as it pertains to the figure of the knight; as such it is an indispensable companion, perhaps preface, to Beate Schmolke-

[78] Evelyn Birge Vitz, 'Rethinking Old French Literature: The Orality of the Octosyllabic Couplet', *Romanic Review* 77 (1986), 307–21; 'Orality, Literacy and the Early Tristan Material: Béroul, Thomas, Marie de France', *Romanic Review* 78 (1987), 299–310; 'Chrétien de Troyes: clerc ou ménestrel? Problèmes des traditions orales et littéraires dans les cours de France au XIIe siècle', *Poétique* 21 (1990), 21–42.

[79] *The Figure of Merlin in Thirteenth-Century French Romance* (Lewiston, Queenston and Lampeter, 1990).

Hasselmann's study.[80] The *fée* has been studied in important books by Laurence Harf-Lancner, Pierre Gallais and Jean-Claude Aubailly.[81] These three works are typical of a kind of Arthurian scholarship currently being produced in France in that they are concerned with mythological and folkloric material which they view from various anthropological and psychoanalytical perspectives. Harf-Lancner's study traces the birth in the Middle Ages of what she considers a new mythological figure, the *fée*, before going on to explore its articulation in figures such as Morgan and Mélusine; a final part of the book considers the rationalization and Christianization of this mythological and folkloric material in medieval literature. Although not restricted to Arthurian romance, this study is particularly important for its treatment of the figure of Morgan and of the widespread 'fairy mistress' theme. Gallais's study, informed by the works of Jung, Bachelard and Gilbert Durand, seeks to establish the figure of the *fée* as an archetype of the feminine *anima* and the rise of the *fée* in literature as an exaltation of feminine values. In addition to its basic thesis, this book is also noteworthy, like that of Harf-Lancner, for much incidental discussion of romance themes and motifs. Similar conclusions are reached by Aubailly, whose book is concerned mainly with the Breton *lais*, two of which, Marie's *Lanval* and the anonymous *Tyolet*, are specifically Arthurian: Jung's principle of *anima*, the collective idea of woman hidden in man's subconscious, is rehabilitated, revealing the restoration of a lost cosmological harmony. While this kind of study is far removed in approach and intent from Beate Schmolke-Hasselmann's book, her view of the relationship between Chrétien and his epigones might be taken as a starting-point when examining the differences between them with respect to folkloric and anthropological issues.

Inseparable from the *fée* and related figures is the concept of the *merveilleux*, the subject of studies by Daniel Poirion and Francis Dubost.[82] Three chapters (IV on the *lais bretons*, V on Arthurian romance and VI on the thirteenth century) of Poirion's study are devoted largely or in part to Arthurian texts. This short monograph is intended as an introductory overview of the subject and provides an excellent starting-point. Dubost's *thèse d'état* is a comprehensive study of 'aspects fantastiques' in twelfth- and thirteenth-century French literature, mainly

80 *Le chevalier errant dans les romans arthuriens en vers des XIIe et XIIIe siècles* (Geneva, 1986).

81 Laurence Harf-Lancner, *Les fées dans la littérature française au Moyen Age: Morgane et Mélusine: la naissance des fées* (Paris, 1984); Pierre Gallais, *La Fée à la Fontaine et à l'Arbre: un archetype du conte merveilleux et du récit courtois* (Amsterdam and Atlanta, 1992); Jean-Claude Aubailly, *La fée et le chevalier* (Paris, 1986).

82 Daniel Poirion, *Le merveilleux dans la littérature française du Moyen Age* (Paris, 1981); Francis Dubost, *Aspects fantastiques de la littérature narrative médiévale (XIIe–XIIIe siècles): l'Autre, l'Ailleurs, l'Autrefois*, 2 vols (Paris, 1991).

romances (many of which are Arthurian) and *chansons de geste*. According to Dubost, the disturbing and inexplicable which define the *fantastique* are generated by 'alterity'. The spaces from which God is absent are likely to be the *loci* of supernatural manifestations and to be inhabited by all manner of fantastic creatures: *chevaliers faés*, dragons, *bestes glastissants*, etc., the Devil and Merlin. Jean-Marie Fritz has published an innovative and interdisciplinary study of madness in twelfth- and thirteenth-century French literature, subtitled 'Étude comparée des discours littéraire, médical, juridique et théologique de la folie'.[83] Amongst the Arthurian romances discussed are Chrétien's *Yvain*, the *Folies Tristan*, the Prose *Lancelot*, the Prose *Tristan* and *Ysaÿe le Triste*. Again, Beate Schmolke-Hasselmann does not deal with matters such as the supernatural and madness directly in her book, but the evolution she has traced will permit us to make comparative studies of these topics in early and later romances. The general differences she has discerned between Chrétien and his epigones suggest that the supernatural is presented in a more spectacular and less mysterious fashion in the later texts. Like many other aspects of Chrétien's *œuvre*, the *merveilleux* becomes demystified in the works of his successors.

Clearly, many of the studies mentioned in the two previous paragraphs deal, both directly and indirectly, with matters of folklore. More avowedly 'folkloristic' in approach is an important article by Anita Guerreau[-Jalabert] on Chrétien's romances and their thematic analogues in folktales.[84] Whilst acknowledging the value of the Stith Thompson *Motif-Index*, Guerreau reveals its shortcomings for the medievalist and revises Thompson's concept of 'motif'. This is achieved by the implementation of a new method of internal analysis and comparative study of the romances, taking into account their meaning in relation to their sources and cultural context. Stith Thompson's *Motif-Index* nevertheless remains the basic model for Guerreau-Jalabert's own important index.[85] In the introduction, Guerreau-Jalabert treats problems of classification, the inevitability of subjectivity and the impossibility of categorical definition. The general motif-index based on Thompson is followed by a motif-analysis of each of the twenty-seven romances in the corpus and an alphabetical motif-index. This will henceforth be an indispensable reference work for students of Arthurian narrative. Another index, by E. H. Ruck, is more restricted in its corpus (Wace's *Brut*, Chrétien's *œuvre*, the verse *Tristan* texts, five *lais*, *Le Bel Inconnu*, *Le Chevalier à l'épée* and *La Mule sans frein*), but more wide-ranging

[83] *Le discours du fou au Moyen Age, XIIe–XIIIe siècles* (Paris, 1992).

[84] 'Romans de Chrétien de Troyes et contes folkloriques: rapprochements thématiques et observations de méthode', *Romania* 104 (1983), 1–48.

[85] *Index des motifs narratifs dans les romans arthuriens français en vers (XIIe–XIIIe siècles) [Motif-Index of French Arthurian Verse Romances (XIIth–XIIIth Cent.)]* (Geneva, 1992).

in that it does not limit itself to narrative motifs; the categories are in essence similar to those used by Mario Roques and Alexandre Micha in the appendices to their editions of Chrétien's *Erec et Enide*, *Yvain* and *Cligés*.[86] Whilst she by no means applies the methods of folklorists, Beate Schmolke-Hasselmann does consider the typology of Arthurian romance in terms of narrative patterns, especially in Chapter 2 of this book. The more properly folkloristic approaches of the studies mentioned above may therefore be seen as a complement to her work.

Joël Grisward has applied Dumézil's work to the domain of Arthurian romance, showing how the Indo-European tri-functional system has been preserved in the stories of Arthur's conception and accession to the throne, and in various transformations of the Grail legend.[87] Although not drawing directly on Dumézil's work, Gaël Milin's study of Aarne-Thompson 782 underlines the associations between the horse and royalty in Indo-European society, and suggests that the episode formed by lines 1303–50 of Béroul's *Tristan* is based on a Celtic tale. This hypothesis allows Milin to show how Béroul modified a traditional tale to fit into the context of his romance.[88] In her book, Beate Schmolke-Hasselmann confirms the centrality of the kingship problem in Arthurian verse romance and how it is directly linked to the intended audience: as political propaganda, romance may either undermine or consolidate the position of the monarchy. As a British king, Arthur is frequently shown to be weak and indecisive by authors writing for audiences of French extraction whose ancestors conquered the island in 1066. It would be extraordinarily interesting to see what the Indo-European approach would reveal about the propagandistic function of romance.

Milin's work is also illustrative of what might be termed a 'new Celticism' on the part of some French and, notably, Breton, scholars. Gwénolé Le Menn's *La Femme au sein d'or* compares recently collected Breton folksongs with the legend of St. Enori and with the Caradoc episode from the First Continuation of Chrétien's *Perceval*. Le Menn concludes that while Welsh tradition may have been the closest source of the romance, the tale can be traced back to a Breton source. The unity and interrelation of Celtic cultures is also stressed in Le Menn's work.[89] Another scholar who has made significant contributions to the

[86] *An Index of Themes and Motifs in Twelfth-Century French Arthurian Poetry* (Cambridge, 1991). A note by Roques at the end of the CFMA *Lancelot* explains the absence of such an index in that volume; Félix Lecoy did not include one in his *Perceval*.

[87] For example, his 'Uter Pendragon, Artur et l'idéologie royale des Indo-Européens: structure trifonctionnelle et roman arthurien', *Europe* n° 654 (October 1983), 111–20.

[88] *Le roi Marc aux oreilles de cheval* (Geneva, 1991).

[89] *La Femme au sein d'or* (St. Brieuc, 1985).

study of the Celtic elements in Arthurian romance is Jean-Claude Lozac'hmeur. Together with Shigemi Sasaki, Lozac'hmeur returns to R. S. Loomis's earlier hypothesis concerning the relations between Celtic tales of vengeance and sovereignty and Chrétien's *Perceval*, concluding, against Frappier, that Loomis was in essence correct. Lozac'hmeur's article on Gauvain's adventures in Chrétien's *Perceval* restates these conclusions, before ingeniously examining the Celtic nature of this part of the narrative, finally justifying its position in the romance as a whole. Similar concerns inform a third contribution in which Lozac'hmeur also underlines the esoteric, Indo-European, nature of the origins of the Grail legend and its relationship to Indo-European rites of royal initiation.[90] This return to the study of Celtic origins is characteristic of the scholarly process in general in so far as approaches and methods once abandoned as obsolete are rejuvenated after a period of neglect in the light of progress made elsewhere. Beate Schmolke-Hasselmann does not deal with matters Celtic in her book, but it is extraordinary to note how Celtic material has been transformed in the French language into what is effectively an instrument of repression.

The theories of Claude Lévi-Strauss are used by Jean-Guy Gouttebroze to elucidate lineage ties in Chrétien's work, notably in the *Perceval*. Perceval is seen as an 'anti-Œdipus' who, by refusing to ask the question at the Grail castle, avoids the danger of incest; the romance is seen as dealing with issues such as stability and instability of lineage, clan and, ultimately, royalty.[91] Another type of psychoanalytical approach is that exemplified in Charles Méla's substantial work on the Grail romances.[92] Largely inspired by post-modernist theory and the work of Lacan, Méla eschews a chronological approach to the Grail romances in favour of a method that elucidates the 'secret life' of the texts, intertextual and intratextual. By examining themes such as the absent father, castration and incest, Méla demonstrates that the itinerary of the hero in the Grail texts corresponds to the manner of their writing and of their reception by the reader. Méla's work was enthusiastically received by Jean-Charles Huchet, who further argues that the homologous structures which exist between psychoanalysis and medieval romance render each capable of elucidating the other: Méla uses

[90] Jean-Claude Lozachmeur and Shigemi Sasaki, 'A propos de deux hypothèses de R. S. Loomis: éléments pour une solution de l'énigme du Graal', *BBSIA* 34 (1982), 207–21; Lozac'hmeur, 'Origines celtiques des aventures de Gauvain au pays de Galvoie dans le *Conte du Graal* de Chrétien de Troyes', in *Actes du 14e Congrès International Arthurien*, edited by C. Foulon *et al.*, 2 vols (Rennes, 1985), I, 406–22; 'Recherches sur les origines indo-européennes et ésotériques de la légende du Graal', *Cahiers de civilisation médiévale* 30 (1987), 44–63.

[91] *Qui perd gagne: le 'Perceval' de Chrétien de Troyes comme représentation de l'Œdipe inversé* (Nice, 1983).

[92] *La reine et le Graal: la 'conjointure' dans les romans du Graal de Chrétien de Troyes au 'Livre de Lancelot'* (Paris, 1984).

psychoanalysis to read medieval romance while Henri Rey-Flaud in *La névrose courtoise* employs medieval romance to refine the results of psychoanalysis. Huchet's study of the Tristan romances is an ingenious and, some might say, subjective, reading of the same persuasion.[93] If Schmolke-Hasselmann's book is about the conscious intent of authors with respect to their audiences, then studies such as those by Méla and Huchet are concerned with the unconscious patterning of the reading and writing of texts.

The Tristan romances have also been studied by Philippe Walter in one of a number of original recent studies on the mythological substructure of Arthurian romance. For Walter, the relationship between the surviving Tristan texts is less important than their ability to reveal the myths, beliefs and superstitions proper to Indo-European society. In particular, the Tristan story shares features with the story of Cinderella. Such superstitions include astrological ones, and Walter has ingeniously proposed that Yvain becomes 'le Chevalier au Lion' because he is under the influence of Sirius ('Canicule', the Dog Star), a bright star of the constellation Canis Major visible in the Summer sky (22 July–23 August) when the sun rejoins the sign of Leo; Sirius brings torrid heat, plague and melancholic rage in 'the dog days of Summer'. Walter's *thèse d'état* is at the same time an analysis of the feasts that punctuate the narratives of Arthurian romance ('nuptial', 'dynastique', 'curial'), and an attempt to recover their mythological and archaic foundations.[94] The method chosen necessarily entails comparison of seemingly quite disparate and distant cultures. Whereas Beate Schmolke-Hasselmann's work seeks to place the romances in their specific cultural and historical context, that of Walter (and some of the other scholars whose work has been discussed in the last few paragraphs) aims to reconstruct the distant context of its origins in the human psyche.

In the USA, Peter Haidu and Eugene Vance have both written post-structuralist, deconstructionist, analyses of Chrétien de Troyes but which attempt to restore a historical dimension.[95] Haidu in particular, in an article on *Yvain*, explicitly aims to show, contrary to de Man's contention, that deconstruction and historicity are not mutually exclusive. The episodes of the hero's meeting

[93] Huchet, 'Psychanalyse et littérature médiévale: rencontre ou méprise? (A propos de deux ouvrages récents)', *Cahiers de civilisation médiévale* 28 (1985), 223–33; *Tristan et le sang de l'écriture* (Paris, 1990); Rey-Flaud, *La névrose courtoise* (Paris, 1983).

[94] *Le gant de verre: le mythe de Tristan et Yseut* (La Gacilly, 1990); *Canicule: essai de mythologie sur 'Yvain' de Chrétien de Troyes* (Paris, 1988); *La mémoire du temps: fêtes et calendriers de Chrétien de Troyes à 'La Mort Artu'* (Paris, 1989).

[95] Peter Haidu, 'The Hermit's Pottage: Deconstruction and History in *Yvain*', *Romanic Review* 74 (1983), 1–15; Eugene Vance, 'Chrétien's *Yvain* and the Ideologies of Change and Exchange', *Yale French Studies* 70 (1986), 42–62.

with the hermit and of the Château de Pesme Aventure are seen as illustrating contemporary economic models of exchange. Similar concerns inform Vance's study, which discusses Yvain's crisis, his relationship with Laudine and the machinations of Lunete in the context of a new view of love as an economic transaction. One chapter of a recent book by Judith Kellogg is also devoted to Chrétien de Troyes, whose romances are said to conceal only skimpily the cracks appearing in the outmoded feudal armour of twelfth-century aristocracy.[96] This type of scholarship clearly pursues another path opened up by the important earlier work of Erich Köhler and effectively uses other means to reach conclusions similar to those of Beate Schmolke-Hasselmann. The difference is that the latter's focus is more specific and local, that of Haidu, Vance and Kellogg more wide-ranging. In a sense, the results of such work are predictable: literature written at a particular time will reflect directly or indirectly the economic concerns and models of that time. Because of Chrétien's status as a 'classic', his romances alone amongst the Arthurian verse corpus have been the object of such analysis. Schmolke-Hasselmann's book offers both an invitation and an opportunity to extend the coverage.

French Arthurian romance has not surprisingly been the object of feminist criticism in the 1980s and 1990s. Particularly active in this field have been E. Jane Burns and Roberta L. Krueger. Burns's major contribution is a polemical examination of gender issues raised by the representation of women in texts inspired by misogynous male imagination and fantasy; foremost amongst these are Chrétien's *Erec et Enide* and Béroul's *Tristan*. Through the speech attributed to them, female protagonists can subvert and restructure the norms of female identity as they are usually perceived in romance.[97] Krueger focuses rather on the relation between the romances and their female audiences, suggesting that such works as *Yvain*, *Lancelot*, *Le Roman de Silence*, *Le Chevalier à l'épée* and *La Vengeance Raguidel* invite their readers to criticize and resist gender roles at the same time as they appear to present idealized models of behaviour.[98] Although Beate Schmolke-Hasselmann does not avail herself of feminist approaches in her book, the question of audience/reader response is crucial both to her work and to the feminist enterprise. What is common to the work of Schmolke-Hasselmann, Burns and Krueger, is the belief that romance can and does subvert

[96] *Medieval Artistry and Exchange: Economic Institutions, Society, and Literary Form in Old French Narrative* (New York, 1989).

[97] *Bodytalk: When Women Speak in Old French Literature* (Philadelphia, 1993).

[98] *Women Readers and the Ideology of Gender in Old French Verse Romance* (Cambridge, 1993). See also a special issue of *Romance Notes* 25, 3 (1985), edited by Burns and Krueger, devoted to *Courtly Ideology and Woman's Place in Medieval French Literature*, and articles on 'The Construction of Manhood in Arthurian Literature', a special section of vol. III of *The Arthurian Yearbook* (1993).

the representation of fundamental social structures and relationships, expressed as political authority or gender roles and identity.

One of the more noticeable trends in medieval literary scholarship in recent years has been the renewed attention being paid to manuscripts. This has not only resulted in the new editions discussed at the outset of this chapter, but more especially in consideration of the manuscript context of the romances and what can be learned from it. I wrote above that Beate Schmolke-Hasselmann does not dwell in detail on the manuscript transmission of romance, yet the medieval codex as physical object, mediated through the performer, is that which carries the text to the audience. As such it is our only tangible link with the reality of the medieval literary enterprise. Studies of romance manuscripts begin to proliferate in the mid-1980s, and are by and large concerned with two, related, areas: the roles of scribes and compilers, and the relationship between text and image. Lori Walters's article on the insertion of Chrétien's romances into the text of Wace's *Brut* in MS Paris, BN fr. 1450 has already become a classic, comparable to Elspeth Kennedy's earlier piece on the manuscripts of the Prose *Lancelot*, in which she coined the phrase 'the scribe as editor'; Walters has also examined BN fr. 1433 (Chrétien's *Yvain*, *L'Atre périlleux*, etc.) as a 'super romance' formed by the conjoining of originally independent works.[99] Here, links between texts are perceived as having been created by the ordering of romances within a codex and interpretations manipulated by the choice of subjects of the miniatures and their placement. Although Sylvia Huot's book on the evolution of Old French manuscripts is not directly concerned with Arthurian literature, it does deal with some romance codices and is a landmark in Old French studies generally.[100] It is an excellent example of what close examination of manuscripts can reveal about the literature they contain and the way in which they were received in the Middle Ages. Such studies clearly add an extra dimension to the reception-oriented work of Beate Schmolke-Hasselmann.

The physical layout of particular manuscripts or groups of manuscripts has been the object of a number of studies: Hans Runte has studied the structuring of Chrétien's romances through the positioning of decorated capitals, Geneviève Hasenohr has discussed the various types of *mise en page* of verse romance manuscripts, while Emmanuèle Baumgartner and Véronique Roland have commented on the opening-page layout of manuscripts of the Prose *Tristan* and

[99] Walters, 'Le rôle du scribe dans l'organisation des manuscrits des romans de Chrétien de Troyes', *Romania* 106 (1985), 303–25; 'The Creation of a "Super-Romance": Paris, Bibliothèque Nationale, fonds français, MS 1433', *The Arthurian Yearbook* 1 (1991), 3–25; Kennedy, 'The Scribe as Editor', in *Mélanges Jean Frappier* (Geneva, 1970), I, 523–31.

[100] *From Song to Book: The Poetics of Writing in Old French Lyric and Lyrical Narrative Poetry* (Ithaca and London, 1987).

Merlin respectively and their implication for the perception of the romances.[101] We should bear in mind generally with respect to codicological study that conclusions drawn with respect to particular manuscripts pertain to their period of manufacture and not necessarily to the original intentions of the authors of the text which they contain. Since many of the manuscripts in which the romances have been preserved are later than their dates of composition, study of them extends the *Rezeptionsgeschichte* beyond the temporal limits of such investigations as that of Beate Schmolke-Hasselmann.

Sandra Hindman has argued that certain of the manuscripts in which Chrétien's romances are preserved were written for the Picard aristocracy in the latter half of the thirteenth century. Basing herself on the scenes chosen for illustration, Hindman suggests that the manuscripts reflect a particular view of chivalry and its social function.[102] Others have looked at the relationship between word and image in the *Perceval* manuscripts and have shown that the visual reception of the romance confirms what can be deduced from more strictly textual sources.[103] Again, the codicological and art historical supplements the textual, the codex as artefact being studied as an integral unit. Alison Stones has provided a basic iconographical update to the Loomises' basic book on *The Arthurian Legends in Medieval Art* (1938) bringing to bear her unrivalled knowledge of vernacular manuscript illumination.[104] Although manuscripts of Gottfried's *Tristan* are richly illustrated, there are few representations of the verse tradition in French. Tony Hunt, however, offers the first analysis of a set

[101] Runte, 'Initial Readers of Chrétien de Troyes', in *Continuations: Essays on Medieval French Literature and Language in Honor of John L. Grigsby*, edited by Norris J. Lacy and Gloria Torrini-Roblin (Birmingham, Ala., 1989), pp. 121–32, and compare Roger Middleton, 'Coloured Capitals in the Manuscripts of *Erec et Enide*', in *The Manuscripts of Chrétien de Troyes*, (below, note 106), I, 149–93; Hasenohr, 'Les romans en vers', in *Mise en page et mise en texte du livre manuscrit*, edited by Henri-Jean Martin and Jean Vezin (Paris, 1990), pp. 245–64; Baumgartner, 'La *première page* dans les manuscrits du *Tristan en prose*', in *La présentation du livre*, edited by Emmanuèle Baumgartner and Nicole Boulestreau (Paris, 1987), pp. 51–63; Roland, 'Folio liminaire et réception du texte: les manuscrits parisiens du *Merlin en prose*', *BBSIA* 43 (1991), 257–69.

[102] *Sealed in Parchment: Rereadings of Knighthood in the Illuminated Manuscripts of Chrétien de Troyes* (Chicago and London, 1994).

[103] Keith Busby, 'The Illustrated Manuscripts of Chrétien's *Perceval*', and 'Text, Miniature, and Rubric in the *Continuations* of Chrétien's *Perceval*', in *The Manuscripts of Chrétien de Troyes* (below, note 106), I, 351–63 and 365–76; Angelica Rieger, 'Neues über Chrétiens Illustratoren: Bild und Text in der ältesten Überlieferung von *Perceval-le-vieil* (*T*)', *BBSIA* 41 (1989), 301–11, and 'Le programme iconographique du *Perceval* montpelliérain, BI, Sect. Méd, H 249 (*M*), avec la description détaillée du manuscrit', in *The Manuscripts of Chrétien de Troyes*, I, 377–435.

[104] 'Arthurian Art since Loomis', in *Arturus Rex*, II, *Acta Conventus Lovanensis 1987*, edited by Willy Van Hoecke, Gilbert Tournoy and Werner Verbeke (Leuven, 1991), 21–78.

of drawings based on Thomas's version in MS London, British Library Add. 11619, which seem to underscore the moral nature of Thomas's text.[105]

An important recent event in Chrétien studies is the two-volume *The Manuscripts of Chrétien de Troyes.*[106] An international, collaborative effort, this work presents a complete catalogue of all Chrétien manuscripts, a photographic inventory of all miniatures, types of decoration and scribal hands, along with numerous studies by literary scholars, art historians, palaeographers and codicologists. The essays it contains illustrate all of the directions discerned in the preceding three paragraphs, and more besides. Space does not permit a full description of its contents here, but in addition to lists, catalogues and descriptions of the manuscripts, there are essays on textual issues, studies of the manuscript transmission and presentation, of the location and significance of coloured initials, on pen-flourishing in some Champenois manuscripts, of the artistic context of the illustrated manuscripts, on the Pierre Sala *Yvain* manuscript, on opening miniatures, on the iconography of *Perceval* and the Continuations, and on fantastic elements of the illustrations.[107] Important sections deal in great detail with the history of all of the manuscripts and what is known about their former owners.[108] While this may seem a long way from Schmolke-Hasselmann's book, study of the manuscripts in fact provides, as I have said, noteworthy support for her claims, both in general and in detail, and extends the coverage of Chrétien-reception well into the fourteenth century by its consideration of later manuscripts.

It is no exaggeration to say that scholarship in Old French Arthurian literature is currently in a healthy, vigorous and robust state. Beate Schmolke-Hasselmann's book will take its place alongside earlier classics of scholarship on French Arthurian literature, such as Roger Sherman Loomis's *Arthurian Tradition and Chrétien de Troyes* and Jean Frappier's *Chrétien de Troyes: l'homme et l'œuvre*. Other studies will in the course of time also emerge as scholarly landmarks to guide us through what often seems at any given moment an impenetrable mass of frequently conflicting ideas. The context of this book in the midst of the kind of scholarly diversity described in the preceding pages reflects not only the fascination Arthurian romance continues to exercise over

105 'The Tristan Illustrations in MS London, BL Add. 11619', in *Rewards and Punishments in the Arthurian Romances and Lyric Poetry of Mediaeval France*, edited by Peter V. Davies and Angus J. Kennedy (Cambridge, 1987), pp. 45–60.

106 *The Manuscripts of Chrétien de Troyes/Les manuscrits de Chrétien de Troyes*, edited by Keith Busby, Terry Nixon, Alison Stones and Lori Walters, 2 vols (Amsterdam, 1993).

107 I do not list the individual articles here; tables of contents are to be found in both volumes.

108 Terry Nixon, 'Catalogue of Manuscripts', II, 1–85; Roger Middleton, 'Index of Former Owners' and 'Additional Notes on the History of Selected Manuscripts', II, 87–176 and 177–243.

scholars but also the passion with which those same scholars debate what they regard as fundamental issues of medieval literary studies. For that, as well as Beate Schmolke-Hasselmann's distinctive contribution, we should be grateful.

Acknowledgements

The study presented here was accepted as a thesis by Göttingen University Faculty of Philosophy in the summer semester of 1978. Its publication as a supplement to *Zeitschrift für deutsche Philologie* was rendered possible by the helpfulness of the series editor, Professor Kurt Baldinger, and by the generous support of both the Faculty of Philosophy at Göttingen and the Deutsche Forschungsgemeinschaft.

My tutors, the late Professors Wilhelm Kellermann and Hanspeter Schelp, awoke my interest in medieval literature and were a source of stimulation in many respects. However, I owe a particular debt of gratitude to Professor Ulrich Mölk, who supervised this thesis. He was always prepared to give me his time and friendly advice, thereby promoting and encouraging my work.

Hannelore Schnorrenberg, Claudia Schöning, Gertrud Meyer, Dr Albert Gier, Michael Heintze and Udo Schöning were kind enough to come to my aid in the correcting process. In addition, I am grateful to my parents and to my husband for their patience and their confidence in me.

Göttingen, April 1980 Beate Schmolke-Hasselmann

Abbreviations

AIV	*Atti del R. Istituto Veneto di Scienze, Lettere ed Arti. Venezia. Classe di scienze morali e lettere*
ALMA	*Arthurian Literature in the Middle Ages*, edited by Roger Sherman Loomis, Oxford, 1959
ArchRom	*Archivum romanicum*
BBSIA	*Bulletin Bibliographique de la Société Internationale Arthurienne*
BLVS	*Bibliothek des litterarischen Vereins in Stuttgart*
CCM	*Cahiers de civilisation médiévale*
CFMA	*Classiques français du moyen âge*
CN	*Cultura Neolatina*
DA	*Dissertation Abstracts International*
DNB	*Dictionary of National Biography*
DU	*Der Deutschunterricht*
FMLS	*Forum for Modern Language Studies*
FS	*French Studies*
GRL	*Gesellschaft für romanische Literatur*
Grundriß	*Grundriß der romanischen Literaturen des Mittelalters*, edited by H. R. Jauss and E. Köhler, Heidelberg, 1968–
HLF	*Histoire Littéraire de la France*
MA	*Le Moyen Age*
MÆ	*Medium Ævum*
MLR	*Modern Language Review*
MPh	*Modern Philology*
NM	*Neuphilologische Mitteilungen*
PBB	*Beiträge zur Geschichte der deutschen Sprache und Literatur*
PL	*Patrologia Latina*, edited by J.-P. Migne, 221 vols, Paris, 1844–64
PMLA	*Publications of the Modern Language Association of America*
RJb	*Romanistisches Jahrbuch*
RPh	*Romance Philology*

RR	*Romanic Review*
SATF	*Société des Anciens Textes Français*
SLF	*Studi di Letteratura Francese*
SRÜ	*Sammlung romanischer Übungstexte*
StPh	*Studies in Philology*
TLF	*Textes Littéraires Français*
UTB	*Uni-Taschenbücher*
ZfSL	*Zeitschrift für französische Sprache und Litteratur*
ZrPh	*Zeitschrift für romanische Philologie*
ZfdPh	*Zeitschrift für deutsche Philologie*

Introduction

Throughout the history of Arthurian research, the works of the poet Chrétien de Troyes have repeatedly proved a rewarding area of study. Chrétien was the first to combine a series of Arthurian motifs and episodes into extensive and carefully organized compositions. In addition, he instilled into those compositions a new meaning, transcending what was originally conveyed by the individual elements. The literary significance of these first Arthurian romances in both the aesthetic and the historical sphere has earned them world-wide recognition, and an examination of the works of later Arthurian poets cannot diminish this significance; on the contrary, it will become apparent that the findings of the present study include new arguments to support and confirm the importance of the early Arthurian literature for several generations of authors in the thirteenth century and beyond. This study is intended as a contribution to both reception history, examining the medieval response to Chrétien's poetry, and genre history, surveying the evolution of Arthurian verse romance in French. The main objective is to describe the evolutionary changes taking place between Chrétien's *Erec et Enide* and Froissart's *Meliador*, the first and last examples of the genre. However, it is not very fruitful to assess the works of later Arthurian writers in terms of a reduction in quality by comparison with Chrétien. Consequently it is not the aim of this investigation to confirm yet again the status of Chrétien's works as the unequalled masterpieces of the whole of Arthurian literature. Instead these works should be understood as the starting-point for the history of their genre, which can subsequently be traced over a period of two centuries in the French-speaking world.

A further focus of interest lies in the analysis of the influence of Chrétien's works, although not as hitherto in the sense of a study of sources and motifs. Instead the investigation focuses on the reception of the Arthurian romances within the same genre and specifically on the response of Chrétien's successors within that genre to the first Arthurian poet. The way in which a succession of thirteenth-century Arthurian romances can be seen to strive for innovation calls for particular attention. At that stage, as the evolution of the genre shows, a tendency towards consolidation was always accompanied by efforts at revitalization. An analysis of the audience for the romances in question and a description of the relationship of the texts to the social and political conditions of the period 1170–1370 form the concluding part of the study.

THE CURRENT STATE OF RESEARCH

Even amongst Arthurian scholars the French Arthurian romances of the thirteenth century are not at all well known. They are usually regarded as the inferior products of several generations of decadent imitators, and are therefore largely excluded from discussions of literary history. They are mentioned with greater frequency only in studies tracing the history of motifs, or when they can shed light on questions of chronology. The proportion of research that has been devoted to them is correspondingly minimal, and until the present study no recent comprehensive evaluation of these romances was available.

Information on the content of post-Chrétien Arthurian literature can be found in the usual works of reference.[1] A sizeable group of studies on the 'post-classical' Arthurian romance appeared around the turn of the century in the form of theses dealing with 'The romance X in relation to Chrétien de Troyes'. They are mainly concerned with the study of style and recurring motifs.[2]

[1] Gaston Paris, 'Romans en vers du cycle de la Table ronde', in *Histoire Littéraire de la France*, Vol. XXX (Paris, 1888), pp. 1–270; this is still the most important and extensive study. G. Gröber (ed.), *Grundriss der romanischen Philologie*, 2 vols in 4 (Strasburg, 1888–1902), Vol. II.1 (Strasburg, 1902), especially 'Artusepen und Graaldichtung', pp. 495–510, 'Artus- und Graalependichtung nach Crestien', pp. 511–23, and 'Artusepen', pp. 785–91. J. D. Bruce, *The Evolution of Arthurian Romance from the Beginnings Down to the Year 1300*, 2 vols (Göttingen and Baltimore, 1923; second edition, Göttingen, 1928, reprinted Gloucester, Mass., 1958), deals with Chrétien's successors in Volume I, Chapter III.I, pp. 100–28, while Volume II contributes the most detailed available accounts of the content of their romances. The literary history by U. T. Holmes, *A History of Old French Literature from the Origins to 1300*, second edition (New York, 1962), contains accounts of content as well as helpful references to manuscripts and dating. Alexandre Micha, 'Miscellaneous French Romances in Verse', in *ALMA*, pp. 358–92, contains the most recent review of scholarship. The new *Grundriß der romanischen Literaturen des Mittelalters*, edited by H. R. Jauss and E. Köhler (Heidelberg, 1968–), includes an article by A. Micha entitled 'Les romans arthuriens', Vol. IV, *Roman* (1978), C.I, pp. 380–99. Wilhelm Kellermann, 'L'éthique chevaleresque et courtoise dans les romans bretons, et son influence' (unpublished paper given at the Eleventh International Arthurian Congress in Exeter, 19 August 1975), and 'Ritterliches und höfisches Ethos am Beispiel des nachklassischen französischen Artusromans in Versen. Mit einem Blick auf den entsprechenden deutschen Roman' (unpublished paper given to the Germanist Seminar at Vienna University, 19 October 1977).

[2] Without the groundwork carried out in these studies, which emanated predominantly from Göttingen, the present investigation would have encountered serious difficulties. The Romance

Hitherto the texts have sometimes been arranged in sequence according to content or approximate chronology, but they have always been studied in isolation from each other. A brief account of the plot would be followed by lists of motifs that also occur in other romances, indications of the episodes and verbatim passages borrowed from Chrétien, a discussion of the possible date and some sort of value-judgement, for which Chrétien's works were the yardstick, even if the writers were sometimes prepared to be benevolent to the extent of acknowledging some ability in a later poet when faced with a particularly nice scene or a witty dialogue.

This individual treatment of the texts has so far prevented any scrutiny of the common ground between examples of the genre, or of what is conveyed by the texts as a sequence. The method applied in the present study has therefore been designed to scan all texts in the category of Arthurian verse romances in search of their persistent shared features, which do indeed exhibit a continuity sufficient to group the texts as a genre.[3] The definition of a particular genre in terms of content can only be derived from a scrutiny of the individual texts for typical elements which can then in turn serve as the basis for generalizations. Only a group of characteristics elicited in this fashion can enable us to define the genre appropriately. The prime concern is thus not to classify but to describe.[4]

Seminar at Göttingen was even able to make available a number of the texts used by former research students, complete with their pencilled annotations, which were particularly stimulating for the current project.

[3] C. Cormeau, *'Wigalois' und 'Diu Crône': zwei Kapitel zur Gattungsgeschichte des nachklassischen Aventiureromans* (Zurich and Munich, 1977), pursues goals comparable with those of this investigation, and he achieves similar results in many respects. There is an extensive correlation between the generic characteristics of German post-classical Arthurian romances and those of the French romances. For the German writers of the thirteenth century the works of Hartmann von Aue and Wolfram von Eschenbach fulfil the same role in their system of references as Chrétien's romances do in France (pp. 68 and 105). In his first section Cormeau deals with questions of generic theory in great detail. In the preface and the introductory chapter he gives notice of a more comprehensive study of the remaining German Arthurian romances not included in his current investigation, and it is to be hoped that this project will soon be realized. Only a complete survey of both French and non-French Arthurian romances in the context of the history of the genre will open the way for an understanding of their more far-reaching links and interrelationships, and of the spread and consolidation of constant elements within the broad supranational genre of Arthurian romance.

[4] The presentation of this material is also intended as a small contribution to a history of the complete network of medieval literary genres. For this reason comparisons and references are introduced whenever possible to other related or contemporary genres and to links with non-French Arthurian literature. See E. Köhler, 'Gattungssystem und Gesellschaftssystem', *Romanistische Zeitschrift für Literaturgeschichte* 1 (1977), 7–22, and H. R. Jauss, 'Theorie der Gattungen und Literatur des Mittelalters', in *Grundriß der romanischen Literaturen des Mittelalters*, edited by H. R. Jauss and E. Köhler, Vol. I (Heidelberg, 1972), pp. 107–38.

THE TEXTS TO BE STUDIED

With the help of the reference works mentioned above it is possible to draw up a list of texts to serve as the basis for the following study. An element of difficulty arises from the fact that some scholars may characterize a work as Arthurian where others deny it this quality. Even the editors of texts sometimes lead us on a false trail. Thus on the one hand many works are termed *roman d'aventure* which could more clearly and precisely be labelled *roman arthurien*, while on the other hand one comes across the subtitle *roman arthurien* in places where this scarcely seems justified, for example in the case of *Le Roman de Silence*. Gröber also classifies *Brun de la Montagne* and *Cristal et Clarie* amongst the Arthurian romances. However, the use of a few Arthurian names and locations or an exceedingly tenuous link between the plot and the Arthurian court does not automatically turn a romance of adventure into an Arthurian romance, if individual examples of the genre are assessed on the basis of their group characteristics. For this reason the above-named texts are disregarded here, as also are romances like *Blandin de Cornouailles*, which has nothing in common with the Arthurian world except the Cornish setting.[5] The metre alone of *Brun de la Montagne* (3962 decasyllabic *laisses* in Meyer's edition) is a clear enough indication that it does not belong to the genre. Similarly, the *Roman de Silence* names King Arthur at the beginning (Thorpe's edition, line 109) and Merlin several times at the end, but there is no other indication of Arthurian connections. The eponymous heroine, Silence, is a woman. This too is un-Arthurian, since the Arthurian romance remains throughout its history a romance of chivalry and must therefore inevitably revolve around a male hero.

A further problem occurs with the prose romances. Nobody can deny their Arthurian character, but if one postulates a wider category of 'Arthurian romance' it soon becomes clear that the form (verse or prose) is a decisive criterion, such that one has to distinguish at the very least between two sub-groups, if not indeed between two separate genres, the verse romances and the prose romances. The verse romances adhere to principles of structure and meaning different from those of the prose romances, even if both sometimes have the same protagonists, similar sequences of *aventure* and much the same length, as well as having their origins during the same period. The concerns of the prose romances are completely different, the mood is serious and the outcome tragic. The inevitability of fate manifested in the death of the king and his knights, a pronounced element of symbolism, the guilt and failure of the heroes in their quests, the admonitory tone of the narration with its call to

[5] R. Lejeune, 'The Troubadours', in *ALMA*, pp. 393–9, classifies *Blandin de Cornouailles* as an Arthurian romance.

self-examination in the face of the fateful events described—these features constitute the essential nature of the prose romances. The interpretation of the narrative as reflecting the process of salvation is seen to place overriding limitations on human individuality, and to leave no room for it to unfold freely in the way that is central to verse romance. The verse romances like the prose romances lay claim to truth, but this is manifested in a different form as a general and exemplary truth in place of the literary and theological interpretation of events.

Further differences in the respective characteristics of prose romances and verse romances can be found in the following pairs of opposites, although this still cannot claim to be a comprehensive list:

Prose	*Verse*
Progression of time and ageing of the characters.	Spiritual maturity without ageing process. Progression of time solely with regard to prescribed goal.
Strong element of symbolism.	Symbolism largely avoided.
Lineage has religious significance.	Lineage of secondary importance.
Narrative time-span covers several generations.	Narrative time-span of one to two years.
Prophetic dreams as omens of impending disaster.	Prophecies serve to glorify the hero.
The reader is moved to fear, emotion and compassion.	The reader is moved to admiration and pleasure.
Lancelot, Guinevere, Morholt, Galahad, Bohort and Perceval are important protagonists.	These characteers are of no significance in the verse romances.
The heroes are predestined to perform deeds of deliverance.	The motif of predestination is largely eliminated.
General avoidance of romantic involvement for the protagonists; love is seen as a harmful force.	The protagonists' love-relationships are central; love is always seen in a positive light.
References to Geoffrey and Wace, and to historical models outside the genre.	References to prototypes within the genre (Chrétien).

The distinctive groups of characteristics make it possible to describe the Arthurian verse romances in isolation from the Arthurian prose romances.

References to the latter are therefore intended to serve merely as points of comparison and as illustrations of the tendencies postulated for the verse romances.

It is not possible to be so unequivocal with regard to whether the *Perceval* Continuations have to be taken into account on the basis of their metrical form, which is identical with that of the verse romances. The romances that are not continuations are characterized by their not touching on the Grail quest in any way, and even the protagonists of the *Perceval* Continuations (apart from Gawain) play only a minimal part or none at all in these other romances. Here too we see that the concerns and aims of the Continuations differ from those of the verse romances; they set out to extend or conclude a given plot begun by Chrétien and this determines their inner structure. By contrast, the verse romances that are not continuations and are independent of the Grail romance are distinguished, like Chrétien's early romances, by their inherent completeness and their purposeful structure. On the other hand, late verse romances like *Escanor* and especially *Claris et Laris* with their sheer bulk, the multiple threads of the plot which can be dropped and picked up again at any time (the technique of *entrelacement*) and also their particular protagonists, are once again so close to the *Perceval* Continuations that it is not possible to effect a rigid separation. However, we are clearly dealing with two different manifestations of the genre of Arthurian verse romances, where the *Perceval* Continuations are to be seen as a specialized off-shoot from the main body of Arthurian verse. The further ramifications of both groups of texts culminate in the prose romances. This assessment of their position accounts for the fact that the Continuations are mentioned only peripherally, albeit repeatedly, in the course of this study.

These fundamental considerations leave us with a genre incorporating the following texts.

The five Arthurian romances by Chrétien:

Erec
Cligés
Lancelot
Yvain
Perceval. [6]

[6] Quotations will be taken from the editions by Roques (*Erec, Lancelot* and *Yvain*), Micha (*Cligés*) and Roach (*Perceval*). Where line numbers are given the additional figures in square brackets refer to the corresponding lines in the editions by Foerster (*Erec, Cligés, Lancelot* and *Yvain*) and Hilka (*Perceval*). Full details of all these editions are given in the Bibliography.

A further fifteen romances (in alphabetical order):

L'Atre périlleux
Beaudous
Le Bel Inconnu
Li Chevaliers as deus espees
Claris et Laris
Durmart
Escanor
Fergus
Floriant et Florete
Hunbaut
Meliador
Meraugis
Les Merveilles de Rigomer
La Vengeance Raguidel
Yder
(Jaufré).[7]

The romance of *Jaufré* has been included in the study despite being composed not in French but in Occitan. In my opinion *Jaufré* does not represent a reworking of a lost Old French original, but is an independent composition. The only truly Arthurian romance to emerge from Occitania is so closely related to the texts from northern France that it has a persuasive case for being allocated to the same genre, albeit with some reservations. The reasons for such a close relationship may lie in the strong cultural and political connections between south and north in the thirteenth century. It will become clear that *Jaufré* shows the same group characteristics as the other Arthurian romances dealt with here; it can even be seen as an especially typical example of the genre.[8]

[7] For editions see the Bibliography. As a rule the quotations will be taken from the older editions, unless the more recent ones offer fundamental editorial improvements, as for example in the cases of *Beaudous, Chevalier à l'épée, Mule, Durmart, Cor* and *Mantel.* [In this translation, quotations from *Beaudous* have been taken from the published edition by Ulrich rather than the unpublished dissertation by Lamarque. Quotations from *Fergus* are taken from the edition by Frescoln, which was not available at the time of this study but is now much more accessible than the two nineteenth-century editions and has the advantage of continuous line-numbering.]

[8] Gaston Paris rightly includes *Jaufré* in his survey in 'Romans en vers', pp. 215ff. In the following study the individual romances will be dealt with at very different levels of intensity. This would seem sensible and indeed necessary in cases where numerous pieces of research have already been carried out (as for example with *Le Bel Inconnu* or the lays of *Cor* and *Mantel*), or where the specific line of inquiry in this study rules out any more detailed work on those texts which contain no significant material relevant to the chosen points of focus.

In addition, there are five fragments to be included:

Les Enfances Gauvain
Gogulor
Ilas et Solvas
Le Vallet a la cote mautaillie
(Melior).[9]

As far as we can judge, these fragments all appear to be the remains of longer romances. In so far as we are able to extract coherent information from them, they can shed important light on the frequency of particular scenes and motifs, and this helps to highlight what may be regarded as typical. For this reason they are included in the study to supplement those texts that have been transmitted in a more complete form.

We shall also be taking account of the lays and shorter Arthurian narratives, and this involves a group of eight texts:

Le Chevalier à l'épée
Lai du cor
Lai du cort mantel
Gliglois
Lanval
La Mule sans frein
Tyolet
Melion.[10]

However, given that Chrétien's romances are taken as the point of reference, the other full-scale romances occupy the bulk of the analysis, since they offer the only chance to observe the evolution of the genre in all its different aspects. Nevertheless, the Arthurian lays and shorter narratives are often cited to illustrate certain tendencies within that evolution and to highlight various themes and motifs. Although their more limited scope renders many of them unsuitable for the elaboration of characteristic structural patterns, the shorter

[9] For editions see the Bibliography. In the case of the fragment *Melior* it is doubtful whether we are really dealing with an Arthurian romance: a queen (Guinevere?) is here unjustly accused of the murder of the king (Arthur?); Melior offers to defend her in a duel. The fragment seems to belong to the beginning of the romance, but in that position the motif would be absolutely unique as the opening of an Arthurian work.

[10] These narratives range in length from 595 lines (*Cor*) to 2942 lines (*Gliglois*). In this study they are distinguished from the verse romances on the basis of their structure, which differs in being limited to one central adventure, with the narrative presented in a concise manner and no sub-plots. For editions see the Bibliography.

texts can still be regarded in many respects as very 'pure' examples of Arthurian narrative.[11]

The working hypothesis of this study is that all the texts listed above belong to a group that we would wish to call a genre. They are united by a series of standard features: the metre, a comparable structure, the shared subject-matter, characteristic plots and themes, similar circumstances of composition and finally their position with respect to other genres.[12] The dominant category of the French Arthurian verse romances, with its fringe groupings of Arthurian lays and Continuations, has a further advantage to offer when studied in terms of the evolution of the genre, for it can be observed as a historical phenomenon, with the first and last examples of the genre spanning a lengthy period of time.[13] The term 'genre' can therefore be understood as a category with a historical role.

THE EVOLUTION OF THE GENRE

Gustav Gröber spoke of the 'Arthurian epic' as a type of narrative poetry already exemplified in the works of Chrétien, its first proponent:

> The individual poems are of roughly similar length, and have a constant metre, standard motifs, characters and groups of characters, and distinct levers and devices to advance or retard the plot, while they deal with the supernatural even more freely than the Tristan poems... The standard characters of these epic poems are the Welsh King Arthur, his wife Guinevere, his nephew Gawain and the steward Kay, who with other elect knights such as Yvain and Lancelot amongst others constitute the king's Round Table... The knights of the Round Table do not normally differ in their fundamental nature but only in degree, and one of them is usually the protagonist of the plot. The poems will recount episodes of his life if he is deemed to be well known (episodic epics), or will present his life and deeds in full if they are only now being made known (biographical epics). The Round Table with Arthur and his court form the background to these works. The plot is made up of adventures, *aventures*, which

[11] The lays of *Cor* and *Mantel* are variations on the theme of the chastity test, just as the lays of *Lanval* and *Melion* represent variations on the theme of fairy mistresses.

[12] Additional characteristic and constant features will be brought to light in the later course of this survey, amongst them for example the signals at the beginning of a romance that indicate its generic grouping, and also the particular political and ideological overtones of the genre.

[13] 'A genre like courtly romance, where the starting-point, the spread and the milieu are so clearly defined, can thereby offer an excellent opportunity for understanding the creation of a literary tradition, not only in terms of individual relationships between authors, but as a wider literary process that transcends individuals and builds on the interplay between authors and their public. Such a study can also help lead to perceptions which have a relevance beyond the individual historical genre.' (Translated from Cormeau, *'Wigalois' und 'Diu Crône'*, p. 1.)

> may be embarked upon at random, or follow upon a departure undertaken for a particular purpose, or be deliberately sought. They serve to highlight the courage and courtly nature of the knight errant, revealing him as a worthy member of the ideal company of knights at Arthur's court.[14]

Chrétien's works reflect at least two different strands of tradition. The first is the written tradition from the British Isles of Latin and vernacular history, which in turn incorporates in its Arthurian sections elements from popular tradition and legend, as in the *Life of Gildas*. Meanwhile an oral tradition of Arthurian story-telling must be postulated for the regions of Celtic settlement. Chrétien combines both strands in his poetic *conjointure* and is thus the first to bring about a change of function or direction in both traditions.[15] From this twofold transformation emerge his verse romances: *Erec, Cligés, Lancelot, Yvain* and *Perceval*; thus Chrétien becomes the innovator of a new genre. It is clear, however, that in the course of his literary development Chrétien adopted a succession of different routes in his quest for a *conjointure* of individual Arthurian elements. After *Erec* he experiments with a completely different kind of structure in *Cligés* (the story extending over two generations, the oriental setting, the dissociation from *Tristan*), while in *Yvain* he returns to the *Erec* pattern. *Lancelot* differs from the previous romances in its new approach to love and in its unprecedented introduction of a second hero who also sets out to seek Queen Guinevere, even if he remains permanently in the shadow of Lancelot, the chief protagonist. When compared with the *Conte du Graal*, all these works are still characterized by unity of action and by the absence of any mystical or religious transcendental dimension. Chrétien's last work combines Arthurian material with the Grail theme, while the division of the action between two protagonists, already foreshadowed in *Lancelot*, becomes a new structural principle.

In terms of literary history Chrétien's romances form the prototypes of a genre; the abundant possibilities contained within them ensure the survival of the genre throughout nearly two centuries. Furthermore, Chrétien's works set the basic pattern that becomes the starting-point for a network of relationships inherent in the genre. The Arthurian romances of the thirteenth century supply variants to this basic pattern, although generally without exploiting extreme situations or speculative elaborations, a tendency recently postulated for the

[14] Translated from Gröber, *Grundriss der romanischen Philologie*, Vol. II.1, pp. 495–6. Gröber uses the misleading term 'Artusepos' (Arthurian epic); however, he intends it to refer to the epic narrative style rather than to a particular genre.

[15] For more on these concepts compare the studies by Jauss, 'Theorie der Gattungen und Literatur des Mittelalters', and Köhler, 'Gattungssystem und Gesellschaftssystem'.

chansons de geste.[16] Nevertheless, the genre of romance also includes contrasts, with light-hearted and serious elements, works that present an apotheosis of moral values (*Gliglois, Tyolet, Durmart, Meraugis*) and those that may use either a comic or a serious approach to reveal the ethical weaknesses of the Arthurian world (*Yder, Mule, Chevalier à l'épée, Cor, Mantel*). But there is scarcely any trace of the movement towards cyclical works. The romances also differ from the heroic epics in that issues of kinship play virtually no part. In the epics the characters only take shape by virtue of their interrelationships extending over more than one work, whereas Durmart has no connection with Fergus, nor Erec with Yder.[17] It therefore seems inappropriate in this context to engage in a synchronic or 'horizontal' study, although this has yet to be put to the test.[18] On the other hand, the correlations permeating the genre sometimes invite a synoptic approach in order to disclose the hidden wealth of possibilities for combination and variation. The Gawain romances are particularly suited to such a procedure, but the danger is that one can become blinded to the scope for alternatives. In looking at too many aspects in parallel it is easy to neglect the fact that each work has different points of emphasis and involves a selection from a range of possibilities.

It is now appropriate to examine a specimen characteristic of the genre as manifested in each of the romances, but without regard to detailed problems of dating. In attempting to present the evolution of Arthurian literature schematically[19] it is helpful to concentrate on one particularly telling characteristic, and just such a feature is provided by a structural peculiarity of Chrétien's romances. The early works present the quest of only one hero (*Erec, Yvain*), while *Lancelot* and *Perceval* set the pattern for the type of romance with two heroes and two

[16] See Köhler, 'Gattungssystem und Gesellschaftssystem', 11, and A. Adler, *Epische Spekulanten, Theorie der Schönen Künste* 3 (Munich, 1975), *passim.*

[17] The knight with the dwarf whose provocative behaviour (the lashes from his whip) sets in motion the action of the *Erec* romance, and who is defeated by Erec at the sparrowhawk contest, is also called 'Ydiers...li filz Nut' (*Erec et Enide*, line 1207). However, there are no allusions to this well-known episode anywhere in the *Yder* romance. The events of the later romance cannot be envisaged as taking place before the *Erec* incident, nor immediately after it, since the knight in *Erec* betakes himself to Arthur's court for the first time after his defeat, and he is as yet unknown to everyone there. The Yder of the later romance is not initially on hostile terms with Arthur's court, indeed he is even a particular friend of the queen, whereas the knight in *Erec* insults her and her *pucele.* The identical names of his hero and the character in *Erec* created opportunities for the author of *Yder* to connect his work with Chrétien's, but whether consciously or unintentionally he did not take them up. In this he differs from most other authors of thirteenth-century Arthurian romances. (See Chapter 6.)

[18] The concept of a synchronic or horizontal method of considering medieval genres dates back to Adler, *Epische Spekulanten.*

[19] See the diagram entitled 'The Evolution of Arthurian literature' on p. 12.

THE EVOLUTION OF ARTHURIAN LITERATURE

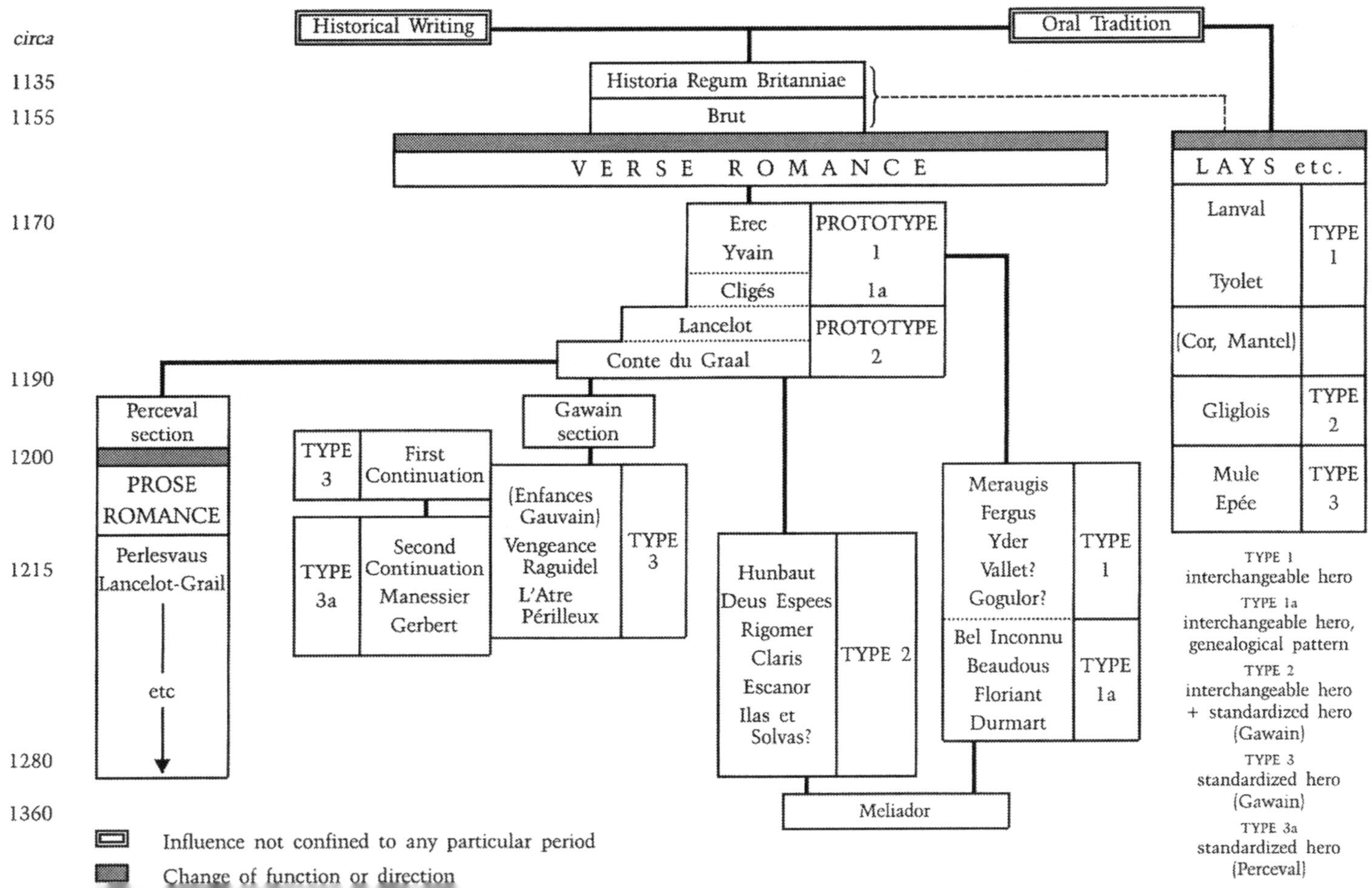

quests. This distinction in the number of protagonists would seem at first to be a rather trivial criterion for distinguishing different types of Arthurian romance, but can be justified by other considerations.

The quest of a single hero has a decisive influence on the *sens* of such romances. The aims of the quest are self-discovery, integration into society and recognition by the Round Table. The spiritual growth of the individual is illustrated by increasingly testing adventures; apparent good fortune is followed by a crisis and then the attainment of lasting harmony, culminating in the auspicious union of the hero and heroine. If two or more knights set out, their main aim is to perform some concrete task, such as freeing the queen or seeking the Grail and the lance, in order to avert a threat of danger or disaster to their community. The prime concern is not apparently to depict the happiness of the individual; this is subordinate to political expediency or the quest for salvation, as can be seen in the relationships between Lancelot and Guinevere or Perceval and Blancheflor. Nor is it Chrétien's overriding concern in these romances to give an account of the individual self-realization of the hero, unlike the authors of many later Arthurian romances.

Erec and *Yvain* represent Prototype 1 for those thirteenth-century verse romances which show comparable characteristics of form and content: *Meraugis, Fergus, Yder,* perhaps *Vallet*; *Bel Inconnu, Beaudous, Floriant et Florete* and *Durmart* also belong to Type 1, but to a greater or lesser degree these romances share an additional characteristic with *Cligés*, namely the role of genealogy in defining the structure. The nine examples of Types 1 and 1a emanating from the prototypes of Chrétien's first three romances represent the strongest group numerically amongst Arthurian works of the thirteenth century.

The two parts of the *Conte du Graal* (the Perceval and the Gawain adventures) furnish the model for three different kinds of subsequent development. The progression observable in Chrétien's works from a single hero to the splitting up of the action between two protagonists finds a parallel in the evolution of the genre as a whole. Romances in imitation of the Grail romance make their appearance after about 1250, with Gawain figuring alongside the eponymous hero in a series of adventures that are often independent of the hero's quest or only very loosely connected (*Hunbaut, Deus espees*). The later manifestations of the genre expand this outline still further and recount in great detail the experiences of a large number of knights errant. The adventures of the nominal hero or heroes and of the king's nephew are accorded only a little more space than those of their other companions, as for example in *Escanor* or *Claris et Laris*. It is possible that the fragment *Ilas et Solvas* also belongs to this second type. *Rigomer* is connected in part with the romance of Lancelot, who does not otherwise reappear in the thirteenth-century verse romances, but here there is a greater role both for the Knight of the Cart himself and for his mythically enhanced rescue mission.

However, before the type of romance just described can develop, the Perceval adventures of the *Conte du Graal* undergo another change of direction to give rise to Arthurian prose romance, which is a genre derived in its entirety from the Grail material. Thus soon after 1200 a clear differentiation of purpose is already becoming visible. The prose romances adopt the character of religious quests for which the seeds were sown in the *Conte du Graal*, while the contemporary verse romances avoid any reference to the search for the Grail and the quests are completely devoid of transcendental overtones.[20] The change of direction is symbolized by the use of prose with its reputation for greater truth, which renders it a more fitting medium for treating questions of salvation; it should also be seen as a formal echo of the historical chronicles from which the romances evolved.

Meanwhile the Gawain adventures of the *Conte du Graal* sow the seeds for those thirteenth-century Arthurian romances which feature Gawain as the sole protagonist. If Type 1 could be defined as a romance with an interchangeable hero, and Type 2 as a composite form with one interchangeable and one additional standardized hero (Gawain), then Type 3 is characterized by Gawain as a single standardized hero. This group is represented by *La Vengeance Raguidel* and *L'Atre périlleux*. Although it shares with Type 1 the characteristic of a linear and self-contained plot, it differs in so far as the quest is episodic and only one of many phases in Gawain's career. The narrative is remarkable in that the hero is not presented as an absolute paragon, but is sometimes subjected to considerable criticism. Moreover, Gawain's adventures do not serve to perfect his *cortoisie*, as is the case with the other protagonists, since he is courtly from

[20] Cormeau comes to a similar conclusion about [Heinrich von dem Türlin's] *Diu Crône*: 'Türlin's Grail has no significance for its deliverer beyond the fame attached to a most difficult and dangerous supreme adventure, and even that is not visible from the dangers of the episode but is merely stated. The Grail is not a goal for a proven and predestined hero, and it has no particular status on a level with, let alone in competition with or surpassing the Arthurian sphere. A mystical and religious or even symbolic significance is completely lacking, and it is merely one of the fairy-tale deliverance adventures of which there are several examples in Arthurian romance...Heinrich's presentation of the Grail world also implies a comment on this development of the genre. In taking up the Grail motif but reducing it once more to an ordinary adventure he is distancing himself from the tendency to extend the romance of adventure into the sphere of religious symbolism. He rejects a surplus of significance and clings emphatically to the code of values of secular chivalry.' (Translated from *'Wigalois' und 'Diu Crône'*, pp. 226–7.) In the French verse romances the Grail has the status of a mere attribute of the knight Perceval, just as the lion is associated with Yvain or the torn dress with Enide.

the start. The First Continuation, dealing with a failed Gawain quest, can be seen in this context as a transitional form.[21] The other three Continuations are related to the Gawain romances of Type 3 in that they too involve a standardized hero, but in this case the hero is Perceval, and the connections with the contemporary prose romances of the Lancelot/Grail cycle become visible. Thus in form and content the Continuations occupy a fluctuating position between the two potential developments of the Grail romance already outlined. Both types of narrative, the Continuations and the Gawain romances, give the appearance of being isolated and fully completed episodes of the *Conte du Graal*.

The fragments of the *Enfances Gauvain* are probably best assigned to the Gawain group for the moment, and yet in content they seem to represent a transition to the prose romances (or indeed the *chansons de geste*); the childhood theme is otherwise foreign to the verse romances.[22] If more fragments were found of this or a similar romance in octosyllabic couplets one could speculate that this might be the beginning of a new change of direction in the evolution of the genre.

At about the same time that Chrétien inaugurated the romance form, oral tradition also gave rise to the genre of the Arthurian lay. The poems of this small peripheral grouping differ strikingly from the wider genre of the verse romances in being restricted to a single central adventure, but even here the three patterns of Arthurian narrative can still be distinguished. *Lanval, Melion* and *Tyolet* relate the experiences of a single hero, and their narratives are still largely composed of fairy-tale elements (Type 1). Probably shortly after 1200 *Gliglois* (Type 2) heralds the merging of the lay, which was becoming increasingly lengthy, with the romance form itself. With almost 3000 lines and the action divided between two protagonists, Gliglois himself and his flawed double Gawain, this work represents a transitional stage. Finally there are parallels in both form and content between the Gawain romances and the shorter narratives

21 The Type 3 Gawain romances were subsequently to prove the most productive of all the variations included under Arthurian romance. They probably appealed so strongly to the public because Gawain had already become a byword for the chivalric ideal at an early stage; in any case it is noticeable that by far the largest number of English, German and Dutch Arthurian works follow the pattern of adopting Gawain as the main hero. For the origins of the prose romances see E. Köhler, *Trobadorlyrik und höfischer Roman* (Berlin, 1962).

22 Compare, however, the childhood of Perceval in the *Conte du Graal*, but even this is only an episode of that text. It is not the main subject of the narrative, as we can assume it was in the *Enfances Gauvain*. On the *enfances* in the *chansons de geste* see F. Wolfzettel, 'Zur Stellung und Bedeutung der *Enfances* in der altfranzösischen Epik', *ZfSL* 83 (1973), 317–48, and 84 (1974), 1–32. A detailed account of the birth and childhood of the hero, such as is attested even for Arthur and Merlin in the prose romances, must not be confused with the so-called genealogical pattern in the construction of some Arthurian verse romances (e.g. *Cligés* and *Durmart*).

of *La Mule sans frein* and *Le Chevalier à l'épée*. Here too Gawain is the sole protagonist and the *Mule* reveals satirical elements which link it with the Gawain parody *La Vengeance Raguidel*. The two lays *Cor* and *Mantel* represent isolated developments, involving neither quests nor adventures. Their burlesque narrative style is directed against the illusory perfection of the Arthurian court, while the anecdotal form of presentation is reminiscent of the *fabliaux*.

PROBLEMS OF CHRONOLOGY

In research conducted by previous generations of scholars an excessive emphasis on chronological relationships was often the first step towards the elaboration of fictitious sequences of development which had little in common with the way the genre actually evolved. By making use of a single characteristic (the unity or division of the action and the different types of romance thus defined), an attempt has been made here to postulate a kind of genealogical system of derivatives for French Arthurian literature. Any more precise chronological considerations have been deliberately ignored for the moment. Nevertheless it should have become clear that the three types of romance, each defined by its particular protagonists, are not just freely available options that may be adopted for the shaping of romances at any time, but rather that these particular changes are evolutionary.

Within the chronological sequence the prose romances should initially be regarded as a sub-genre of the verse romances. For a period of about a hundred years the two co-exist, until the prose romances finally supersede the older genre and become the dominant form. The increasing superficiality of the Arthurian verse romances becomes more apparent after 1250, as they descend to the level of crude entertainment with an element of specific political propaganda. As such they continue to interest a small readership for a few more decades, but the genre is then doomed by the late fourteenth century as the propaganda function disappears. Its off-shoot, the Arthurian lay, was destined for a much shorter existence; the lays merge into the verse romances in the same way as the latter merge into the prose romances at the end of their evolution. The verse romances are the more numerous. The fact that they are shorter than the prose works leads to greater productivity, but their breadth of influence is slight. It is the prose romances that are undoubtedly the more popular with their readers.

The specific concern of this study is the Arthurian literature of the thirteenth century, where research into the relative chronology of the texts has hitherto produced extremely vague and contradictory results. Thus for example West proposes the sequence *Fergus—Chevaliers as deus espees—Durmart—Hunbaut*, whilst Bruce favours *Durmart—Chevaliers as deus espees—Fergus—Hunbaut*, and Levy prefers *Fergus* (1216)—*Durmart* (1240)—*Chevaliers as deus espees* (1250)—*Hunbaut* (first half of the thirteenth century). *Le Bel Inconnu* is almost universally dated very early, between 1185 and 1190, but in her edition Perrie Williams, whom Levy at least should have taken into account, points out quite correctly that there is no reason to suppose the romance was composed much before 1210. The same applies to the *Lai du cor*, which Levy still ascribes to the mid-twelfth century. Yet, none of the commentators has been able to produce any sound arguments for this early dating, and the most recent editor, Philip Bennett, has a convincing case for reassigning the *Cor* together with the *Lai du cort mantel* to the end of the twelfth century at the earliest.

The rigid division of a century into quarters, thirds or even halves is too crudely artificial to do justice to the evolutionary patterns of literature. Within the range of Arthurian verse narrative the texts which can be specifically dated with the greatest precision are *Durmart* (before 1244), *Claris et Laris* (after 1268) and *Escanor* (between 1279 and 1282).[23] The first of these remains hypothetical, but the others are more or less guaranteed. Indeed, the dates of 1268 and 1282 are the only fixed points in the following attempt to reconsider the relative chronology of the texts with the aid of their generic characteristics.

1170–1190	1190–1204	1204–1220	1220–1230
Lanval	*Tyolet*	*Gliglois*	*Jaufré*
Erec	*Melion*	*Bel Inconnu*	*Vengeance Raguidel*
Cligés	*Cor*	*Meraugis*	
Lancelot	*Cort mantel*	*Durmart*	
Yvain	*Mule sans frein*	*Yder*	
Perceval	*Chevalier à l'épée*		
	First Continuation		
	Second Continuation		

1230–1250	1250–1268	1268–1282	after 1360
Fergus	*Rigomer*	*Claris et Laris*	*Meliador*
Ch. as deus espees		*Floriant et Florete*	
Escanor			
Atre périlleux			
Hunbaut			

[23] See the introductions to the editions and G. J. Brault, 'Arthurian Heraldry and the Date of *Escanor*', *BBSIA* 11 (1959), 81–8.

The table on p. 17 sets out a proposed new chronology in which the period 1268–1282 and the other intervals have been chosen on the basis of existing suggestions for approximate dating.[24] The ensuing rough account of the generic evolution of Arthurian verse romance after Chrétien is then intended to explain and justify the relative chronology suggested in the table, but using other methods than those that have hitherto been applied.

From the earliest days of a written tradition in the vernacular there were three possibilities available for the presentation of Arthurian material, namely chronicles, lays and the longer form of romance, represented respectively by Wace's *Brut*, Marie de France's *Lanval* and the romances of Chrétien. There was undoubtedly an active oral tradition of Arthurian narrative in existence at that time, and *Lanval* could still be seen to relate to that tradition. Chrétien, however, with his *conjointure* of disparate elements in the form of romance, created something so unutterably new in the eyes of his contemporaries and successors that for a while after his death no other poet had the temerity to embark on anything comparable to the first Arthurian romances. However, the few years either side of 1200 saw the oral tradition and the poems of Marie de France leading to other lays that bore an Arthurian stamp in form or content finding considerable favour amongst authors; the demands of such works could be met even by less gifted poets. All the surviving works in this short form date from the period of initial reaction to Chrétien's achievement. At the same time the First and Second Continuations were produced in an attempt to make the transition to longer forms.

Around the time that the last surviving examples of Arthurian lays (*Mule, Chevalier à l'épée, Gliglois*) were composed, we can observe the first experimental moves towards breaking the spell cast by Chrétien's unique literary supremacy. Four gifted authors of the next generation, among them Raoul de Houdenc, sought and found their own route to Arthurian romance precisely by not submitting to the schematic demands of the nascent genre. In both form and content the verse romances *Bel Inconnu, Meraugis, Durmart* and *Gliglois* are the most individualistic to be produced by the Arthurian tradition after Chrétien. *Meraugis, Durmart* and *Gliglois* increasingly embody the concept of the *roman à thèse*,[25] but at the same time they are also the furthest removed from the Arthurian sphere. The involvement of Arthurian material is not essential to the themes of these romances.

[24] In accordance with, for example, R. Levy, *Chronologie approximative de la littérature française du moyen âge*, *ZrPh* Beiheft 98 (Tübingen, 1957) and G. D. West, *An Index of Proper Names in French Arthurian Verse Romances 1150–1300* (Toronto, 1969).

[25] See also Chapter 5.

It must be borne in mind that the phase of consolidation of the genre was preceded by another in which Arthurian poets felt themselves called upon, if not indeed compelled, to prove their self-confidence and independence by opposing their own answers to Chrétien's pioneering suggestions. At first these variations threatened to destroy the unity of their group of texts. *Fergus* and *Yder* should also be assessed as further experiments in this direction, even if to a lesser extent. In social terms Fergus travels a longer and more unusual route than all his literary predecessors, from farmer's son to Arthurian knight. Meanwhile Yder refuses to favour the Arthurian court with the customary unconditional respect. However, the thematic dependence of *Fergus* on *Perceval* and of *Durmart* on *Erec* reveals equally clearly a positive approach and an attitude increasingly shaped by close involvement with a particular work by Chrétien.[26]

Jaufré is isolated by its language, yet it embodies a significant crystallization of all the characteristics that have proved to be specific to the genre up to about 1225, and on these generic grounds the dating of 1180 can probably be finally discarded. The period of exploration is over. In terms of its form *Jaufré* is an end-product and, at the same time, the finest example of the genre's characteristics becoming firmly established, while the romance *L'Atre périlleux* (before 1250) is to be seen as a last representative of the movement towards consolidation in the north.[27]

However, *Jaufré* also illustrates the scope that had always been available within the genre from the very beginning of its development for adopting a critical stance towards the motifs and the demands of the idealized Arthurian world. In the opening and closing episodes the narrator's irony is directed against *aventure* as such and sets it in a questionable light. The two lays *Cor* and *Cort mantel* already show a similar tendency to ridicule the ethical values and the excessive demands of the Arthurian world, thus revealing its fragility, although in these cases the distancing is achieved by means of satire and burlesque. The *Mule sans frein* also regards the value of *aventure* with critical irony. Thus the Arthurian lay can be seen to explore an avenue which cannot at first be realized in the more extensive form of romance. The authors of *Meraugis, Bel Inconnu, Durmart* and *Gliglois* are completely unfamiliar with such critical distancing. Their concern is not to oppose the Arthurian ethos, but to integrate this sphere creatively in support of the themes of their romances. After this integration has been satisfactorily achieved, the authors of *Yder, Jaufré* and *Vengeance Raguidel* can once more adopt a critical stance, but this is now directed much more pointedly

[26] See also Chapter 3, pp. 92–103 (*Yder*) and Chapter 5, pp. 158–69 (*Fergus*) and 170–80 (*Durmart*).

[27] This work exhibits the technique of *entrelacement*, and therefore presupposes not only the romances of Chrétien but also the influence of the Vulgate Cycle.

at the essence of the Arthurian world. These romances also differ from the shorter works in having the scope to exercise fundamental criticism in a serious manner (*Yder*) or to resort to the technique of parodying the genre (*Vengeance Raguidel*). However, on no account should an attitude of opposition to Arthurian values and motifs within the genre itself be interpreted as a sign of incipient disintegration. It is more an indication of the undiminished vitality and relevance of the material, to the extent that it is still worth contradicting. Moreover this assessment is supported by the fact that the critical voices do not wait to make their appearance until the development of the genre is nearing its end, but are heard right from the beginning. By contrast there are very few signs of opposition persisting after 1230.

From now on even second-rate authors can venture to compose Arthurian romances, but the poet of *Hunbaut* is already defeated by the project. His work lacks any meaningful superstructure of ideas, and with all the implicit demands which he appears to understand and acknowledge as fundamental to the genre he finds himself unable to complete his romance. There are other arguments available to support the theory that this work was not rendered fragmentary by an accident of transmission, but had been left incomplete in the first place. However, the author's powers of expression are not only limited in terms of content, but are also unequal to the demands of the form he himself has chosen:

> Ja mais ne vos erent dit vers
> De nule rime qui cels sanblent.
> Or entendés con il asanblent
> Et con il sont a dire fort! (34–7)

(Never again will you hear verse that rhymes like this. Now listen to how the lines are joined together and how strong they sound.)

The author puts all his efforts into a sophisticated rhyme scheme (*rime riche*), but this merely serves to highlight even more blatantly the shortcomings of his work.

Floriant et Florete with its servile dependence on *Erec et Enide* represents by about 1250–60 a return to the distant past. Its deliberately archaic idiosyncrasy would merit more extensive examination, but cannot be dealt with in any further detail in this context. At about the same time *Li Chevaliers as deus espees* and *Les Merveilles de Rigomer* mark the beginning of a tendency towards excessive length and an arbitrary expansion of the narrative content. The author of *Li Chevaliers as deus espees* tries to keep this tendency within bounds by dividing the action between two characters, while the author of *Rigomer* attempts a strict but not very compelling division into three formally unconnected plots. To these three parts he proceeds to add a totally arbitrary fourth which has scarcely any connection with the main plot and which moreover he is unable to complete. If aspirations towards self-restraint are nevertheless still detectable in the layout of *Rigomer*, the authors of *Claris et Laris* and *Escanor* have no such aims. It is true that a text extending to 30,000 lines appears to have been acceptable to a readership familiar with the prose cycles, but the excessive expansion, division and final disintegration of the narrative cohesion bear witness to an inherent misunderstanding of the Arthurian features which characterize the genre of romance. Incorporating the popular Arthurian characters and themes can no longer effectively counteract the slow death of the genre. Froissart's *Meliador*, written almost a hundred years later than *Escanor*, is a literary anachronism and only merits our interest because of the skills in synthesis exhibited by its illustrious author. At the time of its composition it must already have been considered delightfully old-fashioned, since the verse romances had long since been replaced by the Arthurian prose romances.[28]

THE POSITION OF CHRETIEN'S WORKS WITHIN THE GENRE

Chrétien's works provide more than just structural models for later Arthurian literature; the first manifestations of the genre also constitute a norm that is equally compelling for both authors and their public. The expectations of all readers and authors of Arthurian romances in the thirteenth century and beyond are shaped by Chrétien's romances, which embody whole patterns for such expectations. Later poets and their works may follow them up, seek to undermine them, or even attack them head-on.[29]

Chrétien's works are linked with the Arthurian romances of the thirteenth and fourteenth centuries in a network of relationships which continues to be both manifested and modified with every new text in the evolution of the genre. Thus a strong sense of tradition is built up at a very early stage. Chrétien becomes an authority, and seemingly as a matter of course he is granted a permanent place in the consciousness of authors and their public in the thirteenth century. The way in which authors refer freely to the reception of Chrétien's works reveals how that conscious reception itself plays a formative role. It is just as powerful a force in the creation of the genre as the Arthurian material itself with its combination of motifs.[30]

[28] For more on Froissart's Arthurian romance see also Chapters 6 and 8.

[29] See R. Warning, 'Rezeptionsästhetik als literaturwissenschaftliche Pragmatik', in R. Warning (ed.), *Rezeptionsästhetik*, *UTB* 303 (Munich, 1975), p. 28.

[30] For more detail on this see Chapters 5 and 6.

A genre arises when the imitation of a prototype amounts to a tradition.[31] Nevertheless the generic evolution of the Arthurian verse romances traces not so much Chrétien's influence and the imitation of his works, which has been the assumption hitherto, but primarily the reactions he stimulated. We are dealing with a different aspect of the same phenomenon. By no means the least interesting approach is to observe which of the potential generic characteristics displayed in Chrétien's works fail to be taken up. Astonishingly, they include precisely those elements which have been considered especially important and characteristic since the nineteenth century. The particular conflicts and tensions of 'conjugal romance' characterize romances like *Erec* and *Yvain*, but are also included for purposes of contrast in *Cligés* and *Lancelot*, yet the concept is not taken up again anywhere in the verse romances of the thirteenth century. There is a similar response to the fundamental theme of the hero's self-imposed guilt and the connected motif of atonement and the purging of that guilt. Only in *Fergus* and *Durmart* do the two still play a part, and that a very minor one in comparison with Chrétien's works. The attitude to love in the romance of *Lancelot* does indeed find its echo once more in the prose romances, but nowhere in the verse romances. These are dominated instead by Chrétien's other favoured love ethic, which owes more to the influence of northern France; its characteristics are mutual affection, partnership, equality of rank and lasting happiness in a marriage which is, however, not concluded until the end of the work.

Chrétien's romances maintain a definite authoritative value for all thirteenth-century Arthurian romances in verse. The earlier narrative material is available to serve as a backdrop for later variations of procedure and presentation.[32] Thus a norm and limits are already set for the genre, which is consolidated as its own internal complexity rapidly increases. This finds expression most forcefully in the increasing appearance of internal literary allusions. Attempts at innovation are directed towards accentuating and drawing out themes from the range of possibilities implanted in the genre since its inception. The increased complexity produces works of a high standard, especially in the first half of the thirteenth century. In social terms this kind of 'negative retrospective link' has an

[31] See M. Waltz, 'Zum Problem der Gattungsgeschichte im Mittelalter. Am Beispiel des Mirakels', *ZrPh* 86 (1970), 31.

[32] This applies to the German as well as the French Arthurian romances of the thirteenth century, as noted by Cormeau [for Wirnt von Grafenberg's *Wigalois*]: 'Wirnt's quotations confirm beyond doubt his knowledge of *Erec*, *Iwein* and *Parzival*; indeed they display a sufficiently thorough knowledge to allow a skilful manipulation of the references. Moreover they testify to an awareness of continuity within the genre.' (Translated from *'Wigalois' und 'Diu Crône'*, p. 118.)

affirming, stabilizing and conservative effect.[33] The verse romances still cling to their traditional form for decades after the rise of the far more influential prose romances; the older form seems to be inseparably bound up with the conservative social and political inclinations of its particular patrons and readership. By contrast, the prose romances are constantly renewed because open to change. Only until the end of the fourteenth century are the verse romances still capable of furnishing a positive role-model for all those conservative forces not wishing to share the doom-laden mood of their counterparts in prose.

THE TERMINOLOGY OF THE GENRE

All the texts have been edited. Most of the editions that still count as authoritative today date from before the turn of the century and were produced in Germany. A second and smaller group of texts were published by English-speaking scholars in the 1930s. Four Arthurian lays have just recently been re-edited in England. Very recently we have witnessed a great deal of editorial activity in North American universities, with the aim of using dissertations, unfortunately only in typescript, to replace the old editions which are for the most part no longer accessible. The only text to have been edited by a Frenchman is *Meliador*.

As mentioned previously, the editors are by no means consistent in labelling their texts. This reveals in the first instance an element of uncertainty, perhaps conditioned by the state of knowledge at the time, in recognizing and classifying texts. For example, even the term 'epic' is used for Arthurian romance, or 'cycle' for the verse romances collectively, though they were never envisaged as cyclical. However, the inconsistency also reflects a very understandable caution, since there was no clearly unambiguous contemporary medieval term at the editors' disposal. Consequently some of them decided upon 'romance of adventure' (*La Vengeance Raguidel, Beaudous, Li Chevaliers as deus espees, Le Bel Inconnu, Jaufré, Meraugis*), or used the terms 'Arthurian romance' or 'romance of the Round Table' (*L'Atre périlleux*). Alternatively some editors visibly avoided having to confront the problem by using headings such as 'Old French romance of Yder' or 'romance of Escanor' on the title pages of their editions.

Nevertheless, the Arthurian poets did not completely omit to give their works some kind of nomenclature.[34] A check through all surviving prologues and

[33] See Köhler, 'Gattungssystem und Gesellschaftssystem', 13.

[34] On the problem of generic indicators see K. Düwel, 'Werkbezeichnungen in der mhd. Erzählliteratur (1050–1250)' (Dissertation, Göttingen).

epilogues (or as appropriate the beginnings and endings of texts) gives the picture below, where the numbers represent the frequency of each term's occurrence:

conte	25
aventure	15
roman	7
livre	4
lai	3
cancon	1
conte d'aventure	2
istoire	1
dis	1
(novas)	3
(canso)	1

Chrétien himself uses the following terms:

conte	8
roman	2
livre	1
estoire	1

Two results stand out from this:

1. The terms *roman d'aventure* (romance of adventure) and *roman arthurien* (Arthurian romance) are not used by the Old French writers within the genre.
2. The term *conte* is the most frequent by a large margin, with both Chrétien and his successors.

However, it is well known that the use of the word *conte* in the twelfth and thirteenth centuries is by no means restricted to works containing Arthurian material, as the following comparison shows:

L'Escoufle	conte	6	
	aventure	1	
	dit	1	
Galeran de Bretaigne	conte	1	(beginning missing)
Amadas et Ydoine	conte	1	

Conte does not normally occur as an isolated term, but predominantly in combination with a name:

Ke c'est *li contes de l'Escoufle*	(*Escoufle*, 39, that this is *the story of the Kite*)
d'Erec, le fil Lac, *est li contes*	(*Erec et Enide*, 19, *the story is of Erec* son of Lac)
Ce est *li Contes del graal*	(*Perceval*, 66, This is *the Story of the grail*)

Thus the word *conte*, like *romant*, seems to denote a longer courtly narrative in general. There is nothing specifically Arthurian about it, but rather it is a term for the broader genre of courtly romance: 'Seignurs, cest cunte est mult divers' (Thomas, *Tristan*, Douce fragment 835, 'My lords, this story is very varied').

The second most common term in the prologues of Arthurian works in verse is *aventure*. The striking fact is that it occurs principally in the shorter form of the Arthurian lay (*La Mule sans frein, Le Chevalier à l'épée, Cort mantel, Cor, Lanval, Tyolet*), where on the other hand *conte* is used only very rarely. In these short forms *aventure* denotes not only the content of the work, i.e. the account of the adventure (usually a single one), but also the literary form of presentation, whereas *lai* is more indicative of the technique of performance.[35] Even though the terms are later blurred so that they overlap and become virtually synonymous, they did originally cover different ground.

The term *aventure* also crops up four times in longer works (*Jaufré, Meraugis, Claris et Laris, Rigomer*). On each occasion it appears to be used with a different nuance:

un'aventura qe avenc / Al rei Artus	(*Jaufré*, 89–90: An adventure that happens to King Arthur)
des bons contes l'aventure / De conter	(*Mer.*, 8–9: to tell the story of the good tales)
escouter bonne aventure	(*CL*, 6: to listen to a good adventure/story)
aventures de Bretaigne	(*Rigomer*, 5: adventures of Britain)

However, the term never seems to be intended to embrace the whole of the work in question, but is always directed towards individual episodes of the plot, as for example in *Jaufré*, where *aventura* encompasses the misfortune that befalls Arthur at the beginning of the romance, but does not denote the whole romance. The impression is thus created that this short but memorable episode

[35] Some useful light is shed on the concept of the *lai* in the studies by Grimes in *The Lays of Desiré, Graelent and Melion*, edited with an introduction by Margaret Grimes (New York, 1928), and by R. Baum, 'Eine neue Etymologie von frz. *lai* und apr. *lais*. Zugleich: Ein Plädoyer für die Zusammenarbeit von Sprach- und Literaturwissenschaft', in K. Baldinger (ed.), *Beiträge zum romanischen Mittelalter, ZrPh* Sonderband (Tübingen, 1977), pp. 17–78, as well as H. Baader, *Die Lais. Zur Geschichte einer Gattung der altfranzösischen Kurzerzählungen, Analecta Romanica* XVI (Frankfurt, 1966).

could equally well be described in isolation, in an *aventure* as a short but self-contained literary form.

This leads to the third term that must be discussed here, namely *conte d'aventure*. It occurs twice with Chrétien's successors and once in his own works.

...veul un roumant estraire
D'un molt biel *conte d'aventure*. (*Bel Inconnu*, 4–5)

(...I want to turn a very fine tale of adventure into a romance.)

J'ai mis mon penser et ma cure
D'un roial *conte d'aventure*
Commencier et dire briement
Sens annioz alongement. (*Durmart*, 13–16)

(I have applied my mind and my efforts to beginning a royal tale of adventure and to narrating it briefly, without tedious elaboration.)

et tret d'un *conte d'avanture*
une molt bele conjointure. (*Erec et Enide*, 13–14)

(and turns a tale of adventure into a very fine composition.)

The authors of both *Le Bel Inconnu* and *Erec* are using *conte d'aventure* to refer not to their own work but to their source, whatever form that may have taken. The author of *Durmart* on the other hand is advertising a 'roial conte d'aventure' which he intends to narrate 'briement' in order not to be thought boring. In fact, however, his romance with its 16,000 lines is the first to go significantly beyond the approximately 6,000 lines that had hitherto been the norm. He may be trying to use a skilful and witty method of distracting his audience's attention from the unusual length of the romance by announcing it as a *conte d'aventure*, a term associated with brevity in the public mind. This theory seems to be supported by findings such as the rapid narrative pace of the first 1,500 lines, the repeated apologies for going into detail, and the numerous assurances that the author wishes to be brief, as well as the astonishing announcement in line 1574 that 'Or primes commence *li contes*' (This is where the tale begins).

If we also take into account the fact that the term *aventure* was primarily used to denote short and possibly Arthurian works ('Li canteor metent lor cures / En dire beles aventures': *Le Bel Inconnu*, 25–6, 'The story-tellers put their efforts into narrating fine adventures'), and that both Chrétien and his two successors quoted above use it to refer to something other than their new work, then we are led to the conclusion that the sources for *Erec et Enide* and *Le Bel Inconnu* are to be sought in Arthurian lays such as have survived in the cases of *Lanval* or *Tyolet*, but can also be perceived in *Le Chevalier à l'épée* and *La Mule sans frein*. The assertions of the two authors are not merely to be understood as a topos. A remark by the narrator in *Tyolet* could, if carefully interpreted, provide additional evidence that in the case of *aventure* we are dealing with a literary term and a literary narrative form:

Aventures beles trovoient,
Qu'il disoient et racontoient;
A la cort érent racontées
Si come eles érent trovées;
Li preude clerc qui donc estoient
Totes escrire les fesoient:
Mises estoient en latin
Et en escrit em parchemin,
Por ce qu'encor tel tens seroit
Que l'en volentiers les orroit.
Or sont dites et racontées
De latin en romanz trovées. (23–34)

(They [the knights] would encounter fine adventures which they would tell and relate; these were told at court just as they had happened; the worthy clerks of that time had them all written down; they were put into Latin and into writing on parchment, because the days would come again when they would be heard with pleasure. Now they are being told and related after being translated from Latin into Romance.)

In the light of this passage the meaning of the passing taunt about 'cil qui de conter vivre vuelent' (*Erec et Enide*, 22, 'those who wish to live by reciting tales') now becomes clearer, since the form of the *aventure* or the *conte d'aventure*, of which many can be told in one day, may well seem inadequate to someone like Chrétien de Troyes who knows he can make more out of such a short episode. After all, if we leave aside the Tristan tradition for the moment, Chrétien's *Erec et Enide* represents the first such attempt to transform the shorter type of Arthurian text into the longer form of romance, with the aid of the combinatory process of *conjointure*. Moreover, if we can rely on the dating, then Renaut de Beaujeu for his part is the first of Chrétien's successors to venture upon a similar task. It is to this fact that he is referring in his prologue. In a similar way, non-Arthurian lays also produced non-Arthurian romances. Thus *Galeran de Bretaigne* is based on the *Lai de Fresne* and *Ille et Galeron* derives at least in part from *Eliduc*.

It has become apparent that the formula 'conte de...' ('tale of...') plus an interchangeable name can be applied to a narrative concerning any courtly hero, any pair of lovers or any event. However, when this freely interchangeable element takes the form of such well-known names as Erec, Yvain or Lancelot, this immediately indicates to the listener the specifically Arthurian context of the work to be recited. These and many other knights can be designated 'cil de la Table Reonde' ('those of the Round Table') and are referred to as such in the romances themselves, for example *Erec*, lines 83 and 1669, or *Perceval*, line 8125. If, therefore, with the benefit of hindsight one wanted to suggest a generic term for this group of texts which at least approximated to medieval French concepts, one could choose 'Conte d'un chevalier de la Table Ronde' ('The tale of a knight of the Round Table'). However, the terms widely adopted by scholars, 'Artusroman', 'roman arthurien' and 'Arthurian romance', are perfectly serviceable as long as they are used unambiguously and not confused with 'Abenteuerroman', 'roman d'aventure' or 'romance of adventure'. They have the advantage of drawing attention to that nucleus in the content around which all the individual elements of the genre are grouped, namely King Arthur himself.

PART ONE

The response to Chrétien: tradition and innovation in Arthurian romance

1

The stigma of decadence

Brogsitter gives the following introduction to German post-classical Arthurian literature under the heading 'Die Epigonenepen' ('The decadent epics'):

> From the very beginning of the thirteenth century the great works of the Master were followed by a number of other Arthurian romances which, despite some fine individual details, reveal all too clearly that they are not independent creations or worthy successors in the great tradition of Arthurian epic, but merely imitations, and limited for the most part to the imitation of narrative elements. Overworked motifs and sequences of motifs are repeated indiscriminately, rearranged and sometimes even cobbled together in utter confusion to create epics that often grow to a considerable length. New characters are introduced to be assigned the plots and events of the classical works. Adventures follow upon adventures, but there is usually no attempt to restructure the material in a sensible way nor even to give it a meaningful wider context.[1]

The history of scholarship shows that the study of thirteenth-century Arthurian romances has always been overshadowed by a preoccupation with the texts of the 'Master'; this is true for France as well as Germany. Being labelled as 'decadent' was to prove their downfall, for this criticism became a commonplace and made access to them considerably more difficult. Thus the assessment of the late nineteenth century seems to remain largely unchallenged and is still found in histories of literature and works of reference. Any attempt at a re-evaluation must inevitably turn its back on the authority of established teachings and in so doing cast doubt upon the results of decades of scholarship. Research on the German side began to tackle this problem not long ago, with the aim of revising the verdicts of Gervinus and Scherer on the post-classical romance and in particular on the 'inferior' Arthurian epic.

> When measured by modern criteria against the romances of the 'Master', these works were all supposed to be second or third rate, but this is not entirely

[1] Translated from K. O. Brogsitter, *Artusepik, Sammlung Metzler* 38, second edition (Stuttgart, 1971), p. 107.

> obvious to the modern literary historian and lover of literature once he has had the patience to read these romances on their own terms and has derived pleasure and satisfaction from them. On the other hand, perhaps he just likes second and third rate literature and should therefore be left to wallow in his own bad taste.[2]

Research into the influence and reception of texts throws up another argument in favour of studying the thirteenth-century romances. Although in modern times they have always been seen as inferior in quality, they were nevertheless much read and admired by their contemporaries and often even centuries later.[3] However, in neither case does such an evaluation represent an entirely objective judgement on the quality of the literature; it is more an expression of the fact that public taste and the value-judgements of literary history cannot be much more than the subjective expression of an aesthetic response conditioned by its own age. This is no reason to despise the judgements of either the thirteenth or the nineteenth centuries, nor to interpret the earlier assessment as evidence of a 'decadent loss of quality' in the medieval reading public, merely because the function of the texts is now no longer apparent.[4]

It is obviously problematic to apply to medieval literature the concept of 'Epigonentum' (decadence) which only became possible with romanticism and the aesthetics of individual genius.[5] Decadence in the sense implied by Scherer's theory of Golden Ages has to be consistently appropriate for a whole generation or epoch and not just for single cases of individual writers. If we try to apply it

[2] Translated from X. von Ertzdorff, *Rudolf von Ems. Untersuchungen zum höfischen Roman im 13. Jahrhundert* (Munich, 1967), p. 23.

[3] On the other hand one could advance the counter-argument, using a more modern German example, that Geibel was also greatly admired by the public of his day and was occasionally treated as being on a par with Goethe, whereas today he has fallen behind in public esteem.

[4] See H. R. Jauss, 'Literaturgeschichte als Provokation der Literaturwissenschaft', in R. Warning (ed.), *Rezeptionsästhetik, UTB* 303 (Munich, 1975), p. 138.

[5] 'When posterity adopted the term once more it acquired a different meaning: a restless hovering between eras turned into slavish dependence on the past, a blind clinging to tradition. The word then became the tool of a new and not entirely unexceptionable interpretation of the historical process and of continuity in cultural development' (translated from C. David, 'Über den Begriff des Epigonischen', in H. Meyer and W. Kohlschmidt [eds], *Tradition und Ursprünglichkeit. Akten des III. Internationalen Germanistenkongresses* 1965 *in Amsterdam* [Berne and Munich, 1966], p. 77). On the problem of decadence see the studies by Brackert, Ertzdorff and Haug on Rudolf von Ems, Monecke and Moret on Konrad von Würzburg, Moelleken and Kern on Stricker's *Daniel vom blühenden Tal*, Rupp on Konrad von Würzburg and Rudolf von Ems, Wehrli on Wirnt's *Wigalois*, Ruh on the *Lanzelet* of Ulrich von Zatzikhoven, Wachinger and Kuhn on Gottfried's *Tristan*. De Boor, David, Windfuhr and Heintz have made decisive contributions to a fundamental examination of the concept of decadent literature. (See Bibliography for details.) The result of these deliberations can be summarized in David's comment (p. 77; here in translation): 'The word decadent [epigonisch] can only obscure the literary realities. It should only be applied to the most inferior specimens, and even then...it will not succeed in shedding much light.'

to French literature of the thirteenth century, or even just the first half of the century, it rapidly becomes clear that this period as a whole cannot be classed as one of decadent decline; on the contrary, the late Arthurian romances are contemporary with the arrival of new forms and epoch-making works such as the prose romances, the *Roman de Renart*, the *Roman de la Rose* and many more. It seems improbable that these could be explained by a general loss of the fundamental creative impulse. The literature of that century abounds in works that continue traditions and conventions (*chansons de geste*, courtly romances, religious and didactic literature), but it also boasts a profusion of innovations.

In resisting any emphasis on the decadent features which are certainly present in the Arthurian romances of later generations, the intention is not to salvage their reputation at all costs but to revise the classifications of previous literary historians and to promote a better understanding of the texts in question. This should lead in turn to a more subtle gradation in the hierarchy from good prototype to poor imitations. Were the authors of the later Arthurian romances conscious of their problematical situation? Did they feel constrained by it? Did they fail to achieve anything new, merely borrowing recipes and devices in slavish dependence on tradition and prototypes? These questions in their various aspects will be dealt with in the first part of this study.

Historical documentation such as letters, diaries or memoranda of conversations, which can shed light on the conscious attitude of authors, does not exist for the period when these romances were composed. Therefore any analysis has to rely entirely on internal literary remarks. Such evidence can still be very revealing, as is shown by H. Ragotzky's exemplary work on the problem of the debate between Gottfried von Straßburg and Wolfram von Eschenbach.[6] Unfortunately, however, we cannot detect a debate on literary criticism of similar intensity or on a comparable scale between the French successors to Chrétien and their illustrious predecessor. Only a small number of passages in later Arthurian romances offer explicit evidence that such a debate did in fact take place. Even though it was probably on a smaller scale, we would certainly not be justified in assuming that it never happened at all, despite the dearth of references, especially since it will become apparent that a debate can be conducted by quite different means.[7]

The relationship between a later author and the work of a predecessor represents one aspect of the reception question. When we witness an author's

[6] H. Ragotzky, *Studien zur Wolfram-Rezeption. Die Entstehung und Verwandlung der Wolfram-Rolle in der deutschen Literatur des* 13. *Jahrhunderts, Studien zur Poetik und Geschichte der Literatur* 20 (Stuttgart, 1971), p. 33.

[7] For further discussion of this see Chapters 5 and 6.

fear of being completely under the influence of earlier works, and the conquering of that fear to produce a new work of which the decisive characteristic is innovation with respect to its predecessor, then we become aware of literary history as the history of relationships between texts. These relationships must inevitably be one-sided, since the later work can no longer influence the earlier one, but it can affect its historical evaluation.[8]

Hitherto, however, theories on aesthetic reception have gone into very little detail on the specific receptive relationship between the new producer and his predecessors or prototype. 'The historical significance of literature as well as its communicative character presuppose a dialogue and even a quasi-juridical debate between text, public and new text.'[9] The dialectic relationship 'text—reader as potential author—new text' represents a significant special case in the study of aesthetic appreciation amongst the reading public at large. Jauss says that the writer who plans his work in the light of positive or negative norms in an earlier work is also initially a reader, before his response to the literature can itself become productive again. The new work is then not only a reaction to the past, but itself an impulse to further historical development. Generally speaking a new work can only make its full aesthetic impact when it stands out against a contrasting background of earlier works,[10] and the author who undergoes the change-over from passive to active reception achieves a renewal of historical continuity.[11]

The generation of authors who were composing romances towards the end of the twelfth and at the beginning of the thirteenth century found themselves in a peculiar situation. Chrétien's name was on everyone's lips, and the significance of his work remained unchallenged for decades. He was admired on all sides. Yet comments openly praising him are to be found only outside the actual Arthurian verse texts which followed directly in his wake. The authors of non-Arthurian literature, including in particular those whose works bear obvious signs of Chrétien's influence, clearly have a freer and less inhibited relationship to the great master. Since they do not intend to succeed him by embarking on the new genre he initiated, they can unreservedly admit to his influence upon them and to their own boundless admiration. For them, reading Chrétien's works is just one reading experience amongst many, admittedly an important one but not one that touches them directly as authors. The well-known quotation from Huon de

[8] These relationships are dealt with in detail by H. Bloom in *The Anxiety of Influence. A Theory of Poetry* (New York, 1973) and *A Map of Misreading* (New York, 1975).

[9] Translated from Jauss, 'Literaturgeschichte als Provokation', p. 127.

[10] See F. V. Vodička, 'Die Rezeptionsgeschichte der literarischen Werke', in R. Warning (ed.), *Rezeptionsästhetik*, *UTB* 303 (Munich, 1975), p. 82.

[11] Jauss, 'Literaturgeschichte als Provokation', pp. 127 and 141.

Mery's *Tornoiement Antecrist* is the most forcefully expressed example of this attitude.

> He already looks back to Chrétien de Troyes and Raoul de Houdenc as if to the inimitable masters of a bygone era. He concludes that everything has already been said (by the courtly poets?), and in his prologue he introduces his own work as new thinking with material never previously employed. The vanished Arthurian world, envisaged and described by Huon de Mery as being at a mythical distance, forms the background for the appearance of the first vernacular version of the *Psychomachia*.[12]

If Huon was plagued by fears of excessive influence, it was mainly on the level of language:

> ...Hugon de Meri,
> Qui a grant peine a fet cest livre,
> Car n'[osoit] pas prendre a delivre
> Le bel françois a son talent,
> Car cil qui troverent avant
> En ont coilli tote l'eslite,
> Pour c'est ceste oevre meins eslite
> Et plus fu fort a achever.
> Molt mis grant peine a [eschiver]
> Les diz Raol et Crestïen,
> C'onques bouche de crestïen
> Ne dist si bien com il disoient. (3526–37)

> (...Huon de Mery, who worked hard to write this book because he did not dare to take liberties of his own with the beautiful French language, for those who wrote before him have gathered the pick of the crop. As a result this work is less polished, and yet it was harder to bring off. He was at pains to avoid the language of Raoul and Chrétien; in all Christendom no one ever spoke as well as they did.)

Huon was striving to find a different type of language for different subject-matter, and was consciously avoiding the linguistic characteristics of the 'inimitable' masters.

Throughout the whole of Arthurian verse romance there are just two places where Chrétien's name is mentioned by subsequent authors in the context of literary procedure. This reserve is easily explained by the dilemma in which his successors found themselves. For them the works of the 'Master' were the great models which they admired and loved, just as for Chrétien in all probability

[12] Translated from H. R. Jauss, 'Entstehung und Strukturwandel der allegorischen Dichtung (4. Allegorische Dichtung in epischer Form)', in H. R. Jauss and E. Köhler (eds), *Grundriß der romanischen Literaturen des Mittelalters*, Vol. VI.1 (Heidelberg, 1968), p. 219.

Wace held that exemplary status. Once Chrétien's first Arthurian romances had appeared on the scene, the other poets of his own and succeeding generations were faced with the startling realization that the theme had been in the air all along; it was after all the literary expression of the political and social circumstances that affected every one of them. Marie de France had accepted the challenge of Arthurian subject-matter in her own way, but now it had been turned into something totally new. Chrétien had to be admired, and above all the new genre that was being evolved was accepted as a positive contribution. On the other hand, Chrétien's successors had to fear their own lack of comparable poetic ability. A simple solution would have been for them to turn aside from the dilemma into other genres; they had the option of writing prose romances, romances of courtly love in the tradition of *Eneas*, didactic works and much besides. As far as we can tell some of them did indeed do this both before and after their Arthurian works, for example Raoul de Houdenc, Robert de Blois, Girart d'Amiens and the author of *Les Merveilles de Rigomer*, who each wrote only one Arthurian romance alongside other works. Clearly, however, they were also enticed into perfecting and transforming the new subject-matter and the new genre. This does not mean imitating in the sense of copying closely; it is precisely those poets who are Chrétien's immediate successors chronologically that are much more individualistic than has previously been supposed. They can certainly not be accused of slavish dependence, but they were faced with a dilemma. On the one hand they wanted to retain the elements which came across as typical of the genre and which were immediately recognized and accepted as such by all authors of Arthurian works in both France and the rest of Europe, as can be seen in the evolution of the genre. These elements had already been subjected to the beginnings of a process of consolidation, partly by Chrétien but also partly by Wace and Marie de France. On the other hand, succeeding poets also wanted to give scope to their own poetic individuality and create something new within the genre, without this new development being suppressed in the strait-jacket of increasingly formalized characteristics. This was the great challenge, and anyone who dared respond to it at the beginning of the new century when faced with Chrétien's daunting supremacy displayed courage and a determination to make their mark. In this context it is hardly surprising that Raoul de Houdenc was one of their number. His romance of *Meraugis* is proof that Arthurian material could be successfully combined with a new plot and a *sens* that Chrétien had not previously touched upon. Raoul and a very small number of his contemporaries were the first to overcome their inhibitions concerning Arthurian literature. Others preferred to hark back to Marie de France in devoting themselves to the shorter Arthurian form, and here too they created independent works. At first glance it seems that imitation of Chrétien dominates in all cases and it looks as though all these writers joined unhesitatingly in riding the Arthurian wave that had borne Chrétien to fame and was to yield success for them as well. But this false impression can only arise if the episodes and motifs are inadmissibly reduced to their generically typical common denominators until they are indeed made to resemble each other. We shall shortly be revealing how Chrétien is in fact interpreted by Raoul and others, for example the authors of *La Vengeance Raguidel*, *Durmart*, *Gliglois* or *L'Atre périlleux*, as they introduce new structures whilst changing, fulfilling and amending Chrétien's original designs.

Firstly, however, the two references to Chrétien already mentioned above have still to be considered. The author of *Le Chevalier à l'épée* upbraids Chrétien for not having written a Gawain romance, thereby shamefully neglecting the great hero.[13] He now regards this as his own task. The writer of *Le Chevalier à l'épée* was looking for the deficiency in Chrétien's work and found it here; the predecessor is reproached with a fault which the successor intends to correct in his own work. The same reproach soon incited numerous other authors to produce their own Gawain romances.

The author of *Hunbaut* defends himself from the start against the accusation that he might have borrowed anything from Chrétien's works; he informs his audience and readers that he has long been engaged in some kind of contest with Chrétien, but that the latter, his friend (or rival?), was eventually the winner:

Fors .I. sorcot sans plus de roube.
Ne dira nus hon que je robe
Les bons dis Crestïen de Troies
Qui jeta anbesas et troies
Por le maistr[i]e avoir deu jeu,
Et juames por ce maint jeu. (185–90)

(With no dress other than a surcoat. No one will say that I am stealing the fine words of Chrétien de Troyes, who threw double one and double three to keep the dice, as a result of which we played many games.)[14]

He now intends to write a romance which has nothing to do with Chrétien's works. He did actually succeed in this, for apart from the indispensable features of the genre *Hunbaut* has very little in common with the romances of his

[13] See Chapter 4.

[14] The allusion is to *Erec et Enide*, lines 739–41 or 2648, or *Yvain*, lines 4368 or 5421. The imagery derives from card or dice games, where in the opinion of the writer of *Hunbaut* Chrétien always had the better cards. Thus his fellow player cannot compete with him in this area, and so he turns to something different, apparently the Gawain material.

predecessor, although this does not prove to be much of an advantage. Nevertheless, even a deliberate rejection of a prototype represents a kind of debate with it.

Other authors found themselves under pressure to justify themselves, as if they had to apologize for offering the traditional genre once more at a time when Arthurian verse romances no longer seemed entirely relevant amid competition from an abundance of modern story-lines, themes and forms. The author of *La Mule sans frein* justifies himself as follows: 'Nowadays the old ways are not esteemed as highly as the new ones, which are thought to be more beautiful, and moreover they do indeed appear to be better. But quite often it turns out that the old are nevertheless more valuable. And so Paien de Maisieres says that one should always keep more to the old ways than to the new.'[15]

The author of *Claris et Laris*, admittedly considerably later, also wants to account for the Arthurian material that he is still serving up to his readers. He concludes a long diatribe against his own day and age with the following explanation: 'I have no desire for martyrdom. Truth is synonymous with misery and torment. I cannot make a pleasant narrative out of the events of the present age if at the same time I am supposed to tell the truth. So I have decided—and I should not be blamed for this—to narrate "aventures de Bretaigne".'[16]

Thus we have been able to show from both a very early and a later example that the composition of Arthurian verse romances is frequently a conscious return, in a positive spirit, to proven traditional material. Raoul also feels that the Arthurian sphere is particularly durable, and places his *Meraugis* within this tradition:

Car joie est de bone oevre fere
De matire qui toz jorz dure. (6–7)

(For it is a pleasure to compose a fine work from material that lasts for ever.)

On the other hand it is precisely such passages which demonstrate that authors who hark back to Arthurian material for their verse romances are quite conscious of what they are doing and possess the inner freedom to choose from a variety of material; they are outwardly dependent, but not inwardly. However, one is entitled to suspect that as poets they belong to more conservative circles, for they resort to 'an older tradition, which they still fully recognize and want to salvage from the ravages of time. This retrospection is no longer regarded as

[15] Translated from the author's German rendering of *La Mule sans frein*, lines 8–16.
[16] Translated from the author's German rendering of *Claris et Laris*, lines 80–8.

a danger, but as beneficial, and this deliberate conservatism after the period of crisis must not be confused with the decadence of naive imitators.'[17]

Judging from the surviving testimonies, the authors of these romances were not striving to surpass Chrétien or to put his work in the shade. However, the few passages that can be considered as explicit comments on their attitude towards their illustrious forerunner do suggest a certain love-hate relationship. Nevertheless, they do not seem on the whole to have suffered unduly from their close chronological proximity to their predecessor. Instead they very quickly came to regard Chrétien, like Benoît de Sainte-Maure or the author of the *Eneas*, as an authority that one accepted without question and certainly did not attempt to equal or surpass. The faith in authority that finds expression in narrators' comments such as 'Si con Crestiens le tesmoine'[18] ('as Chrétien testifies') or 'Crestïen en ai a garant'[19] ('I have Chrétien to vouch for it') implies an attitude towards the first poet of the genre which can hardly come as a surprise, since it is far more in keeping with medieval thinking on matters of tradition than the demand of later centuries for originality in art which may be thoughtlessly applied to medieval texts. But tradition does not signify in the thirteenth century any more than in the rest of the Middle Ages a mere imitation of the hard-won achievements of greater talents. On the contrary, it actually implies constant change. The authority of someone like Chrétien is positive, stimulating and challenging; it does not stifle and curb the poets of subsequent decades to the extent that scholars have hitherto suggested.

The often overwhelming number of similarities between the later Arthurian romances and the works of Chrétien has given rise to the charge of decadent imitation. However, in so far as research into the Old French Arthurian romances was largely confined to the search for parallels and for continuity in form and content, the line of questioning prejudiced the results of these efforts from the start. The process of tracing sources and parallel motifs served to illuminate and clarify relationships of dependence, but at the same time it was often forgotten that the motifs and structures in question did not belong so much to an individual romance as to the genre in general. In other words, they were the common elements of all Arthurian romances, without which they simply would not be Arthurian romances at all. Most scholars can be accused of having been all too easily misled by reducing an episode or a scene to one sentence or one idea and then interpreting quite diverse elements as essentially

[17] Translated from David, 'Über den Begriff des Epigonischen', p. 69.

[18] *Claris et Laris*, line 627.

[19] The First *Perceval* Continuation, MSS *TVD*, line 1234.

the same. M. Tyssens was right to pillory this procedure.[20] If viewed in such a light it is possible to see all the Old French and even all the Middle High German Arthurian romances as decadent variations on the romances of Chrétien. In order to avoid this danger, the present study will dispense with the usual practice of listing similarities in motifs which demonstrate dependence on Chrétien, although this is not to deny that such dependence exists. The formulaic nature of the later Arthurian romances is indicative of a literary type, but the task now is to look for innovation beyond the stereotypes that characterize the genre. We should be searching not for continuity but for discontinuity. This is not exactly the same as the search for originality, because in the case of these Arthurian romances one has to 'assess them from a different standpoint more appropriate to the Middle Ages, that of authority and awareness of tradition... Nothing could be more misguided than to measure the literature of that time against modern demands for originality.'[21]

[20] M. Tyssens, 'Les sources de Renaut de Beaujeu', in *Mélanges J. Frappier*, edited by J.-C. Payen and C. Régnier, 2 vols (Paris, 1970), Vol. II, pp. 1043–55, *passim*.
[21] Translated from de Boor, *Die deutsche Literatur*, pp. 20–1.

2

Consolidation of the form

THE OPENING SEQUENCE OF ARTHURIAN ROMANCES

It is well known that the name of the hero in an Arthurian romance plays a specific and important role, and in many cases is revealed to the audience only towards the end of the narrative. Thus it was not always possible to deduce straightaway when a 'tale of [name]' was announced that the romance to be performed would contain Arthurian material. What distinguishes Arthurian romances from other courtly romances of the period? Is it only the particular characters and the enchanted atmosphere, or is it the structure, the sequence of adventures or the presence of a unified theme? What techniques does an author use to signal to his audience that the material will be specifically Arthurian? In order to be able to answer such questions it will be helpful to investigate the beginnings of the romances (lines 1–500, including the general prologues) with this aspect in mind.[1] For the purposes of this survey the romances of Chrétien and those of his successors will be dealt with separately, so that if there is an evolutionary change it can more easily be observed.

To begin, therefore, with the later works, the typical opening for an Arthurian romance after Chrétien is to name Arthur within the first fifty lines, indeed usually within the first ten. This naming is often associated with an Arthurian eulogy, in other words praise of Arthur's courage and generosity and of that era in the distant past when he and his knights held sway. There may also be an occurrence of the crucial phrase *Table Ronde*. Soon afterwards, normally within the first hundred lines, the name Gawain occurs, either attached to a Gawain-eulogy or incorporated in a list of knights. Next there is the name of a place; this appears predominantly as *Carduel*, but *Carlion* may be regarded as an alternative.[2] The season is also mentioned, and the first scene of such romances takes

[1] For more details about the opening sequences of Arthurian romances, including numerous textual illustrations and a survey in tabular form, see B. Schmolke-Hasselmann, 'Untersuchungen zur Typik des arthurischen Romananfangs', *GRM* 62, new series 31 (1981), 1–13.

[2] As a rule neither Carlion nor Carduel is named in the prose romances.

place almost exclusively at Whitsun. At such a major festival Arthur cannot sit down at table until after some adventure has occurred. The king's waiting for *aventure* and not wanting to eat constitute a further characteristic element of the beginning of an Arthurian romance.[3] If the motif of refusing to eat is missing, then it is replaced by some of the characters either disporting themselves in the solar or watching from a window. These may also occur in combination. However, the suspense is then broken by the arrival of a message or messenger. A lady is in distress, an adventure must be accomplished or a boon must be granted; alternatively, a challenger insults and reviles Arthur in such a way that his knights are provoked into avenging this disgrace.[4] While the king lapses into deep thought, one of the knights sets out and the actual plot of the romance can begin, unless a delaying factor is introduced by the steward Kay claiming the right to accomplish the appointed task himself. In such cases the way is not open for the hero to set off on the adventure until after Kay's lamentable failure. Kay's sortie may be replaced by an exhibition of invective and petty jealousy on his part, directed against the predestined hero. The series of adventures or quest can then begin.[5] As the genre approaches the end of its development the motif of waiting for adventure gradually emerges as the really central Arthurian motif. But it also takes on a life of its own, and its occurrence is no longer restricted to a major festival; instead the Arthurian court is now handicapped on a daily basis by its own custom.

> Even when a literary work first appears it does not present itself as a total novelty in a vacuum devoid of information. Instead the public are predisposed towards a specific type of response by explicit announcements, open and hidden signals, familiar characteristics or implicit clues. Memories of material already read are aroused, inducing a particular emotional frame of mind in the reader, and thus the beginning of the work already creates certain expectations for the middle and the end. As the reader proceeds, these expectations may be maintained or transformed, redirected or even ironically dispelled in accordance with the particular conventions of the genre or type of text involved.[6]

The authorial signals specified above, incorporated in varying numbers and various combinations into the first 500 lines of a romance, enabled the audience to recognize quickly and precisely what kind of courtly romance (in this case an

[3] Arthurian romances in languages other than French exemplify particularly clearly the consolidation of precisely this element; see for example *Sir Gawain and the Green Knight* or *Daniel vom blühenden Tal.*

[4] This motif of challenging the Arthurian court can be observed clearly in *Li Chevaliers as deus espees* and *Ilas et Solvas*; it derives from Chrétien's *Lancelot.*

[5] For the function of Kay's challenge to the hero see Chapter 6, p. 201f.

[6] Translated from Jauss, 'Literaturgeschichte als Provokation', p. 131.

Arthurian romance) the recited text would turn out to be. These signals must be seen as fundamental characteristics of Arthurian verse romances. The same characteristics can also be found in the shorter texts, including the naming of Arthur and Gawain and mention of Carduel and Whitsun, as well as the arrival of a messenger. The motif of waiting for adventure or delaying the feast occurs only once in a shorter text (*Cort mantel*), but on the other hand it is remarkable that Marie's *Lanval*, the earliest Arthurian lay, already has four of these characteristics clearly represented.

The question remains as to which of these typical initial elements of Arthurian romances can already be found in Chrétien and may possibly be derived from him. To begin with, it is noticeable that not one of Chrétien's romances exemplifies an opening schema in the form outlined above. However, even the first Arthurian poet already has the naming of the king at a very early stage.[7] All other elements occur only in isolation, as for example with the early naming of Gawain.[8] In *Cligés*, *Lancelot* and *Perceval* it does not occur until significantly later.[9] *Yvain* and *Perceval* mention Carduel as Arthur's residence at the beginning of the romance, whilst *Erec* has Caradigan, *Cligés* has Guincestre and most manuscripts of *Lancelot* do not specify any particular location. The author of *Fergus*, Guillaume le Clerc, and of course *Floriant et Florete* which is based on *Erec*, take up Caradigan again; Guincestre, however, plays no further part as a setting for later Arthurian literature. Carduel, the place-name used most often by Chrétien, becomes increasingly dominant as the classic Arthurian location.

The festival of Whitsun sees Erec's wedding take place and in *Perceval* the arrival of two prisoners at Arthur's court (line 2785), as well as the intended duel between Guiromelanz and Gawain in Orquenie (lines 8888 and 9103). These latter references to Whitsun are not especially important to the structure or the plot. They are not placed at the beginning, but in the middle of the continuing action. *Yvain* is different; there Whitsun is conspicuously positioned right at the beginning,[10] where it was able to make a particularly memorable impression in the public mind. After the banquet (which in this romance is not yet delayed because of a lack of adventure) the assembled Arthurian knights are amusing themselves, and on this occasion adventure does not occur at first as an actual event, but comes in the form of Calogrenant's story. By contrast, in the scene from *Perceval* mentioned above (line 2785ff.) the naming of Whitsun is linked with the motif of waiting and not being able to eat, and festive joy is not possible

[7] *Erec et Enide*, line 29; *Cligés*, line 10; *Lancelot*, line 31 [33]; *Yvain*, line 1; *Perceval*, line 290.

[8] *Erec et Enide*, line 39; *Yvain*, line 55.

[9] *Cligés*, line 388; *Lancelot*, line 224; *Perceval*, line 4086.

[10] See Chapter 6 for the play on words involving *coste/Pentecoste*.

until the arrival of the two prisoners. The advent of a messenger with a challenge that devastates the Arthurian court is nowhere as well developed as in *Lancelot*. But technically the Red Knight and the Grail messenger in *Perceval* also belong in this category. They trigger a repeated departure of the hero, and their effect is comparable with that of the messenger scenes to be found in the opening sequences of later romances.

Thus the thirteenth-century authors did not have a straightforward or complete prototype for the beginnings of their romances in any of Chrétien's works. The standard pattern for Arthurian romance openings had to be evolved by combining particularly striking individual elements which Chrétien had already used, although for him they had often served a different purpose, and were not necessarily at the beginning of the romance. The gradual consolidation of an Arthurian literary tradition with more and more stereotyped accessories and the fashioning of an almost rigid pattern for the opening of an Arthurian romance becomes particularly apparent when compared with the variety still to be found in Chrétien's works. However, it is very important to realize that precisely in this matter Chrétien himself is already perceived to be within an Arthurian tradition. The relatively complete development of the Arthurian opening manifested in *Lanval* and in the lays *Cor* and *Cort mantel* suggests the need for a survey of Arthurian literature before Chrétien; moreover, in Wace's *Brut* for example, one comes across 'Carlion' (line 10,205) and 'Pentecoste' (line 10,202) as the place and date of Arthur's coronation. Gawain is also mentioned, there is a list of knights, and the Round Table is referred to by name. Thus we have evidence that in this respect the Arthurian tradition was already stronger than all Chrétien's new breadth of variation, and that it persisted without much recourse to his suggestions for possible variants, even if strengthened by them.[11]

In another respect, however, Chrétien proves to be the initiator of a new literary tradition, where the starting-point is his *Cligés*. It is remarkable that it was in fact precisely this 'untypical' Arthurian romance[12] with its two-part structure that should influence the format of a whole group of thirteenth-century Arthurian works, namely *Beaudous, Claris et Laris, Meraugis, Gliglois* and *Durmart*. Moreover, it so happens that the typical romance opening described above is lacking in all these verse romances. Instead they follow the route pioneered by *Cligés*, and here the decisive opening formula runs 'At the

[11] See the First Continuation, MS *L*, line 9169: 'Pasce a Glomorgan', MSS *ASP*, line 9113: 'Pantecoste a Carlion'; *Meliador*, line 2017: 'Carlion', line 2518: 'Pentecouste' (rhyming with 'couste').

[12] Bruce, *The Evolution of Arthurian Romance*, Vol. I, p. 113: '...it is generally agreed that no part of this romance has any genuine connection with the *matière de Bretagne* and the Arthurian affiliation which Chrétien gives it is of the most artificial kind'.

time of King Arthur there dwelt in...King...and his wife. They had a son named...'[13] The opening of *Gliglois* will serve as an example:

Au tans c'Artuz fu en Bretaigne,
Eut a cel jour an Alemaigne
Un castelain preu et gentil.
De sa mouillier eut un bel fil. (1–4)

(In the days when Arthur was alive in Britain, there was at that time in Germany a valiant and noble castellan. His wife had given him a fine son.)

Characteristic elements of this way of beginning an Arthurian romance are the references to Arthur, Britain and the name of the hero. The naming of Arthur is to indicate that the theme of the work belongs within the Arthurian sphere, and it implies a guarantee that sooner or later the young hero will come into contact with the Arthurian court, or perhaps be nominated as a knight of the Round Table at the end of his path to maturity. Britain is mentioned in order to distinguish the hero's country from it and to provide a destination for his developmental journey. The name of the hero is always clearly specified; in that respect this second group of Arthurian romances differs clearly from the type described above, where the name and origin of the hero are often shrouded in secrecy.

However, after the naming of Arthur and Britain as Arthurian signals there is often absolutely no further mention of Arthurian characters or events for thousands of lines. As a rule the marriage of the hero's parents is described first, although we are offered the following reassurance by the poet of *Durmart*: 'Mais je ne vos conterai mie / De chief en chief tote lor vie' (81–2, 'But I shall not tell you the whole of their life-story from beginning to end'). That is what Chrétien had done in devoting the first half of his *Cligés* (2,630 lines out of 6,780) to the life and death of Alixandre and Soredamor. The remark by the author of *Durmart* reveals an expressly critical attitude towards Chrétien's manner of proceeding. Even so, it is worth mentioning that Durmart's parents love each other just as intensely and exclusively as the couple in *Cligés*. Nevertheless, the author wants to get to his main story more quickly than Chrétien:

Mais grans anuis seroit a dire
Ne de conter tot tire a tire
Comment cil enfes est norris. (93–5)

(But it would be a great labour to tell and narrate stage by stage how this child was brought up.)

[13] See P. Rickard, *Britain in Medieval French Literature 1100–1500* (Cambridge, 1956), p. 110 for examples of the literary cliché 'al tans Artu' ('in the days of Arthur').

On the other hand, *Durmart* represents an exception in so far as Arthur is not named at the beginning of this romance.[14] However, it is a common feature of all these romances of the second type (apart from *Beaudous*) that they have no Arthurian scene at the beginning. The narrative initially resembles more a *roman idyllique* or a romance of adventure in general,[15] the link with the Arthurian sphere not being made until relatively late.

The romance of *Floriant et Florete* goes its own way in several respects, including the setting of the bulk of the plot in Sicily and the marriage of Gawain; it also resembles *Beaudous* in combining both techniques for beginning an Arthurian romance. The work begins with a detailed description of Floriant's parents, birth, youth and first heroic deeds. After the young knight has already distinguished himself he comes to the Arthurian court, and as this scene is introduced we then see unfolding yet again the pattern displayed at the beginning of other Arthurian romances:

> *En Sezille ot jadis .I. roi,*
> Preudome et sage sanz desroi,
> Molt fu li rois de bonne vie
> Et plains de grant chevalerie,
> Hardis estoit et redoutez,
> *Elyadus iert apelez.*
> *Fame ot* espousé de grant pris,
> Fille le roi de Clauvegris;
> Ensamble furent longuement
> Qu'il ne porent avoir *enfant*... (33–42)
> Seignor, ce fu a *Penthecouste*
> Que la roïnne sist dejouste
> Le rois *Artus* au mestres dois.
> *Molt i ot dus, contes et rois*;
> Et Queus devant le roi s'en vient,
> .I. bastonet en sa main tient.
> 'Sire, fet il, or m'entendez:
> Vostre *mengier* est aprestez,
> Bien poëz mengier des or mes.'
> 'Keus, fet li rois, laissiez m'en pés
> Que *ja, par Dieu, n'i mengerai*
> Devant que noveles orrai
> Ou de nouvele ou d'*aventure*,
> Quex qu'ele soit ou bone ou dure.'

14 Arthur's name does not appear in *Durmart* until line 4188.

15 See also *Joufrois de Poitiers*, where the function of King Arthur is more realistically replaced by that of 'Roi Henri d'Engleterre' ('King Henry of England').

Ensi li rois a Keus parloit
Et me sires *Gauvains* estoit
Alez *esbastre* a unes loges... (1537–53)
Mon seigneur Yvain en apele:
'Ne veez vous ces *damoisele*,
Fet il, avaler cele angarde?
Se Dex mete m'ame en sa garde,
Je croi que nos orrons noveles,
Ne sai lequel, laides ou beles.' (1573–8)

(*Long ago there was a king in Sicily*, a wise and noble man without fault. The king led an excellent life, and was endowed with great chivalry. Courageous and powerful, *he was called Elyaduc*. He had married a most noble *wife*, the daughter of the king of Clauvegris; they were together for a long time without having any *children*... My lords, it was at *Whitsun* as the queen sat beside King *Arthur* at the high table. *Many dukes, counts and kings are there*. And Kay comes before the king, holding a small rod in his hand. 'Sire,' he says, 'now listen to me, your *meal* is ready and you can eat right away.' 'Kay,' says the king, 'leave me in peace, for *by God I'll not eat any of it* until I hear news of some novelty or *adventure* of whatever kind, whether good or harsh.' The king was speaking to Kay in this way and my lord *Gawain* had gone *for a stroll* in one of the galleries... He calls my lord Yvain and says, 'Do you not see those *damsels* riding down from those outworks? As God may protect my soul, I believe we shall hear news, though I don't know whether it will be good or bad.')

The differences outlined above leave us with two basic types of opening sequence for Arthurian romances. By analogy with Chrétien's works they can be termed the *Yvain* type or Arthurian pattern and the *Cligés* type or genealogical pattern.[16]

REPETITION OF MOTIFS, BIPARTITE STRUCTURE AND DOUBLE COMPOSITION

In searching for other formal features to unite the Arthurian romances as a group, the question arises as to whether the characteristics of repeated motifs, bipartite composition and the deliberate placement of Arthurian scenes still

[16] To a certain extent these types overlap with the concepts of *roman épisodique* and *roman biographique* as defined by Gaston Paris. However, his distinction is based on criteria of content rather than form. He uses *épisodique* to designate those numerous romances which are based on individual episodes from the life of Gawain or some other well-known Arthurian hero (including *L'Atre périlleux, Rigomer, Le Chevalier à l'épée, La Mule sans frein* and *La Vengeance Raguidel*). On the other hand, those romances which describe the path to maturity of a young and still unknown hero as far as his acceptance into the Round Table are termed *biographique*. Arguably, however, there are numerous romances such as *Li Chevaliers as deus espees* or *Yder* which cannot be clearly allocated to either group. See Gaston Paris, 'Romans en vers', pp. 14–15.

occur in the post-Chrétien verse romances. Kellermann and Köhler elevated these characteristics to the status of structural principles for Chrétien's own romances, but are they merely characteristic of Chrétien or are they also to be regarded as fundamental elements of the genre of Arthurian verse romance as a whole?[17]

The doubling of motifs is a frequent phenomenon. The love of Floriant and Florete is developed in parallel with the love of Gawain and Blanchandine; like Gawain, the 'chevaliers as deus espees' (knight with the two swords) is also searching for his name; Agamanor parallels Meliador in trying to win the affection of his beloved; Fergus experiences a similar childhood to that of Perceval, his prototype. There are numerous comparable examples in evidence, and yet hardly any of the later Arthurian verse romances exhibit such a concentration of repeated motifs as one of Chrétien's works.[18]

The technique of doubling motifs was undoubtedly used extensively by romance authors, but in the majority of cases it cannot be seen as the nucleus of double composition, since by no means all the later Arthurian romances follow the principle of bipartite structure at all. That is, unless one wishes to emulate Southworth in revealing examples of double composition by interpreting as a structural division any and every turning-point in the plot which happens to occur in the middle or the second third of the text, and without which it is hard to imagine any literary work of the period.[19]

The incorporation of an Arthurian scene, which in turn occasions a twofold journey, gives a more convincingly bipartite structure in *La Vengeance Raguidel*, where Gawain sets out twice, in *Li Chevaliers as deus espees*, where the hero Meriadeuc cannot linger at Arthur's court because he still has to investigate the mystery of the blood-stained sword, in *Floriant et Florete*, where Floriant sets out with Florete on a quest for adventure after the wedding and subsequent period of *recreantise*, and in *Hunbaut*, an incomplete romance of which only 3,617 lines have survived (or were ever written?), but where the existing narrative ends with the words 'Mais ai[n]s qu'il lievent de la table' (3618, 'But before they rise from the table'). Perhaps a second part was intended to follow on from there, which might have contained about the same number of lines and would have been in a better position than the first part, which can be regarded as a Gawain romance, to justify the romance's title of *Hunbaut*.

17 W. Kellermann, *Aufbaustil und Weltbild Chrestiens von Troyes im Percevalroman*, *ZrPh* Beiheft 88 (Halle, 1936, reprinted Darmstadt, 1967); E. Köhler, *Ideal und Wirklichkeit in der höfischen Epik*, *ZrPh* Beiheft 97, second edition (Tübingen, 1970).

18 On this topic see W. Brand, *Chrétien de Troyes* (Munich, 1972).

19 M. J. Southworth, *Etude comparée de quatre romans médiévaux: Jaufre, Fergus, Durmart, Blancandin* (Paris, 1973).

In the case of *Durmart* the hero's visit to the Arthurian court with the test of the perilous seat can be taken as the clearest indication of bipartite structure; although this is Durmart's first contact with the Arthurian court, the episode still has all the hallmarks of a key Arthurian scene, since it brings about the hero's renewed departure: 'Car li Galois s'en vuet partir / Por achiever son grant desir' (10,325–6, 'For the Welshman wants to leave in order to fulfil his great desire').

If one is prepared to concede that a bipartite structure does not have to be strictly linked to the occurrence of Arthurian scenes, then *Meraugis*, *Jaufré* and *Fergus* as well as *Durmart* can be interpreted as examples of double composition. In *Durmart* the author himself announces a division: 'Or primes commence li contes' (1574, 'This is where the tale begins'), and the first section bears some resemblance to the *premerain vers* in *Erec*. However, the relationship of the two parts is approximately 1,600 to 14,000 lines, which does not remotely correspond to the proportions suggested by Chrétien. Another characteristic of bipartite structure, observable not only in *Durmart* but also in *Meraugis*, *Jaufré* and *Fergus*, is the sudden loss of the hero's lady. This separation from the beloved leads to the reawakening and maturing of the hero, whether he is to blame or not, and enables him to begin growing in awareness. As in *Yvain*, the loss in *Durmart* and *Fergus* is followed by a time of *égarement*, the madness caused by the pain of love and the awareness of guilt. However, it must be stressed yet again that these divisions and the resulting bipartite structure of the narrative are not always formally supported by an Arthurian scene and must not therefore be seen as indications of Arthurian double composition in the sense intended by Kellermannn and Köhler. On the other hand, it is equally true that the absence of double composition or of a fully-fledged structure based on Arthurian scenes is no indication of faulty composition or of inferior literary quality, as could be amply demonstrated on the evidence of romances such as *L'Atre périlleux*, *Le Bel Inconnu*, *Durmart* and *Meraugis*.

Both *L'Atre périlleux* and *Le Bel Inconnu* have only opening and closing Arthurian scenes; in between no more than a tenuous contact is maintained with the Arthurian court by dispatching prisoners to it. *Beaudous*, although undoubtedly an Arthurian romance, has no Arthurian scene at all until the end of the work. In this context, however, it is also relevant to recall what was mentioned in connection with double composition: not every scene in a romance that takes place at the Arthurian court should be termed an Arthurian scene, because otherwise we would create a decidedly misleading picture of romance structure. Thus only scenes having the following characteristics are to be treated as Arthurian scenes for these purposes:

1. Arthur and several knights of the Round Table must be present, and it must be to a certain extent a public occasion.
2. The scene must not focus merely on prisoners or messengers; the hero of the romance must be at court in person.
3. Something of relevance to the hero must take place.
4. The hero must depart again (in the case of the main Arthurian scene).

A theory about the structural role of Arthurian scenes developed on the basis of Chrétien's romances can only be expected to transfer successfully to the more extensive of the later Arthurian verse epics. The shorter Arthurian texts and the fragments will therefore be accorded only peripheral consideration in the following section. There are three types of structure represented in the short works:

1. *One Arthurian scene*
   The action takes place at Arthur's court from beginning to end with no change of scene (*Cor, Cort mantel*).
2. *Two Arthurian scenes*
   The hero departs, and returns to Arthur's court after successfully accomplishing his task in one change of location (*Le Chevalier à l'épée, Gliglois, Tyolet*). *Lanval* and *Melion* are special cases because the hero withdraws from court and returns, only then to face the crisis and turning-point, after which he withdraws for ever.
3. *Three Arthurian scenes*
   The first hero departs and returns, then the second hero departs and returns, but only the second is successful, i.e. double composition with two protagonists (*La Mule sans frein*).

A more detailed picture can now be drawn to show the structural role of Arthurian scenes in the sixteen full-length Arthurian romances. *Beaudous* has an Arthurian scene only at the end of the work, but this is exceptional. The hero, who knows from the start that he is Gawain's son, does not need to appear at Arthur's court before the perfecting of his chivalry has been completed, because his lineage guarantees his unproblematic entry into the circle of Arthurian knights. The romance merely describes his many adventures on the journey from his native country to the Arthurian court. However, the author Robert de Blois did not devise this romance in isolation but as an integral part of an extensive didactic work, and he therefore differed from many other Arthurian writers in the function he envisaged for both the form and the content of his romance. Thus it was possible for him to dispense with the normally obligatory first Arthurian scene. The assumption that such a first Arthurian scene is a standard requirement follows from the observation that it can be found in eleven of the sixteen romances. Furthermore these are instances of a first Arthurian scene in the strict sense; in other words, the scene takes place before the reader knows any details about the hero or the object of his quest, and before the hero sets out on his series of adventures. In this first Arthurian scene the knight is allotted a specific task which he undertakes to accomplish (*Fergus*), or he sets himself a clearly defined goal (searching for his father in *Yder*, finding out his own name in *Li Chevaliers as deus espees*, or proving himself to a lady in *Durmart* and *Meraugis*). A combination of both alternatives is also possible (*Fergus*), and had already occurred in *Lancelot*.

Sometimes the first Arthurian scene can occur so late that it takes over the function of the main Arthurian scene. This is true of *Durmart*, where the hero goes through half the romance (about 8,500 lines) before coming into contact with Arthur's court. In *Floriant et Florete* the hero Floriant is also an accomplished knight before he comes to Arthur's court, but he wins the tournament while still unrecognized. Gawain becomes his comrade-in-arms when they are faced with freeing Floriant's mother from the clutches of a wicked steward. At the end of this rescue mission to Sicily (during which Arthur and his knights are present throughout), we have the wedding of Floriant and Florete. Arthur and Gawain return to London, while Floriant succumbs to the temptation of *recreantise*, then sets off with Florete on a journey to Arthur's court, frees Rome from the heathens on the way, reaches Arthur (second and last Arthurian scene), learns of the death of his father-in-law and returns home as Emperor of Constantinople. For their part, the friends Claris and Laris travel repeatedly to the Arthurian court and thence to their native Gascony, so that the structure of the romance is shaped by their four journeys. On each journey they support Arthur in a military undertaking, fighting against Rome, Spain, Denmark and Hungary; however, these are not examples of quests, but simply demonstrations of military virtues that were never in doubt. In the course of the narrative both heroes marry ladies they had chosen for themselves at the beginning of the romance, but this love-element is not connected with the accomplishment of adventures. Both strands of the narrative, the romantic and the military, proceed in parallel but are also swamped by the adventures of countless other knights, inflating the romance to a length of 30,000 lines. As we saw in *Floriant et Florete*, the Arthurian scenes do not lend themselves to precise demarcation because Arthur and his army are usually travelling with Claris and Laris. Such Arthurian scenes do not function as points of rest or stability, and they contribute little to the structure. None of them is characterized by the tension of latent conflict to be found in Chrétien's Arthurian scenes.

Meliador also runs to more than 30,000 lines, but in this case Froissart has constructed his Arthurian romance much more rigidly and purposefully. The beginning and the end both have an Arthurian scene. In between lies a time-span of five years during which 240 knights contend for the accolade of being the boldest knight and for the hand of Hermonete; however, only two, Meliador and Agamanor, have their efforts described in detail, whilst a third important rival, the somnambulant Camel, is rapidly eliminated by Meliador within the first third of the romance.

Finally, the romance of *Escanor* breaks away completely from the Arthurian format. It too contains about 30,000 lines. There are at least three protagonists, Kay, Gawain and Escanor, and of these the eponymous hero Escanor has the least influence on the narrative, since he plays only an indirect role. His supposed murder by Gawain and the resultant complexities of the vindication process, as well as Kay's love for the beautiful Andriuete with all its ramifications, form the basis of the narrative. There are at least seven Arthurian scenes, even if they are often relevant only to Kay or Gawain separately. Kay returns to court repeatedly, either because he is in doubt about the success of his wooing or in order to demand Arthur's help in freeing his lady. He sets off three times for 'Norhombrelande', the home of his future wife, and the last occasion does not even come until after the wedding. Gawain also sets off three times, to quell a rebellion in Brittany, to clear up the accusations against him and to seek his brother Gifflet. The romance ends in a most unusual fashion with the death of Escanor as a hermit and the death of Gifflet's wife, the Queen of Traverses. The criticism so unjustly levelled at many of the romances by Chrétien's successors is justified for once in this case; the structure of the work is disjointed and tortuous. Unlike Froissart, the author Girart d'Amiens failed to recognize the latent structural force of Arthurian scenes, although in purely chronological terms his work is about a hundred years closer to Chrétien's than is *Meliador*. The same can also be said of the authors of *Floriant et Florete* and *Claris et Laris*.

Wherever there is a first Arthurian scene there is also a corresponding final one, the exception being *Durmart*, where there is another important section of narrative after the final Arthurian scene and the wedding. As in fairy-tales, almost all the final Arthurian scenes include wedding celebrations, and the Arthurian court provides the framework for these festivities. The probable inspiration for this is the coronation of Erec and Enide. The wedding of hero and heroine taking place at the end of a romance points to the fact that in the last resort the winning of the beloved lady represents the hero's main motivation and greatest reward. The additional honour of now belonging to the Round Table is a secondary consideration, even though success in chivalry constitutes an important prerequisite for the hero to win the love of his life. Only the romances in which Gawain is the chief protagonist lack this motivation, at least for the hero himself. But even in the romances of this group there are still numerous weddings celebrated in the final scenes, especially in *L'Atre périlleux* where no fewer than four couples are brought together through Gawain's beneficial influence.

Chrétien's romances have the winning of Enide and Laudine depicted separately from the main action, and in a position to be regarded as the starting-point for that action. The main Arthurian scene separates the first part from the subsequent main narrative. This particular formal procedure of Chrétien's and its structural significance were not pursued by very many of his successors, and indeed the idea of the conjugal romance itself makes no further appearances in any of the texts. *Floriant et Florete* is alone in following the structural pattern of *Erec et Enide*; the other romances do not unite the hero with his lady until the end of the narrative.

The problem of the main Arthurian scene is very closely bound up with that of double composition. Only a few romances with a bipartite structure have an example of such a scene. A rigid structural pattern based on Arthurian scenes in the spirit of Chrétien's romances (or even in the sense of a hypothetically idealized version of Arthurian structure) occurs in only three romances, namely *Floriant et Florete* as mentioned above, *Yder* and *La Vengeance Raguidel*. These contain at least three Arthurian scenes. *Hunbaut* could be added to the list, but only on a hypothetical basis, since the part after the postulated main Arthurian scene has not come down to us. *La Vengeance Raguidel* illustrates the basic arrangement with three Arthurian scenes:

1. *First Arthurian scene*
   The hero Gawain departs. He has a definite task of interest to the company in general.
2. *Main Arthurian scene*
   Gawain returns to Arthur's court and has to admit that he failed to reach his goal because he forgot the necessary means to achieve it when he set off. Renewed departure, to the accompaniment of reproaches and invective.
3. *Final Arthurian scene*
   Gawain returns home after successfully accomplishing the task; celebrations at Arthur's court.

The arrangement in *Yder* is more complex because the author has inserted an interim Arthurian scene both between the first and the main Arthurian scenes and again between the main and final scenes.

1. *First Arthurian scene*
   The hero Yder meets Arthur but distances himself from him in disappointment and continues on the quest that had previously been his incentive, namely the search for his father.
2. *First interim scene*
   Yder comes across Arthur's army and fights against him on the opposing side, because he considers Arthur's motives for war to be unjust.
3. *Main Arthurian scene*
   Yder allows himself to be accepted as one of the Round Table, but only reluctantly; soon he moves on of his own accord to seek his father.
4. *Second interim scene*
   Return to Arthur's court after finding his father. Renewed departure to accomplish a task maliciously set by Arthur, and on which the winning of his beloved lady also depends.
5. *Final Arthurian scene*
   Return to Arthur's court after successfully performing the deed, marriage to the lady, marriage of Yder's parents and reconciliation with Arthur.

The structure of both romances is very rigid. However, amongst all the later romances only *La Vengeance Raguidel* and perhaps *Floriant et Florete* follow Chrétien's structural model, in so far as their main Arthurian scenes contain an accusation of guilt or a source of conflict. This then entails the condemnation of the hero and his expulsion from the Arthurian community, and at the same time lends the second expedition the character of a journey of atonement and purification. In general, however, Chrétien's pattern of composition clearly did not appear to the Arthurian poets of the thirteenth century to be an essential element in shaping this type of romance.

The absence of the main Arthurian scene in most of the romances after Chrétien raises the question as to whether the function of this scene in so far as it is typical of the genre could be transferred to other scenes in the romance. Chrétien's *Lancelot* is already devoid of a main Arthurian scene, and it is precisely this romance which has also been shown to be particularly close in structure to most of the later romances in its use of the motif of the messenger who unleashes shock waves at Arthur's court. Fergus and the Bel Inconnu, but also Jaufré and Meriadeuc, the knight with the two swords, already find themselves in a state of conflict in the first Arthurian scene. This conflict, generally articulated in the form of invective from Kay and/or the presence of a lady who still has to be won by heroic deeds (and of whom the hero is not yet worthy), motivates the departure of the knight. On this basis one could postulate for the later Arthurian verse romances a transfer of the function of the main Arthurian scene to the first Arthurian scene. This transfer renders superfluous the temporary return of the hero to Arthur's court and his renewed departure with the goals of purification and the search for his identity.

At the same time these considerations apparently confirm that neither a main Arthurian scene nor double composition are obligatory characteristics of the whole genre of Arthurian verse romances, as has hitherto been supposed. Even Chrétien does not observe the principle of a rigid pattern of Arthurian scenes in all his romances; the first Arthurian poet offers instead a variety of structural prototypes. However, a review of all the manifestations of the genre does seem to show that the obligatory first Arthurian scene and the final Arthurian scene can be classified as standard characteristics of that genre, in conjunction with some sort of central break, although this is differently organized and less formal than with Chrétien. Some works such as *L'Atre périlleux* and *Fergus* were composed to a clearly defined pattern, even if without a rigid structure along the same lines as Chrétien's romances. The revealing fact remains, however, that precisely those romances which adopt a critical stance towards Chrétien's works or towards particular tendencies of the genre (as we shall be seeing in the cases of *Yder, La Vengeance Raguidel* and *Durmart*) are in structural terms the most closely oriented towards the first Arthurian romances; thus they bear witness to the authors' recognition, understanding and subsequent remodelling of Chrétien's structural designs.

3

Changes in the relationship between ideals and reality

THE FRAGILE IDEAL OF THE ROUND TABLE

The romance of *Li Chevaliers as deus espees* begins with a description of Arthur's court, the hub of the Arthurian world. Whereas Chrétien had always confined himself to brief generalized indications of where the first phase of the narrative was taking place,[1] the author of *Li Chevaliers as deus espees* presents us with a detailed enumeration of the characteristic features of the Arthurian court and the king as its chief representative:

Tenue a sans quinte de guerre
Lonc tans li rois Artus sa terre
Et ot trestous ses anemis
A son voloir desous lui mis,
S'iert lies et la roine ert lie
Et la cours fu mout envoisie,
Et li boins rois ki tant valoit
Se pourpensa lors k'il tenroit
Court la plus bele et la grignour
K'il onques tenist a nul iour,
Dont de mout grans tenir soloit;
Car ch'est la riens k'il plus voloit
Et ki plus li plaisoit a faire
Pour aloier et pour atraire
A lui les cuers des chevaliers.
Tant les amoit et tenoit chiers,
Ke ia nuls d'els, se il peust,
D'entor lui ne se remeust.
Et rice et grant et noble estoient
Li don ke toute iour avoient,
Car de ce n'iert ratiers ne chices.

[1] *Yvain*, lines 1–7; *Erec et Enide*, lines 27–34; *Lancelot*, lines 30–33 [31–35].

Pour eus honnerer estre rices
Voloit sans autre baerie.
Ainc ne fu sa mains desgarnie
Toutes eures de grans dons faire,
Et il, li frans, li deboinaire,
Ke plus donna, et il plus ot.
Ainc sa larguece ne le pot
Apourir, bien le vous plevis,
Ains le monteploia tous dis.
Tant ert preus et de grant afaire,
Ke onques riens pour honnor faire
Ne li sambla travaus ne paine.
Li plus bas iours de la semaine,
Quant plus priveement estoit,
Pasques d'un autre roi sambloit.
Un iour a les baillius mandes
Et ses clers dont il ot asses;
Et quant il devant lui les vit,
Tost lor a commande et dit,
Ke par tout laissaissent savoir
A tous ceus ki sous son pooir
Tenoient fief ne seignourie
De lui, k'il ne laissaissent mie
K'a Pentecouste ne venissent
A Cardueil et se li tenissent
Compaignie. Ki n'i venroit,
De voir seust k'il fourferoit
Tout sans pardon et sans pitie
L'amour de lui et tout son fie. (1–50)

(King Arthur had held his lands for a long time without having to pay the price of war, and had subjected all his enemies to his will, so that he and the queen were both joyful and the court was in high spirits. Then the good and worthy king thought that he would hold the greatest and most splendid court that he had ever held, though he always held court on a very large scale. For it was his greatest wish and what pleased him most, to attract and bind to himself the hearts of his knights. He loved them so much and held them so dear that none of them left his entourage if he could prevent it. Rich and noble were the great gifts they received every day, for in this matter he was neither miserly nor mean. He wanted to be rich only in order to honour them, without any other ambition. His hand had never lacked the means to give great gifts at all times. Worthy and noble as he was, the more he gave the more he had. I can assure you that his generosity had never been able to impoverish him; rather it never ceased to enrich him. He was so noble and magnanimous that nothing conducive to honour ever seemed a burden or an effort for him. The most ordinary day of the week when he was at his most private seemed like Easter for any other king. One day he summoned his bailiffs and his clerks, of whom he had plenty, and when he saw them all assembled before him he immediately commanded them to let it be known everywhere amongst all those holding a fief or a lordship from him that they should not fail to come to Cardueil at Whitsun to keep him company. Anyone who did not come should know for certain that he would forfeit without pardon or mercy the king's affection and his fief.)

This passage has all the appearance of a résumé of the genre's development. None of the company of knights will leave Arthur's court willingly, such is the attraction of its peaceful state,[2] resulting from the king's claim to absolute sovereignty, manifested in the subjection of all his enemies and in his efforts to make even the festivities surpass all that has gone before. Arthur loves his knights; he bestows lavish gifts on them, and his *largesse* (generosity) is richly rewarded by the tribute of their affection. In *Durmart* the king testifies explicitly to the value he places on his knights:

Li rois se prent a esjoïr;
Ne se puet de parler tenir
Cant il voit sa chevalerie
Par cui il maintient saignorie.
'Dex! dist li rois a Saigremor,
Com est riches de bial tresor
Qui bons chevaliers a o lui!
Mout riches et mout manans sui,
Quar j'ai les millors chevaliers
Que puist avoir rois ne princiers.
Ja vers eaz ne tenrai avoir,
Car rois ne puet onor avoir
Se de chevaliers ne li vient.
Quant del roi Daire me sovient
Qui les chevaliers avilla
Et les vilains tos ensaucha,
Mout sui joians quant on me conte
Qu'il en fu mors viement a honte.
Il ensaucha sers et vilains,
Et cil l'ocisent de lor mains.
Mar avilla les chevaliers;
Rendus l'en fu ses drois loiers.
Mout doit on riche home blamer
Qui chevaliers ne vuet amer.' (8153–76)

[2] This is probably a direct reference to Wace, from whom the author of *Li Chevaliers as deus espees* also derives other motifs. On this point see M. Pelan, *L'influence du* Brut *de Wace sur les romanciers français de son temps* (Paris, 1931), Part IV, pp. 133–46.

(The king begins to rejoice. He cannot help speaking when he sees all his knights that are a symbol of his lordship. 'God!' said the king to Segremor, 'How rich is the man who has a fine treasury of good knights around him. I am very rich and very well provided for, since I have the best knights that any king or prince can have. Indeed, I shall never possess any wealth that can compare to them, for a king cannot have honour unless it comes from his knights. When I remember King Darius who despised knights and honoured villeins, I am very happy to hear the story of how he died in shame and dishonour. He favoured serfs and villeins, and they killed him with their own hands. He was wrong to despise the knights, and he received his just deserts. A rich man who refuses to hold knights in affection must be severely criticized.')[3]

According to the prologue of *Li Chevaliers as deus espees*, courage and honour are cherished at Arthur's court, and every day seems like a festival. But if anyone dares to oppose the wishes of the king, even in the most trivial matter, he loses his sovereign's affection and his fief. In that prologue we have a combination of all the features that the audience for Arthurian literature could possibly associate with the notion of 'Arthur's court' before about the middle of the thirteenth century. It is certainly a place of joy, but not of moderation, giving rather the impression of a world of superlatives and extremes. Here the cream of chivalry, the noblest and the bravest, are gathered under the symbolic title of the Round Table. Wace explains this image:[4] the Round Table was instituted so that all would be equal and no one would have priority in the seating arrangements. Yet this equality appears to be a theory that was never put into practice, since we can detect a hierarchical principle at work in the Arthurian world from the very start. Gawain is deemed to be the *crème de la crème*, no one can measure up to him, and as the king's favourite nephew he enjoys a privileged position at court even above his brothers. Kay's position and function are not comparable with those of any other knight, and according to *Erec et Enide*, lines 1671–1706, he is not a knight of the Round Table. Lancelot stands out from the mass of his equals because of his special relationship with the queen. Finally, only one chosen knight at a time can fulfil each particular adventure, and this separate destiny inevitably renders that knight no longer equal.

There is no scene to be found anywhere in Chrétien's works where the knights' claim to equal status is realized symbolically even for a moment by their sitting around a circular table for a feast. The later romances also lack any such

3 This passage is extremely interesting in view of the audience for which *Durmart* was intended; it even appears to include a message from the patron to the monarchy of the time. It also contradicts Köhler's theory that warnings against drawing upon *vilains* as advisers to the king do not occur in Arthurian literature (Köhler, *Ideal und Wirklichkeit*, p. 18).

4 *La Partie Arthurienne du Roman de Brut par Wace*, edited by I. D. O. Arnold and M. M. Pelan, *Bibliothèque Française et Romane*, Series B, Vol. I (Paris, 1962), lines 1207–20.

image.[5] This forces us to the conclusion that the Round Table failed to materialize either as a symbol or as a tangible object in the minds of the authors of Arthurian verse romances. Nor is the idea of equality revived, either explicitly or implicitly, in any of these works. On the contrary, the king and his knights are explicitly described on several occasions as not sitting at the same table, and this is far more in keeping with the hierarchical attitudes of the Middle Ages than is the notion of a Round Table. In so far as the verse romances contain any comments at all on seating arrangements, the emphasis is always on the fact that Arthur and a few select companions are seated on a *dais* or raised platform.[6] All the examples indicate that the Round Table with its demands as formulated by Wace remained a fiction within fiction. The concept retains a specific function only as the usual label for the Arthurian knights ('cil de la Table Reonde'), when it generally rhymes with 'li mieldres del monde' ('the best in the world').

The Round Table has to remain a fiction, because there is a fundamental distinction between this community of knights and the disciples at the Last Supper or Charlemagne's Twelve Peers, in that the membership can be extended *ad infinitum*. Arthur's ambition is to gather the whole of chivalry to his court. Every knight who comes within the sphere of influence of the court is generously invited to prolong his stay and is asked to become a member of the Round Table.[7] The personalities of the members are of secondary importance in this process. They are after all a whole collection of former opponents, exponents of negative forces, frequently evil and cowardly characters,[8] former Arthurian knights who have turned traitor,[9] abductors and insurgents.[10] They are sent to the court defeated and apparently penitent. Originally they were probably intended to receive their punishment there (as with Guinevere's abductor Meleagant, who in Chrétien's version has to die). But their actual (moral) punishment lies in their enforced integration into the company of exemplary knights. The Arthurian court enjoys an absolutely unlimited ability to integrate; its unchallenged claim to perfection has the effect of subjecting even

[5] The opening episode of the *Queste del Saint Graal* represents an exception.

[6] Examples include *Fergus*, line 6196, *Floriant et Florete*, lines 1537–9, *Tyolet*, line 285, Wace's *Brut*, line 2073 (contrast lines 1207–20), and *Li Chevaliers as deus espees*, lines 1888 and 11,832. The problem of *Table Ronde* versus *dais* is to be discussed more fully in a separate study. [This has now appeared: B. Schmolke-Hasselmann, 'The Round Table: Ideal, Fiction, Reality', *Arthurian Literature* 2 (1982), 41–75.]

[7] In *Le Bel Inconnu* (199–227) the hero asks Arthur to grant him the boon of being allowed to pursue a particular adventure. Arthur objects on the grounds that he is too young for it, and offers him a place at the Round Table as compensation!

[8] *Hunbaut*, lines 64–5.

[9] *Li Chevaliers as deus espees*, lines 10,702–3.

[10] *Hunbaut*, lines 3607–12.

antagonistic elements to its automatic perfecting process. As has already been suggested, opposition is not only not tolerated but is resisted until the opponent submits unconditionally. As if by magic, all negative forces at the Arthurian court are neutralized. Integration is thus the most important function of the Arthurian court in the verse romances of the thirteenth century, whilst re-integration is of secondary importance.

ARTHUR'S LACK OF PERFECTION

The number of Arthurian knights is extended to the point of being potentially unlimited. The inevitable consequence is a watering down of the ideal of perfection, exemplified most clearly in the person of the king himself.[11]

The personality of the king fluctuates from the start (indeed even in Wace) between the poles of activity and inactivity. These two basic aspects of his nature still appear to be fundamentally unchanged in the verse romances of the thirteenth century; in comparison with Chrétien there is even an increase in his readiness to take action, but his habit of *penser* also plays a significant role. Arthur now quite frequently goes to war (for example in *Durmart, Escanor, Yder* and *Rigomer*), fights a duel himself (*Rigomer*, lines 16,036–44 and 17,075–229) or takes part in tournaments in person (*Claris et Laris*, line 13,141, and at the end of *Le Bel Inconnu*). However, this urge to be involved in the action rarely if ever turns out to his advantage. If he goes to war the reader discovers forthwith that he has been encouraged by bad advisers and is fighting on the wrong side.[12] Without knowing or wishing it—but precisely this is typical of Arthur—he supports the villain who is under attack from the hero. If he wants to be like his knights and ride off in search of adventure for once, his close friends advise him against it, fearing the worst. However, his wishes prevail:

> 'Lors me convient', fait il, 'aler
> Ausi bien aventure querre
> Con les autres fors de ma terre.'
> 'Sire,' çou dist se baronie,
> 'Par no consel n'irés vos mie!
> Por vos i voist li uns de nos.'
> 'Dont soie jou honis et cous',
> Dist li rois, 'se ja i envoi
> Nul autre chevalier que moi.' (*Rigomer*, 16,036–44)

[11] Compare K. R. Gürttler, 'Künec Artus der guote. Das Artusbild der höfischen Epik des 12. und 13. Jahrhunderts' (Dissertation, Bonn, 1976), p. 279.

[12] For example *Durmart*, lines 13,629–41, and again in *Yder*, where he is partly motivated by greed—he has been promised a town and twenty castles as a reward.

('Now it's my turn', he says, 'to do as the others do and go in search of adventure outside my own land.' 'Sire,' said his barons, 'if you take our advice you will not go. One of us will go for you.' 'That would bring me shame and brand me a coward,' said the king, 'if I were to send any other knight but myself.')

Later in the same text, in a duel against a man who is disputing his niece's inheritance, Arthur behaves with laborious politeness, as if he is still having to learn from scratch the rules of courtesy operating at his court. After he has lifted his opponent out of the saddle he remembers the noble custom of Gawain and Lancelot, that they themselves always dismount in order not to have a dishonourable advantage over their opponent. Arthur then continues to fight on foot, but soon afterwards he cleaves the lawbreaker's body from head to chest in a most uncourtly fashion, as if he were a warrior in a *chanson de geste* (lines 17,134–89).

Arthur's lust for power and his territorial greed can be seen as another facet of his active side. There are several instances of the motif whereby the king at the beginning of the romance narrative asks the question: 'Do you know anyone whose land is still not enfeoffed to me?'; *Hunbaut* provides one example:

'Hunbaut,' fait li rois, 'or me di,
Qui tant as erré par le mont,
Est il dont nus n'a val n'a mont
Qui ne tiengne de moi sa terre?
Il n'a si cointe en Engleterre,
En France n'en Constantinoble,
N'en soit iriés, ja tant n'iert noble,
Se mon conmandement depieche.' (90–7)

('Hunbaut,' says the king, 'you have travelled the world so much; now tell me, is there anyone anywhere, up hill or down dale, who does not hold his land from me? There is no one so valiant in England, France or Constantinople that he will not be made to regret it, however noble he may be, if he disregards my command.')

When Hunbaut tells him of a King of the Isles who has inherited his country from his forefathers and rules it independently, Arthur decides to send Gawain to him with a warning:

'Et dira li que j'ai voé
—Cil qui bien li savra aprendre—
Se il ne vient de moi reprendre
Sa terre et service me face,
Si voie je Diu en la face,

Bien li porra dire por voir
Que je vaurai sor lui mouvoir
Tot le premerain jor d'esté.' (118–25)

('And [Gawain] who can make it quite plain to him will tell him that I have vowed, as God is my witness, that if he does not come to receive his land as a fief from me and do me homage, he can tell him this for a fact, that I shall prepare to move against him on the very first day of summer.')

No objections can deter Arthur from his plan; anyone who does not submit to him voluntarily must expect war. Ilas and Solvas are neighbouring kings, and in the surviving fragment, where the pattern of motifs suggests that it belongs to the beginning of the romance, they accuse Arthur of having treated them unjustly; for that reason they no longer wish to be his vassals and they renounce their homage, which makes Arthur very angry (line 21ff.).

For similar reasons the grasping and power-hungry king in *Yder* is not willing to rush to the aid of a damsel who invokes his promise; he justifies this breach of feudal loyalty in the following terms:

'Mes [i]cil sevent qui ci sunt
Qu'asseoir doi le Rougemunt.
Talac ne.l volt de moi tenir,
Si l'en voil feire repentir.
Jo li metrai le siege entor,
Ço sace de voir, einz tierz jor.' (103–8)

('But those who are here know that I have to go and lay siege to Rougemont. Talac does not want to hold it as a fief from me, and I intend to make him regret it. I shall most certainly besiege him within three days.')

Arthur is always glad of easy prey; if two others are fighting over a country he is quickly on the spot to seize it for himself. He is also quick-tempered and easily offended if he thinks, as he often mistakenly does, that he has been provoked. He is then liberal with threats of death.[13] In order to achieve his own ends he does not shrink from endangering even his favourite knights. The author of *Hunbaut* reproaches him with this:

Li rois povrement se nature
Vers Gauvain, qu'isi l'en envoie
En tel contree ne en voie
U il ait tant peril ne doute. (198–201)

[*Translator's note*: There are difficulties here with both text and grammar. *En tel* is Breuer's emendation; Winters preserves *Que en*, but her note fails to give

[13] *Li Chevaliers as deus espees*, line 1887ff., especially lines 2054–5.

a satisfactory explanation of the grammar. Breuer's *qu'isi l'en* is punctuated by Winters *qui si l'en*, without any significant difference to the meaning. The object pronoun may be either masculine (= Gawain) or feminine (= his sister, the subject of the previous lines), but if we assume that *isi* ('in this way') refers to the fact that Gawain is to have no travelling companion but his sister we may translate: 'The king is behaving badly towards Gawain, in sending him and his sister on a journey to a land in which he may meet so much peril and danger.']

Without suspecting what awaits him Gawain arms himself and sets off. Arthur has made him take his own sister as a companion, because the king does not want to spare any other knights. Soon afterwards, when the girl falls into the hands of a villain, the knights who have remained behind express their anger at Arthur's rashness:[14]

Hunbaus l'en a souvent repris
Et a biaus mos l'en aparole
Et en tel guisse a lui parole,
Que li rois en connoist sa coupe.
Et cil Hunbaus mout l'en encoupe,
Que voirement li dist li roi:
'Par foi, Hunbaut, mal sai mon roi,
Quant je sui .I. poi carciés d'ire'...
'Qui a folie, sen(t) aliue,'
Fait Hunbaus; 'tel tient on a saje
Qui tos est plains de forsenaje.' (250–7; 286–8)

(Hunbaut has often taken him to task for it and now addresses him on the matter in fine words, speaking to him in such a way that the king realizes he is at fault. And Hunbaut criticizes him severely for it so that in truth the king said to him: 'By my faith, Hunbaut, I do not know what I am doing when I get at all angry'... [*Translator's note*: Winters rejects Breuer's emendation of *sent* to *sen* in line 286 and proposes: 'He who smells of madness for a league,' says Hunbaut, 'such a man is considered wise, who is full of madness.' With or without emendation line 286 does not connect well with the proverb that follows.])

Arthur, who is universally held to be wise, often behaves extremely stupidly in practice. In the thirteenth-century romances he is no longer the well-adjusted sovereign full of kindness and justice who still seems to predominate in Chrétien's works. Although he sometimes realizes that his behaviour can best be termed *vilenie* (baseness),[15] he is in the main portrayed as having become unjust and arrogant as power and fame have gone to his head. In the fragment of *Le Vallet a la cote mautaillie* a young knight who wants to join the king's

[14] See also *Lancelot*, lines 226–7, where Arthur is reproached by Gawain.
[15] *Yder*, lines 2447–58.

household is rejected by Arthur with contemptuous laughter because he is too poorly dressed. Arthur tells him: 'I have more than two thousand knights who all possess rich weapons and furs to serve me properly. I have no use for you' (compare lines 9–18). The young knight is greatly distressed and decides to look for another overlord. When he has gone, Gawain takes Arthur to task:

> 'Rois, or te voi affaibloier
> Et ta grant court et ta poissance.' (50–1)

('Sire, now I see you diminishing both your great court and your power.')

Arthur has offended against the accepted 'custom' that 'Es dras ne gist pas la prouece' (59, 'prowess does not lie in the clothes'). Gawain as intermediary succeeds in persuading the young man to return to the court.[16]

Aggression, injustice and a lust for power are only some of the new characteristics ascribed to the king in the thirteenth-century Arthurian romances, and which thus destroy the positive impression prevailing in the earlier texts.[17] However, the older image of Arthur does also live on in a considerable number of works,[18] but his traditional characteristics are sufficiently well known not to need more detailed discussion here.[19]

A further crucial indication of the change in the king's personality is his jealousy, which in some cases amounts to a pathological state. In the *Lai du cor* Arthur is already seen reaching for a knife to stab Queen Guinevere when he is the first to be exposed by the horn test. Gawain, Yvain and others have to wrest the weapon from his grasp:

[16] To judge from its structure and content, the scene belongs at the beginning of the lost romance; the hero will prove that appearances are not decisive for the true worth of a knight. The theme of this work would therefore place it alongside *Meraugis*, *Gliglois* and *Durmart* as a *roman à thèse*. 'Cil a la cote mautaillie' is mentioned in the prologue of *Le Bel Inconnu* at line 49, in a list of knights, as well as in *Rigomer* at lines 7075, 10,391 and 13,596, but these passages have apparently not yet attracted any attention. However, the hero has a part to play in the Prose *Tristan* where he bears the name Brunor. It therefore seems that the romance was quite well known.

[17] The newly developed aspects all have a negative bias. A comparable development also emerges in the *chansons de geste*, where the image of Charlemagne becomes increasingly tarnished, likewise after about 1200. However, *Lanval* already portrays Arthur as thoughtless and unjust.

[18] For example in *Claris et Laris*, *Fergus* and *Escanor*.

[19] The role of the *don* (boon) with its attendant concern for honour is an example of an aspect which is subject to hardly any change. On the other hand, it is striking that Arthur's much-vaunted *largesse* hardly ever finds illustration in a tangible form in the narrative of the romances. What the knights possess is what they have either inherited from their forefathers, won for themselves in battle or acquired by means of a fortunate marriage. The concept of *largesse*, as a relic of a positive image of Arthur, is incompatible with what we can actually see becoming thematically significant, namely the king's greed. However, Arthur is often introduced in a negative light at first, only to emerge at the end as better than all the rest; his opponents, who thought at first that they had grounds for contempt, eventually stand corrected (see *Li Chevaliers as deus espees*, lines 2330–47).

Durement le blamerent.
'Sire,' ceo dist Iuwains,
'Ne soiez si vilains,
Kar n'i est femme nee
[Quei] que soit espousee
Qui n'eyt pensé folie.' (306–11)

(They reproached him severely. 'Sire,' said Yvain, 'do not be so base, for there is no woman born, whoever she is married to, who has not had foolish thoughts.')

In the romances of Chrétien such an incident would be unthinkable, whereas here King Arthur, the symbol of chivalry, is rightly accused of behaving despicably.

In *Durmart* (lines 4966–9) the king insists on twenty knights swearing an oath that the queen's honour has not been besmirched during an abduction episode. The last part of *Les Merveilles de Rigomer* contains a bitter quarrel between Arthur and Guinevere. The king has mounted his horse and is intending to ride off in pursuit of *aventure*. While Guinevere is crying because she believes he is in danger the king starts to laugh. When questioned as to the grounds for his unusual behaviour, he replies that he is laughing for joy, because in the first place he is the greatest person on earth after God and secondly he is mounted on the best war-horse in the world. The queen agrees with both claims. But when Arthur asserts that Gawain, who is holding his stirrup for him, is the best knight in the world and that this is a third reason for laughter, the queen is silent. This makes Arthur furious. 'Lady,' he says, 'you owe it to me as a duty to approve of everything that I approve of.'[20] Thereupon Guinevere ventures the assertion that there is another knight better than Gawain, but she does not reveal his name. Arthur threatens to have her beheaded if she does not produce this knight within a day:

Li rois la röine manace
Et a talent que mal li face.
Tout a ceval vers li s'adrece,
Ja l'evust prise par le trece
Et si l'ëust vers lui tiree
Et de son cors mal atiree,
Se ne fusent li haut baron
Qui sont entor et environ.
'Sire', font il, 'çou n'i a mie,
Car trop seroit grant *vilonie*...'
Mout le laidist cascuns et cose. (16,247–60)

[20] Translated from the author's German rendering of lines 16,213–16.

> (The king threatens the queen and wants to do her harm. He rides towards her without dismounting, and he would have seized her by the hair, dragged her towards him and ill-treated her but for the high-born nobles who were present. 'Sire,' they say, 'this must not be, for it would be an act of extreme baseness...' They all criticized the deed severely.)

In order to resolve the dispute Gawain offers a public acknowledgement that he is not the best knight. Then he tries to soothe Arthur, which he manages only with difficulty; like Arthur and the rest of the knights, he suspects that it is Lancelot, Guinevere's lover, whose fame she is defending so emphatically. This also accounts for Arthur's outbursts of aggression. Jealousy and fear of those around him have warped his character. *La Mort le Roi Artu* gives a graphic account of how jealousy drives him inexorably to pursue its consequences and thus becomes a contributory factor in the downfall of Arthur's kingdom.[21] It is possible that in this case the verse romances have been influenced by motifs from the prose romances. Arthur becomes increasingly stereotyped as jealous, and the verse romances go further in this respect than their counterparts in prose. Such behaviour is undoubtedly an instance of the lack of courtliness already highlighted by the accusation of baseness or *vilenie*.

In barely two hundred lines this scene from *Rigomer* makes a significant link between Arthur's jealousy and his sovereign pride, which borders upon hubris, for both he and his entourage are constantly aware of the deep humiliation brought upon him by the infidelity of the queen. It tarnishes his dignity and casts the shadow of ridicule over his political ambitions.[22] Conscious of his image as a cuckold, he is unsure how to behave; aggression alternates with passivity and depression. Arthur is certainly not the undisputed model of chivalry any more, and this development is epitomized in the repeated association of his name with the concept of *vilenie*. His behaviour leads the knights of the Round Table to take an increasingly critical view of him, whilst the outside world that has not yet been absorbed into his sphere of influence often goes so far as to hold him in contempt.

THE ROLE OF CONFLICT IN THE ARTHURIAN COMMUNITY

The constant need for the outside world to seek renewed contact with the Arthurian court, even if only through provocation, reveals that its contempt for Arthur always subconsciously embraces aspects of its former (and secretly

[21] Charlemagne's jealousy becomes the factor which triggers the action in the *Pelerinage Charlemagne*; perhaps this helped the motif to become more influential.

[22] Arthur also appears ridiculous in the judgement scene of *Meraugis*.

longed-for) intense admiration. A representative of the outside world challenging the Round Table and in particular the king as its central figure is not only a typical structural element of Arthurian verse romances but is also characteristic of the relationship between the Arthurian court and its surroundings. There is an excellent example of this in an episode from *Li Chevaliers as deus espees*, line 145ff. At court a glittering festival is under way when the king is overcome by great sorrow. A messenger from King Ris of Outre-Ombre suddenly appears in the hall and informs Arthur that his master intends to have a cloak-lining made for his mistress from the beards of nine conquered kings. Because Arthur is the second-best king in the world after Ris, the lady wants the tasselled fastening of the cloak to be made from Arthur's beard. If Arthur is not prepared to donate his beard and moreover to accept his kingdom as a fief from Ris, then the latter will wage war on him and not rest until he has conquered the whole kingdom, captured the queen and handed her over to the King of Northumberland. He has already invaded the country and is currently besieging one of Arthur's vassals.[23] When Arthur hears these insulting demands he becomes angry, but in particular he is extremely embarrassed that all the knights gathered at court should have witnessed this impudent challenge.[24] *Aventure* had been a long time coming that day, but this kind of adventure is not to Arthur's taste. The provocation is directed against him personally, so that his thirst for new experiences is being punished through his own shame (267 and 270).

The Arthurian community bears all the hallmarks of a militant organization. The knights at Arthur's court form a relatively closed group with the aim of propagating and defending courtesy as their fundamental *raison d'être*. If there were no outside world refusing immediate acceptance of this ideal or enemies deliberately contravening it, then the knights of the Round Table would not be able to create any group identity for themselves and their endeavours would lack purpose. Only a state of conflict with other groups can help to create and confirm their identity, and to maintain the necessary barriers between themselves and society at large. In order to avoid the dissolution which is a constant threat after successful efforts at integration, the elimination of their original enemies (representatives of the non-courtly approach) must be followed by the search for new antagonists, so that the group can still remain in a state of

[23] The beard motif derives from Wace's *Brut*, where it is not given comic treatment. The name Ris suggests the Welsh leader Rhys ap Gryffydd who was in conflict with the English king. Was Wace already intending to stigmatize the uncourtly behaviour and primitive manners of the Welsh?

[24] In lines 11,140ff. and 11,183ff. we are told in so many words that Arthur always puts on a brave face in humiliating circumstances in order to maintain his dignity; he is also afraid of being criticized by Gawain.

conflict and thus preserve its structure, which it would lose if there were no more enemies.[25]

When King Arthur waits longingly for *aventure* and the court seems inhibited and paralysed until it arrives, this can be understood as the search for a new conflict which can once more protect the Arthurian court, even if only temporarily, from emptiness and disintegration. Arthur's craving for *aventure* has to be understood as his existential need for conflict. Because the ending of each romance involves the integration of an enemy, the beginning of each new romance must therefore bring on another enemy. Since only a new conflict can save the Arthurian community from the constant threat of dissolving into futility, this explains why the romance *La Vengeance Raguidel* has Arthur saying a prayer of thanksgiving to God when *aventure* finally arrives, after he has already given up all hope:

> 'Dius m'a aventure envoïe
> Dont ma cors ert joians et lie,
> Et j'en sui liés, si doi je estre!' (137–9)

('God has sent me an adventure that will bring joy and rejoicing to my court, and I am glad of it, and so I should be!')

Apart from Arthur's own longing for conflict, the other possibility for staging a dispute lies in external provocation, of which there are numerous examples. As long as challengers of the Meleagant type shatter the *joie* at Arthur's court the provocation is meant to be taken seriously and the subsequent confrontations may be a matter of life and death; such conflicts have mythical overtones. In the verse romances of the thirteenth century, however, it is quite often the case that the outside world and the audience, in other words everyone except the affected characters at Arthur's court itself, know that the provocation is a pretence, that the challenge is a playful hoax, and more or less the only purpose it still serves is to drag the Arthurian court out of its lethargy, to satisfy its desire for *aventure*, or to create the coveted opportunity for the challenger to fight a knight as famous as Gawain.

At the beginning of *L'Atre périlleux* a youth comes to the court and abducts a maiden currently under Arthur's and Gawain's protection. After he has insulted and disparaged the court, the youth rides away provocatively slowly and even lets them know his route, in order to give one of the Arthurian knights for whom he has shown such contempt an opportunity to pursue him.

[25] The model of a militant organization that is here applied to Arthur's court is based on L. A. Coser, *Theorie sozialer Konflikte* (Neuwied, 1972), especially Chapter 5, which discusses group structure and conflict with alien groups.

'Savés por quoi je vous devis
Par u je m'en doi repairier?
S'il avoit çaiens chevalier
Qui par savoir u par folie
Rien nule que je ci vous die
Vuelle desdire par bataille,
Ne die pas que jou m'en aille
Par une autre voie fuiant.
Voiant tox ensanle me vant
Que par icele m'en irai,
Ne ja del petit pas n'istrai
Desi la qu'i m'avesperra.
Je weul que cil qui me suirra
M'ait a aise, s'il ne se faint,
Ains que je viegne au bos, ataint.' (186–200)

('Do you know why I am telling you which way I am to go? If there were a knight here, be he wise or foolish, who wants to contradict by force of arms anything that I have said to you here, then let him not say that I ran away by a different route. In the sight of you all I declare that I shall go this way and I shall ride at no more than walking pace until nightfall. It is my wish that whoever follows me can easily catch up with me before I come to the woods, if he does not lose heart.')

Kay follows him, but as expected he is thrown from his horse. Then at last Gawain decides to pursue the knight, after having to face the dilemma as to whether he should finish his meal first or not. But because he has delayed too long he does not immediately succeed in avenging the disgrace of the abduction. In a manner reminiscent of *La Vengeance Raguidel* he becomes embroiled in other adventures.

Si qu'il ne set que il fera,
La quele aventure il suirra,
La premiere u la daraine. (639–41)

(So that he does not know what to do, which adventure to pursue, the first or the last.)

In any case it soon emerges that the abduction was a pre-arranged trick on the part of the girl and the knight, and was intended solely to provoke Gawain.

In clarifying the differences between this abduction motif and Chrétien's *Lancelot*, it is easy to recognize the considerable implications of the change that has taken place, and in particular also its direction; this and numerous other romances illustrate the loss of purpose of the Arthurian court and its growing incapacity to fulfil its own ideals. Provocation from the outside world to pursue an adventure that is merely illusory or even non-existent, although its emptiness is barely recognized by even the best Arthurian knights,[26] degenerates into a source of almost malicious amusement for the fictional outside world in the romance itself, but also and not least for the author and his public. After Chrétien nearly all authors of Arthurian verse, from the *Cor* onwards until after 1250, feel the need to a greater or lesser extent to reveal the fragility and unreality of Arthurian pretensions to perfection, and on occasion even to make fun of them.

Conflict as a structural model has a further possible application in explaining another phenomenon of the quest for *aventure* in the thirteenth-century verse romances, namely the search for a fictitious enemy. Arthur's waiting for something to happen to release the tension has just been interpreted as a yearning for that state of conflict without which his society cannot exist. However, in the last phase of the Arthurian verse romances all aggressive enemies have finally been disposed of and even the most distant potential opponents have been definitively integrated. In that situation only one last course of action remains to prop up any feeling of group identity: an external enemy has to be invented in order to give expression to those aggressions which would otherwise be directed inwards and would destroy the cohesion of the Arthurian community. Bickering and hostility amongst the knights at court are not unusual; Kay and Arthur represent one pole, which attracts an assortment of increasingly negative elements, whilst Yvain and Gawain form another pole in adopting a positive stance towards whoever is the current hero.[27] The resultant danger of an internal split is countered by the institutionalization of the fictitious enemy, who may be invented by a member of the Round Table itself as in *Jaufré*, or concocted by outsiders as a joke in order to provoke the court.[28] The imaginary adventure is designed to entice the Arthurian court to rise to the bait and thus be stimulated into action.

If a threat is seen as real, then its consequences will be real. One of these consequences is an increased feeling of group solidarity, and the opening episode of *Jaufré* offers a fine example of this. An Arthurian knight with magic powers, transformed into a giant bird, kidnaps Arthur in order to put an end to the agonizing state of waiting for something to happen. In so doing he fulfils two requirements; the necessary *aventure* comes about and at the same time the court is plunged into fear and horror which awaken it from its state of lethargy. On this occasion it is of no consequence that the danger is only an illusion, as

[26] See also below, pp. 79f.

[27] See also below, p. 97ff.

[28] For example in *L'Atre périlleux* and *La Mule sans frein*.

everyone finally recognizes; the decisive factors are the sudden unanimity, the bonds created by a common concern for the king and the unifying as well as activating effect of desperation. The playful element and the comedy inherent in this particular kind of situation have another obvious consequence, in that the audience's laughter cannot be directed at anyone except Arthur himself. How could he possibly have been taken in by such nonsense? Presumably only because he takes himself too seriously. The awe-inspiring ruler has become a figure of fun and object of ridicule as he is seen wriggling and squealing in the clutches of a clown. This example of taking ideas to extremes is further evidence that here as in other respects the romance of *Jaufré* is merely following to its logical conclusion the trend suggested by a number of the verse romances from northern France.

THE CRUMBLING ETHOS OF *AVENTURE*

Arthur's knights lose much of their good reputation at the hands of Chrétien's successors. At one time it may have been possible to arouse universal admiration merely by establishing that a knight was one of the Round Table, but throughout the romances of the thirteenth century emphasis is placed on the unwillingness of those knights to become involved.[29] Just as Arthur often hesitates to fulfil his moral and practical obligations, so too his knights lack the courage and drive to set off in search of adventure. The court is generally regarded as feeble and devoid of good knights, and the abductor in *L'Atre périlleux* voices this with great clarity; he would never have dared to steal his mistress from any other court:

> 'Mais je senc la toie a si tendre
> Et de bons chevaliers si vuie
> (Je di por ce qu'i lor anuie,
> Et que de li la saisine ai)
> Que ja par ex ne la perdrai,
> Ains l'en porterai sans dangier:
> Ja par le cors d'un chevalier
> De cex qui çaiens sont assis
> N'en ert vers moi son escu pris.' (174–82)

('But I perceive your [court] to be so feeble and so lacking in good knights—I am saying this to annoy them and because I have her in my possession—that I shall never lose her because of them, but carry her away without resistance. Of the knights seated here none will ever take up his shield against me.')

[29] *Le Bel Inconnu*, line 249, and *Rigomer*, lines 75–84.

In *Li Chevaliers as deus espees* the court is so lethargic that even a lady in distress finds it better to take up the sword herself in her own defence than to wait for help from Arthur's knights; because she has lost her land through Arthur's negligence she has no choice 'fors ke me mete en aventure' (563, 'except to undertake the adventure'). It seems as if the knights of the Round Table are actually afraid of the dangers of *aventure*:

> Li rois esgarde et atendoit
> Qui le don li demanderoit;
> Mais n'i trove demandeor,
> Car n'i ot nul qui n'ot *paor*
> Que il aler ne li comant. (*Bel Inconnu*, 199–203)

(The king looks around, waiting to see who would ask the boon of him, but he does not find any claimants, for there was nobody who was not in fear of the king commanding him to go.)

In *Meraugis* the knights are summoned by a dwarf to look for Gawain, who has not been heard of for a year and is probably in danger. However, to the great distress of the king, none of his friends looks up or says a word, until Meraugis finally announces that he is prepared to go in search of Gawain (line 1326ff.).

When all the famous knights refuse to be involved in an adventure the young unknown knight can seize his opportunity. It should certainly not be overlooked that a recurrent motif of this kind is also primarily a literary device designed to give prominence to the hero of the romance, usually an unknown figure, by contrasting him with the traditional heroes of the Arthurian world. Nevertheless, the image of the court in general has undeniably changed for the worse. Thus Fergus is criticized when he admits to being an Arthurian knight:

> 'Iés tu des chevaliers Artu,
> Le tres mauvais roi abatu?...
> Il n'est pas dignes d'estre rois.' (2303–6)

('Are you one of the knights of Arthur, that worthless and feeble king? He is not worthy to be a king.')

There are also instances of women messengers cursing the court from which they cannot obtain the assistance they had hoped for.

> 'De cort m'en vois come faillie!
> Dehé ait la Table Reonde
> Et cil qui sïent a l'esponde,
> Qui le secors ne veulent faire!
> Ha! doce dame debonaire,
> De secors point ne vos amain.

N'est mervelle se je me plain,
Qu'Artus ne vos secorra mie;
Ains i sui bien de tot faillie.' (*Bel Inconnu*, 248–56)

('I leave the court having failed. Cursed be the Round Table and those who sit around it, who do not want to help anyone. Alas, sweet noble lady, I do not bring you any help at all. It is not surprising that I lament, when Arthur will not help you. My mission there has been a complete failure.')

A similar complaint is voiced in *Jaufré*, lines 8042–70. However, the situation can also arise when the knights are so terrified that they forget to ask the messenger where the advertised adventure can be found or how it can be overcome.[30]

Adventure can no longer entice the knights to leave the court, and the court no longer attends to its traditional duties. One reason for this probably lies in the fact that Arthur is afraid of his household dispersing and leaving him behind on his own, deserted by all his knights. The knights are the symbol of his power, and so increasingly he prevents them leaving the court for fear they may not return, as in *Li Chevaliers as deus espees* (17ff.) or in *Rigomer*:

'Comment, diauble! por un cors
Esvuidera tote ma cors
De ma millor chevalerie!
Autant ne m'en demore mie.
Se jou [Lancelot tant n'amaise,]
Nesun aler n'en i laisaise;
Car çou est tot paine pierdue:
Ja ne venrés sans revenue...' (7121–8)
'Asés en serés en quarante—
Voir', dist li rois, 'jusq'a sisante
Le vos consentirai mout bien,
Mais plus n'en otroie jo rien.' (7135–8)

('By the devil! Is my court to be emptied of my best knights for one person? I have hardly any left. If I did not love Lancelot so much I should not let anyone go, for this is all a waste of effort. You will never return unscathed...' 'Forty of you will be enough', said the king. 'In fact I am quite happy to let you have as many as sixty, but I shall not allow one more than that.')

Arthur speaks in similar terms in *Hunbaut* when Gawain wants companions for his journey to the King of the Isles:

...'Trop sui escars
De chevaliers, dont mout me poisse.' (166–7)

('I am very short of knights, which grieves me greatly.')

[30] *Rigomer*, lines 112–18; *La Vengeance Raguidel*.

In the verse romances the king strives by every available means to bind the knights to his court, in order to avoid the development that has already taken place in the contemporary prose romances, where all the knights have departed on a quest and where this is one of the factors in the downfall of Arthur's kingdom.

Under these circumstances the concept of *aventure* acquires some new aspects. A reading of Chrétien's works still tends to create the impression that the poet is using his representation of the Arthurian world to discuss the problems and ideals of his own time,[31] whereas Chrétien's successors usually make it quite clear to their audience that they are reporting events from the distant past. The Arthurian world is no longer merely admirable and exemplary,[32] but henceforth, as testimony to a vanished era, it also takes on the curiosity value of an achievement that can never really be repeated. The ideals described there are far removed from the practice of the writer's own age, as the author of *Tyolet* points out in a passage reminiscent of the beginning of *Yvain*:

> Jadis au tens qu'Artur regna,
> Que il Bretaingne governa
> Qui Engleterre est apelée,
> Dont n'estoit mie si puplée
> Conme ele ore est, ce m'est avis;
> Mes Artur, qui ert de grant pris,
> Avoit o lui tex chevaliers
> Qui molt érent hardiz et fiers:
> Encor en i a il assez
> Qui molt sont preuz et alosez,
> Mes ne sont pas de la maniére
> Qu'il estoient du tens ariére,
> Que li chevalier plus poissant,
> Li miedre, li plus despendant,
> Soloient molt par nuit errer,
> Aventures querre et trover,
> Et par jor ensement erroient
> Que il escuier nen avoient,
> Si erroient si toute jor
> Ne trovassent meson ne tor,
> Ou dui ou troi par aventure,
> Et ensement par nuit oscure
> Aventures beles trovoient,

[31] It has been assumed that this applies for example to the Pesme Aventure episode in *Yvain*, line 5101ff. [5107ff.]

[32] Hence the numerous passages praising former times in the prologues.

Qu'il disoient et racontoient;
A la cort érent racontées
Si come eles érent trovées. (1–26)

(Long ago in the time when Arthur reigned and when he ruled over Britain which is now called England, it was, as I believe, not so densely populated as it is now. But Arthur, who was of great renown, had such knights with him as were very bold and valiant. There are still many there who are most brave and praiseworthy, but they are not like they were in that earlier age, when the most powerful, best and most generous knights were in the habit of roving at night, seeking and finding adventures. They wandered in a similar way by day without any squires, and they travelled all day, or perhaps even two or three days, without finding any house or tower, and in this way in the dead of night they would encounter fine adventures which they would tell and relate; these were told at court just as they had happened.)

It seems as though the narrator has to make a point of explaining to his audience what is actually meant by *aventure* and what the knights of that former age were aiming to achieve on their excursions. So also in *Li Chevaliers as deus espees* and *Durmart*:

...par le monde
Por leur aventures trouver,
Pour eus connoistre et esprouver. (*Deus espees*, 116–18)

(...away from court to find themselves adventures, to test and prove themselves.)

Mais il ert costume a cel tens
Que les aventures queroient
Li fil as rois qui dont estoient.
Quant il pooient eschiver
Et en lor païs retorner,
Adont tenoient les grans cors. (*Durmart*, 1476–81)

(But it was the custom in those days that the sons of the kings of that time would seek adventures. When they managed to survive and return to their own country, they would hold their great courts.)

It emerges from other comments by narrators that *aventure* is mainly the province of impetuous youngsters, as in *Li Chevaliers as deus espees*, lines 7105–7. Indeed the quests in the thirteenth-century verse romances, in direct contradiction to the concept of *aventure* in *Erec* and *Yvain*, are almost exclusively a means of self-discovery for inexperienced young men. They are a kind of initiation in the sense of a training method for young knights. A young man who has only just reached adulthood can try out his strength, accumulate successes, get to know the world and win his future wife; after the wedding he can settle down in peace. He will hardly ever feel the need for adventure or be confronted by it again. It was part of the *Sturm und Drang* years of his turbulent youth, a phase of his development which is now terminated.

Anyone who has successfully left that period of his life behind him does not need to expose himself to danger any more. This reflects a keen awareness amongst the authors of the late verse romances as well as their public that adventures on knightly quests do not always turn out well (after all, one out of the two combatants in any fight must always suffer defeat), and that some knights lose their lives in the process; this awareness enters the works themselves in the form of a sceptical attitude towards the chivalric ideal of *aventure*, which has meanwhile come to seem exaggerated and unrealistic. *Aventure* is now no longer seen exclusively from the perspective of the ever-victorious hero. In a way the criticism follows on from the bitter reflections of Perceval's mother when she learns to her distress that now even her last surviving son is about to set off on the dangerous path of knighthood. She was hoping to protect him from it (408–11), since her husband and two of her sons had died either in duels or from their consequences. As a result she sees knights as those 'dont la gent se plaignent, / Qui ocïent quanqui'il ataignent' (399–400, 'of whom the people complain, who kill whoever they get hold of'). This thought is taken up again in a more emphatic form by the author of *Tyolet*.[33] When the young Tyolet, who has grown up in the forest, meets a knight and naively puts the question 'Quel beste chevalier estoit' (137, 'what kind of animal a knight might be'), the knight replies:

> 'Par foi,' fet il, 'jel te dirai,
> Que ja mot ne t'en mentirai:
> C'est une beste molt cremue,
> Autres bestes prent et menjue,
> El bois converse molt souvent,
> Et a plainne terre ensement.' (139–44)

('In faith,' he says, 'I shall tell you and not one word will be a lie: it is a much feared animal that captures and eats other animals; very often it lives in the woods but also in open country.')

Then he shows Tyolet another group of two hundred knights who are just returning from a plundering expedition: 'Une fort meson orent prise / Et en feu et en charbon mise' (201–2, 'They had captured a strong house and burnt it to cinders'). Now Tyolet also feels the urge to become a 'chevalier beste', but the

[33] The work also contains other close parallels with the beginning of *Perceval*, but the textual relationship of the two poems has not been fully explained. See the comments by Gaston Paris in his edition.

knight warns the boy that his mother will be furious when she finds out 'Que tu as tel beste veue, / Qui autre engingne et autre tue' (235–6, 'that you have seen such creatures who trap and kill others').

In the lay of *Tyolet* knights are presented as the wildest, most dangerous and most bloodthirsty of all animals, and this is even put in the mouth of a representative from the ranks of knighthood itself. Ascribing such self-irony and acknowledgement of his own weaknesses to an Arthurian knight is evidence of a corresponding scepticism on the part of the author towards the ideals of knighthood. Unfortunately he cannot explicitly pursue this idea any further in such a short work, but the subsequent use of the old motif of the cowardly scoundrel who adorns himself with the achievements of a real hero (familiar from the Tristan story) is further evidence in this context that the author does not think very highly of most specimens of knighthood, and wishes to make known that he has seen through their pretence of perfection.

In *Meraugis* we hear of a knight who has taken a strange oath; he intends to ride for a whole year without reins or bridle, wherever his horse takes him. He is a knight-errant par excellence, perhaps the last of his kind:[34]

'Me porpensai que je feroie
Tel veu que nus n'oseroit fere
Autel: lor dis, ses fis toz tere,
Que de tot l'an n'avroie frain
N'esperon ne verge en ma main
Por ce que ja mes ne ferroie
Mon cheval, ne ne li toudroie
Chemin por nul autre doner,
Mes tot cest an sanz demorer
Iroie tant que troveroie
Plus fort de moi. Que vos diroie?
Einsi ai tenu mon chemin
Tant qu'or sui venuz a la fin:
Je ne puis dire ne savoir
Quel part j'arriverai le soir.'
Cil li respont qui a droiture
Li dit: 'Tu vas par aventure
Plus que nus...' (1810–27)

('I resolved to take a vow such as no one else would dare to take: I told them, silencing them all, that for the whole year I should have neither reins nor spurs nor a riding-whip in my hand because I should never spur or whip my horse, nor would I turn him from one path to another, but for the whole of this year

[34] There is a similar knight-errant figure in the *Conte du Graal.*

> without respite I should ride until I found someone stronger than me. What can I tell you? I have kept going in this way until I have now reached the end. I cannot know or tell where I shall arrive this evening.' The other answers him by telling him quite rightly: 'You ride at random more than anyone else...')

However, in the verse romances of the thirteenth century we now also come across increasingly frequent examples of knights who declare emphatically that their life is dearer to them than the fame derived from a successful adventure. In the forefront of this group is Kay, always an ambivalent figure, but who now acquires the additional characteristics of a coward—or of a realist with both feet firmly on the ground. In *La Mule sans frein* he cuts a particularly poor figure, but even the great hero Gawain fares no better, and his journey of adventure, though fraught with dangers, proves to have been in vain because the promised reward does not materialize. The narrative tells of a girl who comes to Arthur's court and laments that she cannot find her mule's valuable bridle. All the knights are challenged to take part in the search, and she offers herself as the reward for finding it. Kay volunteers to go first, but wants a foretaste of the joys to come in the form of a kiss before his departure; this he is refused. He then sets off, but in the wood he trembles with fear as he comes across numerous wild animals; however, they kneel down out of respect for the girl's mule which he is riding. Nevertheless, Kay is pleased when he emerges from the wood. Now he has to go through a deep and dangerous valley full of serpents, and once again he is very afraid.[35] Next he comes to a broad black stretch of water without a ferry. He does actually find a very narrow plank but he is too frightened and turns back, not wishing to endanger himself unnecessarily for a bauble like the lost bridle, 'por tel noient, por tel oiseuse' (253, 'for such a worthless, trivial thing'). Following Kay's failure, Gawain undergoes many taxing adventures before bringing back the bridle. He then wants the due reward, but does not receive it. It emerges that the young lady was wilfully keeping her bridle hidden to hoax the Arthurian knights. In retrospect the knights can see that they have been tricked. The spurious *aventure* has served to entice one of them on a journey of adventure which remains completely meaningless because it achieves nothing. The 'heroes' do not save anyone from distress, nor does the quest contribute to their purification. Even the reward is denied them. Here a mere girl can get away with making fun of the Arthurian knights' naive desire for adventure, which anyone with an invented story can arouse. Timid heroes endure pointless dangers for a meaningless goal. The Arthurian court's ideal of *aventure* has become the laughing-stock of the public at large.[36]

[35] Lines 141, 180, 185, 190, 244, 254 and 276; these all contain *paor* or equivalent.

[36] See also Chapter 4, p. 120.

In *Claris et Laris*, lines 23,309–15, Kay expresses the opinion that itinerant chivalry is much too strenuous for him, and the narrator comments that fear of disgrace is the only thing keeping the steward in his post; otherwise he would have given up his chivalric career long ago. But Kay is not alone; other knights would also prefer to spend their lives in peace and security. In *Les Merveilles de Rigomer* (6577–98) the prospect of an adventure splits the Arthurian court into two opposing parties, one in favour but the other warning of the dangers of an unspecified *aventure*. In *Claris et Laris* (26,750ff.) Dodinel makes an excuse to decamp before a dangerous duel. Kay is representative of all these voices that are beginning to deny the idealistic view of chivalry and *aventure* when he asserts:

> Que il n'a en cest mont terrien
> Si sote gent con chevalier,
> Car querant vont lor encombrier... (10,098–100)

(That in the whole of this world there is no race of people as stupid as knights, for they go seeking their own hardship...)

Kay sees knights as totally foolish in seeking their own misfortune, and he longs for the times in the past when he could still enjoy peaceful days at Arthur's court, and could ensure for himself the tastiest titbits from the kitchen.

Later in the same text the knight Biaus Mauvais thinks he has achieved a splendid victory, but to his embarrassment his opponents turn out to have been ladies in disguise (27,664ff.). Meanwhile, in *Fergus* the hero sets out to fight a dangerous giant and is supposed to prove himself thereby, but then to his shame he has to recognize that the dreaded enemy is a statue which cannot intend any harm to anyone and which he is able to topple from its plinth without exertion. Thus chivalric expeditions increasingly appear as devoid of their original significance, and *aventure* becomes tilting at windmills.

The author of *Escanor* lashes out in particular at the customs surrounding hard-fought tournaments and criticizes their absurdity. In almost all tournaments the participants are seriously wounded: 'de si faites aventures/souvent em Bretaigne avenoient' (4220–1, 'such things often happened in Britain'). The watching ladies are extremely fearful that something may happen to their knights, and one of them laments: 'je ne sai, mais si crueuz juz/ne fu en cest siecle trouvez' (5607–8, 'I don't know, but this is the cruellest game in the world.') [37]

[37] In *Durmart* there is condemnation of wars, where it is primarily the civilian population that suffers. The *terre gaste* (wasteland) in *Durmart* is not some half-mythical landscape subjected to a mysterious curse as it appears in Chrétien's version, but is an absolutely concrete example of a country devastated by war and overrun by plundering and death.

...eles n'erent pas a aise;
ainz estoient a tel mesaise
qu'il sambloit c'on les acoroit,
quant on sor lor amis feroit:
et quant il cheoient a terre,
plus grant paor n'esteust querre
ne plus grant mal qu'eles avoient. (5624–30)

(...they were not contented but rather in such anxiety that it seemed as if their hearts were torn out whenever anyone struck the knights they loved. And when the knights fell to the ground no greater fear could be found nor greater distress than they experienced.)

The author declares (lines 5668–72) that the knights are striking each other for no reason. The tournament is a dreadful thing, because the knights are not behaving like the friends they are but like deadly enemies bent on murdering each other 'sanz raison' (5672, 'without cause'). He puts the following words into the mouth of Dinadan:

...bien sont avugle
li chevalier de la Bretaingne,
car l'unz l'autre ocist et mehaingne
sanz achoison et sanz meffait.
'Mout a,' dist il, 'cil vassal fait
vers cel autre bele acointance:
el cors li a mise sa lance,
mout a or ci bele achoison,
d'ocirre .I. honme sanz raison. (12,316–24)

(...the knights of Britain must be blind, for they are killing and maiming each other without cause and without previous injury. 'This fellow', he said, 'has certainly made the very close acquaintance of the other one: he has put his lance in his body, and now he has a fine opportunity to kill a man for no reason.')

Any exemplary aspect to the plot of the romance is here denied. Dinadan decries the custom which dictates that two knights are obliged to fight a duel as soon as they notice each other, and in the same way he also declines to go off in search of adventure for the sake of any lady:

'pour dame ne pour damoisele,
tant soit savereuse ne bele,
ne me quier metre en aventure...
je sui de les amer si las
que quite lor claim lor solas,
lor deduit et lor cortoisie...' (11,827ff.)

('I have no desire to put myself at risk for a lady or a maiden, however charming or beautiful... I am so tired of loving them that I renounce their solace, their delights and their courtesy...')

In any case the custom appears to have been undermined long since; in *Meraugis* (lines 316–35) the author reveals that for a long time it has not been the best knights who win tournaments any more but the ones most beloved of their friends and their ladies. In *Escanor* there is a scene where the Arthurian knights argue for a whole day as to who did actually win the previous day's tournament. Everyone has a favourite, and knightly qualities are no longer clearly perceptible in the way that they were in Chrétien's works. There is a similar situation in *Durmart*:

Li jugeor sont en effroi
Li quex a vencu le tornoi;
De monsaignor Durmart disoient
Li plusor qu'a lui se tenoient.
N'est pas finés li jugemens,
Ains s'acordent de tos lor sens
Li un a monsaignor Gavain,
Li autre a monsaignor Yvain;
Maint en velent doner le pris
A Lancelot, ce m'est avis,
Et a Percheval le Galois,
Et li alquant Brun de Morois.
De Galehet de Cornillon
Sunt li plusor en grant tenchon;
Del roi des Isles ensement
Font li plusor grant parlement.
Chascuns i a ramenteü
Ce qu'il a endroit soi veü.
Cel jor ne sot on pas de fi
Qui le tornoiement venqui. (8123–42)

(There is consternation amongst the judges as to who had won the tournament. The majority were saying they supported my lord Durmart, but the judging does not end there. Instead some are wholeheartedly in favour of my lord Gawain, and others of my lord Yvain. Many want to give the prize to Lancelot, I think, and many to Perceval le Galois, and others to Brun de Morois. Several argue strongly for Galehet de Cornillon and similarly many speak in favour of the King of the Isles. Everyone has remembered what he has seen near himself. That day they did not know for certain who was the victor in the tournament.)

The author of *Escanor* directs his sharpest criticism against tournaments and duels as abuses of the desire for *aventure*. In so doing he is probably at the same time passing an opinion on an undesirable practice of his own age. His extensive work also reveals some other peculiarities, which show up particularly clearly in the central figure of Kay, who in this instance has some successful fights and finally ends up in the haven of marriage. Moreover, this change in the figure of Kay is not presented with any trace of the comic stylization that the genre would traditionally have required. Thus the author negates many of the traditional aspects of the Arthurian verse romance. Does this imply lack of understanding or a conscious attempt to construct an alternative pattern? *Escanor* is an erratic offshoot of the genre, but the surprising aspect is that the author, such a decided opponent of the world of chivalry, should still have written a romance of chivalry running to 26,000 lines.

However, this is not the only example of an aversion to the senseless shedding of blood. Robert de Blois, author of *Beaudous*, describes in lines 1052–73 how a lady weeps for her badly wounded companion and admits that she provoked the fight herself to test his courage. Now she regrets having gambled with his life so pointlessly.[38] In the course of the fight his opponent, the young Beaudous, repeatedly asks him to surrender because it would grieve him to have to kill him. Slowly the knight Ermaleüs allows himself to be persuaded that his life is worth more than his honour and that his mistress will still love him in spite of his defeat.

> Il a bien tant soffert por li,
> Bien le doit tenir ai ami... (1296–7)
> Ermaleüs est apensez,
> Que cil [Beaudous] li dist grant cortoisie;
> N'est pas preudom ki het sa vie.
> 'Tenez m'espee, je me rent...' (1317–20)

(He has suffered so much for her that she really ought to accept him as her *ami*... Ermaleüs considers that he [Beaudous] is giving him very courtly advice; no noble person hates his life. 'Take my sword, I surrender...')

On the occasion of a great battle Robert de Blois describes the misery of more than three hundred wounded and dying men, whose screams can be heard a mile away. The battle is supposed to continue on the following day, but Beaudous is not interested in a victory at the expense of humanity, so he suggests that he could fight the king of the opposing party in single combat to prevent further bloodshed:

> 'Voire', fait il, 'mais trop doloir
> Poez, et grant corrous avoir,
> Vos ki la fors avez laissié

[38] There is a similar scene in *L'Atre périlleux*, lines 2209–24.

Vos amis a mort detrenchiez...
Mais trop est grans dolors de mort,
C'om voit tant franc home morir
Ne nuns ne c'en doit esjoïr.
Por ce, ce vos le consilliez
Et tant en moi vos fiesiez,
Bien fust la bataille de moi
Cors a cors encontre le roi...' (3072–89)

('I know', he says, 'that you are now feeling great grief and great sorrow, those of you who have left your friends out there, hacked to death... But the sorrow of death is great indeed when one sees so many noble men die, and no one can rejoice at this. Therefore, if you approved of it and were willing to put your faith in me to that extent, a good plan would be a single combat between myself and the king...')

This kind of motivation for a duel that the hero cannot afford to lose is certainly new. In the older Arthurian romances the chief preoccupation in descriptions of *aventures* was to demonstrate courage in battle, but now increasing use is made of other techniques to reveal values which could once be tested by the sword, even when they were of a purely ethical nature. Of this too an example is to be found in *Beaudous*; before the planned duel the hero suddenly runs to his opponent and holds his stirrup:[39]

Et quant li rois tenir le vit,
Merveille s'en por quoi le fist
Si dist: 'chevaliers, par ta foi,
Di moi la veritei por quoi
Tu venis mon estrier tenir.'
'Sire,' fait il, 'bien doit servir
Par tot li plus haut li plus bas;
Rois estes et je nel sui pas.'
'Mout estes,' dist li rois, 'garnis
De grant proesce, et bien apris.' (3230–9)

(And when the king saw him hold it, he marvelled at why he did it. So he said: 'Knight, by your faith, tell me the truth as to why you came and held my stirrup.' 'Sire,' he said, 'the lower should always serve the higher. You are a king and I am not.' The king said: 'You are richly endowed with great nobility, and well instructed.')

[39] Robert de Blois says expressly that the story of Beaudous is intended to serve as a warning and an example: 'Car je wel por toz chastoier / Un novial dit encomencier' (209–10, 'I intend to begin a new story for the instruction of all').

A new feature of *cortoisie* is the promise quite commonly given by messengers and other knights not to abuse a *don contraignant* (a binding pledge) or turn it against the generous donor.[40] Similarly, maidens no longer exploit the granting of a boon, as they did in Chrétien, to obtain vengeance through the killing of a knight; on the contrary, they use it to terminate a fight. This occurs in *Escanor*, but also especially in *Durmart*:

> 'A! fait ele, rois debonaire,
> Vos qui les grans biens solés faire,
> Je vos vien un don demander
> Que vos me devés bien doner;
> Certes n'est pas drois que g'i faille.
> Sire, apaisiés ceste bataille:
> C'est li dons que je vos demant.
> Li chevalier sunt si vaillant
> Que trop grans damages seroit
> S'a nul d'eaz deus i mescheoit.' (10,269–78)

('Ah, noble king,' she says, 'it is your custom to do much good. I come to ask a boon of you that you really must grant me. It would certainly not be right for me to be refused. Sire, put an end to this battle; that is the boon I ask of you. The knights are so valiant that it would be the greatest misfortune if it turned out badly for either of them.')

The custom of the *don* is thus mitigated and rendered more humane.[41] *Beaudous* and other contemporary romances exemplify the proposition that the virtues of modesty, goodness and loyalty count for more than victory in a duel.

The author of *Durmart* concerns himself with another idea related to this problem: how is one still supposed to tell the difference between good and bad knights in the face of deception and false courage? The poet has to contend with the difficult question of whose life and deeds he should describe, since one can often distinguish between brave and cowardly knights only after the event. He himself shows how the young Durmart, who was morally on the wrong track at the beginning of the narrative, nevertheless emerges later as an exemplary knight. But only the adventures of a knight such as he are worth recounting and of interest to posterity:

> Encor en i a mout de teuz
> Cui les dames quident mout preuz

[40] In *L'Atre périlleux*, lines 39–41, the messenger who appears at court promises not to abuse the boon granted by Arthur. See also the arrival of Meleagant in Chrétien's *Lancelot*.

[41] On the problem of the *don contraignant* see Köhler, *Ideal und Wirklichkeit*, pp. 33–6, and J. Frappier, *Amour Courtois et Table Ronde* (Geneva, 1973), p. 225ff.

Por ce que il lor font acroire
Mainte chose qui n'est pas voire.
I[l] lor dïent qu'il font mervelles,
Et les chaitives ont orelles,
Mais s'eles a tornoi alassent,
Je ne quit pas qu'eles amassent
Les coars beubenciers mavais
Qui devant eles sont crïais.
Por escoter si quident bien
Que cil ne lor mentent de rien,
Mais tot cil ne sont pas vallant
Qui devant eles vont beubant.
Recreans chevaliers vanteres,
Cointes et coars et borderes,
Cil tient de lui mout grant sermon
Cant il ne voit se mavais non;
Mais quant il est entre les buens,
Adont n'est mie li plais suens,
Ains est tos mus et tos tapis
Por ce qu'il ne vaut un tapis.
Qui tel chevalier vuet amer
Trop a son cuer nice et amer,
Mout doivent bien estre reprises
Les dames qui la se sont prises.
Mais je quit bien avoir mespris
Cant j'ai cest afaire repris,
Car les sages bien entendans
Aiment les preuz et les vallans,
Et les chaitives, les chaitis;
Ensi est li siecles assis,
Si le nos covient esgarder. (7581–613)

(There are also many whom the ladies consider very brave because they make them believe a lot of things that are not true. They tell them that they do wonders, and the poor women listen, but if they went to a tournament I don't think they would love the boastful and miserable cowards who sing their own praises to them. Through listening they become convinced that these are not lying to them in any way, but not all those who go around boasting before them are really valiant. An arrogant but craven knight, elegant but cowardly and untruthful, will say many fine words about himself when surrounded by his own kind, but when he is amongst true knights, then he cannot do the talking, but instead is completely silent and withdrawn, since he is not worth a doormat. Anyone who wants to love such a knight has a very naive and bitter heart. The ladies who have been caught like that are to be thoroughly reproached. But I believe I have been wrong to take up this matter, because women who are wise

> and of good understanding love the brave and the valiant, whilst foolish women love the cowards. That is the way of the world, and that is how we have to look at it.)

Criticism of the particular aspect of *aventure* that one would be inclined to regard as essential to the whole concept reaches a climax in *Jaufré*. *Aventure* is thrust upon Arthur himself—which never happens anywhere else—in the form of his abduction, when he is carried through the air defenceless and unarmed (and therefore completely unlike a knight). We can discern in this incident that the Arthurian knight who used his knowledge of magic to set it up as a joke wanted to deliver a reprimand to the king on his greed for *aventure*. At that moment the other knights also begin to doubt the wisdom of *aventure* at all costs, and in their anxiety about the king they curse adventures in general as if they were vowing to renounce them for ever:

> Aqui viras tirar cabels
> A cavaliers e a donzels,
> Que tuit rompon.s lor vestiduras
> E maldizon las aventuras
> Qu'en la forest son atrobadas,
> Qu'a gran dolor lor sun tornadas. (363–8)

> (They were seen to tear their hair, both knights and squires, they were all rending their clothes and cursing the adventures which are found in the forest, and which have brought them great distress.)

It is becoming clear without needing to enlarge on the texts any further that this criticism of *aventure*, perceptible everywhere and recognizable as a persistent motif throughout the Arthurian verse romances of the thirteenth century, is still not capable of rocking the foundations of the traditional narrative structures of Arthurian romance; *aventure* is much too vital an element in romances of chivalry. The increasing frequency with which criticisms of *aventure* and *chevalerie* are expressed is primarily an indication of the changing attitude of authors and public towards certain exaggerated and sometimes absurd aspects of this sphere as represented in the romances of the twelfth century. It would not be appropriate to see this characteristic merely as an example of a kind of realism on a specific point. Clearly the reality of the thirteenth century is so far removed from the plots of the romances that these have to be expressly located in a bygone age and viewed from a sceptical and critical distance if they are not to appear ludicrous and therefore comic, which is not at all what is intended. Adventures which focus on a fight scene no longer have the meaningful context that Chrétien gave them; instead they become increasingly rare, or else pointless and therefore arbitrary, because it is manifestly no longer acceptable for an unconditional jeopardizing of life and health to contribute more than any other pattern of human behaviour to the attainment of honour and of love.

THE PROBLEM OF CUSTOMS

The principle of maintaining a custom (*costume*) undergoes a similar transformation to that of the notion of *aventure*.[42] Chrétien subjects every hero to its magic compulsion; they have to come to terms with it despite (or because of) its being so unjust, arbitrary and incomprehensible. The method of settling scores with evil is the duel; the stronger contestant is then in a position to dissolve or modify the custom as he pleases. Victory over such a phenomenon of mythical dimensions serves as a basis for measuring the hero's value and significance.

In the thirteenth-century romances the first difference is that customs of mythical proportions are much rarer than in Chrétien's works. As an example of a custom being stripped of its mythical element one could cite the Joie de la Cort (Joy of the Court) from *Erec* reflected in the episode of the Isle sanz non (Island without a name) in *Meraugis*, in which the custom is a wanton man-made device and can be obviated by cunning. The Arthurian court is generally regarded as a place of good customs.[43] The most important tradition, which becomes very forcefully established, is the custom of waiting for *aventure*. In *La Vengeance Raguidel* Arthur defends it with the same vehemence and with similar arguments as he used for the hunt of the white stag in *Erec*:

Li rois Artus ert coustumiers
Que ja a feste ne mangast
Devant ce qu'en sa cort entrast
Novele d'aucune aventure.
Tels fu lors la mesaventure
Que li jors passe et la nuis vint
C'onques nule n'en i avint,
S'en fu la cors torble et oscure.
Tant atendirent l'aventure
Que l'ore del mangier passa.
Li rois fu mus et si penssa
A ce qu'aventure ne vint;
Dedens son cuer cest corols tint
Que poi s'en faut qu'il ne muert d'ire;

[42] On the concept of the *costume* see E. Köhler, *Trobadorlyrik und höfischer Roman* (Berlin, 1962), pp. 205–12.

[43] Arthur complains in *Beaudous*, lines 3588–601, that it is now the custom for all and sundry to come to the court festivals wanting to be honoured in the same way, but he cannot treat all equally. See also *Li Chevaliers as deus espees*, lines 7715–23.

Et li baron li vienent dire:
'Sire, por Diu, laissiés ester!
Vos n'i poés rien conquester
En dol faire, venés mangier!
Veés que vostre chevalier
Vont esbahi ça .x., ça .xx.'
'Onques', dist li rois, 'ne m'avint
A si haut jor ne n'avenra
Que je manjuce, ançois venra
Aventure d'aucune part.
Dius qui tos biens donne et depart
M'a le costume maintenue;
S'or ne vieut que plus soit tenue,
D'auques per ge ma dingnité,
Et si m'en a desireté.
Bien vuel morir puis que le pert!
Ce vos di je tot en apert.' (18–48)

(It was King Arthur's custom never to eat at festivals until news of some adventure came to his court. Such was his misfortune on this occasion that the day passed and the night came without any news being brought, and the court was troubled and gloomy. They waited so long for the adventure that the time for eating passed. The king was silent, for he was thinking about the fact that adventure did not come. He kept this distress locked in his heart until he nearly died of frustration. Then the barons came to speak to him: 'Sire, for Heaven's sake let it be. You will not achieve anything by being miserable, so come and eat. Look how your knights are confused, wandering around in groups of ten or twenty.' The king said: 'It never happened before nor will it now that I should eat on such a high day before some adventure occurs. God who gives and takes away all good things has maintained the custom for me. If He no longer wishes that it should be kept, and He has indeed taken it from me, much of my dignity is lost. Since I am losing it, I tell you quite openly that I want to die.')

Maintaining the custom which he sees as instituted by God himself is absolutely vital for Arthur; his royal dignity depends upon it. The non-arrival of *aventure* is an existential disaster from the king's point of view, and abandoning the custom of waiting would lead to the downfall of both the king and his kingdom. In that respect nothing has changed since Chrétien.

On the other hand, almost every reference to a tradition of this type appears with the formula 'costume ert a cel tens' ('it was the custom at that time'), indicating that it belongs to the past and requires explanation. Thus, for example, the public has to be enlightened as to why a knight who has been defeated in a duel may not first let his wounds heal: 'at that time custom required that the knight should go to Arthur's court and place himself under the jurisdiction of the king by the fastest possible means, whatever state he was in'.[44]

The characteristic use of 'at that time', 'formerly' or 'in earlier times' marks out such details as evidence of a historical development; alternatively, if one wishes to regard the noble behaviour of knights as a literary fiction, the use of such phrases does at least imply something about what was customary at the time when the romance in question was composed. An example of this lies in the striking frequency with which an elucidation of the rules of knightly combat recurs, always accompanied by emphatic comments on how it differs from contemporary practice. Examples may be found in *Le Bel Inconnu* and in one version of *L'Atre périlleux*:

> Et *a cel tans* costume estoit
> Que quant uns hom se conbatoit,
> N'avoit garde que de celui
> Qui faissoit sa bataille a lui.
> *Or* va li tans afebloiant
> Et cis usages decaant,
> Que vint et cinc enprendent un;
> Cis afaires est si comun
> Que tuit le tienent de or mes.
> La force paist le pré adiés:
> *Tos est mués* en autre guisse;
> Mais dont estoit fois et francisse,
> Pitiés, proece et cortoisie,
> Et largece sans vilonnie;
> *Or* fait cascuns tot son pooir,
> Tot entendent au decevoir. (*Bel Inconnu*, 1067–82)

(And *at that time* it was the custom that when a man fought he did not need to fear attack from anyone except the man he was fighting. But *our times* are becoming less honourable and this practice is on the decline so that twenty-five may take on one; this sort of thing is so common that now everyone is behaving in this way. Now force rules the roost. *Everything has changed* its style but at that time there was faith and honesty, pity, prowess, courtesy and generosity, without wickedness. *Now* everyone puts all their efforts into deception.)

> Qu'il estoit costume a *cel jor*
> S'uns chevaliers en un estor
> Venoit por joster ne por poindre,
> N'en doit que uns seus a lui jondre,
> Et se doi i vienent ensanble
> Il serroient, si com moi sanble,

[44] Translated from the author's German rendering of *Beaudous*, lines 3378–85.

Trestot recreant et honni:
Ja mais ne serroient servi
En cort a roi, s'il ert seü.[45]

(Because it was the custom *in those days* that if a knight entered a battle to joust or to fight, only one single opponent was allowed to engage him, and if two attacked together it seems that they would be branded utter cowards and disgraced; never again would they be served in a royal court if it became known.)

Laments directed against the practices of a non-fictional reality are directly related to the tendency outlined above for the romances to feature a hero who proves his worth not in a duel but by his humanity. The ideal presented as a model in the romances represents the exact reverse of the actual state of affairs. In *Les Merveilles de Rigomer* (11,847–902) Gawain has to fight first against one, then against two, four, eight and finally against all the opposing knights at the same time.[46] However, the fundamentally dishonourable nature of such a fight is pointed out over and over again.[47] In *Le Bel Inconnu* a knight who has been defeated in a duel does not simply accept his fate, but incites three of his friends to take revenge on the handsome stranger (557). In *Beaudous* the jealous Madoine sets fifteen of his vassals on to the hero of the romance who is his rival. The change of attitude becomes clear if one compares such conduct retrospectively with Chrétien's account of Erec's combats against the robbers, where the increasing numerical superiority functions solely to emphasize Erec's courage and strength. In the Arthurian verse romances the same contempt shown for fights on unequal terms is likewise accorded to attacks on unarmed opponents.[48] The encounters with an armed knight defending a ford, rendered familiar by Chrétien's romances, are also seen in a new light; the hero of *Le Bel Inconnu* tries to convey to one such knight of a ford that his behaviour represents an unlawful custom, being simple robbery (427). There is, moreover, a practice governing the relationship between potential opponents in a duel: one cannot first greet an opponent and then fight him, but only the other way round, because the greeting as such already implies an offer of peace; see for example *Li Chevaliers as deus espees*, lines 2916–20. Finally, mention should be made of a custom in the romance of *Yder* (787–839): a vavasour draws Yder's attention to the traditional requirement that no knight should be allowed to continue on his

[45] Woledge's edition of *L'Atre périlleux*, p. 187, lines 15–23 of the variant. See also *Erec et Enide*, lines 2821–6.

[46] Similarly in *Li Chevaliers as deus espees*, lines 7658–64.

[47] See also *Le Bel Inconnu*, line 1025, *Rigomer*, lines 8512–19, and *Escanor*, lines 2234–7.

[48] *Le Bel Inconnu* (1015–24), *L'Atre périlleux* and *Le Chevalier à l'épée*.

way in the morning on an empty stomach; the hero responds with pleasure at having found an agreeable custom for once.[49]

YDER: AN ANTI-ARTHURIAN ROMANCE

Yder is the illegitimate son of an impoverished young noblewoman. He does not know his father and so when he has barely reached maturity he sets out to look for him. On his journey he meets Queen Guenloie, but their mutual affection does not reach fulfilment because Guenloie utters a 'dur mot' (6487, 'hard words') against Yder and thus drives him away. This outline of the narrative from the missing opening section of the romance can be reconstructed from the references to it in the surviving text, and Gelzer did indeed piece together most of it in the preface to his edition, but he did not venture to suggest what the *dur mot* might have been. However, one can deduce from some unobtrusive remarks by Guenloie and from certain elements of the narrative what those harsh words of the young queen may have been about, namely that Yder as a young man without wealth or lineage did not represent a husband of suitable standing for a queen. Guenloie may have urged Yder to find his father and to make good these deficiencies with admirable deeds of chivalry. This would then also explain her excessive relief later on (5034–42) when she hears that Yder's father is the rich and powerful Duke Nut l'Alman. In the end Arthur is prepared to crown Yder king in order to make his marriage to Guenloie possible. It seems therefore that, like *Fergus*, *Yder* is concerned not least with problems of rank, but this is not its only remarkable feature. What is particularly new and surprising in this work is the literary treatment accorded to King Arthur and his steward Kay.

It is mainly this aspect of the romance of *Yder* that will now be considered, because it reveals in a concentrated form all those developmental tendencies which have just been shown to be fundamental or more generally characteristic of Arthur and the Arthurian community in the verse romances of the thirteenth century. At this point a more detailed account of the narrative content is necessary before any attempt at interpretation; on the other hand, we can omit all the narrative elements which do not directly concern the relationship of the hero to the Arthurian court and to its most important representatives, Arthur, Kay and Gawain.

> In the forest Yder meets a knight who has lost his way while hunting. He serves him as his squire and kills two enemies who threaten the knight. The next morning Yder learns to his great joy that the stranger is King Arthur himself. He hopes to be dubbed a knight by the king as a reward for his overnight assistance, but they have

[49] See also *Durmart*, lines 2669–72.

scarcely reached the hunters' camp when Yder has to face the realization that his companion from the forest has completely forgotten him. A short time later the young lad is witness to an embarrassing incident: Arthur refuses to go to the aid of a lady in distress to whom he has promised support, because his attention is focused on another project; he is more interested in forcing the subjection of the knight Talac de Rougemont without any justification for so doing, merely because the latter has so far refused to become his vassal. Yder is appalled at the ingratitude, unreliability and injustice of the king of whom previously he had heard only good reports. In his disappointment he decides to seek another lord; he would rather have no lord at all than one like Arthur.

> 'Ja Deus', dist il, 'moi nen äit,
> Si jo por estre sanz seignor
> Od icesti plus me demor(e);
> En poi de tens l'ai bel (de) servi,
> Si m'at si tost mis en obli,
> Ne il de moi ne li sovient,
> Ne il nul covenant ne tient.' (130–6)

> ('May God never help me', he said, 'if I stay with this man any longer, even if it means being without a lord. I have served him well in a short time, and he has forgotten me so quickly, he neither remembers me nor keeps any of his promises.')

Yder then rides away. Arthur is made aware of his unjust behaviour by the knights of the Round Table and sends after him, but in vain. Yder refuses to return to the court and soon afterwards has himself knighted by another ruler; then he sets off to lend support to Talac de Rougemont against Arthur's attack. In the general mêlée of the battle against Arthur's troops he knocks Kay from his horse several times. As a result the steward becomes his mortal enemy. In his hatred of the better knight Kay thinks up a cunning plan: he intends to ambush Yder's small troop with thirty knights and thus see his enemy disposed of. However, Yder defends himself bravely and defeats them all. The next day he embarks on a fight against Gawain. He feels great respect for this knight and would even see it as an honour to be defeated by him, but the outcome is rather different (2281–3); he is able to get the better of Gawain, who falls together with his horse. The other knights of the Round Table are horrified. Such a thing is unprecedented—Gawain as the loser in a duel! Yder feels he is the winner and claims Gawain's charger as his prize. As he is about to lead it away, Arthur intervenes personally. In his rage at the defeat of his best knight he wants to deny the victor's right to the horse. Since a violent verbal dispute leads nowhere, Arthur resorts to physical means and tries to take hold of the animal by force. Yder resists and both pull at the bridle:

> Cist le sache, si(l) le recule,
> Cist li di io, cil le soufraine,
> Le cheval est en male peine.

Cist le resache e cil le tire,
Ja montast entr'els dous grant ire. (2315–9)

(One pulls the horse this way, the other that, one says 'Gee up', and the other reins it back; the horse is in cruel distress. One tugs it his way and the other pulls; the two men would have become very angry.)

At this point Kay intervenes. Fired with rage and filled with hatred he plunges a sword into Yder's body from behind and is even so base as to turn it several times in the wound, with the result that the point of the weapon breaks off and remains lodged in Yder's body. Yder falls to the ground as if dead. For the second time Arthur now realizes that his behaviour towards Yder has been reprehensible. Filled with sudden remorse, he attends to the lifeless knight as if he were a doctor. Gawain, who was watching the whole episode, weeps with compassion for the wounded man, whilst Arthur reproaches himself bitterly and accuses himself of *vilenie* not only on Yder's account but also because he failed to help the lady in her hour of need and is conducting an unjust war against Talac instead. He attributes the blame to his steward, who advised him to take that course, and his speech ends with a wish that God may curse Kay for his wickedness.

'Allas', dist il, 'mal[e] soit l'ure
Ke jo le Rogemont assis.
La *vilanie* que jo fis,
Quant jo failli a la pucele
Qui m'envea sa demoisele,
M'a chargié grieve penitance.
Ki par *vilanie* s'avance
De suen buen et [de] son prou feire,
Al chief del tor en a contraire.
El s'ert mise en ma garantie;
Ja nuls ne fera *vilanie*
Qu'il ne.l compert ou loins ou prez.
Cest siege pris trop a engrés;
E ço fist Quois qui.l conseilla,
Qui onques bien n'aparailla;
Maudit seit il de Chesu Crist,
Ke onques bien pur bien ne fist,
E Deu maudie il suen sen.'
Assez i out qui dist amen. (2447–65)

('Alas!' he said, 'cursed be the hour when I laid siege to Rougemont. The wrong (*vilanie*) that I committed when I failed the lady who sent me her maid has brought me a heavy penance. Anyone who promotes his own well-being and advantage through wrongdoing (*vilanie*) will eventually reap its opposite. She had placed herself under my protection. No one will ever do wrong (*vilanie*) without paying for it sooner or later. I undertook this siege too impetuously, and that was Kay's doing because he advised it, and he never planned anything good. May he be cursed by Jesus Christ for never having done good for its own sake, and may God curse his designs.' There were plenty who said amen.)

Gawain demands that Kay's crime should be punished by death, and he cannot understand how the king can still tolerate his presence (3115–39). Yder survives this attempted murder, and his mistress Guenloie, who is having all his activities secretly observed, brings him to an abbey where he is healed within a few weeks. When Queen Guinevere learns that Yder is alive and well, she asks Arthur to accept him as one of the Round Table. However, the king is not immediately ready to do so, and his dislike of Yder, fuelled by the first traces of an unfounded jealousy, once more gains the upper hand, banishing discernment and remorse. Arthur is annoyed that Yder enjoys such respect in his wife's eyes. Although he eventually gives in to her request and allows Gawain to deliver the invitation to Yder to join the Round Table, the latter cannot immediately make up his mind to accept the king's offer, so unfavourable has been his experience hitherto of the knights of the Round Table and their lord. From Yder's point of view acceptance into this circle does not represent an honour. Only when Gawain and Yvain offer to be his friends and comrades-in-arms does he agree for their sakes and return to court, although still inwardly reluctant. A short time later he rescues the queen from a great bear which had escaped from its cage and found its way into the ladies' apartments; this gives Arthur renewed grounds for jealousy. Similarly, Kay can hardly contain his fury and envy.

Meanwhile Talac, who surrendered to Arthur after Yder was wounded and is now the king's vassal, is being besieged by his enemies, and so he asks his new feudal lord for support. However, Arthur once more looks for excuses; he claims that he has to take the field against the black knight and cannot therefore help Talac for the moment. Talac was firmly relying on Arthur's support and is dismayed and offended. He leaves without any form of salutation, and deep in thought:

'Tenir', dist il, 'me puis por sot,
Mult ai bien prochacié ma honte.' (3492–3)

('I can consider myself a fool,' he said. 'I've been intent on pursuing my own shame.')

For the second time Arthur is doing him a grave injustice, and he perceives that the king's word of honour no longer counts for anything. Gawain and Yvain are ashamed for their lord. In order to make good his breach of faith, at least in part, they decide to support Talac on their own responsibility and ride after him in secret, but without taking Yder, their comrade-in-arms, because they are afraid that his wounds, which have only just healed, could open again in a fight. Yder interprets this as a further sign of the unreliability and wickedness of the once so exemplary Arthurian knights. He believes that his friends have deserted him. Saddened, he sets off alone in search of adventure, and thereby eventually finds his father, whereupon he returns to Arthur's court.

Everyone rejoices with him except Arthur and Kay. The steward is jealous of Yder's successes, whilst the king is increasingly upset that Guinevere entertains such great admiration for Yder. One day he asks his wife what she would do if he, Arthur, were dead. She assures him of her love, but he questions her more closely and wants to know whom she would marry after his death. In her embarrassment and confusion she replies that if such were the case then Sir Yder would be the most likely candidate. This appears to seal Yder's fate, and Arthur now thinks only of revenge. When Yder's mistress Guenloie demands that the king grant her as a husband the man who can kill two dangerous giants and gain possession of their famous magic knife, a task which Yder and a few others declare themselves prepared to undertake, Arthur recognizes the possibility of sending the hated knight into a fight from which he will probably never return. Kay is sent on ahead to reconnoitre, but at the sight of the terrible giants he is overcome by cowardice and hides in the undergrowth. Now Arthur sends Yder into the giants' house, to what he hopes will be certain death. However, Yder kills the giants and gathers up the knife to serve as evidence of his victory. Then he calmly waits for the other Arthurian knights. They have heard the cries of battle; Gawain and Yvain want to rush to Yder's aid, but Arthur forbids it. Then Kay emerges from his hiding-place and reports that Yder is dead; he pretends to have killed the giants himself, but Yder's friends find the real victor sitting on a bench safe and sound.

Kay and Arthur are infuriated by the outcome of this adventure. When Yder complains of thirst, Kay is prepared to go to the lengths of procuring water from a poisonous spring to bring to him. The drink produces such a drastic change in Yder that he resembles a piece of dry wood. His friends lament this terrible death, while Kay explains that he was killed by the poisonous breath of the dead giants. To pre-empt further disaster Arthur and his knights leave the vicinity. A little later two knights from Ireland who are skilled in medicine recognize that Yder has been put under a spell and cure him again with the aid of an antidote.

At Arthur's court, meanwhile, the king and his accomplice indulge in unqualified rejoicing at Yder's death, while Yvain and Gawain mourn their friend. When the Irish knights inform the court that Yder is still alive and explain what really happened to him, everyone realizes what a crime Kay has committed. Gawain severely reproaches his uncle; he cannot understand why Arthur still remains so fond of his steward.

> 'Boens reis', dist il, 'gentil e francs,
> Mult devrïez Keis tenir vil,
> Car fels et träitres est il;
> Vos l'amez, si.l tienc en damage.
> De (vos) prover l'en vos tent mon gage,
> Qu[e] il est träitres mortels,
> Se il le nie, e il est tels,
> Li fel träitres ramposnos,
> Qu'il ne deit converser od nos.' (6335–43)

('Good, noble, high-born king,' he said, 'you should consider Kay to be very base, for he's evil and a traitor; you love him, and I think that's wrong. I offer you my pledge to prove that he's a deadly traitor, and if he denies it, and he's the sort who might, evil, foul-tongued traitor that he is, let him be forbidden to associate with us.')

Gawain wants to arrange a trial by ordeal and oppose Kay there himself. The cowardly Kay tries to flee but is locked in a room. Yder returns to court just in time and Guenloie recognizes him as her fiancé, whereupon no one is more eager to provide Yder with a wife than the jealous king. The wedding and coronation are duly celebrated and Kay arranges a safe-conduct for himself during the festivities because he fears reprisals from Yder. However, with exemplary generosity the hero forgives him his evil deeds; he even kisses and embraces him, although not without one last commentary on Kay's evil characteristics (6627–31).

No other thirteenth-century Arthurian poet went as far as the author of this romance in his negative stereotyping of the Arthurian court. We were able to show above that many other texts do have a perceptible tendency to belittle the king and his immediate entourage in order to highlight other forces, but in this romance Arthur and Kay are painted in the blackest of colours, whilst the idealized nature of the court and its exemplary role have been dispensed with. The norm to which the chivalric world accepts it must conform is no longer represented by the courtly king and his Round Table. The new norm is based on the exemplary character of the hero, and it is this point of comparison that makes sense of the king's extremely negative image.

The unexpected confrontation with this Arthur who is ungrateful, false, jealous and, in a word, *vilain*, and who no longer corresponds in the slightest to his fame and reputation, comes as a profound disappointment to the young idealistic knight. His view of the world is shattered. His attitude to the values of chivalry still corresponds to the traditional concepts, and he finds himself forced to draw his own conclusions; his repugnance is symbolized by his refusal to join the Round Table. Yder is noble, courtly, loyal and generous. No one can persuade him to do wrong and he has no desire to join forces with Arthur and Kay. Instead he distances himself from this 'courtly' society which does not live up to its own demands and which is epitomized by a king of weak character who succumbs to the disastrous advice of a corrupt *baron* (Kay). Arthur is not presented as wicked through and through, but he lets himself be drawn far too quickly into actions which can scarcely redound to his credit. He is equally quick to show remorse, but as soon as his material advantage is in question again all his good intentions are forgotten. In *Yder* the king is fickle and swayed by the force of his own emotions. Instead of recognizing his responsibility, which no one can lift from him, he puts all the blame on others, specifically Kay and

Guinevere. Arthur's jealousy, which gets him ever more deeply entangled in moral guilt, makes its appearance as a motif in other romances too, but here it has become a theme, like his *vilenie*. The narrator remarks upon this jealousy (5142–67); he sees it as the root of all evil which can plunge even the noblest person into the abyss. He introduces two other characters besides Arthur who succumbed to this vice, one being Yder's father Nut and the other the lord of a castle who is not only jealous of his mistress but who also lets himself be provoked into all kinds of wicked deeds by his adviser, a dwarf. It is not hard to see this as an analogy in both structure and content to the relationship of Arthur and Kay.

The king's jealousy brings him closer to a literary stereotype not otherwise represented in the Arthurian verse romances, namely the jealous husband (*gelos* or *mari*) of the lyrics and the *fabliaux*. Although there are similarities with the Tristan material and the jealousy of Arthur in the prose romances, in those instances the sovereigns are made to become either tragic or comic figures, but not wicked criminals as in *Yder*. In non-Arthurian literature the jealous figure is normally a negative stereotype, whilst in Arthurian works apart from *Yder* the king's jealousy tends to lend him a comical aspect precisely because it is apparently justified. In *Yder* itself, however, the vice has no basis in Yder's irreproachable behaviour, yet its palpable consequences lend the work dramatic qualities as they lead to a bloody conflict between the king and the hero. The fact that an older narrative tradition identifies Yder with Lancelot[50] is of interest in this context but is of secondary importance with regard to the romance of *Yder* itself.

However, the actual villain of the piece here is not Arthur but Kay, as is demonstrated by the epithets applied to this character. Criticism of Arthur himself is restricted to the reproach of *vilenie*, which seems quite serious enough, but Kay, who admittedly was always known for his fault-finding, mockery and boasting, although not previously seen as wholly wicked, is now submerged in a torrent of derogatory nouns and adjectives. In *Yder* he is a disgrace to chivalry (1148–58), a traitor, a criminal and an assassin (2746). He is accused of *deshonor* (2347, dishonour), *felonie* (2327, 2746 and 3126, betrayal), *damage*, *mesprison* and *traïson* (3129–30, harm, outrage and treachery). The word *traïtres* (traitor) occurs about twenty times, used both by the positive characters of the romance (Gawain, Yvain and Yder) and by the narrator himself to refer to Kay. Envy, ill-will and cunning are typical of him. Not only the other knights of the Round Table but even the narrator himself invokes the wrath and curse of God upon him (2344, 2462 and 2464–5).

[50] See Gelzer's introduction to his edition of *Yder*, p. LVf.

E cels de la ro[o]nde table
Mult tenoient Keis por metable
D'armes, s'il fust de bones mors,
Mes onques hoen ne.s out peiors. (6628–31)

(And the knights of the Round Table thought Kay very skilled in arms, if only he had been of good character, but no man ever had worse.)

The fact that Kay makes three attempts to murder the hero is already sufficient to indicate a change; that Arthur should be his accomplice is seen as quite inconceivable for the characters in the romance and must also have seemed unusual to the audience, unless their own image of a ruler at the time happened to correspond to the portrayal in *Yder*. How are we to interpret the picture of Arthur as the supposed lord of all knightly adventure unscrupulously misusing the notion of *aventure* and hypocritically entrusting a knight of his Round Table with a supposedly impossible task in order to eliminate him? The disintegration of the concept of *aventure* in the later Arthurian romances is nowhere more clearly seen than in this extreme manifestation. The king is the only one who holds Kay in affection. This fact puts him in the worst possible light, since it indicates his own moral and ethical inadequacy. In *Yder* Kay's actions, his pernicious characteristics and his bad influence on the king lead to a split in the Arthurian community. The knights are no longer united in their endeavours or wishes; this leads to a polarization, with Kay and Arthur on the side of evil whilst Gawain, Yvain and the hero are on the side of good. The more negative the image of one group, the more positive the other becomes.

In Chrétien's works the polarity of good and evil had not yet taken on this particular form. 'Good' was equated with the courtly Arthurian community, whilst 'evil' meant both what was uncourtly and what was beyond the court. In *Yder* evil is now no longer a feature of the world outside the court but is a component of the Arthurian community itself, and one to which Arthur and Kay have succumbed. The world embodied in the person of the king has become hostile in the consciousness of the hero; in this romance that is a world riddled with dark forces as was the outside world in the earlier evolution of the genre. Thus *Yder* takes on the role of an anti-Arthurian romance. The Arthurian court is characterized by the dualism of good and evil; in the eyes of the hero this renders it a hostile world where all that remains for him to uphold is his own individual integrity.

The evolution of the genre had for a long time been working towards this final outcome, which should be understood as an element in the inherent dynamic potential of the genre. Chrétien had already envisaged Arthur and Kay as ambivalent characters;[51] they combined positive and negative traits, and precisely because of their predetermined exemplary role they had always been vulnerable to criticism. Other characters such as the protagonists of the romances are allowed to make mistakes and then atone for them, and this is seen as a necessary ingredient in their personal development. In general, however, no such allowances are made for Arthur and Kay, any more than for Gawain who in the group of Gawain romances is also ascribed increasingly unpleasant characteristics. It is inherent in the nature of the genre that within any given text these characters should remain static, and should not be permitted to hesitate or vacillate between the poles of good and evil; either they are absolutely exemplary or they are turned into a negative stereotype to counterbalance the idealization of the hero, which becomes increasingly pronounced as the genre evolves. This can be summarized in the formula that the more exemplary the protagonist, the worse the image of the king. This is especially true of *Yder* and seems also to apply to the romance of *Le Vallet a la cote mautaillie*, of which only one fragment survives, albeit a very informative one. It would not be going too far to suggest a strong resemblance to *Yder* in the outline of this lost romance; the *vilenie* of the king is central to both texts. Arthur's *proece*, undisputed in Chrétien, survives only as wishful thinking in some later specimens of the genre. The hero has to face the fact that his striving for ideals and for morally acceptable self-fulfilment can now only be realized whilst he remains independent of the demands and judgements of the Arthurian court. In Chrétien's works there were still two moral arbiters, the collective consciousness of the court and the separate awareness of the individual knight, but heroes like Yder, Durmart and Meraugis have absorbed the ideal so thoroughly that their own self-awareness alone can supply the guiding principle for their thoughts and actions. Thus it is also the case, as *Yder* shows, that at the end of the romance the gap between the Arthurian court and the individual knight can no longer really be bridged. In other romances Arthur may perceive his unfairness and realize his own limitations, but in *Yder* a superficial reconciliation of the king, Kay and the hero is only brought about because of Yder's magnanimity and *cortoisie*. Arthur and Kay do not change and show no perception of their despicable behaviour. As a result, the situation at the end of this romance merely resembles a truce rather than the traditional state of *joie*.

In view of this process of isolating the hero as an individual knight in opposition to the Arthurian community, there is a need to re-examine Köhler's

[51] See Gürttler, 'Künec Artus der guote', and J. Haupt, *Der Truchsess Keie im Artusroman. Untersuchungen zur Gesellschaftsstruktur im höfischen Roman, Philologische Studien und Quellen* 57 (Berlin, 1971).

ideas on the separation of the individual from society in Arthurian romance. It becomes debatable whether the theories developed on the basis of Chrétien's romances and then accepted as fundamental to this whole category of romance can in fact be applied in the same way and without extensive modifications to Arthurian romances after Chrétien.

The heroes of the early romances (Erec, Yvain or Lancelot) are envisaged as integrated members of the Arthurian community before the action begins. Whenever the Arthurian court as a place of *joie* has its harmonious state disrupted, then one of the knights sets off on his own, an elect representative, to come to terms with a hostile environment through the medium of *aventure* and finally to restore the ideal social order. However, in his capacity as a heroic fighter for the interests of the Arthurian court and the ideals of chivalry he is able at the same time to complete a process of self-discovery which changes his character, and enables him to return to the bosom of the community with a broadened understanding.

> The function of *aventure* as a way of restoring a disrupted state of harmony means that the quest becomes a search for the meaning of life as a whole, but that meaning can no longer be found in the immediate situation, with the antagonisms of feudal society on the increase rather than the decrease. The hero of a courtly romance undergoes a process of purification leading to complete individual perfection, and this process at the same time constantly reinforces a community that has been called into question; the significance of this is that the individual comes to prominence as the basis on which the community can be established, although the concept of the primacy of the community cannot be abandoned without endangering the very status of knighthood itself and the principle of a hierarchical society.[52]

In the real world *aventure* can never be more than an experiment, and can never lead to a renewed conflation of the internal and the external, since in Köhler's view the dichotomy between the individual and his milieu can never be resolved.[53] In Chrétien's Arthurian romances, on the other hand, the alienation is overcome, even if only on the level of fantasy, and this is represented in the state of *joie* which is restored from time to time, even if only temporarily.

There are, however, differences to be observed in the thirteenth-century Arthurian romances. Many heroes of later Arthurian romances, including Durmart, Fergus, Yder, the Vallet, Gliglois, Beaudous, Meriadeuc and the Bel Inconnu, do not belong to the Arthurian court at the time that they set off in

[52] Translated from Köhler, *Ideal und Wirklichkeit*, p. 83.
[53] Köhler, *Ideal und Wirklichkeit*, pp. 82–3.

pursuit of adventure;[54] they are unknown youths who still have to win fame and earn their place within the chivalric community. Their fleeting contact with the knights of the Round Table is often less important than their decisive encounter with their future beloved. The young hero undergoes his adventures for her and for himself, but not to avert a threat to the Arthurian court. His actions serve the Arthurian community only in the limited sense that every good deed is beneficial to society. Self-discovery is paramount.

This means that the young hero cannot have the function of restoring a disrupted state of harmony at the Arthurian court. He is not sent out by the court, nor is he pre-destined in Chrétien's sense.[55] When he presents himself as a stranger at court he is not entrusted with a task but is sent away. Thus there is no alienation of the individual from society in the form suggested by Köhler for the early romances, since an emotional bond between the individual knight and the Arthurian court has never even been established. The knight's isolation from society only exists in so far as he adopts the idealistic ethics of the Arthurian court as a personal requirement for himself. The Round Table does not acknowledge and claim him as a worthy member until the end of his quest, and consequently he can at best be integrated, but not reintegrated, into the court.

Integration into the Arthurian community is far from being the ultimate goal for individual knights such as Yder, Durmart or the Vallet, since they can no longer regard Arthur's court as the refuge of an ideal social order. This rejection of an illusory perfection and of an Arthurian community which can no longer meet its own demands results in the knight withdrawing into himself. Perfection materializes in the individual when he succeeds in his own eyes. A state of joy and harmony, independent of the now secondary *joie* of the court, arises from the knight's awareness that he has successfully mastered the world and has thereby eliminated any risk of alienation between himself as an individual and his environment. In the last resort these individuals are self-reliant and no longer depend on recognition by the knights of the Round Table; on the contrary, they accept the admiration of the Arthurian community without any sense of having fulfilled a life-long ambition by belonging to it. Their alienation from Arthur's court is thus total and insuperable.

[54] The Perceval section of the *Conte du Graal* furnishes the prototype for this structural arrangement.

[55] Erec and Yvain are not sent out either; Erec himself undertakes to withdraw from the court in order to avenge an insult inflicted on himself and therefore by implication also on the court. Yvain goes to the fountain to salvage on the one hand the honour of his own kin, but on the other hand also the honour of all Arthurian knights. This dual purpose of the quest, which features even more clearly in *Lancelot* (although there the elect aspect also has a role to play), distinguishes these three Chrétien romances from many of the later ones.

However, this phenomenon of alienation should not be seen as the end-result of a linear development. The negative stereotyping of the character of the sovereign and the associated emphasis on the exemplary nature of individual knights reflect the attitude of poet, patron and audience, but they show no tendency to increase in later texts. Instead, criticism of Arthur and the illusory perfection of the court are fundamental characteristics of the genre from the start. Works such as *Cor*, *Mantel*, *Yder* or *Vallet* show that the exhibition of these characteristics may co-exist with other contemporary texts, for example *Fergus* or *Le Bel Inconnu*, which emphasize the exemplary nature of the king and the Round Table. The final manifestations of the genre contain a thoroughly positive image of the sovereign. Thus the presentation of King Arthur acts as a barometer showing the degree of identity or divergence between the interests of royalty and the *baronie*, and depends on the particular group by which each romance was commissioned.[56]

[56] For a detailed discussion of this aspect see Part Two.

4

Knight or lover: Gawain as a paragon divided

From the very earliest examples of Arthurian literature Gawain, the king's nephew, was one of that relatively small group of characters who form the human nucleus of the Arthurian world; a verse romance in this genre is inconceivable without him.[1] Gawain has particular functions in which he is as irreplaceable as Arthur, Kay or Guinevere, whereas the same cannot be said of Erec, Yvain, Lancelot or Perceval. These protagonists of Chrétien's romances are replaced in each of the later romances by the new hero of that particular text, and thus their role in Arthurian narrative after Chrétien is just as peripheral as it was in the earlier texts that Chrétien himself drew upon.

A reading of the earliest Arthurian texts conveys a clear and comprehensive image of Gawain's literary persona. In William of Malmesbury he is already noted for his exceptional *virtus* (strength), and in the early stages of the genre's development this becomes his decisive characteristic. Geoffrey of Monmouth also emphasizes this feature, and Wace rarely mentions Gawain without praising his outstanding qualities. Finally, Chrétien's Gawain is a model of *proece*, *charité*, *san* and *cortoisie* (prowess, compassion, good sense and courtesy), the incarnation of chivalric and courtly virtues, the first and the best, in short the very sun of chivalry:

> Cil qui des chevaliers fu sire
> et qui sor toz fu reclamez
> doit bien estre solauz clamez.
> Por mon seignor Gauvain le di,
> que de lui est tot autresi
> chevalerie anluminee,
> come solauz la matinee... (*Yvain*, 2402–8)

[1] On the function of the Gawain figure in Chrétien's works see H. Emmel, 'Formprobleme des Artusromans und der Graaldichtung' (Dissertation, Berne, 1951), p. 26ff.

(He who was supreme amongst knights and honoured above them all may rightly be called the sun. I am referring to my lord Gawain because he lends brilliance to chivalry just like the sun in the morning...)[2]

The late Arthurian romances as a group include quite a large number of texts dominated by the figure of Gawain. In these narratives he is no longer merely an idealized model and thereby implicitly condemned to a peripheral role ('rôle accessoire'), or to being the secondary hero.[3] Instead he takes on the role of the titular hero or at least the main character, and steps into the position and function previously occupied by a succession of different heroes including Yvain and Erec. This change in the persona of Gawain is evident in *L'Atre périlleux*, *Gliglois*, *Li Chevaliers as deus espees*, *La Mule sans frein*, *La Vengeance Raguidel* and *Le Chevalier à l'épée*.[4]

Despite his functions as the king's nearest relative, as an adviser and as comrade-in-arms to Lancelot and Perceval, Chrétien's Gawain is a relatively passive figure. How then does he come to be the main hero of so many of the later Arthurian romances? The reason may lie precisely in his idealization, which is given ever-increasing emphasis through the sequence of the early works. A literary figure with exclusively exemplary characteristics is in danger of being boring and colourless, and even Gaston Paris noted a lack of distinctive traits in the figure of Gawain.[5] A study of the later Arthurian romances, especially those of the Gawain group, suggests that in subsequent generations both authors and their public begin to react in some measure against the excessive and therefore rather tedious idealization of Gawain.

Another reason for making Gawain the main character is explicitly stated by several authors, who feel that it was distinctly remiss on Chrétien's part not to have composed a Gawain romance:

L'en en doit Crestïen de Troies,
Ce m'est vis, par raison blasmer,
Qui sot dou roi Artu conter,
De sa cort et de sa mesniee
Qui tant fu loee et prisiee

2 See also *Erec et Enide*, lines 2232–3.

3 Gaston Paris, 'Romans en vers', p. 33. Emmel, 'Formprobleme', p. 67, sees the Gawain romances as manifestations of structural disintegration and claims that they lack one ingredient essential to the composition of a genuine Arthurian romance, namely the relationship of the hero to the norm of Arthurian chivalry as represented by the figure of Gawain.

4 In these works Gawain is either the main protagonist or else serves as comrade-in-arms to another hero of whom he is the equal. Within certain limitations this could also be said of *Gliglois* and *Hunbaut*. See K. Busby, *Gauvain in Old French Literature* (Amsterdam, 1980).

5 Gaston Paris, 'Romans en vers', p. 29.

Et qui les fez des autres conte
Et onques de lui ne tint conte.
Trop ert preudon a oblïer.[6]

(In my opinion it is right to criticize Chrétien de Troyes, who knew how to tell stories about King Arthur, his court and his company of knights who were so highly praised and esteemed, and who told the deeds of others but who never told a story about him [Gawain]. He was too worthy a man to be forgotten.)

Chrétien had neglected to devote a work to Gawain, and so here was a task just waiting for his successors, and one which they undertook with much enthusiasm, as the evidence still shows. Writing about Gawain represents a deliberate policy of rectifying past omissions:

Roumans a faire m'aparel
De celui qui ainc n'ot parel
De pris ne de valor el mont. (*Hunbaut*, 145–7)

(I am about to compose a romance about the one who never had his equal in all the world for worth or valour.)

Et tos li plus vaillans del mont
Et cil dont plus dire vos doi... (*Hunbaut*, 662–3)

[*Translator's note*: 'And the most valiant in the world, and he of whom I am to tell you more...' Following the printed edition, Schmolke-Hasselmann apparently takes the first phrase as well as the second to refer to Gawain, but this may not be what the author intended for it is by no means certain that successive editors have supplied the correct punctuation.]

Je cont de monsaignor Gauvain,
Qui tant par ert bien ensaigniez
Et qui fu des armes prisiez
Que nus reconter ne savroit.
Qui ses bones teches voudroit
Totes retrere et metre en brief,
Il n'en vendroit onques a chief.
Se je nes puis totes retrere,
Por ce ne me doi je pas tere
Que je ne die totes voies. (*Chevalier à l'épée*, 8–17)

(I am telling a story about my lord Gawain, who was so very well bred and so esteemed for deeds of arms that no one could adequately tell of it. Whoever attempted to give an account of all his good qualities and set it down in writing

[6] *Le Chevalier à l'épée*, lines 18–25. [*Translator's note*: The unique manuscript (Bern 354) has 'L'en *ne* doit...blasmer' ('It is *not* right to criticize...'). The text used by Schmolke-Hasselmann relies upon an emendation that prejudges the interpretation that follows. See Owen's edition.]

would never get to the end of them. Nevertheless, even if I cannot recount them all, that is no reason for me to keep silent and not have my say.)

Moreover, according to the author of *Hunbaut*, if a poet writes about Gawain rather than the central characters chosen by Chrétien he cannot be accused of deriving all his ideas from his great predecessor, which could be seen as a kind of robbery:[7]

Ne dira nus hon que je robe
Les bons dis Crestïen de Troies... (186–7)

(No one will say that I am stealing the fine words of Chrétien de Troyes...)

Les Merveilles de Rigomer could not be called a Gawain romance, but it also contains a passage that is none the less important in this context when the poet asserts:

Mais cil ouevre par grant delit,
Qui de tel ome fait son dit
Con mesire Gavains estoit,
Quant on nul millor ne savoit. (10,969–72)

(But it is a joy to work if one is telling the story of such a man as my lord Gawain, knowing none better.)

This focus is also reflected at the beginning of the romance: 'Del roi Artu *et de ses houmes*' (7, 'Of King Arthur and of his men'), as well as in lines 10,605–12.

Just as Chrétien's successors turned against their model, so also the poet of Branch I of the *Roman de Renart* directs his criticism against Pierre de Saint Cloud, whom he reproaches for not having described the trial and sentencing of the fox:

[Perroz] laissa le mieuz de sa matiere
quant il entroblia les plaiz
et le jugement qui fu faiz... (Roques' edition, 4–6)

(Pierre left out the best part of the story when he forgot the pleas to the court and the verdict that was delivered.)

For the modern reader there is a certain element of contradiction in the more critical statements made by Chrétien's successors, since we know (or think we know) that Chrétien did in fact give detailed attention to the king's nephew; after all, several thousand lines of the *Conte du Graal* are devoted to him.[8] Is it

[7] See also Chapter 1, p. 37.

[8] On the dispute about the authorship of the Gawain section of the *Conte du Graal* see L. Pollmann, *Chrétien de Troyes und der Conte del Graal*, *ZrPh* Beiheft 110 (Tübingen, 1965), and E. Köhler, 'Zur Diskussion über die Einheit von Chrestiens *Li Contes del Graal*', *ZrPh* 75 (1959), 523–39.

conceivable that the later authors were ignorant of this, despite their exhibiting an otherwise intimate knowledge of Chrétien's works, including *Perceval*? Or is it not more likely that they saw the role of Gawain in the *Conte du Graal* as a mere 'rôle accessoire', just as in *Lancelot*. An examination of the *Perceval* Continuations shows that in the pseudo-Wauchier section for example the narrative alternates the adventures of Perceval and Gawain; however, Gawain's quest eventually runs out of steam in the search for Perceval. The pseudo-Wauchier text makes it clear that Gawain is not destined to win the Grail. He fails to put the broken sword back together, omits to enquire about the Grail and goes to sleep before he has been given an explanation of the mysterious proceedings.[9] It is entirely possible that in this portrayal the poets of the *Perceval* Continuations were in agreement with Chrétien's original intentions. However, other Arthurian poets clearly wanted to compose works in which their ideal but neglected knight was to be the sole hero and at the centre of the action for once. It is reasonable to assume that in realizing this desire they were also meeting the expectations of that section of the public interested in Arthurian verse:

> Ma dame me conmande et prie
> Que une aventure li die
> Qu'il avint au Bon Chevalier,
> Et je nel puis mie laiscier
> Quant ele le m'a commandé,
> Des qu'il li plaist et vient a gré. (*L'Atre périlleux*, 1–6)

(My lady asks and commands me to tell her of an adventure that happened to the Good Knight, and since she has commanded me I cannot fail to do it, given that it pleases her and that she finds it agreeable.)

Even if we regard it as a topos when the author asserts that his lady assigned him the task of composing a Gawain romance, the fact that he can pretend to have received an explicit commission speaks for itself.

However, anyone who expects Gawain to bask in unqualified admiration in the works wholly devoted to him will be disappointed. His function as a model of chivalry is often very much relegated to the background. He is criticized, makes mistakes and fails to fulfil the obligations imposed upon him. Yet he still meets public expectations in other respects; a literary tradition as old and firmly established as the one associated with the name of Gawain cannot be transformed into its opposite without a transitional phase. Thus he still continues to function as a good adviser to the king, he receives guests at court, people turn to him when they need help, and for the inexperienced young men coming to the

9 However, in Arthurian romances in languages other than French it is possible to find Gawain elevated to the position of hero of the Grail adventure and thus also of deliverer.

court he is still the shining example of a perfect knight that they wish to spend their lives emulating. For this reason he is held in great esteem as a teacher of squires. Boys are sent to him from far and wide, even from beyond Arthur's kingdom. Gliglois, hero of the romance of that name, is the son of a rich German chatelain, and when he has reached his fourteenth year his father sends him to Arthur's court:

Jou vuel que vous alliéz a court
Pour aprendre sens et savoir...
Gavain pressentés vo service;
S'i vous retient, n'aiéz cointize,
Mais servéz le dessy qu'al pié
Si chier con avés m'amistié. (24–32)

(I want you to go to court to acquire sense and knowledge... Offer your service to Gawain, and if he accepts you do not give yourself airs but serve him meticulously if you value my affection.)

Meriadeuc, later to become 'li Chevaliers as deus espees' (the knight with the two swords), is also one of Gawain's squires until the day when he suddenly shows signs of exceptional qualities and sets off in pursuit of *aventure*.

Gawain is the travelling-companion and comrade-in-arms of Fergus, Meriadeuc, Durmart, Meraugis and Yder, for he knows how to recognize chivalry better than other knights at court, even when it has not yet been proved by great deeds. The sequence of adventures which a hero has to undergo, and through which he proves his worth to himself and the world, often culminates in his having to hold his own in a fight with Gawain. The function of the Gawain fight in its various forms will be discussed again elsewhere.[10]

Gawain is also shown as a ruler; in *Beaudous* he acquires a country of his own and great wealth on the death of his father. The romance begins with Arthur inviting the barons to his nephew's coronation festival. Gawain's acquisition of his own territory is an isolated case but is nevertheless a further indication of the way in which his character is made progressively more active and autonomous.

Quite apart from these indications in the content of the romances, which vary in significance depending on the line pursued by each text, it is noticeable that virtually none of the authors can mention Gawain's name without immediately launching into a eulogy of him. This can be illustrated from various different romances:

Une aventure qui avint
Au bon chevalier qui maintint
Loiauté, proëce et anor,

[10] See Chapter 6, p. 202.

Et qui n'ama onques nul jor
Home coart, faus, ne vilain. (*Chevalier à l'épée*, 3–7)

(An adventure that happened to the Good Knight who upheld loyalty, prowess and honour, and who never at any time loved a cowardly, false or unworthy man.)

...icil
Qui d'autres homes valoit mil
Por amor, honor et francise. (*L'Atre périlleux*, 2737–9)

(...this man who in love, honour and nobility was worth a thousand other men.)

Et si est preus et biaus et gent,
Bien parlans et cortois et sage... (*Hunbaut*, 112–13)

(And he is also noble and handsome and well bred, fluent of speech, courteous and wise...)

...cil en cui Dix avoit mise
Loiauté, prouece et francise,
K'il avoit fait cortois et sage,
Sans vilounie et sans outrage,
Sans orguel et sans desmesure... (*L'Atre périlleux*, 4994–8)

(...he to whom God had given loyalty, prowess and nobility, whom He had made courteous and wise, without baseness and without infamy, without pride and without arrogance...)

Loiauté, *proece*, *honor*, *franchise*, *amor*, *cortoisie*, *sagesse*, *largesse*, *biauté*, *gentilesse* (loyalty, prowess, honour, nobility, love, courtesy, wisdom, generosity, beauty, gentility)—the epithets used to praise Gawain reveal the extent to which he is credited with all the characteristics of the chivalric ideal. No other hero in the whole field of Arthurian narrative combines so many positive characteristics. The first impression created by William of Malmesbury continues to find total confirmation in most of the Arthurian romances even after Chrétien.[11]

TRIUMPHS AND FAILURES OF THE 'CHEVALIER AS DAMOISELES'

There is a further characteristic which, like those touched upon above, was ascribed to Gawain right from the start, and which is reflected in the title *chevalier as damoiseles* (knight of the damsels).[12] This aspect, however, is not

[11] In the *Roman de la Rose* (lines 2081–2 in Lecoy's edition) Gawain is praised as the ideal of a courtly person and as an absolute model of behaviour.

[12] This title first appears in *Meraugis*, line 1348.

merely confirmed by the later Arthurian romances but is emphatically expanded and accentuated; Gawain's special relationship with women has a part to play in almost all the romances, and in many of the texts it becomes the decisive element in structuring the narrative.

Gawain has a reputation for hastening promptly to the aid of any lady in distress:

> Bien puet trestox li mondes dire
> Que c'est ci le Bon Chevalier,
> Et cil qui tox jors seut aidier
> As damoiseles au besoig. (*L'Atre périlleux*, 1410–13)

(The whole world may well say that this is the Good Knight and the one who was always able to help maidens in their hour of need.)

Indeed, Arthur almost regards this as Gawain's sole purpose in life:

> Vous ki estes tous iors vescus
> Por poures dames soustenir,
> Vous ki solies si maintenir
> Les puceles desiretees... (*Deus espees*, 3310–13)

(You who have always lived to succour poor ladies and are accustomed to supporting deserted maidens...)

When for once he is not immediately on hand, Yvain enquires:

> —Et mes sire Gauvain, chaeles,
> li frans, li dolz, ou ert il donques?
> A s'aïe ne failli onques
> dameisele desconseilliee. (*Yvain*, 3692–5 [3698–701])

('And what of my noble and gentle lord Gawain, where was he then? His aid was always available to any damsel in need of help.')

In this respect Gawain is of course merely fulfilling one of the requirements of the chivalric code. But this is also a task which he carries out with particular willingness, and his nickname does not derive merely from his role as a liberator from distress in the way that Gaston Paris supposed:

> We can be certain that he never fails a lady who needs protection... Thus he has earned the title of 'Chevalier aux demoiselles' which is ascribed to him in *Meraugis*.[13]

In fact, however, he has such a good reputation as a lover amongst the ladies of the Arthurian world that some of them believe him to be the only person they

[13] Translated from Gaston Paris, 'Romans en vers', p. 34.

could possibly consider for their *ami*. Hence they reject all other suitors and cause the latter to develop a quite understandable hatred of Gawain. This motif is brought into several of the later Arthurian romances, either peripherally or as the starting-point for an entire narrative sequence.

Gawain's role as the perfect knight is suitably complemented by his role as the perfect lover, and he seems able to combine harmoniously the demands of both *chevalerie* and *amour*. However, whilst doubt is scarcely ever cast on the first of these roles, the second proves exceedingly complex in its diverse manifestations. It is clearly difficult for Gawain to fulfil all the amorous expectations that people have of him. The problem may lie in the fact that as a rule those ladies who dream of him have never yet seen him. Thus they adore Gawain not as an individual but as an idealized and de-personalized stereotype, the archetypal chivalrous lover.

A couple of observations on points of detail will help to make this clear. When the real Gawain suddenly appears before these ladies they do not recognize him, for he is in reality quite different from the image proclaimed by his exaggerated reputation. In *La Vengeance Raguidel* Gawain comes to the castle of the Dame del Gaut Destroit. This lady's affection had once been offered as the prize at a tournament which our hero had won, but he had disdained the prize. Nevertheless, years later he begs the lady for overnight accommodation in her castle. Ever since the occasion of that previous rejection the lady has been consumed by a love-hatred for Gawain. She has taken his brother prisoner and tortures him every day in Gawain's stead. She has also prepared an imaginatively constructed trap for Gawain himself. While he examines the craftsmanship of a sarcophagus which is intended as the communal burial place for himself and the Dame del Gaut Destroit, a guillotine is supposed to decapitate him. However, the lady fails to recognize him:

> La dame ne connissoit mie
> Monsignor Gavain qu'ele amot. (1772–3)

(The lady did not know my lord Gawain whom she once loved.)

Without suspecting his identity she tells him the story of her love and characterizes Gawain in these words:

> Molt est plains de grant vilonnie,
> Quant il de m'amor ot le don,
> Que puis ne vint en ma maisson...
> Je cuit qu'il ait honte de moi! (2262–7)

(He is nothing but a low-born wretch. He had the gift of my love and yet never came into my house... I think he is ashamed of me.)

She explains that if he fell into her hands she would kill him first and then herself. Thus he would have to bear her company in the grave, since he had declined to do so when he was alive.

This strange *amour de loin* (love from afar) has some very remarkable consequences, both here and in other romances. If the real Gawain seems unapproachable and unattainable, the ladies in question provide themselves with a substitute to symbolize his constant presence. The Pucele de Lis in the First Continuation has had a wall-hanging embroidered for her by a Saracen woman with scenes from Gawain's life, a tapestry which runs all round her bedroom. When a knight comes claiming to be Gawain she asks him to take off his armour and then compares him with the representation that is so familiar to her, whereupon she recognizes that the knight has been telling the truth and surrenders herself joyfully and unhesitatingly to the idol of her youth:

Et avoit ens portrait l'image
Monseignor Gavain en cel bort.
Ne l'ot pas fait bochu ne tort,
Mais tot ausi come il estoit,
Come il s'armoit et desarmoit,
Ses bones teches, sa biauté,
Sa cortoisie, sa bonté.
Tot i ot portrait si tres bien
Que l'image sor tote rien
Monseignor Gavain par painture
Sambloit et fu de tel figure. (2682–92)

(And she had the image of Sir Gawain portrayed within its borders. He had not been shown humpbacked or twisted but exactly as he was, putting on and taking off his armour, his good qualities and good looks, his courtesy and kindness. Everything was portrayed there so well that the painted image of Sir Gawain was just like him.)

In *Hunbaut*, on the other hand, a certain chatelaine has such a lifelike statue of Gawain standing in her bedroom that the steward Kay takes fright when he catches sight of it and is firmly convinced that the king's nephew himself is secretly staying in the lady's chamber. This image is nothing less than an idol:

En la canbre la pucele ot
Une imagene si entaillie
—C'uns engingnieres ot taillie
Si adroit que n'i ot que dire—
Que de sanblant n'i ot a dire,
Con mesires Gauvains avoit.

A tesmong celui qui le voit,
Que l'image(s) itels ne fust.
Si ert entaillie de fust
Si adroit et en tel sanblant
Que ja nus hon por nul sanblant,
Tant fust ne percevans ne cointe
Qui tant fust [de] Gauvain acointe,
Se l'imagene esgardast el vis
Qu'il ne [li] fust mout [bien] avis
Qu'il veïst Gauvain en apert. (3104–19)

[*Translator's note*: This passage is difficult and neither the punctuation that is reproduced above nor the emendations proposed by Winters make sense of it. The text itself may be allowed to stand provided that the editor's full stop after *avoit* is changed to a comma. A fairly literal translation preserving the structure (and the clumsiness) of the original would then be:

> In her chamber the maiden had a statue—carved by such a skilful craftsman that it could not be faulted—that resembled the appearance of my lord Gawain so exactly that, on the evidence of anyone who sees it, it was not a statue at all. It was carved in wood with such skill and to such a likeness that no one who looked the statue in the face, however observant or clever he may be, or however well he knew Gawain, could possibly believe that he was not seeing Gawain himself.]

Gawain's function as an image of male perfection for women who have never seen him leads to complications and cases of mistaken identity in *Hunbaut*, *La Vengeance Raguidel*, *Li Chevaliers as deus espees*, *Le Bel Inconnu* and even as early as in the Gawain section of the *Conte du Graal*, as well as in the First Continuation. In general Gawain cannot live up to the ladies' exaggerated expectations of him. As a result, the traditional image of Gawain as active or even impetuous in his courting of ladies changes to one where Gawain has to ward off the ladies' affection.

However, the custom sometimes demands that a lady falls to his lot for a particular deed of arms, because the gift of her person was tied to the resolution of the preceding conflict. Or he may be obliged to spend the night with the daughter of the household. This occurs for example in *Li Chevalier as deus espees* and in *Le Chevalier à l'épée*; in the former Gawain has suddenly fallen in love with an innocent young girl. In gratitude for his successful support in battle the parents allow him to enjoy their daughter's love. It is true that no one yet knows his name, but such a reward for having just rescued them from their distressed state seems to be entirely appropriate. The mother escorts the girl to Gawain's bed and says:

Si vous proi, k'ele ne s'en liet
Pas tele ke i couchera. (4896–7)

(And I pray you that she will not get up in the condition in which she goes to bed.)

Left alone with Gawain, the girl begins to cry and informs him that long ago she heard about Sir Gawain; she has been deeply in love with him since her fifteenth year and has vowed to give her virginity only to him. In happy anticipation Gawain now reveals his identity, but the girl does not believe him. Only recently she has been told that the hero is no longer alive. All Gawain's assurances are to no avail, and he has to let the maiden go again without having achieved his purpose. Deeply disappointed, he passes a sleepless night. The girl travels to Arthur's court in order to clarify whether Gawain is still alive. There the two meet again and she has to admit her mistake. She then explains to her lover after their long-awaited union why she had previously been sceptical:

Ne dui croire, se dix m'ait,
Que ia ior mes sire Gauvains
Fust si lasques ne si vilains,
Que por plaindre ne por plorer
Peust de lui feme escaper,
Qu'il eust si en son voloir
Que vous avies moi la endroit. (12,072–8)

(As God is my helper, I could not believe that my lord Gawain would ever be so feeble or so boorish that a woman could escape from him by crying and protesting, if he had her in his power as you had me then.)

Gawain's impetuous lack of consideration in matters erotic seems to be as much feared as admired by the women of the Arthurian world. Many a girl is reduced to fear and trembling when Gawain arrives, for example in the *Conte du Graal*:

'...je sai bien que vos pensez.'
— 'Et coi?' fait il. — 'Vos me volez
Prendre et porter ci contreval
Sor le col de vostre cheval.'
— 'Voir vos avez dit, damoisele.'
— 'Je le savoie bien, fait ele;
Mais dehez ait qui ce quida,
Garde nel te penser tu ja
Que tu sor ton cheval me metes.
Ne sui pas de ces foles bretes
Dont cist chevalier se deportent...' (6697–707)

('I know very well what you have in mind.' 'And what is that?' he says. 'You want to seize me and carry me off on your horse's neck.' 'Damsel, you're quite right.' 'I knew it,' she says. 'But a curse on the one who thought that, and make sure you never think of putting me on your horse. I am not one of those silly foolish girls that the knights take along for their amusement...')

Se tu avoies rien tenue
Qui sor moi fust, de ta main nue
Ne maniie ne sentie,
Je quideroie estre honie. (6843–6)

(If your bare hand had held or handled or felt any part of me, I'd consider myself dishonoured.)

It is appropriate at this point to quote Kay's verdict on Gawain as found in *Hunbaut*:

Mout est fols mauvais qui lui prise,
Ce vos vel bien entreconter...
Se n'est de ses putains torser:
De cel mestier est il tot baut. (3180–3)

(Anyone who admires him is making a stupid mistake, I can tell you, unless it's for lifting the skirts of his whores—he's slick enough at that trade.)

Thus there is widespread support amongst the characters of the later Arthurian romances for the belief that if Gawain has won fame, this is not so much as a knight but principally as a Casanova. Version B of the First Continuation probably goes furthest in this direction.[14] In this text a girl is raped by Gawain, a scene 'without precedent in Arthurian literature...it must have shocked a great many people, both audiences and authors'.[15] There are also ironic comments scattered throughout other Arthurian verse romances which clearly allude to an image of Gawain such as appears later on in the Prose *Tristan*, the pseudo-Robert de Boron and the *Suite du Merlin* as well as other prose romances. This tendency has been present from the earliest stages of the genre's development; Gawain is already credited with both military and romantic qualities in Geoffrey and Wace. His love-affairs are also given ironic treatment in Chrétien's *Lancelot*.

Included in the fluctuating image of Gawain which Chrétien bequeathed to his continuators it is easy to discern a paragon of worldly chivalry and courtly

[14] Version B, manuscripts *MQETV*, line 13,611ff. In *Le Chevalier à l'épée*, lines 581–9 and 625–36, Gawain is afraid that it might be to his disadvantage if it became known that he had spent a whole night lying with a girl without managing to fulfil his desires. He would rather be killed by the sword suspended over him than have to bear this disgrace.

[15] Translated from P. Gallais, 'Gauvain et la Pucelle de Lis', in *Mélanges M. Delbouille*, edited by J. Renson (Vol. I) and M. Tyssens (Vol. II), 2 vols (Gembloux, 1964), Vol. II, p. 210.

> elegance, a ready but inconstant lover with a touch of the Don Juan about him, and in the last resort a hero who is out of his depth when his adventures lead him into the domain of marvels and the supernatural.[16]

The examples already adduced have served to emphasize Gawain's reputation as a perfect lover in the eyes of many women, whilst the men criticize him for this, seeing him as a seducer with no thoughts in his head beyond easy conquests.

At this point it is interesting to observe, particularly in *Gliglois*, *La Vengeance Raguidel* and *Le Chevalier à l'épée*, that for precisely these reasons Gawain is also disdained as a lover and husband by ladies of nobility or prominence. This is especially clear in *Gliglois*, and it will therefore be useful to take a quick look at this somewhat lengthy example of a lay:

A beautiful girl named Belté comes to Arthur's court, and the king entrusts her to Gawain, who falls so passionately in love with her that he loses no time in proposing to her, only to be immediately and unambiguously refused:

> Gavains rougy, molt ot gran honte,
> Ly sans del courps el viz ly monte,
> Ly cuers ly bat en la poitrisne... (261–3)

(Gawain blushes and feels very great shame. The blood rises from his body to his face and his heart pounds in his breast.)

He asks the queen to mediate for him, and Guinevere is furious at Belté's behaviour. Never before has any woman been known to reject Gawain rather than feeling highly honoured 'Se vous le daingnïez avoir' (297, 'If you deign to have her'). Gawain's self-confidence is severely shaken and he begins to doubt himself: 'Si n'ay s'amour, moult poy me pris' (319, 'If I do not have her love, I consider myself to be of very little worth').

In order to change Belté's mind, Gawain sends her his best squire, Gliglois, to serve her at table. But Gliglois falls in love with the beautiful girl himself, and as a result he finds himself in a difficult dilemma, for his young love is in conflict with the loyalty he owes to Gawain. He is afraid that his master will regard him with mortal hatred if he should hear about this love. At meal times he is so pensive and spellbound by Belté's beauty that he forgets to carve for her. Belté makes fun of him. Weeks later when he meets her early one morning in the garden he confesses his love to her. Her reaction is hard and arrogant; she informs him that he is presumptuous to want to love her, for he is only an insignificant little squire, and he has after all seen her reject even Gawain. She threatens to tell his master everything.

At this point a tournament is announced, but Gliglois is not allowed to go with the others. Gawain tells him he is confident that his victory in the tournament will finally win Belté for him, whereupon the squire becomes jealous in earnest:

[16] Translated from J. Frappier, 'Le personnage de Gauvain dans la *Première Continuation de Perceval (Conte du Graal)*', *RPh* 11 (1958), 333, as quoted by the author. See also Köhler, *Ideal und Wirklichkeit*, pp. 182 and 193.

> Entre ses dens dist: 'Vous l'amés?
> Miex l'aim jou, voir, de vous assés.' (975–6)

(He said between his teeth: 'You love her? Well, I love her a great deal better than you.')

Belté also wants to stay at home, in order to avoid giving Gawain the impression that she is his *amie*. However, she would like to be able to go to the tournament with a different knight. Gliglois unselfishly procures an escort for her, but he cannot bear to lose sight of her, so he follows her at a distance, dressed just as he is and without armour or a horse. Soon his feet are bleeding and he is on the verge of fainting in the hot sun. Belté repeatedly orders him to turn back and ridicules him in front of her companion, but the reader is already beginning to suspect that all this is a test of love. She sends Gliglois to a lady who she says will kill him; Gliglois replies that he is looking forward to death as long as it comes at her command. The squire's devotion is total (lines 1580–4); he is willing to become a martyr to love. But the lady knights him instead of killing him; she does so in response to a request from her sister Belté.

When Gawain catches sight of Gliglois at the tournament, in armour and with a large retinue, his respect for him grows. He can hardly believe that this should be his former squire. Gliglois wins one part of the tournament, and he receives a falcon from Belté as his prize:

> Tenés, fait elle, biaus amis.
> Certes, fait elle, Dieu merchy,
> Vous l'avés tres bien deservi. (2654–6)

('Here you are, my fair friend,' she says, 'and, God knows, you certainly have a right to it.')

Gawain is not envious of Gliglois' victory, but when he learns that the latter has also won Belté's love he is disappointed and dejected:

> Gavains l'oï, si s'enbroncha,
> Dolans en fu, si souspira
> Quant il ot de l'amour parler,
> Car il cuidoit Biauté amer... (2875–8)

(When he heard that, Gawain bowed his head in sadness, and sighed when he heard talk of that love, for he thought he loved Belté.)

'Il cuidoit...' ('he thought...'), yet he did not really love her with his whole heart. The narrator concludes his work with the remark that Love has richly compensated Gliglois for all his suffering, and we should model ourselves on his example. Some people (and this is undoubtedly aimed at Gawain) believe that they understand a great deal about *fine amor*, and yet they know nothing about it. They think that the purpose of love is to avoid suffering, but that is a lie:

> Qu'amours ne vient mie de gas;
> Trop en seroit amours volage...

Amours ne brule mie, ains art.[17] (2924–8)

(Love is not to be taken lightly—that would make it too flighty... Love doesn't just burn, it's a conflagration.)

In this romance we see the fickle affection of the great Gawain rejected in favour of a young, unknown and naive squire who is capable of true love. Heartfelt and sacrificial love carries the day against *amour-vanité*.

The situation is rather different in *La Vengeance Raguidel* and in *Le Chevalier à l'épée*.[18] In both works Gawain's erotic potential is called into question. The lady that Gawain appears to be seriously in love with runs off with the first knight she comes across standing by the roadside after she has spent a night of love with the *chevalier as damoiseles*. In these texts, however, unlike Belté in *Gliglois*, the female character is portrayed in an exclusively negative light; her unfaithful behaviour has offended Gawain and made him look ridiculous at court, and he reacts with a long tirade against women:

Tel foi, tel amor, tel nature
Puet l'en sovent trover en feme:
Qui autre blef que il n'i same
Voudroit recoillir en sa terre
Et cil qui en feme vialt querre
Fors sa nature n'est pas sage—
Toz jorz l'ont eü en usage
Puis que Dieus fist la premerainne...
Cil qui fainte et fause la trueve
Et la cherist et ainme et garde,
Ja puis Dieus ne l'ait en sa garde. *(Épée,* 1168–88)

(Such faith, such love, such a nature can often be found in women. Whoever expects to reap from his land a corn other than what he sows, or whoever expects to find in women anything other than their nature, is not wise—they have always been like that, ever since God made the first one... Whoever finds a woman false and deceitful, yet still cherishes her, loves her and keeps her, may God never more protect him.)

Ja mais nule n'en amerai
De cuer! Damesdius le[s] confonde!
Car eles honissent le monde. *(Raguidel,* 4634–6)

[17] The author of *Durmart* expresses similar thoughts; see lines 5151–72.

[18] *Le Chevalier à l'épée* turns this episode into a brief self-contained narrative, whereas *La Vengeance Raguidel* makes it an integral part of the plot. The repeated inclusion of the episode probably indicates that such a daring scene, contradicting as it does the older Gawain tradition, could nevertheless meet with audience approval.

(I shall never give my heart to another one. May God confound them! They bring shame upon the world.)

The 'perfect lover' is now of the opinion that Kay's attitude to women is the only proper one, and in future he intends to follow the steward's example.

La Mule sans frein differs from the texts already mentioned in the way that Gawain's affection is disdained. In this instance his hope of a romantic adventure is not fulfilled, and instead a woman makes a complete fool of him.[19] After Kay has returned without success from his search for the lost bridle, Gawain wants to set out to find it. In view of the reward which he seems certain to attain he is not refused a kiss. He then endures the same adventures as Kay but he does manage to cross the narrow bridge, although according to the narrator the credit for that must go to the mule rather than to the hero. Later he chops off the head of a dwarf (who immediately puts it back on again), and kills two lions and a dragon. The dwarf informs him that he is to be thanked by being invited to a meal by a lady. Moreover, this lady will grant him whatever he desires of her. But to begin with, instead of making romantic advances to him the lady only utters slanderous reproaches against him. However, she then pulls herself together, praises him and offers him herself and thirty-nine castles if he should wish to stay with her. It turns out that she is the sister of the girl at whose bidding Gawain undertook this journey, and that her sister had given her the bridle to look after. Gawain takes possession of it and rides back to the court, where the *demoisele* is very pleased to have her bridle back. She says that many knights have already lost their lives because of it. Gawain then gives a detailed account of the taxing adventures he has undergone on her behalf (1092–1112); he now wants to be thanked accordingly. But the *demoisele* does not keep her promise. She rides away without a word as soon as she has the bridle in her hands.

Although on many occasions Gawain had proved a failure as champion of the ladies and as a lover, the Arthurian poets of the thirteenth century still had the option of marrying him off along the lines of Erec or Yvain and creating a conjugal romance with Gawain as the male protagonist. But despite repeated forays in that direction the concept was never really successful; Gaston Paris suggests one possible reason:

> Although some later narratives tell us of his marriage to various women, there is none whose name is associated with his like those of Enide, Iseut, Blancheflor and Guinevere with Erec, Tristan, Perceval and Lancelot.[20]

[19] See Chapter 3, pp. 79–80. The episode is also contained in *Diu Crône*.

[20] Translated from Gaston Paris, 'Romans en vers', p. 34.

We have already seen that Gawain has many female admirers, whilst various texts also record the presence of ladies who have been introduced as *amie de Gauvain* and have received recognition as such at Arthur's court. Their names include Yde, Venelaus, Guinloie and Florie.[21] Repeated attempts have been made to place Gawain in a stable relationship with one partner, but the First Continuation already contains an implication that Gawain is not very amenable to such attempts. In that text he is accused of not having married the sister of Bran de Lis even though he had made her pregnant. When her father and brother try to bring Gawain to justice he kills one and injures the other. In some manuscripts[22] there is a touching scene where years later the mother tries to send in her little son in the hope of preventing a fight to the death between her brother and Gawain:

> Et li anfes antr'ax s'an vet.
> Tres parmi la janbe anbraça
> Son oncle, et trois foiz li beisa,
> Et dist: 'Sire, ce dit ma mere
> Que vos n'ocïez pas mon pere.'[23]

(And the child puts himself between them. He embraced his uncle tightly round his leg, kissed him three times and said: 'Sir, my mother says you are not to kill my father.')

This boy is not the only son ascribed to Gawain in the later Arthurian romances. Beaudous and the handsome stranger Guinglain are further illegitimate offspring of the great lover. However, this fact is in no way a disadvantage to them in Arthurian society; they are allowed to take pride in having Gawain as their father. On the other hand, the relationship of the father himself to these sons of his, whom he usually only gets to know when they are already adolescents, is scarcely any different from the way he treats every other promising young squire at Arthur's court. Thus the revelation by a fairy of the hero's true parentage is the climax of the plot in *Le Bel Inconnu*, whilst the beginning of the romance of *Beaudous* even gives notice of Gawain's eventual wedding to the hero's mother, the Dame de Galles (lines 398–400). However, the end of the story breaks off before the great court festivities can take place. Thus Gawain's traditional role in French Arthurian romance has remained unaltered, and he is still the bachelor and Don Juan who can flirt with a different woman in each romance. He remains freely available because his character is constructed

[21] In *La Vengeance Raguidel*, the *Lai du cort mantel*, *Li Chevaliers as deus espees* and *Diu Crône* respectively.

[22] Manuscripts *LASPU* of the First Continuation.

[23] Manuscripts *ASP* of the First Continuation, lines 5072–6.

in such a way that he is incapable of entering into a lasting union with a woman. However, although we have seen him desert numerous women after flirtations pursued to varying lengths, it is Gawain of all people who repeatedly sets himself up as the guardian of decency and morality. Thus he reprimands a knight who, after having at last been permitted to consummate his love, has left his once adored lady in the lurch because she had deliberately kept him waiting too long.[24] Gawain impels him by force of arms to swear eternal fidelity to the girl and to marry her. Furthermore the whole romance of *L'Atre périlleux* (but see especially line 6604ff.) deals with Gawain's repeated involvement as a marriage broker for a succession of couples who have quarrelled or become estranged. In the same romance (905ff.) Gawain keeps watch in person to make sure that a knight does not spend the night with a young lady (although they are both in love with each other) because property matters have not yet been clarified. But he only applies these moral distinctions to others, not to himself.

We can thus confirm that virtually none of the writers succeeded in steering Gawain into the haven of marriage, because the literary tradition of the amorous hero proved stronger than other tendencies and always prevailed. The long-established characteristics of the Gawain figure make it a law unto itself and incompatible with the role of husband.[25]

A NEW MOTIF: GAWAIN'S APPARENT DEATH

Gawain always has numerous enemies who are seeking his life for the most diverse reasons. In the romances of *Li Chevaliers as deus espees* and *L'Atre périlleux* the narrative pattern involves one of these enemies meeting either Gawain himself or a knight whom he wrongly believes to be Gawain, whereupon he attacks him and severely wounds him (if it really is Gawain) or kills him (if he was mistaken). A rumour subsequently spreads throughout the whole of the Arthurian world that Gawain is dead, and all who love him (in particular, of course, the ladies) sink into deep mourning and melancholy. Gawain himself must now avenge the 'murder' and make good the injustice done to his double. The misunderstanding has to be cleared up, and Gawain also has to find his identity again after being temporarily deprived of it by the rumour of his death. Which of the thirteenth-century authors first hit on this particular device of making the apparently dead Gawain the hero of his work remains as yet unclear

[24] *L'Atre périlleux*, line 3051ff., and *Hunbaut*, lines 1864–2163.

[25] *Floriant et Florete* includes a reference to Gawain getting married, but this plays no significant part in the plot of the romance. In *Wigalois* Gawain marries Florie (line 961ff.) but soon leaves her to go to Arthur's court, and once there, since he has not taken the magic girdle with him, he never returns.

and in any case it is perhaps not that important. Nevertheless, we are dealing here with the most original contributory element in transforming the structural function of the Gawain figure within the romances of the Gawain group.[26]

The fact that our hero is thought to be dead, with only the reader and Gawain himself knowing otherwise, makes it possible to compose scenes of tension and literary piquancy which have few equals in Arthurian verse romance. Gawain travels around incognito. This is not unusual in itself, but now he himself believes that he is no longer Gawain and that he has lost his name and with it his identity for as long as he is unable to prove that he is still alive, a fact which sheds some interesting light on the self-perception of this Arthurian character. His attitude to his own name virtually amounts to a personal fetish, and on other occasions he would rather be killed than keep his name secret, but here he becomes *cil sans non* (the nameless one), and even refers to himself in that way.

The first example of this type of Gawain romance to be examined here is *Li Chevaliers as deus espees*, with 12,053 lines the longest romance of the group. The title refers to Meriadeuc, the knight with the two swords, who is also searching for his name and identity. The second protagonist, and no less important for the development of the plot, is Gawain who enters the narrative at line 2373:

> Arthur sees a totally dishevelled knight approaching on Gringalet and deduces that someone has killed Gawain and now intends to boast about the deed at court with the horse as proof. However, Arthur is eventually obliged to acknowledge that it is Gawain himself returning from an exhausting adventure. The whole town now rides to meet him, and he is shown affection and honour by all and sundry. After exchanging news, everyone goes to bed.
>
> However, Gawain has always been an early riser and he is already up before sunrise:

Et vit le soleil ki levoit
Mout clers et ou vergier avoit,
Ce li sambloit, oiseles tans
En tantes manieres cantans
Ke tous li cuers l'en esioist
Et souslieve tant ke il dist
A soi meisme ke dormir
Ne devoit nus hon ne gesir
Par tel tans tant k'il fust haities. (2637–45)

[26] Gawain's death is already mentioned by Geoffrey of Monmouth, who reports that his grave has been found. The motif becomes important in the Prose *Lancelot*. Gaston Paris, 'Romans en vers', p. 198, mentions the motif of Gawain's apparent death and voices his belief that there was originally an independent lay on this subject, a short episodic Gawain narrative which he suggests might be numbered amongst the most successful story-lines ever conceived.

(And he saw the sun rising brightly, and in the orchard there were so many birds singing in so many different ways that it seemed to him as if his whole heart was glad and so uplifted that he thought no man should sleep or stay in bed in such a season, as long as he was in good health.)

Richly dressed but unarmed, Gawain makes his way into the garden:

Puis se part d'iluec et si treuve
L'uis du gardin tout desferme,
Si s'en ist et passe le gue,
S'entre es pres plains d'erbe et de flors,
Formians de maintes colours,
Si voit la forest et va la
Tout son pas et il esgarda
Enmi une lande petite
Une place le plus eslite
Por deduire et la plus plaisant,
K'il veist ainc en son vivant,
Et en mi liu un fou avoit,
Dont il nul plus biel ne savoit,
S'ert par desous vers les praiaus,
Mais nul ki de loing fust si biaus
Ne vit nus ainc ne frans ne sers.
Et li fous estoit tous couvers
De tantes manieres d'oisiaus
Que c'estoit deduis et aviaus
D'oir la joie k'il faisoient,
Car en lor langage cantoient
Chascuns endroit soi si tres bel
Et por l'amor du tans nouvel
Et por la douce matinee,
Ke nule riens de mere nee
Onques mais tel joie ne fist. (2700–25)

(Then he leaves that spot and finds the garden gate undone, so he goes through it, crosses the ford and enters the meadows full of grass and flowers, shimmering with many colours. Then he sees the forest and heads for it as fast as he can, and in a small copse he beheld the finest and most delightful pleasure spot that he had seen in all his life. And in the middle of it there was a beech tree, the most beautiful he knew. It was on the lower side towards the meadows, but no one, whether free man or serf, had ever seen one looking anywhere near as handsome. And the beech tree was completely covered with so many kinds of birds that it was a pleasure and a delight to hear them rejoicing, for in their language each one was singing for himself, both for love of spring and for the mild morning, so beautifully that no creature ever born rejoiced like that ever again.)

Gawain kneels down and thanks his creator for all the good things that have been granted to him. This idyllic scene is remarkable in that it expresses a feeling for nature, but it is closely followed by misfortune. Moments later Gawain comes across a knight who refuses to greet him. The knight tells of a lady who has turned away all her suitors; he wants to risk everything to become her *ami*, but she has rejected him because he is only the son of a vavasour and not of noble descent (2799 and 2824). For her part, she claims to be one of the most beautiful of women and does not want to bestow her love on any but the most handsome and most nobly born of knights. She is prepared to admit that her admirer is attractive and brave, and one of the best knights in the country, but there is still a knight who is much better, namely Gawain. In response to her suitor's assertion that he is even more good-looking and brave than Gawain, she told him that if she was to believe it he would have to go and cut off Gawain's head and bring it to her as proof of his courage. Since then the knight has been travelling the length and breadth of the country searching for Gawain. He never greets anyone until he knows who he is talking to by name. Only when it emerges that he is not talking to Gawain does he become friendlier. Now he asks the other knight's name. Gawain is caught in a dramatic dilemma, because he owes it to his reputation always to make himself known, but on the other hand he is unarmed and cannot defend himself against the attack which he has just been led to expect. Yet even in this potentially disastrous situation (2935ff.) he decides not to keep his name secret. The other knight thanks heaven that he has found Gawain and wants to fight him straight away. Gawain draws his attention to the conventions of chivalry, but the other knight does not care; he sees only his long-awaited goal. It would be simple enough for Gawain to flee at this stage, since without armour he could ride faster than his opponent, but even when fearing for his life he will not do anything that might tarnish his reputation (3000–13). After a brief fight he is badly wounded and falls unconscious from his horse. His opponent, thinking he is dead, claps his hands for joy and cries out:

> Or ai de la table reonde
> Ocis la rose et le rubi,
> Quant mes sire Gauvains gist chi. (3064–6)

(Now I have killed the ruby and the rose of the Round Table, now that my lord Gawain is lying here.)

Nevertheless he has no inclination either to cut off Gawain's head or to take Gringalet away with him, since that could be held against him as uncourtly behaviour:

> Car trop aves el monde amis
> Et trop estes bien conneus. (3076–7)

(For you have very many friends in the world and you are very well known.)

Happy to have attained his goal, the knight rides away:

> Et dist ke li est avenue
> A volente et a droiture
> Toute la plus biele aventure
> Ki a chevalier avenist. (3088–91)

(And he said that he had had his wish and his deserts and had met with the best adventure that ever happened to a knight.)

During his recovery Gawain thinks only of revenge; he is overcome with rage at the thought that the other knight exhibited so much rejoicing over his supposed death:

> Ce me grieve certes plus fort
> Ke de ce ke ie sui navres. (3406–7)

(And indeed that hurts me more than the fact that I am wounded.)

One morning he rides away to find his murderer and combines this with the king's commission to seek the Knight with the Two Swords. During his journey Gawain is denounced as an impostor whenever he says who he is. Moreover, almost all the people he encounters at first are in some way related to his adversary; consequently they are annoyed to hear that Gawain is still alive and could frustrate all their ambitious plans. Some of them make a second attempt to kill him, in the hope that after his death their relative can marry the rich lady and become king.

Meriadeuc teams up with Gawain in the town of Rades, where the wedding is due to take place between the murderer (Brien) and the young queen, who for her part still continues to dream of Gawain. At the reading of the banns Brien once again boasts that now, after Gawain's death, he is the best knight in the world. Gawain, unrecognized, defends his own claim in a duel, which he wins. Then he rides away with Meriadeuc. When the lady learns that Gawain is still alive she renews her vow to seek to belong only to him, 'K'encor n'a pas feme espousee' (5987, 'since he still has no wife').

This Gawain episode in *Li Chevaliers as deus espees* is allocated a total of approximately 3500 lines. Obviously Gawain plays an important part in the further progress of the narrative as well. Nevertheless it becomes clear that the motif of Gawain's apparent death is not the fundamental element of the plot as a whole. There is no sign of its having a functional position within the overall structure of the romance.[27]

In *L'Atre périlleux*, on the other hand, Gawain's apparent death is no longer a peripheral motif but is the driving force of the plot from beginning to end. In this romance Gawain meets three maidens lamenting in the forest. Beside them lies a young squire whose eyes have been put out. A short time previously, according to the maidens, three villains had ambushed the unarmed Gawain, killed him and hacked him to pieces; then they had taken his head and limbs

[27] This suggests that the motif did not originate in *Li Chevaliers as deus espees*.

away with them. The maidens' companion had witnessed this and the villains had blinded him for fear of being betrayed. But this was not nearly as tragic as the death of the knight who was held to be the 'flower of chivalry' (500, 'flor de chevalerie').

Gawain tries to make them realize that there must have been some mistake, but they refuse to believe him. He then swears to avenge the dead knight and the blinded squire, and sets off in search of the murderers. Since no one will believe that he is Gawain, and the whole country is overwhelmed by grief at his death, he calls himself *cil sans non* (the nameless one).[28]

> Mais l'uevre est ja par tout seüe,
> K'el ne porroit estre teüe...
> Ahi! Dix, tant fortune het
> Les dames et les damoiseles!
> Quant eles saront ces noveles... (4987–91)

(But the deed is already known everywhere and cannot be hushed up. Alas! God, how fortune must hate ladies and maidens! When they hear this news...)

Numerous adventures encountered along the way deflect Gawain temporarily from his main purpose, but he never loses sight of his goal, as the narrator indicates:

> A tant se part des chevaliers
> Gavains, et va querre son non
> Entre lui et son conpaignon. (4866–8)

(Then Gawain takes leave of the knights and goes to seek his name, just him and his companion.)

> Or me restuet dire conment
> Cil qui aloit por son non querre
> En aventure par la terre
> Puet traire a cief de son afaire. (4894–7)

(Now I must tell how the knight who set out to roam the land in search of his name manages to succeed in his task.)

Gawain's supposed death splits the Arthurian world into two camps. The ladies and his friends mourn, whereas there is rejoicing amongst his numerous enemies, almost all of whom, however, only became his enemies because the ladies are constantly comparing them unfavourably with Gawain, leaving them unable to fulfil their own desires. We have seen several examples of how far this hatred of Gawain can go, but there are also many cases where admiration of him

[28] See in particular lines 4382, 4395, 4446, 4567 and 4806.

knows no bounds. The Gawain statue, the sarcophagus of the Dame del Gaut Destroit and the tapestry of the Pucele de Lis testify to this.

In *L'Atre périlleux* this idolization of Gawain goes another step further, and at the same time it is noticeable that it makes itself felt more widely than merely amongst ladies who have fallen for the hero. The three villains are reported to have visited one of Gawain's friends and hosts. They had the head and limbs of a knight with them and claimed that the dead person was Gawain. On their departure they left the right arm behind, and the host, Tristan who never laughs, has now had a casket made for this arm:

> Onques nus bras a nul cors saint
> Ne fu mais si ricement mis. (5180–1)

(Never was any arm from the body of a saint given so rich a shrine.)

The supposed arm of the best of all knights is thus treated like a precious holy relic, comparable with the remains of a saint. The cult of Gawain is taken so far here that it must surely have created a comic effect for its readers, especially as they knew that Gawain was still alive and that the relic was spurious.[29] On top of this, the dismembered corpse is put back together again at the end of the narrative and is brought back to life; the whole sequence of events turns out to have been an example of sorcery. When Arthur tries to punish the 'murderer' and sorcerer Orguellous Faé, Gawain asks him to have mercy on the offender. There follows a great feast.

If this is compared with the complex issues surrounding good and evil, guilt and justice in Chrétien's *Lancelot*, and if furthermore we consider the role played by Meleagant in that text and the serious way in which the stylized conflict between positive and negative forces is acted out, we are in a position to see how much the basic ethos of later Arthurian romance differs from that of Chrétien's works.

However, the comic elements in *L'Atre périlleux* occur only sporadically, and any deliberate criticism there may be is not directed against the figure of Gawain himself, even though for reasons already mentioned his position within the Arthurian sphere is becoming increasingly problematic. Yet quite apart from the difficulties encountered by our hero in his dealings with ladies and rivals, it is remarkable how often Gawain is blamed for things he has not done (where the truth may or may not emerge later). Thus he is accused several times of being a murderer himself.[30] Apart from such crimes and uncourtly behaviour he is

[29] The faking of relics was a problem with which thirteenth-century readers would be familiar, and a parallel instance from the Arthurian world must have been a source of amusement for them.

[30] See for example the Gawain section of the *Conte du Graal*, lines 4759 and 5863; the true circumstances are never explained. In *Li Chevaliers as deus espees* (line 6859ff.) Gawain has killed

further reproached with a number of other misdeeds such as rape, treachery and thoughtlessness. Moreover he is often simply the object of hatred for whole clans, without the reason for it ever becoming apparent to the reader. Within the Arthurian world no other figure apart from Arthur and Kay, and then only to a lesser extent, encounters both affection and antipathy in such powerful measure as Gawain.

PARODYING THE IDEAL IN AN ANTI-GAWAIN ROMANCE: *LA VENGEANCE RAGUIDEL*

Authors of the second and third generation who intend to make Gawain into the focal point of their work can incline more towards either a positive or a negative image according to their own preferences or according to the supposed requirements of their public. The most usual approach is one of affectionate but critical irony; not one of the narrators of this time and this genre dares to make Gawain as evil as he appears in the contemporary prose romances. One of them, however, chooses a third course, that of parody. He gives his name as Raoul and is the author of *La Vengeance Raguidel*. In terms of the development of the genre this romance can be regarded as the most interesting of the Gawain group and it therefore calls for the following detailed analysis of how it functions as a parody.

According to Friedwagner, who edited the text, the chivalric undertaking narrated in *La Vengeance Raguidel* represents 'only one of the countless deeds of the hero, a mere episode. It could just as easily be omitted from a verse chronicle of Gawain without his image being noticeably altered.'[31] In fact, some features of *La Vengeance Raguidel* seem distinctly unusual by comparison with the colourful but nevertheless firmly circumscribed literary representation of Gawain within the tradition of the genre.

In *La Vengeance Raguidel* Gawain is presented in his well-known dual role as the bravest of all knights and the most courtly of all lovers. As a knight he is intent upon adventure in the form of fighting, and as a lover his target is what Kellermann has called *amour-flirt*.[32] Amongst all the knights at Arthur's court, Gawain is the only one who succeeds in removing from the chest of the dead

the father of the hero Meriadeuc, admittedly under orders and in the armour of another knight to whom he had promised this action as a *don*, without reviewing all the consequences of his actions. He is also denounced as a murderer in *Escanor*, lines 6972–4, and in *Les Merveilles de Rigomer*, lines 7351–442.

[31] Translated from the introduction in Friedwagner's edition, p. CLIV.

[32] W. Kellermann, 'Les types psychologiques de l'amour dans les romans de Chrétien de Troyes', *Marche Romane* 20 (1970), 31–9, *passim*.

Raguidel the section of broken lance left by his murderer. It emerges from a prophetic message left with the dead man that it is a magic weapon; only with this *tronçon* can revenge on the murderer be carried out, because he cannot be killed except with his own weapon.

Gawain rides off with all speed in order to carry out his task as chosen avenger as quickly as possible. (We learn later that he was selected for it by a fairy.) However, the reader is very soon informed that our exemplary hero has forgotten to bring the broken lance with him, and that his journey will therefore be in vain:

Car sans le tronçon de la lance
N'en prendroit il nule vengance.
Il s'en vait, si l'a oublié. (547–9)

(For without the remains of the lance he would not take any vengeance at all. He sets off, having forgotten it.)

Gawain does not realize this oversight until he has already been travelling for some considerable time and has experienced numerous adventures. The reason is that he pushes the purpose of his journey more and more into the back of his mind, until he has soon forgotten this as well. In complete contrast to Chrétien's Lancelot, who is pursuing a definite route and does not allow himself to be diverted from it by anyone or anything, Gawain in this romance is literally a knight errant. Although it is part of the code of chivalry for a knight to complete without delay a task that he has been set or that he has taken up voluntarily, Gawain deliberately seeks out accommodation for the first night where he knows that he will be delayed for a long time.[33] The adventure with the Black Knight (Maduc le Noir) that has to be undergone there results in Gawain not remembering until more than half way through the narrative of the romance that he has forgotten to bring the enchanted weapon with him from Arthur's court:

A icest mot li muet et lance
Li cuers et lors s'est apensés
Del tronçon qui fu obliés,
Dont il dut la vengance faire.
Lors li veïst on .i. dol faire
Et demener et corecier,
Les iols movoir, le cuer lancier,
Les bras estendre et tresalir... (3124–31)

[33] Compare the way in which both Erec and Perceval vow to spend no more than one night under the same roof. Similarly, Yvain suffers anguish when the sisters of Noir Espine delay his quest to help Lunete. It is in comparison with such episodes as these that Gawain's behaviour is to be assessed.

(Hearing these words, his heart stirs and bounds, and then he remembers the broken lance that he had left behind and with which he must carry out the vengeance. Then he could be seen grieving and lamenting in his despair, eyes rolling, heart pounding, arms waving and trembling all over...)

The poet makes this scene particularly ironic by having Gawain in the immediately preceding lines give his vassal the Black Knight a very detailed explanation as to why, in the latter's hour of greatest need, he cannot fetch help for him from Arthur's court, because he cannot possibly show his face there without having carried out his mission to avenge Raguidel:

Je vois .i. aventure querre,
Ja mais n'enterra[i] en ma terre
Devant que je l'arai trovee.
Trop serroit ma *honte* provee
S'a la cort retornoie issi... (3113–17)

(I am going in search of an adventure, and I shall never again return to my own country until I have found it. My great shame would be all too obvious if I were to return to the court like this...)

He will indeed have to face shame at Arthur's court because he now has to go back to fetch the broken lance, whereupon Arthur will ask him about the *aventure* and he will have to admit that he has not achieved anything so far:

'Si m'aït Dius, sire, je non!
Tant nel soic querre ne cherkier.
Le tronçon dont je duc vengier
Obliai, ne ne m'en souviunt.' (4052–5)

('May God help me, sire, no I haven't. I was unable to seek it or search for it. I forgot about the piece of lance that I had to use for the vengeance, and left it behind.')

However, the return to Arthur's court does not proceed very swiftly either; Gawain is once more only too willing to let himself be delayed. He frees a girl from the clutches of two vicious knights, although his own brother, apparently contradicting normal courtly standards, urges him not to do it.

After Gawain has been scorned by Kay and rebuked by Arthur, and then, having equipped himself with the piece of lance, has finally sworn to set off next morning on his mission of vengeance (all of which has taken fifty days, the time between Easter and Whitsun), then regrettably something again occurs to hinder him. He is challenged to a duel over his beloved Yde and has to appear at the court of King Badamaguz within forty days to fight Druidain. Again he encounters sundry misfortunes on the way there, and the promised act of vengeance is once more quite forgotten. Only after the duel (when five-sixths of the plot of the romance are already over) does Gawain think about the *aventure* that is still unresolved, and even then with more reluctance than enthusiasm for action. This time he cannot avoid getting into the ship that has been provided for him; it even comes sailing after him. At the same time he is afraid, and immediately regrets his resolve:

> De ce quë il a ensi fait
> Se tint por fol et s'en repent,
> Mais il ne puet estre autrement. (4930–2)

(He thinks himself a fool for doing what he has just done, and regrets it, but it cannot be otherwise.)

The ship takes him to Scotland, which is to be the setting for the act of vengeance. Once there he begins by learning from Raguidel's mistress, who does not recognize him, how his coming has been long awaited and yearned for. She complains:

> 'Mais il va tant et ci et la
> Par tot le mont querre aventure,
> Que c'est trop grans mesaventure
> Quë il n'arive en cest païs.' (5200–3)

('But he [Gawain] has been wandering here and there, seeking adventure all over the world for so long that it is the greatest misfortune that he has not yet come to this country.')

> 'Mais trop demeure, ce me sanble,
> Mesire Gavains longement!' (5312–13)

('But it seems to me that my lord Gawain is delaying too long.')

By delaying he has caused anxiety and pain. The comrade-in-arms without whom, according to the prophecy, the deed of vengeance cannot be accomplished has been on the spot for a long time and is only waiting for him. But just as Gawain set off too hastily at the beginning of the adventure and failed to take the magic weapon with him, so now he acts hastily and without thinking, indeed almost boorishly once more. Guengasouain can only be defeated by two knights, but Gawain tries to attack him in haste before his companion Yder is present. Then in the fight he sets about Raguidel's murderer without using the broken lance, because in the first instance he wants to see if he can perhaps manage to vanquish him using only his own strength. This results in his suffering a humiliating defeat. His opponent wounds him, kills his horse Gringalet and pours scorn upon him into the bargain. Even when he eventually resorts to using the *tronçon*, he still cannot achieve anything. Guengasouain, who is escorted by a giant bear, can only be conquered by two knights together. Gawain in his stubborn arrogance will not keep to the terms of the prophecy. Finally Yder comes to his aid after all, kills the terrifying bear and shields the unfortunate Gawain, who no longer has a horse. Gawain and Guengasouain decide to fight each other once more, with ordinary instead of enchanted weapons, and before an assembly of all the knights of the land. This time Gawain does indeed succeed in defeating his opponent, but this is no longer a very spectacular deed, because without his magic weapons and the bear Guengasouain is a very average and not particularly courageous knight; he even volunteers to surrender his life. So Gawain is able to appear a great hero for the moment, although his part in the revenge on Raguidel's murderer was no great achievement.

In this romance Gawain cuts an even less glorious figure in his role as a lover. The reader gradually discovers that Gawain's dealings with ladies directly or indirectly bring trouble and misfortune to those concerned, and that, as a consequence of meeting Gawain, good and loving people turn into wicked creatures seething with hatred. This is what happens to Maduc le Noir, whose mistress, the Dame del Gaut Destroit, loved him at first but then directed all her passion towards Gawain. Disappointment over his spurned affection and his unfaithful mistress has turned Maduc into the scourge of the land. He kills every knight who ventures to his castle in the hope that Gawain, whom he does not know by sight, may be amongst the ones he has slaughtered. In this way he hopes to win back his beloved. He hates no one more than Gawain, and furthermore he also accuses him of being quite incapable of appreciating the love of the Dame del Gaut Destroit:

'Ne la prisse mie .i. bouton... (1408)
Qui ne le prisse .i. sol denier... (1414)
Si ne he nule creature
Com faiç cel Gavain que je di.' (1420–1)

('He does not think her worth a button... Who does not think her worth a single penny... And I hate no other creature as I do this Gawain I'm telling you about.')

Gawain defeats Maduc and ends his evil custom by making him his vassal. He then travels on, to the Dame del Gaut Destroit of all people, where in fear of her revenge he claims to be Kay. Whilst there he is able to find out what she thinks of him without being recognized. She seems unable to come to terms with the notion that he has rejected her:

'Je cuit qu'il ait honte de moi!
Mais s'il ert fius au plus haut roi
Quë on peüst el mont trover,

> Ne deüst il pas refuser
> M'amor s'il le peüst avoir!
> Je sui rice de grant avoir,
> Asés bele, asés jentius feme...' (2267–73)

('I think that he is ashamed of me. But if he were the son of the greatest king to be found in the world he still ought not to refuse my love if he could have it. I am rich and wealthy, a woman of the noblest birth and the greatest beauty.')

Even if he now fell at her feet in remorse she would not be able to forgive him. In her bitterness she says of Gawain: 'Even if he had married me, he would still have been on his way again by the next day, and would soon have forgotten me, because he would have seen someone even more beautiful than me.'[34]

She thus delivers a verdict on our hero which seems to correspond in large measure to the image of this literary figure held by the general public at the time.[35] Gawain is the courtly but uncommitted lover who seems incapable of *amors de cuer* (love from the heart). Kelly sees this as the reason why in the last resort Gawain is not on a par with the other heroes of Arthurian romances.[36] With the Dame del Gaut Destroit as with Maduc le Noir, Gawain again causes the transformation of a good person into a wicked and vengeful one. Both plan to take their revenge on Gawain, and unlike him they do not hesitate to go into action. The third person to have been made unhappy because of Gawain is Raguidel's mistress, who has to wait in vain for a long time before Gawain finally comes to avenge her companion. She has vowed to go around with her clothes the wrong way round and to sit backwards on her horse until that time. Thus Gawain takes a very careless attitude to the feelings of others, although not without eventually having to atone for it. Just as the Dame del Gaut Destroit suffers from unrequited love for him (and she is not the first case that we know of where Gawain initially made promises to a lady and then left her),[37] so in *La Vengeance Raguidel* we are offered for the first time a picture of Gawain, now in love in his turn, being himself scorned and deserted by a woman, his mistress Yde.[38] The great Gawain in person, who could have loved so many noble and

[34] Translated from the author's German rendering of *La Vengeance Raguidel*, line 2345ff.

[35] On one occasion in *La Vengeance Raguidel* (line 1339) Gawain is openly called a *leceor*.

[36] D. Kelly, 'Gauvain and *Fin'Amors* in the Poems of Chrétien de Troyes', *StPh* 67 (1970), 458: 'We find in Gauvain's failures and shortcomings evidence for the superiority of the *chevalier-amant* over the knight pure and simple.'

[37] Other examples are Lunete in *Yvain*, and the girl with the small sleeves or the daughter of the King of Escavalon in *Perceval*.

[38] Yde is not the only lady in *La Vengeance Raguidel* who does not want Gawain as a husband; the daughter of Guengasouain, who is destined by the custom to become Gawain's bride, also reacts in exactly the same way: 'Vos meïsmes a cui je sui / Ne me plaissiés tant com'il fait' (5978–9, 'You yourself to whom I belong do not please me as much as he does').

worthy ladies in the course of his literary development, but who could only ever flirt and who never lost his heart, is punished here in *La Vengeance Raguidel* by Amor, who makes him fall head over heels in love with one of the most unworthy female characters in the whole Arthurian romance tradition, the beautiful but depraved and perfidious Yde.

As mentioned above, this episode, which can be regarded as the central part of the romance, begins with a familiar scene: away to the side of the road Gawain hears a girl crying aloud and lamenting, and he hurries to her aid.[39] No knight can shirk this task; they have to regard it as a sacred duty to lend support to people in distress. It is therefore all the more surprising that on this occasion Gawain's brother Gaheriet earnestly advises him not to help:

'C'est folie! fols, laissiés lor
La damoissele qui est lor,
Venés! de li n'avés que faire,
S'irons porchacier nostre afaire,
Ne devés pas ci arester!'
'Fui toi de ci, laisse moi ester!'
Fait mesire Gavains, 'par foi,
Je n'en lairoie riens por toi!' (3463–70)

('It's madness. Fool, leave that girl to them; she is theirs. Come on! It is none of your business, so let's go and see to our own affairs; you mustn't stop here.' 'Go away and leave me be,' says my lord Gawain, 'in faith, I shall certainly not give up because of you.')

The knights who are ill-treating the girl are not much inclined to fight Gawain over her:

... 'Laissiés le li!
Vos volés vos meller por li?' (3475–6)

('Leave her to him. Do you want to get into a fight over her?')

'Je le vos lais, ce vos afi,'
Fait li chevaliers, 'prendés la!' (3562–3)

('I'll leave her to you, I assure you,' says the knight. 'Take her!')

Thus Gawain acquires Yde like a free gift, and she gives herself to him unhesitatingly:

'Dous amis, mesire Gavains,
A vos me doins, a vos me rent!' (3574–5)

('Dear friend, sweet Sir Gawain, I give myself to you, I am yours!')

[39] See also *Erec et Enide*, line 4280ff.

Just like the Dame del Gaut Destroit, Yde offers herself to Gawain even though she has never seen him before; his reputation as the most courtly of all lovers is sufficient incentive.[40] For his part, Gawain reacts as if he has taken to heart the reproaches of the Dame del Gaut Destroit:

> 'Plains serroie de grant orguel
> Se je refusoie tel don.' (3606–7)

('It would be the height of arrogance for me to refuse such a gift.')

This is because his love for Yde has already been strongly aroused:

> Endementiers li amors nest
> Qui monsignor Gavain sousprist:
> Tos jors ala, tos jors esprist,
> Or l'ainme, or dist qu'amer le veut,
> Or l'ainme il plus quë il ne seut,
> Or l'ainme .i. poi, or l'ainme il mius,
> Or l'ainme autant c'un de ses iols,
> Or l'ainme il bien, ce vuelt qu'il l'aint,
> Or l'ainme, or l'a amors ataint,
> Or l'ainme molt, or l'ainme asés,
> Or l'ainme trop, ja n'iert lasés—
> Ce li est vis—de li amer,
> Or l'ainme il molt sans point d'amer,
> Or l'ainme tant, or croist, or monte,
> Or n'en set nus ne fin ne conte
> Com'il plus l'ainme et plus li plest,
> Ains qu'il issent de la forest
> Fu si ses cuers d'amors soupris
> Qu'il n'i remest fronce ne plis
> Qui ne soit pas tos rasés et plains. (3624–43)

(Meanwhile love was born and took my lord Gawain by surprise. It continued to grow and to burn; now he loves her, and says he wants to love her; now he loves her more than he realized; now he loves her a little, now he loves her more; now he loves her as much as one of his own eyes; now he loves her well and wants to love her; now he loves her and love has seized him; now he loves her much, then completely; now he loves her very much and thinks he will never tire of loving her; now he loves her much without any bitterness; now he loves her so much, his love grows and increases; now no one can tell the story or bring it to an end, for the more she delights him the more he loves her. Before they emerge from the forest his heart has been so overpowered by love

[40] This is reminiscent of the Pucele de Lis in Redaction A of the First Continuation (manuscripts *TVD*): 'Amis, fait ele, en abandon / Vos met mon cors et vos presant. / Vostre serai tot mon vivant' (2702–4, 'Friend,' she says, 'I give and surrender myself to you. I shall be yours all my life').

that there is not a fold or a crease in it that has not been made completely flat and smooth.)

Amor, who punishes all who only flirt or who even make fun of love, has now taken vengeance on Gawain. In this context the anaphora is a means of comic exaggeration; for a public familiar with Gawain's traditional image in literature, the hero is here completely transformed into a figure of fun, especially since we are further informed only a few lines later that he loves Yde much more than she loves him.

After they have spent a night together Gawain takes Yde with him in order to present her at Arthur's court:

Mesire Gavains qui en mainne
Ydain dou Castiel de l'Angarde,
Souvent le voit, souvent l'esgarde,
Sovent l'acole et si le baisse.
Molt estoient andoi a aisse. (3806–10)

(My lord Gawain, who is escorting Yde of Castle Angarde, keeps eyeing her, keeps looking at her, keeps embracing her and kisses her; both are very contented.)

The wording is reminiscent of a similar situation in *Erec et Enide*, and it is probably deliberate that the audience is led to make this association, because in the context of this scene Yde is to be understood as a contrast to Enide's image of courtly perfection:

Because of her excellent character Enide is a worthy object of Erec's love; Yde with her vices of wantonness and hypocrisy is not worthy of Gawain's affection.

The climax of the comparable passage in *Erec* (line 1459ff.) emphasizes the equal rank of both partners, whereas in *La Vengeance Raguidel* the point being underlined is that Gawain loves Yde more than she loves him.

Both knights take their *amies* to Arthur's court in order to present them there. Whilst Enide with her simple dress and her modesty wins everyone's hearts, Yde tries to look particularly magnificent and is only shown respect at court for Gawain's sake.

Whilst Erec does not venture to do more than kiss Enide before the wedding, Gawain and Yde after they met immediately spent the first night together.

Like Enide, Yde carries a sparrowhawk, and at Gawain's bidding she rides in front of him; unlike Enide, however, she does not stay silent but tells him a pack of lies.

Enide remains faithful to Erec even after his supposed death, whereas Yde in her lasciviousness is unfaithful to Gawain at the very first opportunity.

> When Enide is supposed to marry the Count of Limors she resists in every way she can; when Yde is claimed by Druidain as his own she says absolutely nothing to indicate that she would prefer to stay with Gawain.

In this romance Yde turns Gawain from a seducer into a cuckold, in just the way that Kay hoped it would happen to him:

> 'Quë ele vos face wihot
> Tant que soiés de li jalous.' (4096–7)

('May she make a cuckold of you and turn you into a jealous husband.')

For as she is riding with Gawain she notices a knight urinating at the side of the road and at his request she immediately leaves Gawain in the hope of obtaining greater satisfaction from the other. It seems, therefore, that her night of love with the 'perfect lover' has not left her with a particularly good impression of his virility.[41]

The author of *La Vengeance Raguidel* has used the Yde episode to parody the corresponding passage in *Erec et Enide*.[42] However, the parody is not directed against Chrétien as an author for his works or his style; here, as almost invariably in the thirteenth century, it is directed against a literary tradition. In the new work the parody of a single episode, which in content is quite unrelated to the figure of Gawain, has been incorporated into a parody of Gawain's traditional image. Within *La Vengeance Raguidel* it is not an isolated case of creating the effect of parody for the audience, but fits smoothly into the overall atmosphere of the work, for we have seen that Gawain is ridiculed not only as a lover but also as a knight errant, and here specifically as an avenger, since he forgets the instrument of vengeance when he sets off, and after delay and disobedience with respect to the prophecy can only carry out his commission of vengeance with Yder's assistance.

This leaves the question as to which technique of characterization the author employs in order to make his hero fail at every opportunity. Gawain's behaviour invariably conforms to the courtly code of conduct. He sets out in search of *aventure*, fulfils the norms of *fin'amor* and defeats the wicked Guengasouain; however, in so doing he only ever follows the letter of courtly requirements without understanding the spirit behind them. He sets off in haste on his quest but forgets the means by which he can prevail in that *aventure*; he does

[41] This scene is generally regarded as the most improper in the whole of French Arthurian literature; see A. Micha, 'Miscellaneous French Romances in Verse', in *ALMA*, p. 365.

[42] The abduction scene from *Lancelot* is also parodied in *La Vengeance Raguidel*: Druidain is not fearsome like Meleagant, but has a childish simplicity, whilst Yde unlike Guinevere is not a worthy object for a self-sacrificing *queste*. In the end Gawain bestows Yde on Druidain because he is glad to be rid of her, whilst in *Lancelot* the hero and Gawain bring the queen back to court.

eventually reach his destination, but only after dawdling for so long that it is almost too late. He loves with exemplary devotion, but has chosen the wrong lady; instead of reacting with understanding, as Durmart does, the experience makes him a woman-hater. He overcomes his opponent, but without his magic weapons the latter is no fitting adversary for 'the best knight in the world'. Gawain is nevertheless proud of his victory and allows himself to be fêted by the Arthurian court.

Each of Gawain's experiences is shown to be essentially hollow; he seems to lack insight into the fundamentals of life, yet the courtly norms can only be fulfilled to perfection if they are not divorced from the insights of human experience or the requirements of the individual situation.[43] In *La Vengeance Raguidel* Gawain is the opposite of a courtly knight, and it is significant that precisely this hero was chosen for such a role. He is a failure all along the line, in other words an anti-hero. Kay's scornful remarks about him can be seen as representative of public reaction to this portrayal of Gawain as the object of parody. This time, for once, Kay's mockery is more than justified:

> 'Certes, je ne m'en vul atendre
> En vos de faire la vengance...
> Si laissiés la vengance ester,
> Vos n'i poés rien conquester
> Fors honte et vilenie et paine!
> Chevaliers qui s'amie mainne
> Ne doit pas tel fes comencier.' (4418–25)

('I certainly don't want to rely on you to take vengeance... Give up the vengeance, you'll get nothing from it except shame and dishonour and suffering. A knight who has his mistress in tow shouldn't start on deeds like that.')

The author of *La Vengeance Raguidel* has two main concerns. His comic style of presentation does not preclude a hidden didactic element in the work, for he wants to show that a knight like Gawain, who is neither ready for nor capable of true love, cannot have any success in *chevalerie* either. In addition he wants to create an image to contrast with the colourless and excessively idealized Gawain figure of the early Arthurian romances, parodying it by means of an ironic exaggeration both of Gawain's conventional features and of his weaknesses.

A parody demands a witty and very gifted narrator; that may explain why this particular literary possibility was not employed more frequently in the course of the genre's evolution.[44] Parodying Gawain's traditional image can be seen as

[43] This viewpoint in *La Vengeance Raguidel* is reminiscent of *Meraugis*.
[44] Distinctly satirical elements are to be found in the majority of the shorter narratives.

a most original solution to the problem of writing about this particular character, although Gawain is also especially well suited to being subjected to parody; he is one of the best-known figures in the Arthurian sphere alongside Kay and Arthur himself, and is even more popular than either of them. His name is generally associated with the concept of perfect chivalry, and his good qualities are known to all. These are the most important preconditions for the success of a Gawain parody.

La Vengeance Raguidel represents a turning-point in the development of the Gawain tradition, and constitutes an exception within the evolution of the genre of verse romance. The prose romances take the negative stylization still further. Yet the parody of Gawain is not a late phenomenon within the tradition, but only one of several possible reactions to the traditional literary image of this hero. Gawain is the literary figure that arouses the greatest level of interest amongst narrators and their public; the fragments of a verse romance dealing with Gawain's childhood and youth are further evidence of this. Whereas in the earlier Arthurian romances his role rendered him inevitably one of the least colourful characters, in the course of the genre's evolution he becomes the most glittering and complex personality of the Arthurian verse romances. Perfect knight, failure, idol of women and rejected lover, helper and brute, guardian of morality and murderer—his colourful image could scarcely be more diverse. Initially the positive assessment of the hero still dominates in the public mind, despite the repeated tarnishing of his image. He is also seen by many Arthurian scholars as the embodiment of the essential knightly and courtly virtues, and when they adopt Chrétien's explicit comments on Gawain uncritically they are then often deaf to the discordant note which is already sounded by the first Arthurian poet in spite of all his extravagant praise, but which is even more common amongst his successors.[45] The two basic attributes of 'perfect knight' and 'perfect lover', which have shaped Gawain's literary career from Wace onwards, remain constant right through to the end of the genre's development.

[45] Positive assessments are to be found in W. A. Nitze, 'The Character of Gauvain in the Romances of Chrétien de Troyes', *MPh* 50 (1952/3), 219–25, Charles Foulon, 'Le rôle de Gauvain dans *Erec et Enide*', *Annales de Bretagne* 65 (1958), 147–58, and Frappier, 'Le personnage de Gauvain'. Kelly, 'Gauvain et *Fin'Amors*', is relatively unusual in pointing out a contradiction in the personality of this literary character (p. 458): 'Not that Gauvain and his values are evil or wrong; but they possess obvious limitations when compared with what the values of a Lancelot and an Yvain permit these two knights to achieve.' Negative traits in the character of Gawain occur in three Chrétien romances. In *Yvain* he is the cause of the hero's separation from Laudine and thus ultimately of the entire sequence of unhappy events in the romance. In *Lancelot* he achieves nothing in his search for Guinevere, in other words he is unsuccessful, and on top of that he even takes a pathetic tumble into the water and has to be rescued by others. In *Perceval* he is the victim of unexplained misunderstandings and is repeatedly the object of a hatred which from the reader's point of view appears to be unmotivated.

These are the constant features of a literary stereotype, one of which, the knightly aspect, is universally accepted and therefore, although always brought into play, has only a minor role; by contrast the other characteristic is called into question and extensively developed. In almost all romances of the Gawain group, doubts are cast upon his status as perfect lover; thus the focal point changes in the thirteenth century. Gawain as a model of chivalry is not a particularly interesting concept for the audiences of the later Arthurian verse romances. In the prose romances the ethical values he represents are widely negated. Here they are called into question and subjected to doubt. An increasing alienation from the concept of perfect chivalry goes hand in hand with the humanization of Arthurian characters in the sense of emphasizing their human weaknesses, thus bridging the gap between them and the average person.

5

Old *matiere*, new *sens*: innovations in thought and content

It is characteristic of the authors of *Meraugis*, *Fergus* and *Durmart* that their works continually make deliberate references to Chrétien's Arthurian romances; thus it is equally true for thirteenth-century readers and for modern commentators that the three later texts cannot be properly understood unless seen against the background of the Arthurian romances that preceded them. The authors presuppose that their public is familiar with even the details of Chrétien's works; it is only on this premiss that they can be fully effective in the presentation of their own attitudes, their carefully considered insertions of motifs and scenes, their playful handling of familiar *matiere* and also their criticism of the earlier author, both implicit and explicit. Persistent allusions to the pattern of expectations predetermined by Chrétien's works create a specific kind of generic development going beyond mere similarities of form and content.

All three romances bear witness to a renewed flowering of Arthurian verse romances in the period up to about 1250, a trend more conspicuous in terms of the quality rather than the quantity of the output. Some decades after Chrétien's death a series of gifted authors undertook the attempt to put new impetus into the genre of Arthurian romance in verse, which in the meantime had either confined itself to shorter lays and episodic continuations of an older work, or had abdicated its dominant position in favour of romances in prose. These thirteenth-century innovations in the verse romances are just as evident in the content as they are in the *sens* or the form. The conflicting requirements of the individual and society, of *amour* and *chevalerie*, already central themes in Chrétien's works, are now presented in a different light. The problem of *cortoisie* in particular is given greater emphasis than before in *Gliglois* and *Meraugis*, yet the Arthurian court retains scarcely more than a subordinate role; the scenes located there betray the formal principles inherent in the norms of the genre rather than any organic relationship of their narrative content to its *sens*.

Here as in *Yder*, the realization of the individual and the personal development of the hero are the foremost areas of interest, and are no longer directly dependent on recognition by the Arthurian community. Didactic considerations also have a certain part to play. Battle scenes are increasingly subject to ethical demands: they no longer set out to prove knightly courage, but demonstrate instead the hero's capacity for love and perfect *cortoisie*. Thus the plot is primarily a romantic narrative with the aim of drawing both protagonists closer together, in accordance with the principle of complete equality, and concluding with the wedding of the lovers. The crisis, in the form of the loss of the beloved and usually without the accompaniment of any intermediate Arthurian scene, is the formal basis for a bipartite structure. The crisis affects not only the hero but his beloved as well, whereas the Round Table has no part in it.

MERAUGIS: EXTENDING THE CONCEPT OF *CORTOISIE*

Unlike most of the other authors of verse romances, we have more information about the author of *Meraugis* than merely his name. Huon de Mery names him in one breath with Chrétien, and both are accorded an elevated position in the *Tornoiement Antecrist*: 'C'onques bouche de crestïen / Ne dist si bien com il disoient' (1336–7, 'No Christian ever wrote as well as they did'). Around 1225 both are regarded as unattainable models, especially in terms of their language and style: '[apres eus] n'ont rien guerpi' (1341, 'they left nothing for their successors to do'). The fact that Raoul de Houdenc was a gifted author is substantiated by more than just this quotation; there are also two more of his works that have come down to us. These are allegorical poems, the *Roman des Ailes* (Romance of the Wings) and the *Songe d'Enfer* (Dream of Hell); the latter is probably his last work, composed around 1214/15.[1] Fourrier has attempted a historical identification of this author, and although he is very cautious in formulating his suggestion that Raoul de Houdenc can be identified with Radufus de Hosdenc, from Hosdenc near Beauvais, the hypothesis is nevertheless thoroughly convincing.[2] This would make Raoul de Houdenc a knight of inferior rank who had influential relatives and came from the same area as Huon de Mery. The last documentary reference to him bears the date October 1220. He was born around 1165–70, and probably died between 1221 and 1230.

[1] For more on Raoul's works see V. Kundert-Forrer, *Raoul de Houdenc, ein französischer Erzähler des XIII. Jahrhunderts* (Berne, 1960).

[2] A. Fourrier, 'Raoul de Hodenc: est-ce lui?', in *Mélanges M. Delbouille*, edited by J. Renson (Vol. I) and M. Tyssens (Vol. II), 2 vols (Gembloux, 1964), Vol. II, pp. 165–93.

Thus Raoul de Houdenc was a younger contemporary of Chrétien. It is possibly less true for him than for other later authors in subsequent phases of the genre that Chrétien's works were felt to be authoritative, requiring unquestioning acceptance. Raoul is a poet of considerable talent, and whilst he does allow himself certain borrowings from his predecessor in his Arthurian romance, it is also characteristic of him to transform Arthurian romance motifs already well-known from Chrétien's works, sometimes even deliberately reversing their significance. This implies an independent and critical attitude towards the older poet; in many respects he gives the impression of being a pupil of Chrétien's who wants to go his own way with what he has learned.

This duly results in *Meraugis* being even less like the usual kind of Arthurian romance than others of the genre. In fact, for those commentators accustomed to visualizing the genre in terms of constant features, it represents at first a confusing conglomerate of the usual and the unusual in its themes, motifs and patterns of meaning. It is therefore not surprising that the work has even been criticized for a lack of consistency in its execution.[3] However, it would appear that the meaning and purpose of this romance are especially difficult to grasp precisely when commentators measure it rigorously against the well-known representatives of the genre with which they are familiar (in other words, Chrétien's romances), and then judge the work simply according to its degree of convergence with or divergence from those texts.

Meraugis is an Arthurian romance of a quite individual type for the reason that it makes use of Arthurian *matiere* for its motifs and characters, but at the same time it does not in every context meet the requirements set by Chrétien's works in terms of *sens*. Thus, for example, even in this relatively early romance the concept of love clearly outweighs that of chivalry or of benefiting society. As the genre requires, Meraugis' journey of adventure begins at Arthur's court and leads back to it in the end, but he is acting in the interests of the court only in so far as he releases Gawain from a difficult situation. The adventure of the Ile sanz non (Island without a name), which exhibits motifs strongly reminiscent of the Joie de la Cort (Joy of the Court) in *Erec*, is not turned to the advantage of the community as in *Erec*, but benefits only Gawain himself, whilst the evil custom lives on. Meraugis, initially unaware of whom he is rescuing, fights primarily to give proof of his love for Lidoine. That is probably also the reason why the Arthurian court scarcely takes cognizance of this act of deliverance. The only consequence of the aid accorded to Gawain is that having been released he is enabled in turn to come to the aid of Meraugis when the latter finds himself in difficulties.

[3] See the introduction to Friedwagner's edition, p. 69, and Gaston Paris, 'Romans en vers', p. 236.

The plot of *Meraugis* starts with an unfamiliar motif for an Arthurian romance: two inseparable friends, Gorvain Cadruz and Meraugis, simultaneously fall in love with the beautiful Lidoine. On the other hand, this rivalry between the two friends is not, as Micha supposes,[4] the central theme, but only the initial trigger for the action, and the friendship breaks up over Lidoine. The motif helps to pose an exercise in casuistry: Gorvain loves Lidoine because of her agreeable external appearance (*beauté*) and would still love her even if she were the devil in person, a ghost or a serpent. Meraugis on the other hand values Lidoine's inner qualities (*valor* and *cortoisie*); his heart would still be hers even if she were 'baucenz ou noire / Ou fauve' (610–11, 'dappled, black or tawny'). On the other hand, if she did not possess *cortoisie* she could be another thousand times more beautiful without his finding her at all agreeable.

The quarrel leads to a bitter duel between the friends. Lidoine puts an end to the confrontation by referring the dispute to Arthur's court, where there is to be a *jugement* to which all the parties involved must submit. Until that time she puts both contestants under an obligation to go in search of *aventure* and 'de pris conquerre' (802, 'to win fame').

The frame of reference of the genre might have led one to expect an account of two sequences of *aventure*, designed to reveal who is to win the contest by the quality of the adventures they withstand on the way. However, the reality is entirely different; instead Raoul proceeds without digression to a description of the *jugement*. Guinevere and the ladies of her court announce their verdict in favour of Meraugis. They give as their reasoning that *beauté* and *cortoisie* are actually unthinkable one without the other: 'Li uns sanz l'autre ne vaut rien' (962, 'the one is worthless without the other'), but because beauty alone often results only in pride and arrogance, the prize should go to the admirer of *cortoisie*:

> ...amor doit cortoisie amer...
> Donc aime Meraugis a droit;
> Qu'il l'aime por sa cortoisie. (1016–19)

(...love should love courtliness...thus Meraugis loves properly since he loves her for her courtliness.)

However, Gorvain proves to be in total disagreement with this most chivalrous decision; in fact, he rages against the injustice of the court: '...en ceste cort clochent li droit' (1110, 'in this court the laws are lame'). But even Meraugis is still a long way from the fulfilment of his wishes, for Lidoine imposes the condition that he is first to prove himself and show himself worthy of her. At

[4] Micha, 'Miscellaneous French Romances', p. 373.

the end of a year she intends to decide whether or not she can grant this passionate admirer her favour in return:

> Selonc ce que j'avrai oï
> De lui bien dire, itant vos di
> D'itant avra le guerredon:
> Ou lors li ferai .I. beau don,
> Ou lors m'avra dou tot perdue. (1145–9)

(I assure you that his reward shall be in accordance with what good I hear of him. At that time either I shall give him a fine gift or he will have entirely lost me.)

Lidoine fulfils the role of *dame* in every respect. She is rich and independent, and holds sway over a country of her own, which she rules with justice and circumspection. She is not ready to give her hand to the first person who happens to woo her. The authority which she is both determined and accustomed to exercise manifests itself with abundant clarity in her manner of speaking. She begins almost all her speeches with 'ne vueil', 'ne voudroie', 'einsi me plest', 'por ce vueil gié', 'vos comant'[5] ('It is not my wish', 'I should not wish', 'It is my pleasure', 'Therefore it is my wish', 'I command you') and similar turns of phrase. Moreover she is the embodiment of *cortoisie*. The author illustrates the effect of this characteristic by means of comic exaggeration:

> S'en la damoisele ot beauté,
> Plus i ot sens et plus bonté;
> Qu'ele fu dou tot si cortoise
> Qu'environ li a une toise
> N'avoit se cortoisie non.
> Pucele estoit de grant renon
> Et escole de bien aprendre.
> Environ li peüst l'en prendre
> Totes les honors a plain poing,
> Et les puceles de mout loing,
> De Cornoaille et d'Engleterre,
> La venoient par non requerre
> Por veoir et oïr parler.
> Toz li monz i soloit aler
> A si cortois pelerinage;
> Car la pucele estoit si sage
> Que ja si cortois n'i parlast
> Qui plus cortois ne s'en alast
> S'il vousist ses diz retenir.

[5] Lines 753, 772, 782, 792 and 795.

A cel tens la sieut l'en tenir
Por la plus gentil damoisele.
S'ele ert gentiz et preuz et bele,
Parmi tot ce fu el si digne;
Car qui de li veoir se digne,
Ja le jor ne li mescheïst,
Non, par mon chief! nes s'il cheïst
D'autresi haut com un clochier;
Ja por ce n'esteüst clochier
Puis qu'il l'eüst le jor veüe. (111–39)

(If the damsel had beauty, she had even more good sense and kindness. She was in all things so courtly that there could be nothing but courtliness within a yard of her. She was a maiden of great reputation and a school for fine manners. In her vicinity all that was honourable could be gathered by the handful, and indeed maidens from far away came seeking her, from Cornwall and England, to see her and to hear her talk. Everyone used to make this courtly pilgrimage. For the maiden was so wise that no one, however courtly, spoke to her without going away even more courtly, if he took to heart what she said. At that time she was by common consent the most noble of damsels. If she was noble and high-born and beautiful, all these qualities made her a person of great worth; for anyone who did himself the honour of seeing her could not suffer any misfortune for the rest of that day. No, upon my life, not even if he fell from as high as a bell tower. That would not prevent him walking away unhurt because he had seen her that day.)

Lidoine's relationship with Meraugis is at first confined to her gracious acceptance of his service. By setting her conditions, she makes it possible for him to demonstrate the extent of his love and his endurance. She makes the granting of her affection dependent on '...s'il fet ce qu'a chevalier / Afiert a fere por s'amie' (1134–5, 'whether he does what a knight undertakes to do for his mistress'). In the event that Meraugis should fail to live up to expectations, she regards herself as free of any obligations towards him. However, when it comes to the journey itself on which the young knight has to prove himself, she is not inclined to be dependent on the reports of others:

'Et neporquant mieuz me puet plere
La proece s'ele est en lui
Par mon veoir que par autrui.
C'est voirs, en ce n'a que redire:
Savoir vaut mieuz que oïr dire.' (1380–4)

('And nevertheless I can gain more pleasure by seeing for myself rather than through the eyes of someone else the prowess that he may possess. It is true and cannot be contradicted: knowledge is worth more than hearsay.')

Even the outward circumstances of this incipient relationship between the principal characters bear all the marks of a feudal relationship between lord and vassal. *Dame* and *chevalier* arrange what amounts to a contract, publicly witnessed by the Arthurian community at large (line 1151) and sealed with a kiss as the official act of seisin:

> ... Lors fu li besiers
> Donez. Voire sanz nul arrest
> Dist Lidoine: 'Je vos revest
> De m'amor si com je devis.' (1160–3)

(Then the kiss was given. And in truth Lidoine said without hesitation: 'I invest you with my love on the terms that I have just stated.')

When the Gawain adventure is announced shortly afterwards, Meraugis duly behaves as one who has no will other than that of his mistress; he says to Arthur:

> 'Sire, se ma dame plesoit,
> Li chevaliers ma dame iroit
> En ceste queste; priez li.' (1355–7)

('Sire, if it pleased my lady, my lady's knight would go on this quest; beseech her.')

Lidoine is in agreement with Meraugis' wish, although she voices her desire to accompany him. Meraugis is astonished but submits to her will without questioning it:

> Li chevaliers respont aprés:
> 'Vos portez la trieve et la pes,
> Que poez vos plus demander?
> Il ne vos faut que comander,
> Ja ne vos desdirai de rien.' (1367–71)

(Afterwards the knight replies: 'The truce and the peace is yours. What more could you ask? You have only to command, for I shall never disobey you in anything.')

However, Lidoine's relationship with Meraugis has already undergone one decisive change, against her will and not in the way that she had expected. Her whole philosophy of life together with her role as the dominant courtly lady in a one-sided amorous relationship are called into question by the fact that on the occasion of the feudal kiss the flame of love already burning in Meraugis quite suddenly spreads to her as well. Since she now no longer wants to be parted from him (and not merely, as she pretends, because she wishes to observe his deeds of arms with her own eyes), she changes her mind and wants to accompany her beloved on his journey. She already regrets having imposed the one-year delay. Raoul's linguistic and psychological skills are fully demonstrated in his very impressive account of the effect of this kiss upon Lidoine (lines 1164–1254). As he reflects on the events he skilfully involves his audience. Rhetorical questions, exclamations, the use of direct and reported speech, and the introduction both of outlandish metaphors and of a simultaneous irony directed against this procedure—all these contribute to the success of an extremely lively and yet utterly artistic section of narrative poetry which is in no way inferior to Chrétien's poetic writing at its very best, as the following brief example shows:

> Lors, einsi come por taster,
> Le feri des ieuz une foiz.
> Et amor se fiert en la roiz.—
> Queus roiz? Qu'apel je roiz?—Les ieuz.—
> Et donc nes sai je nomer mieuz?—
> Nenil.—Por quoi?—L'en voit au cors
> Que li oeil peschent les amors.
> Par tant poez des ieuz aprendre
> Que c'est la roiz as amors prendre. (1222–30)

(Then, tentatively, she darted one glance at him with her eyes, and love plunged into the net. What net? What am I calling a net? The eyes. And yet, can I not find a better name for them? Not at all. Why not? We can see that within the body it is the eyes that go fishing for love. Thus you can learn something about the eyes, namely that they are the net for catching love.)[6]

Raoul has certainly been learning from Chrétien here. But is the adoption of one author's stylistic innovations by another to be equated in every case with an uncritical inability to create anything new? In this instance Raoul has not merely copied Chrétien's mannerisms; instead he has embraced the linguistic initiative of his predecessor in order to apply and perfect it with supreme irony. Amongst the authors of Arthurian verse romances he is the only one to have succeeded in reaching Chrétien's level in terms of style; in this respect Huon de Méry's verdict is still accepted even today. The charge of preciosity that has been levelled against him does not seem to be justified.[7] It would be nearer the mark to say that he plays with the concept of preciosity, just as he does with other stylistic devices and clichés such as the catalogue of beauty, and with just as

[6] The fishing metaphor already occurs in Andreas Capellanus. Raoul de Houdenc's customary way of working leads us to suspect that this passage is an ironic allusion to the metaphors of that treatise on love, or indeed of *Artes amandi* in general.

[7] Micha, 'Miscellaneous French Romances', p. 373; see also Kundert-Forrer's reference to rhetorical acrobatics (*Raoul de Houdenc*, p. 79) and Friedwagner's use of 'Spitzfindigkeit' ('sophistry'; p. LXIX of his edition).

much self-confidence as he employs in his treatment of the *matiere de Bretagne*, without subjecting himself to the rigours of Arthurian formulas.

In *Cligés* Chrétien had combined the Byzantine romance with the Arthurian. Raoul's capacity for innovation *vis-à-vis* the specimens of the genre already in existence before the composition of *Meraugis* manifests itself amongst other things in his combining Arthurian *matiere* with a kind of *roman à thèse*, in this instance a discussion of the niceties of love. There are also elements of the Byzantine romances of destiny creeping into his work, for example in the separation of the lovers by the malice of Fate. From time to time *Erec* and *Yvain* have also been called *romans à thèse*,[8] but *Meraugis* differs from them in that the points for discussion are here explicitly formulated and analysed, and a decision is reached. However, the amalgam of the two kinds of romance did not create any great following within the genre, where the other works all adhere to the pattern for the opening of an Arthurian romance that has already been outlined. What is Raoul hoping to achieve with his unusual and not very 'Arthurian' opening section? It seems as though he wants to make clear that matters of love cannot be decided by a tribunal; on the other hand, this does not mean that their decision is necessarily wrong. Love, however, concerns only those involved, the couple themselves. Raoul is also interested in demonstrating that the Provençal concept of *fin'amor*, which is paraded with great emphasis for the first thousand lines or so, is doomed to failure the moment true love affecting both partners becomes involved. Thus the romance has been constructed on this level as the story of two courtly people, where the man works his way up in the course of his experiences and his personal development to the level and social standing of the lady, whereas the superior lady is moved by her acquiring insights into the nature of love (which has nothing in common with the aloofness imposed by a feudal relationship), as well as by her experience of suffering, to descend from her exaggeratedly lofty position. At the end of the narrative a potentially happy partnership is achieved only by both parties drawing closer to each other. In much the same way as with Erec and Enide, their setting out together on their journey is thus simultaneously a prerequisite for arriving at this goal and also the means to achieve it.

In the course of his adventures the hero Meraugis undergoes an astonishing development which can be seen as his progress to maturity. Deeds of arms, whilst not without their importance, play only a secondary role in this development. The tournament at the beginning of the romance was already sufficient proof that Meraugis was one of the best (lines 355 and 464), and

[8] For example Wendelin Foerster uses the term 'Thesenroman', *Kristian von Troyes. Wörterbuch zu seinen sämtlichen Werken, Romanische Bibliothek* 21 (Halle, 1914), pp. 43–4.

therefore in all probability it is not the attainment of perfection in this sphere that Lidoine expects of him. Rather she seems to sense that Meraugis, although amiable and good-natured, is too shy and lacking in self-confidence, and especially so when compared with Gorvain Cadruz. One of the ways this is revealed is in his readiness to submit to Lidoine herself. The difference in character between Meraugis and Gorvain is clearly brought out; in contrast to Meraugis' friendly attitude, Gorvain immediately adopts a stance of irreconcilable hatred towards his friend and rival when he learns of his love for the same woman. Gorvain Cadruz is the reckless type, and within minutes he manages to avow his newly-awakened love to Lidoine and demand her for himself. Meraugis, on the other hand, is so overwhelmed by his new feelings that the sight of Lidoine leaves him speechless:

> Voirs, il est si d'amors espris
> Enfin qu'il n'i a que redire.
> Ja Deu ne place s'il puet dire
> Sol tant qu'il demandast congié;
> Mes com home qui a songié
> Remest toz pris en mi la voie.
> Dou cuer et des ieuz la convoie,
> Qu'il n'a pooir d'aler avant. (506–13)

(In truth, he is finally so overwhelmed by love that there is no denying it. As God is my witness he cannot say one word, not even so much as to take his leave. But like a man who has been dreaming he remains in a daze in the middle of the road. He escorts her with his heart and eyes for he lacks the power to move any further.)

This facet of the hero's character, which includes indecision, credulity, shyness and a lack of independence, is dismantled in the course of his adventures without losing the positive aspects of such characteristics. The hero's journey falls into two sections, with the break coming at line 3440 when the lovers are separated by a misunderstanding. Up to this point virtually all the adventures that Meraugis embarks upon are characterized by one unusual feature; he intends to do good, but every good deed unfailingly brings trouble in its wake. Dishonour ensues from an honourable impulse, and *honor* is transformed into *honte* (shame). The relationship between *honte* and *honor*, involving both the desire for honour and the fear of disgrace, is thematic in the first part of the work and determines all the hero's actions.

It seems as if Meraugis is constantly being led up the garden path and made fun of because he is too unsure of himself to be taken seriously. A dwarf and an old lady enlist him for their purposes, abuse him thoroughly and make promises which they do not keep. The inhabitants of the Esplumeor Merlin, from whom he had been assured of help and advice when he set off, simply laugh in his face when he enquires about Gawain. When he asks for information as to where he can find the Esplumeor Merlin they ridicule him for not knowing that he is standing right in front of it. Whilst Meraugis strives to be a model knight, his opponent Outredouté makes no pretence of keeping to the fundamental rules of chivalrous behaviour; Meraugis had not allowed for that and only gradually realizes it. The hero can no longer make sense of the world; although he makes every effort to appear pleasant and helpful, nothing turns out right for him, and yet he cannot understand where he is going wrong. The feeling of powerlessness confuses him totally, and he repeatedly expresses his growing insecurity:

> Cil qui entent qu'il est gabez
> Respont: 'Hui mes ne sai je rien,
> Mes je cuidai fere mout bien.' (1584–6)

(Realizing that he is being mocked, he replies: 'Now it seems I know nothing, but I thought I was doing the right thing at the time.')

> 'Deus, tant m'en poise! C'est par moi
> Que cil dieus est, ne je ne voi
> Par quoi j'en puisse oïr noveles.' (1599–1601)

('God knows it grieves me very much. That sorrow has come about because of me, and yet I do not see how I can find out about it.')

> Li chevaliers s'est corrociez
> Et dit: 'Or sui je maneciez,
> Si ne sai de cui ne por quoi.' (1627–9)

(The knight grows angry and says: 'Now I am being threatened and I don't know why or by whom.')

It happens again and again that Meraugis cannot grasp what people are intending to do to him. His uncertainty is expressed in the great variety of ways in which he states his ignorance: 'ne sai je rien', 'je ne voi', 'ne sai', 'Or sui je maneciez', 'Or sui je fous', 'Vos me donez si ne sai quoi', 'est ce gabois', 'Or sai, por fol me tient / Cele qui ci m'a fet venir. / Hé! Deus, que porrai devenir! /... / Qui me conseillera? Ne sai' (1585, 'I know nothing'; 1600, 'I don't see'; 1629, 'I don't know'; 1628, 'now I am being threatened'; 2290, 'now I am mad'; 2350, 'I don't know what you are giving me'; 2709, 'is this a joke?'; 2734ff., 'now I know that the lady who sent me here thinks I am mad. Alas, God, what will become of me?... Who will advise me? I don't know.')

Whilst Meraugis finds himself helplessly at the mercy of most of the situations in the first part of his sequence of adventures, despite never infringing the established rules of *cortoisie*, the picture changes in the second part. On the occasion of Gawain's rescue, which, in line with the thematic pattern just outlined for the first part, has to result in the separation from Lidoine (punishment instead of reward), the hero comes increasingly to realize that he can often only extract himself from difficult situations by using cunning. *Chevalerie* and *cortoisie* come into conflict with one another. Where nothing further can be achieved by force of arms and the rules of the chivalric code of behaviour, then knowledge of people and inventiveness can help. Thus he releases Gawain and himself from the clutches of the lady of the island first by pretending to be dead and then by dressing in ladies' clothing, 'Plus acesmez qu'une popine' (3340, 'prettier than a doll'), thus outwitting the guards, who think he is their mistress. At this stage of his spiritual development it is possible for the hero to defeat his opponent Outredouté, a success which eluded him before his separation from Lidoine. Later he frees (and wins) Lidoine with the help of another clever stratagem: her abductors are unaware of which side he is on, and he talks them into swearing feudal allegiance to him so that at the decisive moment he can order them what to do; they cannot refuse without infringing the law, and have to make the best of a bad job.

Before the works of Raoul de Houdenc there were no cunning heroes in Arthurian romance.[9] Raoul exemplifies through his heroes the view that not all problems can be solved by strength or by courage in battle; on the contrary, employing such powers uncritically can frequently entail *honte*. In many instances the qualities of intelligence and humanity are to be given precedence, and these virtues are not to be pushed into the background by an interpretation of chivalry based purely on courage and strength. Perfect *chevalerie* and total *cortoisie* involve the use of whichever means are appropriate for each situation. Thus the development of the hero is presented as the route along which the naive and credulous youth becomes an experienced and cautious man, combining all the positive characteristics of one who is both courtly and chivalrous.

Lidoine also undergoes a development. At the beginning of the narrative she still pulls all the strings; she is self-confident and superior, a mistress in the *fin'amor* sense. She exercises *signorie* (lordship), and sometimes in the early stages it even looks as though she is orchestrating her companion's quest for adventure herself, with the dwarf as her agent. Everything proceeds according to expectations as far as the crossroads, but here she loses her commanding view

[9] Tristan bears some of the hallmarks of the cunning hero; Chrétien probably has no concept as yet of a conflict between *cortoisie* and *chevalerie*. Arthurian romance in Germany develops a comparable image of the knight in *Daniel vom blühenden Tal*. Lunete and Enide are corresponding examples of female characters.

of the situation; she is just as much at a loss as Meraugis, and from here onwards, in total contrast to her behaviour at the beginning of the romance, she submits unreservedly to the decisions of her beloved. Spiritually, both protagonists have reached a low ebb; their understanding of the world is shattered, their disorientation absolute. Meraugis now has to take over responsibility. Whereas previously he has always unthinkingly obeyed the promptings of others, following the commands of Lidoine, the dwarf or the old woman, he now sees himself forced to make a decision for himself and choose one of the three ways:

> 'Qu'en diroie? A la parclose
> Choisir m'estuet, ce covient mon.
> Dame,' fet il, 'Quel la feron?'
> 'Ne sai.' 'Comment? Si ne savez?'
> 'Je non,' fet ele, 'mes alez
> Ou que ce soit, je vos siurai.'
> Il li respont: 'Dame, j'irai
> Cele sanz non; einsi me plest...' (2790–7)

('What shall I say? In the end I have to choose, and that is what I must do. Lady', he says, 'which way shall we go?' 'I don't know.' 'What? You really don't know?' 'Not I', she says, 'but go any way at all, I shall follow you.' He answers her: 'Lady, I shall take the way without a name; that is the one that appeals to me...')

At this point Lidoine abandons her claim to superiority. The unexpected adventure plunges her into misfortune, and the false report of Meraugis' death punishes her for having wanted at first to be too much of a *dame* and not enough of an *amie*. The separation is a testing period, bringing Lidoine to a concept of love which no longer has anything in common with doctrines in the Provençal mould. She has to progress from her initially lofty and distant bearing to a spontaneous humanity which makes it possible for her to love Meraugis even when his head has been shaved bald and he is sick and ugly. In this scene (line 4901ff.) it becomes clear that the discussion about the value of inner and outward beauty and about the relationship between *beauté* and *cortoisie* runs through the whole work and is not confined to the opening section. When Lidoine catches sight of the sick Meraugis in all his ugliness, and love flares up in her again for the one she had believed to be already dead, it becomes obvious that she loves his soul more than his body—and that therefore she loves him in the same way as he loves her. *Cortoisie* and *amor* triumph over *beauté*.

This personal insight and the change of heart which it entails distinguish Lidoine very sharply from the usual image of the hero's female partner in Arthurian romances. In this case she is not merely a parallel or subordinate entity serving as a necessary adjunct of the genre; instead she develops a life of her own, thereby acquiring a new importance within the romance as a whole. Both partners have to move closer to each other, and Raoul's romance is concerned with showing how that happens.

There is much in Lidoine's initial behaviour as a superior lady which is reminiscent of the problematical issues in *Yvain*. It is possible that Raoul is thereby resurrecting a theme which his predecessor had already addressed, although Chrétien had treated it with different points of emphasis and had resolved it in a different way. The decisive distinction seems to lie in the fact that Laudine is a rather static figure by comparison with Lidoine. Perhaps the similarity in the names is intended to indicate a thematic analogy. On the other hand, Lidoine also has many of Enide's characteristics, and indeed finds herself placed in similar situations to Enide's, so that one is led to suspect that Raoul wanted his female protagonist to combine the virtues of both her predecessors, whilst expurgating through her own spiritual development the more negative manifestations of their characters (Laudine being too superior and Enide too passive).

The romance of *Meraugis* exhibits a causal relationship between the individual adventures; this too distinguishes it from most of the other representatives of the genre. Almost every *aventure* arises from the preceding one, although not in a logical fashion, but in a way that is equally surprising for both protagonists and public. Because Meraugis wants to help the dwarf he provokes the wrath of the old woman; his desire to mollify the old woman arouses the anger of Outredouté; because he wants to justify himself to the latter his messenger loses an eye; because he has to avenge this offence, he pursues Outredouté; having managed to kill him, he is so highly esteemed by Lidoine's abductors that they swear the oath of allegiance to him. The causal sequence thus produced is quite unusual in Arthurian romance, and it can safely be said of this romance that the adventures cannot be interchanged at will, since they have a clear function in the overall pattern of meaning.[10] So far this has been suggested only tentatively for other romances, even Chrétien's.

Because of the links with other types of romance and the use of motifs unfamiliar to the genre, the Arthurian element is reduced to a peripheral position. Meraugis is already a member of the Round Table before the action begins, but this fact is irrelevant to the way the action proceeds. Only the most

[10] Even Kundert-Forrer does not believe that the succession of adventures is random, although she is of the opinion that the connections are limited to thematic correspondences. She lists the themes in question as aimlessness, self-assurance, immoderation (cruelty and arbitrariness) and covetousness (*Raoul de Houdenc*, p. 84).

fundamental Arthurian characters make their appearance (Arthur, Gawain, Kay, Calogrenant, Guinevere and Melianz de Lis). The only fully developed Arthurian scene (lines 855–1407) focuses on the *jugement*, which is already an unusual feature in itself. However, the verdict is not pronounced by Arthur and the knights but by the ladies of the court. Moreover, there is restrained comedy in the stylized way the Arthurian court is presented here, exemplified when Guinevere shoos King Arthur and his barons out of the hall, enraged at the presumption of the men for wanting to pass judgement in a love case. It is possible that here the queen is intended to embody a contrast to Raoul's idea of the perfect woman who should be prepared to renounce any authority.

Meanwhile, the testing and development of the hero do not take place with a view to increasing his status at Arthur's court, nor to integrating (or reintegrating) him into the security and fellowship of the Round Table. The romance also neglects any suggestion of a discrepancy between the demands of society and the behaviour of individuals.

In formal terms *Meraugis* is modelled not so much on the classic structure of a double sequence (which also implies an Arthurian scene at the division, a crisis and a second departure) as on the bipartite pattern more typical of the genre. An Arthurian scene forms the conclusion, but is not very elaborately developed, whilst the court supplies the framework for the reconciliation of the rivals Gorvain Cadruz and Meraugis. A renewed state of harmony is thus achieved, as it existed at the beginning of the narrative. This element is also found in Chrétien, but no longer occurs in the later Arthurian romances, which culminate in the union of the lovers. As already mentioned, a state of harmony with the Arthurian court does not need to be created for the simple reason that it was never disturbed. Nevertheless, the fact that the hero is now finally united with his *amie* dispels Gorvain's criticism of the verdict pronounced by the Arthurian court. In retrospect it becomes apparent why Meraugis loves 'better' than Gorvain: he loves in Lidoine not her transitory beauty but her lasting qualities,[11] he has greater generosity and intelligence than Gorvain, and last but not least Lidoine reciprocates his love. The concept that the virtues of *valor*, *cortoisie* and *amor* are victorious over external beauty is illustrated by various other characters in the romance as well as the main protagonists.[12] The best example is the marital union of the ugliest of all male dwarfs with the ugliest of all female dwarfs, for which Meraugis himself helps to pave the way. The two partners match each other in every respect, and they love and esteem one another. In spite of their

[11] R. M. Spensley, 'The Theme of *Meraugis de Portlesguez*', *FS* 27 (1973), 130ff.

[12] Spensley, 'The Theme of *Meraugis*', *passim*.

physical disfigurement they are courtly people of royal descent;[13] it is not beauty which is crucial for them, but the ethical and moral values which they exemplify. Meraugis and Lidoine have also demonstrated in the course of their shared journey that they are worthy of one another. The verdict of the Arthurian court proves to be right, and this brings about the final state of *joie* which is typical of the genre.

The romance of *Meraugis* is a treatise on the nature of courtly love as shaped in northern France. At the same time it serves as an *exemplum* demonstrating the educative force of this love in the protagonists' changes of heart. This general theme enables the work to dovetail with the traditions of the genre, yet by comparison with Chrétien Raoul has adopted a new and free approach to the dialectic, and to the practical development of the idea which is in outline a constant of the genre. The outstanding quality of *Meraugis* was already recognized by earlier scholars, but without being accounted for in detail.[14] Only Kundert-Forrer is fundamentally critical of this work. Her method of interpretation is based on rather elementary opinions about Chrétien's work, so that she is primarily checking Raoul's romance to see whether or not, like *Erec*, it focuses on 'the organic expansion of a human relationship'.[15] She then declares *Meraugis* to be lacking this prerequisite quality, and states that the work is 'based on the idea that any claim must be justified by deeds' (translated from p. 85). 'In *Meraugis* we seek in vain for any kind of human relationship... The lack of human relationships is not, however, the theme or the dilemma in Raoul's romance; he is never even aware of it. He thinks he only has to use the word *amor* for that to create a relationship in itself' (translated from p. 75). Moreover, 'the simple level of Raoul's thinking is a further indication that he has not managed to penetrate the courtly world...thus *Meraugis*, like Beroul's *Tristran*, is an example of courtly romance sinking to the level of the bourgeoisie' (translated from p. 80).

The preceding analysis of the romance has shown that to reproach it with a lack of human relationships is certainly not justified. The final conclusion drawn from this reading, that Raoul wrote an uncourtly or even bourgeois romance, is equally erroneous. Fourrier has shown that in all probability Raoul was not a citizen of a town. Furthermore, the poet expressly emphasizes in his prologue that his narrative is for a courtly audience and only a courtly one (lines 30–1). The discussion of the relationship between *beauté* and *cortoisie* in a literary

[13] On this point see B. Schmolke-Hasselmann, 'Camuse chose. Das Häßliche als ästhetisches und menschliches Problem in der altfranzösischen Literatur', *Miscellanea mediaevalia* 11 (1977), 442–52.

[14] Gaston Paris, 'Romans en vers', p. 223; Micha, 'Miscellaneous French Romances', p. 372.

[15] Translated from Kundert-Forrer, *Raoul de Houdenc*, p. 85.

work is an eminently courtly theme, and it is Raoul's desire and intention that the romance should be about *cortoisie*:

> Il n'i a mot de vilainie,
> Ainz est contes de cortoisie
> Et de beaus moz et de plesanz. (27–9)

(There is not one word of baseness in it. Quite the opposite, it is a story of courtliness, told in fine and pleasing words.)

However, *cortoisie* is at the heart of all human relationships in French medieval romances. Raoul wants to show that it can be understood in a general sense as a way of life and is then the only possible basis for a love and a marriage that will last. He is not alone in this concern; the authors of *Durmart* and *Gliglois* follow in his footsteps, whilst Chrétien had preceded him in giving expression to the principle. The wanderings of the heroes in the thirteenth-century Arthurian romances are primarily designed to further the acquisition of *cortoisie* and through it the perfection of the person. This thematic field is a constant of the genre, and the romance of *Meraugis* is one of the most successful examples of a text shaped by these ideals.

THE PRINCIPLE OF VARIATION: *FERGUS* AS A NEW *PERCEVAL*

The romance of *Fergus* by Guillaume le Clerc begins by describing a court festivity at Caradigan. After the meal, unnoticed at first, Arthur mingles with his knights who are passing the time by giving accounts of their adventures. Gawain notices the king and wants to make room for him, but Arthur orders the horses to be saddled, because he wants to hunt the white stag. The hunt lasts a whole day. It is Perceval who slays the stag and is rewarded with a golden goblet. On the way back the company of riders passes a boy ploughing a field. He is the eldest son of the rich peasant Soumilloit and his nobly-born wife. The boy is afraid and thinks he is under threat, but then he learns that these are the knights of the Round Table. Since he has already heard a lot about the fame of King Arthur he decides to become a member of his household forthwith and to serve the king in the role of counsellor.

These few sentences should suffice to give a first impression of Guillaume's method of working. One after another he evokes the opening sections of Chrétien's *Yvain*, *Erec* and *Perceval*. Scarcely has he led the expectations of his audience in one particular direction when he wheels around and leads into another dead-end; only at the third attempt does he keep to the route he has begun, which is now that of *Perceval*. This playing with audience expectations colours the entire romance. Guillaume knows Chrétien's works very precisely, and he also presupposes such knowledge on the part of his readers. Such familiarity with another work on the part of both an author and his public gives a common point of reference, permitting an effortless pattern of associations that results in a very direct impact. Material that has already been stored more or less subconsciously on a previous occasion is combined with what is now to be assimilated and the different point of view that it entails. The author of *Fergus* guides this process by means of explicit signals—citing names, recalling particular episodes, and supplying clear allusions and quotations; this is an extremely literary procedure. The result is a work for connoisseurs and thus a particularly interesting example of the genre.

The close relationship between *Fergus* and Chrétien's *Perceval* has already aroused interest. Moreover, *Fergus* is the only Arthurian verse romance to make any such detailed references to *Perceval*. The others confine themselves to isolated allusions, with *Tyolet* using only the opening episode. Martin when he edited *Fergus* had already supplied a list of narrative and stylistic borrowings, whilst Marquardt observes: 'The introduction to his romance, the account of Fergus' early years, his appearance at court and the encounter with the Black Knight (a Red Knight in *Perceval*) are all copied from *Perceval* and only thinly disguised.'[16] In fact the corresponding features are so numerous and so striking, even in points of detail, that it is all too easy to gain the impression that Guillaume was 'cribbing' from Chrétien. The author's real and rather surprising purpose only emerges when we look at the differences from Chrétien's *Perceval* and especially at the way the familiar scenes are placed in different contexts; we then become aware that this is anything but a mere copy. The apparently superficial differences are the key to an understanding of this work.

It is important to recognize from the start that Guillaume le Clerc does not intend to hide the similarities between his composition and *Perceval*; instead he deliberately emphasizes them with repeated references to the earlier romance: 'Perceval, / Qui tant pena por le Garal' (13–14, 'Perceval, who endured so much for the Grail'), or 'Percheval, / Ki seoit sor molt bon cheval / C'au vermel chevalier toli' (145–7, 'Perceval, who was riding on a very good horse which he took from the Red Knight'). The fictional events of Chrétien's romance are thus integrated on the assumption that they are common knowledge. In *Fergus*, unlike other romances, Perceval does not merely put in an appearance but has an active role supporting the young hero in a fatherly manner and even making him a present of a good sword; in this romance he is a character with his own

[16] Translated from W. Marquardt, *Der Einfluss Kristians von Troyes auf den Roman 'Fergus' des Guillaume le Clerc* (Dissertation, Göttingen, 1905; published, Göttingen, 1906), p. 31.

individual past history. Such a concept is otherwise rare in Arthurian verse compositions. As a rule the well-known figures have no individual history and carry out their current function as if neither Chrétien nor any other author of a romance had ever subjected them to experiences that were irreversibly character-forming. They are eternally youthful and eternally identical. In *Fergus* it is different; here Perceval is the one who in his time has already experienced and can remember everything that now awaits the youthful hero. In this sense the romance is a historical continuation of the earlier work, bringing Arthurian history within the genre.

This was part of the author's intention, as the following scene illustrates: the naive youth from the country[17] comes to Arthur's court in his father's rusty old armour and asks the king to accept him as a *conseiller* (adviser) of the Round Table. On this occasion, just as in the earlier instance when Perceval wanted to be knighted, Kay is again unable to curb his tongue. He takes a malicious pleasure in the fact that at last someone has come who is willing to take on the adventure with the Black Knight, which none of those present has so far dared to do. Fergus does not notice at first that Kay is thus trying to send him to his doom. Gawain, on the other hand, is very angry at his wicked words. Although he can no longer prevent Fergus from taking up Kay's challenge, he advises the king to furnish the young lad with a good suit of armour forthwith; surely he can still remember what had happened with Perceval on a previous occasion. The latter had misunderstood Kay's mockery and as a result had killed the Red Knight, whereupon he had kept his distance from the Arthurian court for too long:

> 'Souviegne vos de Perceval
> Que vos *toli* mesire Kois.
> Par ses dis et par ses destrois
> Le vos *toli*, bien le savés.' (1338–41)

('Remember Perceval, of whom you were *robbed* by my lord Kay. He *robbed* you of him, as you well know, through his tormenting words.')

These words allude to Arthur's sorrow in the romance of *Perceval*, where the king repeatedly complains about Kay being responsible for Perceval's prolonged absence:

> 'Ha! Keu, com avez hui fait mal!
> Par vostre lange, l'enuiouse,
> Qui avra dite mainte oisouse,
> M'avez vos le valet *tolu*
> Qui molt m'a hui cest jor valu.' (1240–4)

[17] 'ome nice' (909, 'naive man'); 'qu[i] a peu de sen' (797, 'who has little sense').

('Ah, Kay, how badly you have acted today. Through your cruel tongue with all its stupid remarks you have *robbed* me of the youth who was of great service to me this day.')

Elsewhere he comments:

'Par ton gabois *tolu* le m'as,
Si que jamais nel quit veoir.' (4080–1; see also 2880–1)

('Through your mockery you've *robbed* me of him so that I don't expect ever to see him again.')

After the author has used these means to establish beyond doubt the connection with Chrétien's romance, he can now give new weight and particular emphasis to the points where he deviates from his model. These require special attention.

It is significant that in *Fergus* the whole of the Grail narrative as well as the mythical and religious themes that go with it are totally excluded. In this respect Guillaume le Clerc is proceeding in conformity with the genre, since the Grail and all the motifs and scenes connected with it have no part in the remainder of Arthurian verse literature either. In the prose romances, by contrast, this element of the Perceval narrative is picked out for reinforcement and becomes one of the central motifs of the whole Vulgate Cycle. The romance of *Fergus* reduces the narrative of *Perceval* to its amorous element and thus embarks on the same course as the other texts of the genre. The love-story with its female protagonist, merely initiated and hinted at by Chrétien, now becomes the centre of interest. The heroine Galiene, resembling Blancheflor in every aspect, becomes the goal of the quest. In this respect *Fergus* is comparable to the *Perceval* Continuations; it completes what Chrétien left unsaid.

The relationship with the heroine also serves as the basis for the guilt element, which takes on a very distinct form here, once again distinguishing this work from the other Arthurian verse romances. For when Galiene approaches the young hero's bed in the night, wakes him with her tears and confesses her love to him (Blancheflor had merely asked for support against her enemies), the hero does not draw her to him on the bed as Perceval does, but primly dismisses her, reminding her that he still has to accomplish the adventure with the Black Knight. Fergus here places *chevalerie* above *amour*, for he is still completely inexperienced in matters of love and is not quite sure what Galiene is talking about. The metaphors of love which she uses are completely unfamiliar to him:

'Vostre gens cors, vostre biautés,
Vostre valors, vostre proëche
M'a mis en si tres grant destrece
Que jamais jor joie n'arai

Ne delit se par vos ne l'ai.
En vostres main, ne doutés mie,
Tenés et ma mort et ma vie.'
Fergus li respont en rïant
'Pucele, je vois el querant
Que amors ne que drüerie.
J'ai une bataille aatie
Que je vaurai avant parfaire;
Mais quant je verrai el repaire,
Se je en puis vis escaper,
Par chi m'en vaurai retorner...
Car il n'est riens, se Dius me voie,
Qui me peüst metre en la v[o]ie
Que me drüerie donnaisse
A pucele. Ne point l'amaisse
Desi que jo aie conquis,
Maté d'armes u mort u pris
Le chevalier mal enginnos.' (1954–81)

('Your noble body, your beauty, your valour, your prowess have put me in such very great distress that I shall never have joy or delight unless it comes from you. Have no doubt that in your hand you hold my death and my life.' Fergus laughs and replies: 'Maiden, I am seeking neither love nor its pleasures. I am committed to a fight that I should like to settle first. But when I return, if I come out of it alive, I should like to pass this way again... For, as God is my witness, there is nothing in the world that could lead me into giving my affection to a maiden or loving her at all until I have defeated, overcome by force of arms and either killed or captured that scheming knight.')

Fergus has not yet grasped the fact that love and chivalry are not mutually exclusive and that they need to be combined before a knight can achieve perfection. He rejects the love that would have enriched his life of chivalry and in so doing he incurs guilt, rather like Yvain, who also sometimes places the requirements of chivalry above those of love. Galiene feels she has been profoundly hurt and humiliated by this youth

U ele n'a pité trové,
Ne amisté ne drüerie. (1990–1)

(in whom she has found no pity, friendship or love.)

Not long afterwards Fergus recognizes his guilt, and without anyone having to point it out to him as they did with Perceval; he then goes mad with grief:

'C'est mervelle que je n'enrage;
Ce serroit drois, quant j'e[s]condis

Celi qui d'amor me requist.
A grant honte me doit torner.' (2704–7)

('It is a wonder that I do not go mad. It would only be fitting, considering that I refused the one who was asking for my love. I am heading for great shame.')

For a year he lives like an animal in the forest (reminiscent of *Yvain*), thin and covered in hair, and knowing only raw meat for food, 'dont le mangoit / Comme ciens' (3662–3, 'which he ate in the manner of a dog'). When he has come to his senses again, it is another year before he has found and won his beloved. The idea of harmony and discord in the relationship between love and chivalry, and of Fergus' sin against the demands of *cortoisie*, is taken up again right at the end of the work. Here it is Gawain (the one who provoked the conflict in *Yvain*) who once again draws the attention of Fergus, his comrade-in-arms, to the danger which could now be awaiting him after the wedding, namely that he might make the opposite mistake and lapse into idleness with his young wife:

Et se li amoneste et prie
Qu'il ne laist pas chevalerie
Por sa feme, que n'est pas drois:
'De pluissors gabés serrois.'
Fergus bien li afie et jure;
Ja n'ora parler d'aventure
Qu'il n'i aille, s'il a santé. (6989–95)[18]

(And he urges and begs him not to give up chivalry because of his wife, for it would not be right: 'Many would mock you for it.' Fergus gives him his full assurance and vows that he will never hear talk of an adventure without undertaking it, if he is in good health.)

The recognition of personal guilt entails a crisis, and with it a division into two parts. Fergus may have defeated the Black Knight, sent him to Arthur and thus performed the task he had undertaken, but he still does not return to court, and his uncourtly behaviour towards Galiene is never publicly acknowledged; thus also it is not the joy of the court which is destroyed but specifically the personal happiness of the hero himself. He has made a mistake which affects Galiene and himself, but not society at large as it did in *Perceval*. He has to atone for his mistake, and has to set off again to find Galiene. The second part of his journey of adventure serves purely personal ends, even though in the course of his journey he also accomplishes a number of deeds which benefit society.[19] If the wedding of the protagonists is nevertheless celebrated in the presence of Arthur

[18] See Southworth, *Etude comparée*, p. 95.

[19] Southworth, *Etude comparée*, p. 81, asserts that Fergus' mission is above all for his personal glory and gain, and is only indirectly connected with serving Arthur, the guardian of honour and justice.

and his knights, then this is only because the format of Arthurian romance requires a final Arthurian scene; there is no internal necessity for it in this text.

The other burden of guilt that Perceval incurs when he leaves his mother undergoes a similarly significant transformation in order to make its appearance in *Fergus*. Unlike Perceval's, Fergus' lineage is not amongst the most illustrious, and the romance also omits any mystery about his name. He has not been deliberately kept at a distance from the courtly world like Perceval, nor has there been any conscious attempt to dress him as a fool. He is the son of a rich peasant, and it is not necessity but a matter of principle which makes his father keep him working in the fields, because he believes this to be appropriate for someone of his class. The mother, who is of noble birth, takes a different view. When Fergus expresses a desire to go to Arthur's court his father is about to beat him, but she supports her son and is prepared to engage in a violent war of words with her husband on his behalf:

> Lors commenche ses felons dis,
> Itels com a vilain covient:
> 'Fius a putain, dont vos souvient
> D'armes requerre et demander?
> Bués et vaches devés garder...'
> 'Avoi! sire, par Saint Mangon,
> Fait li dame, vos avés tort.
> N'avés qui tesmoig vos en port
> De la honte que m'avés dite;
> De putage cuic estre cuite...
> Et si vos di de cest vallet,
> Se de prouëce s'entremet,
> Ne vos en devés mervillier,
> Car il a maint bon chevalier
> En son lingnage de par moi.
> Si i retrait, si com je croi,
> Et se men consel volés croire,
> Ja ne destorberés son o[i]rre.' (478–502)

(Then he begins to utter base words suited to a peasant. 'Son of a whore, where did you get the idea of asking to be given arms? Your job is to look after cows and cattle...' 'Look here, sir, by Saint Mungo,' the lady says, 'you're wrong. You'll not find anyone to support the shameful thing you've said about me. I don't think I can be accused of whoring... And let me tell you that you shouldn't be surprised if this lad turns to a life of prowess, for he has many good knights amongst his ancestors on my side. Thus I believe that he is now taking after them, and if you want my advice you'll not interfere with his journey.')

Fergus' mother can understand her son's striving for knightly honour. She is proud of the handsome youth who is eager to continue the tradition of her own family, whereas the uncourtly father draws the conclusion from Fergus' aspirations that anyone who wants to become a knight cannot be his son. The mother's attitude explains why Fergus does not incur any guilt by leaving her, and also why he feels no particular sense of urgency about seeing her again to make good an offence. Textual examples such as this show the nature of the relationship between *Fergus* and *Perceval*: the motif is the same, but the location and treatment are different.

Fergus leaves home unencumbered by well-intentioned but misinterpreted advice. Thus he also avoids bringing misfortune upon others in the way that Perceval does to the *amie* of Orguelleus de la Lande or to the Fisher King. Fergus is not as ignorant of the world as his predecessor and moreover he learns faster (his tutor being the king's chamberlain). He has more sound common sense as well as a conspicuous fund of wit at his disposal.[20] One example of this occurs when Fergus is stopped by a knight at a ford, and is supposed to surrender his horse as a toll; this leads to a duel. When the knight realizes his impending defeat he is filled with fear and runs off into his castle. Fergus, who has not yet punished him sufficiently, sets off after him shouting:

> 'Ça tornés, sire chevalier!
> Je vos amainne mon destrier
> Por ce que vel estre aquités
> Del paiage que demandés;
> Nel vauroie en nulle maniere.
> Vos me tenrïés por trechiere,
> Por vilain et por trop engrés
> Se j'enportoie vo travers.' (3175–82)

[*Translator's note*: The text printed here, from Frescoln's edition (see above, p. ix), gives: 'Come back here, sir knight! I'm bringing you my horse because I want to pay the toll you are demanding. I do not at all want to do so. You will think me deceitful, base or in too much of a hurry if I go off with your crossing fee.' But this does not make good sense of the incident, and the text printed by Schmolke-Hasselmann from Martin's edition (Ne vauroie en nule maniere / Que me tenissiés...) is clearly preferable. D. D. R. Owen, in translating Frescoln, silently takes the same view, producing: 'I wouldn't on any account want you to think me a trickster...']

On another occasion Fergus says to the Black Knight, who is bleeding after their duel: 'The surgeon was still rather inexperienced and didn't find the right artery

[20] On this point see Micha, 'Miscellaneous French Romances', p. 364.

straight away. Therefore I fear that you will suffer some pain from this blood-letting.'[21] This ironically exaggerated politeness towards an unworthy opponent is characteristic of Fergus' behaviour and is a clear expression of his superiority. Perceval is also excessively polite, but in his case because of insecurity and social inexperience. There is also a significant difference in the scene where Fergus, after taking revenge on Kay for his wicked mockery in a manner modelled on *Perceval*, then proceeds to indulge in mockery himself. After he has thrown Kay from his horse, head over heels into a muddy stream, he begins to laugh aloud and calls to him:

'... En moie foi, biaus sire,
Vos estes trop mal afaitiés
Qui en ma riviere peschiés
Quant n'en avés congié de moi,
Si avés fait trop grant desroi.
Or puet li rois bien tornoier;
A plenté ara a mangier,
Au soir poisson se vos pöés.
Ne puet estre mal conreés
Nus hom qui ait tel connestable.' (6462–71)

('By my faith, fine sir, your manners are very bad, fishing in my river without my permission. You really have behaved very badly. Now the king can have a fine tournament. He'll have plenty of fish to eat this evening, if you can manage it. No man can be poorly provided for if he has such a constable.')

It has already been pointed out that despite following the narrative material of *Perceval* so closely, the author of *Fergus* has largely if not totally eliminated the problem of the hero's name, his guilt and all the Grail material, and taken in conjunction such factors demand a fundamental change from the interpretation of Chrétien's work. The Grail experience belongs to the personal history of the knight Perceval, and cannot be repeated or transferred, at least not in a verse romance. Fergus is not the saviour of the world, nor is he a child prodigy like Perceval, whose adventures result from his lineage and are predestined. Is the romance of *Fergus* no more than a witty game using literary associations? What *sens* did Guillaume intend to give his work? Jordan calls the poet a democrat and a rationalist,[22] because he wants to draw attention in the first place to the unusual factor that Fergus as the son of a *vilain* knocks some of the most famous knights out of their saddles (p. 154), and secondly to the numerous examples of realistic detail, alongside which the element of the marvellous is largely dispensed with:

[21] Translated from the author's German rendering of line 2406–9.
[22] L. Jordan, 'Zum altfranzösischen Fergusroman', *ZrPh* 43 (1923), 185.

'And just as the poet refuses to have anything to do with the prejudices of the nobility against the less well-born, so he reacts similarly in the face of epic mysticism... Guillaume is basically much more original than Chrétien's other imitators...the aristocratic element is missing.'[23]

This seems a fair assessment initially,[24] but the conclusion points in a misleading direction. Had it been Guillaume's purpose to illustrate the contention that the son of a peasant can become a knight of the Round Table just as well as, or better than, the sons of the nobility, and to do so by writing a romance about a social climber, whose story he could have used to demonstrate the fading power and strength of the hereditary nobility, then this aspect would surely have been more strongly accentuated and presented as a contentious issue. In fact, however, the nobility as represented by society at Arthur's court is at no point viewed critically in this romance in the way that pervades the other romances. Indeed, one could assert the opposite view, that Fergus can only rise precisely because he does have noble blood. Through his decision to become a knight he is moving towards his natural calling. Thus the message of this romance could be seen as lying in the maxim that *natura* is more powerful than *nutritura*.[25] Through his mother Fergus possesses a high degree of *hardiment*, *cuer* and *vaselage* (4602–3, boldness, courage and valour); these qualities have simply been obscured by his uncourtly peasant upbringing and are set to emerge. He has to follow the path that conforms to his true nature.

In a lengthy speech after the realization of his guilt, at the peak of the crisis, Fergus reflects on his status between two worlds. His crisis is also a problem of self-discovery:

> 'E las! que j'ai bien porchacié
> Ceste dolor par mon pecié!
> Pechié? Mais par male aventure.
> Certes ainc me vint de nature
> Que je ne doi faire fors honte.
> Qui sui je donc? A moi qu'en monte?
> D'amors d'uiseuse m'entremet.
> Onques mes pere Soumillet,
> Onques a nul jor qu'il vesquist,
> De tel ouvre ne s'entremist.
> Et li fius s'en veut entremetre!
> Dius, quel eschar! qui me vel metre

[23] Translated from Jordan, 'Zum altfranzösischen Fergusroman', 186.

[24] According to Jordan, 'Zum altfranzösischen Fergusroman', 154, Foerster also holds this view.

[25] See Micha, 'Miscellaneous French Romances', p. 378: 'Guillaume's purpose was not to describe how a plough-boy became a knight, but rather to show that nature is stronger than nurture.'

El renc de cels qui nuit et jor
Por saudees seervent Amor!
Et je, por choi ne m'i metroie?
Car jou mius orë en vauroie.' (683–98)

('Alas, I really have brought about this sorrow through my own fault. Fault? Bad luck would be more like it. Or, indeed, it is in my nature that I can do nothing that is not shameful. Who am I after all? What does it matter to me? It is pointless my meddling in love. My father Soumillet in all the days of his life never got involved in such things. And the son wants to try his hand at it. God, what a joke, wanting to join the ranks of those who serve in love's army night and day. And why shouldn't I join them? For then I'd increase my worth.')

Fergus is unsure of himself because he wonders if it is inherent in his *nature*, in his descent and upbringing, that he should have treated Galiene in that way. Is *honte* part of his destiny and an inescapable fate? Is it permissible for him to venture the desire to belong to the ranks of those whose origins, unlike his, are not in conflict with the essential nature of courtly love? But there again, why shouldn't he? His conflicting feelings are resolved in a victory for his maternal inheritance, the courtly and aristocratic component which proves to be the hero's true nature once it has fully unfolded. He has the essential characteristics of a knight in abundance, but the son of a peasant does not become a truly courtly person until he has experienced love and its attendant sufferings. Perceval experiences no such conflicts, undergoes no crisis in this sense, and never doubts his noble ancestry. Nevertheless, by setting his hero's childhood in a forest, far away from the influence of the courtly sphere, Chrétien has likewise prepared the ground for a potential conflict between *natura* and *nutritura*; on the other hand, it does not erupt with quite the same trenchancy in *Perceval* as in *Fergus*. In his later romance Guillaume le Clerc has taken up the beginnings of an idea from Chrétien and has expanded it with extra emphasis.

Emmel in her work on problems of form in Arthurian romances cites Fergus as an example of formal constraints being relaxed; although Guillaume had been endeavouring to preserve the structure employed by Chrétien,[26] he had omitted the interim return of the hero and thereby weakened the significance of Chrétien's symbolism.[27] It is a fact that Fergus puts in only two appearances at Arthur's court, and these two Arthurian scenes flank his journey of adventure. The romance does also include another three more limited Arthurian scenes

[26] Emmel, 'Formprobleme', p. 147.

[27] Emmel, 'Formprobleme', p. 155. It is astonishing that although Emmel's study is chiefly concerned with the narrative material of *Perceval*, she does not refer anywhere to the similarities of content between *Fergus* and *Perceval*, nor does she even acknowledge the special relationship binding the two romances so closely together.

where the hero is not present, namely the familiar messenger scenes. To conclude from the absence of a central Arthurian scene (which is already missing in Chrétien's *Lancelot*) that formal constraints are being relaxed, one must start from the premiss that three of Chrétien's five Arthurian romances (*Erec*, *Yvain* and *Perceval*) are to have their particular form held up as the absolute norm, and are to be termed 'genuine' Arthurian romances.[28] Measured against this 'genuine' form, all other possible variations amongst the later specimens of the genre must logically be counted as deviations and evidence of formal degeneration. However, Chrétien himself already envisaged various possibilities for the structure of a romance; not only that, but if we judge *Fergus* according to our knowledge of what is actually typical of the genre, then its omission of the central Arthurian scene is in conformity with a large number of the other Arthurian romances. In both form and content it is oriented towards a generic norm which has scope for precisely this omission. In terms of form, Guillaume looks not to Chrétien but to the Arthurian romances of his own time. In the later Arthurian romances the function of the interim return, Chrétien's central Arthurian scene, is sometimes absorbed by the Arthurian scene at the beginning of the romance, but on other occasions it may equally well be detached from the Arthurian court, appearing as a personal crisis symbolized by the loss of the beloved. This formal principle emerges particularly clearly in *Fergus*.

Fergus is a new and different *Perceval*. The author uses Chrétien's *matiere*, works with the literary knowledge already possessed by his audience and plays with their expectations. His method is that of variations on a familiar theme. He organizes the narrative material, the scenes and the details in a different way and thus arrives at a new theme for his work. By forgoing the Grail material and accentuating the romantic element of the plot he brings his work within the generic system which has been developing an increasing rigidity since Chrétien's time and which can no longer tolerate the religious mythology that is now relinquished to the prose romances. The subtle procedure adopted by the poet Guillaume le Clerc allows us an insight into the social composition of his intended audience, their intellectual dimensions and their high degree of literary awareness. However, as a working method Guillaume's procedure was not without its imitators; to name just two works which in places draw either upon the Arthurian tradition or upon romances by Chrétien, *Aucassin et Nicolette* and Huon de Mery's *Tornoiement Antecrist* both employ a comparable technique of literary allusions.[29]

[28] Emmel, 'Formprobleme', p. 171.

[29] Huon de Mery makes special reference to *Yvain*, as does *Aucassin et Nicolette*, with a shepherd modelled on the wild herdsman in *Yvain*.

THE SOCIAL EQUALITY OF THE COUPLE: *DURMART* AS AN ANTI-*EREC* ROMANCE

Soon after 1210 the author of *Durmart* composed a romance of 16,000 lines in which the prerequisites of the genre and Chrétien's concept of it are taken up and transformed in yet another way. The sheer bulk of the romance is already an indication of its fundamental independence from its generic prototypes; it is almost three times as long as the Arthurian verse romances (apart from *Perceval*) which preceded it. Nevertheless, despite this unusual bulk *Durmart* is clearly built upon a coherent and deliberate structure, to which even the earlier generation of scholars already gave due recognition.[30] Stengel, the first editor of the romance, divides the work into five parts: loss of innocence (I), the struggle to atone for past errors (II, III, IV), and the glory of fame after victory has been won (V); these are for Stengel the decisive stages and at the same time 'the poem's clearly emerging sequence of ideas'.[31] Southworth sees it as tripartite, with divisions coming at the loss of the Red Tent and at the test of the Perilous Seat. This alternative proposal for the divisions is less convincing, because Southworth denies the beginning of the romance, dealing with Durmart's formative years, any real place in its structure.[32] Moreover, even the author's strong hint in line 1574, 'Or primes commence li contes' ('This is where the tale begins'), is not taken into account, or indeed mentioned at all. By contrast it is the intention of the present study to air the conviction that precisely this opening section holds the key to an understanding of the romance and reveals its *sens*. It is then this *sens* which is to be evaluated as the decisive innovation with respect to Chrétien's works, although the form of the romance also represents an independent attempt to structure an Arthurian verse romance, with Arthurian double composition undergoing a characteristic transformation.

Unlike Chrétien's romances with their structural use of Arthurian scenes, *Durmart* contains neither an initial Arthurian scene nor a final one. In fact the hero does not come into contact with Arthur's court or his knights until a stage when he has already attained a decisive degree of perfection. His desire for purification and perfection is not oriented towards Arthur's court; he has no need or desire to be judged by Arthurian society, but has to try to prove himself in his own eyes and in those of his parents, and it is for this reason that his parents have to hear of every new achievement. Their son sends his defeated opponents to his mother instead of Arthur, and his knightly deeds are performed

[30] Foerster [no further reference given]; Gaston Paris, 'Romans en vers'; Southworth, *Etude comparée*, p. 117.

[31] Translated from *Li Romans de Durmart le Galois*, edited by Edmund Stengel, *BLVS* 116 (Tübingen, 1873), p. 510.

[32] Southworth, *Etude comparée*, p. 108.

in her service, whilst his father Jozefent has to be present as an observer to witness his final test, the battle in Limeri. Although he is a close relative of the king, Durmart does not at first seek any encounter with the Arthurian court. It eventually comes about by chance, and even after it has taken place it is clearly not essential to the hero's moral purification. It is significant that Durmart repeatedly and definitively resists Arthur's summons to join his household. The Arthurian court plays only a subordinate role in his life, and his contact with it is thus only sporadic. The author of *Durmart* has made an attempt to link the aspirations of his work to the courtly standards and authoritative jurisdiction of the Arthurian court without submitting to the formal constraints of the genre.[33] He retains only the main Arthurian scene with the test of the Perilous Seat, which forms the conclusion of Durmart's first trial phase, and ensures him public recognition of his purification. The hero wins the esteem of King Arthur himself but cannot stay at Arthur's court because the more important part of his quest, winning the bride who will be appropriate for him, has still to be accomplished. At this point he is still not worthy of the *fin'amor* of the Queen of Ireland, as he himself is all too well aware, even if the others fail to notice. However, the queen's love and recognition are fundamental to his earthly happiness, whereas the esteem of Arthur and his knights is purely secondary.

The author of *Durmart* presents his audience with a kind of case study. He introduces a hero who before reaching manhood commits an offence against morality which belies his noble origin and thus also his *nature*, and who is at odds with the obligations imposed on him by his background. He is a *beaz malvais*, a handsome good-for-nothing. He is the son of a powerful king but falls in love with the young wife of a seneschal, and for three years he lives with her in a sinful adulterous relationship. In so doing he excludes himself from the company of his social equals. His parents and the outside world despise him, whilst his future subjects fear that he will rule them like a chambermaid, since he has learned nothing and is living in a manner unworthy of his rank. His father threatens to turn him out of the house, imprison him or disinherit him, but Durmart is young and stubborn. It is a long time before he realizes the error of his ways. His offence, i.e. his sin against society and religion, is a combination of *mavaistié* (wickedness), *perece* (sloth) and *luxurie* (lust). The wife of the seneschal is not worthy of him and he himself is not yet worthy of love. His behaviour is *folie*, and ill becomes the son of a king. He has done nothing to earn the love of a woman, and his first mistress was at fault in nevertheless granting him her love without hesitation. She has no time for knights who go on begging

[33] The elements of an Arthurian romance opening are echoed in the Arthurian scene to be found at lines 9322–10,347.

for too long, nor for the ladies who keep them begging. *Fin'amor*, however, demands that trouble and effort be expended in its pursuit. Not until he is eighteen does Durmart realize that his love-affair has been diverting him from his true destiny. One beautiful spring morning he awakens from his aberration. He becomes conscious that he is a coward and can be of no use to anyone; he has not learned the art of handling weapons because he has isolated himself from the company of his contemporaries. He now perceives that he must give up a love which is making him more degenerate with every day that passes:

> 'Trop ai ceste amor maintenue,
> Je doi mais bien issir de mue.
> Miech ain de la dame a partir
> Que moi abaissier ne honir,
> Quar on doit bien l'amor laissier
> Dont on ne fait fors empirier.' (611–16)

('I have persisted in this love for too long; henceforth I must leave the mews. I prefer to part from the lady rather than degrade and shame myself, for one should abandon love that only leads one into degeneration.')

When Durmart has just been knighted, having been provisionally reconciled with his parents, a wise old pilgrim informs him that there is a lady who must become the sole object of his desires, since she is a perfect match for him in every respect. However, the way to her will be difficult and onerous. Durmart recognizes his vocation immediately; he must seek the Queen of Ireland, even though he has never seen her, because she is the appropriate bride for him. From now on, undeterred by mockery and disappointment, he keeps to his course; marriage to Queen Fenise is both the goal of his quest and its reward.

Durmart's journey to Ireland is a journey of atonement and purification. The narrator of the romance leaves us in no doubt that his hero will follow the true path to the end:

> Nus ne se doit desesperer,
> Mais plus et plus al bien penser. (639–40)

(No one must despair but must think more and more about what is good.)

> D'une chose bien certains sui:
> Que Durmars vuet querre son pris. (896–7)

(Of one thing I am certain: Durmart intends to follow the path of honour.)

The young good-for-nothing will eventually become an exemplary person, and thus we have here another example of the fundamentally optimistic approach typical of Arthurian verse romance. The author intends the narrative of

Durmart to illustrate a succession of propositions which in combination represent the *sens* of the romance:

> The son of a king may only love and marry the daughter of a king, for complete compatibility at all levels is the only guarantee of a happy relationship. Only a wife of equal rank and exhibiting equal beauty and moral excellence will be able to share his life in a way that brings fame and advantage to both partners.
>
> Only someone doing his very best can hope to win *fin'amor*. It must be the object of desire over a long period and must be laboriously fought for. The man must continue to prove himself until he is worthy of it (1620–8; 10,365–404). A love that lacks any educational force is worthless (8835–52).
>
> Anyone who is loved by his mistress and who loves her with *fin'amor* must enter into marriage with her; otherwise he is playing a dangerous game with love (14,995–15,012). True love lasts as long as marriage, and marriage is indissoluble (5168; 15,015).
>
> Anyone who takes a mistress (*amie*) of equal rank as his wife (*moillier*) need not fear that his reputation will be diminished by marriage. His intelligent wife will ensure that he continues to put his chivalric capabilities to the test, since she is concerned for his welfare and his good name. A man must continue to test his valour repeatedly well into old age (15,728–30).
>
> Prowess (*proece*) and good looks (*beauté*) are of little value without goodness (*bonté*); it is only the combination of these characteristics that constitutes perfection, whether in a man or in a woman.
>
> Anyone whom nature has blessed with good qualities but who fails to use them is committing a sin (10,402–4). No one can win fame without exposing himself to danger (10,755–6), and it takes a crisis to reveal a truly valiant man (12,425–6, *preudon*). If knights do not undertake anything involving effort, then no chronicle will be able to tell us anything about them. Anyone who seeks degenerate company becomes degenerate himself, so good people must cultivate the friendship only of exemplary companions.

The author presents these views in the form of maxims, aphorisms and numerous comments from the narrator, but also via the narrative content in a variety of different ways, so that they permeate the entire text. Thus the prologue already contains the information that the work is intended to be a *conte roial* (a royal tale):

> Por cho est li contes roial
> Que *filz de roi* fu li vassal
> Dont li contes est devisés. (17–19)

(The tale is royal because the young man of whom the tale is told was the son of a king.)

This remark seems strangely superfluous at first, but it gains increasing significance when we realize that it is already addressing a theme of the romance.

The idea finds further expression in the father's admonitions:

'Tu aimes luxure et perece;
Dehés ait bealtés sens proëce.
Tres beaz malvais, enten a moi:
Sez que doit faire filz de roi?
Il doit amer les chevaliers
Et honorer et tenir chiers;
Doner lor doit les riches dons,
Si doit haïr faus et felons,
Si doit le siecle resbadir,
Joie et proëce maintenir.
Filz de roi doit estre loialz,
Dignes et vrais et de cuer halz;
Ne doit estre luxurios,
Quar c'est uns plais vilz et hontoz.
Tu fais pechié mout desloial
De la femme le seneschal
Que tu tiens...
E! quar laisse ester ta folie,
Si feras sens et cortoisie!' (457–80)

('You love wantonness and idleness. A curse upon beauty without prowess. Pay attention to me, you handsome failure. *Do you know what the son of a king should do*? He should love knights, honour them and hold them dear; he should give them rich gifts, and should hate the false and the disloyal. He should be an encouragement to the world, maintaining joy and prowess. The *son of a king* should be loyal, worthy, honest and noble of heart. He should not be wanton, for that is a vile and shameful state to be in. You are guilty of great disloyalty in consorting with the seneschal's wife... Listen! Put an end to your madness, and you will be acting sensibly and in a courtly fashion.')

On another occasion he explains to his son the error of his ways:

'N'est pas amors de *fil a roi*
Vers la feme d'un vavassor.
Filz de roi doit avoir amor
A haute pucelle roial
Ou a roïne emperïal.
Mais vavassor et bacheler
Cil doivent haut et bas amer;
De *fil a roi* n'est pas ensi.' (860–7)

('Love for the wife of a vavasour is not a love for the *son of a king*. The *son of a king* should have the love of a high-born royal princess or a sovereign queen. A vavasour or a landless knight may love high or low, but not the *son of a king*.)

The wise old pilgrim tells Durmart that he is miraculously good-looking, and that the Queen of Ireland is another miracle of beauty. It is she who must be the object of his love. She is a queen and he is the son of a king, and thus it will be a good thing for them to unite their beauty. It will be the talk of the whole world, and Durmart's fame will be increased by his love for her (1153–6). On the eve of the wedding, the queen herself tells Durmart:

> 'Cil doit bien avoir haute amie
> Qui hautement l'oze conquerre,
> Mais ne doit hate amor requerre
> Nus hom qui deservir ne l'ose...
> Vos estes *fiex de riche roi,*
> Et je sui par verité fine
> *Fille de roi et de roïne,*
> Se m'est avis, se bel vos semble,
> Que nos avenons bien ensemble;
> Et Deus nos doinst si assenbler
> Qu'a tot le monde pui[s]t senbler
> Que bone soit nostre assenblee.' (14,858–77)

('It is fitting that any who dares to win her through high deeds should have a high-born mistress, but no man should pursue a noble love who does not dare to earn it... You are the *son of a mighty king* and I am in very truth the *daughter of a king and queen,* and thus it seems to me, if you agree, that we are well matched, and may God so join us that our union may be seen as good by everyone.')

The author of *Durmart* has already propounded the idea of an exemplary marriage on the basis of equal status by telling the story of the hero's parents, Jozefent and Andelise. Both are of royal blood and they love each other right through to old age; they do not wish to be separated for a single day, and Jozefent has always remained his wife's knight, for she remains his *amie* even in marriage. Jozefent never succumbs to the danger of *recreantise* (cowardice), and he admonishes his son to follow the example of his mother and himself.[34]

It is God's will that Durmart should fight against *mavaisté* (wickedness), *perece* (sloth) and *desloialté* (treachery; see line 5838). Where he has sinned, he has to make up for it in his dealings with other people. Thus the conflicts in which Durmart becomes involved during his probationary journey take the form predominantly of fights against characters who embody these vices. However, it is a crucial feature of these conflicts that he does not merely overthrow and

[34] The knights of the Ten Maidens likewise illustrate the author's concerns; despite their amorous relationships they do not neglect their chivalric duties, for 'mavaisté he[en]t et perece' (6145, 'they hate wickedness and sloth').

humiliate his opponents but also converts them to doing good. This is illustrated by, for example, Creoreas (*mavaisté*) and Brun de Morois (*luxurie* and *desloiauté*); they promise that 'Prodom serai d'or en avant' (5700, 'From henceforth I shall behave nobly'). Because Durmart is fighting against vice (and he has already proved in himself that it is possible to conquer evil) he is able to overthrow all his opponents without difficulty. It is not the case that from the time of his own conversion Durmart undergoes no further development.[35] He has, for example, reached a decisive turning-point in proving himself and gaining insight when on the occasion of a dubbing ceremony he is now able to pass on to other young men the teachings of his father which he refused to accept in his youth. The hero's step-by-step development is also reflected in the degree of esteem in which he is held by the Arthurian court and by his own parents. Having graduated from being worthless to being a good knight who performs ever more impressive deeds, he scales the ladder of fame to become the 'miedres chevaliers / Et as armes li plus maniers / Qui soit en la crestïenté' (13,475–7, 'the best knight and the most skilled in arms throughout Christendom'). It is expressly stated that as such he is superior to the best knights of the Round Table, even to Gawain since he was able to defeat him (see lines 13,472–8). Not long beforehand, Arthur had still rated him as the best knight apart from four of the Arthurian court (lines 13,164–5). Because Durmart is the best knight in Christendom by the end of his journey of atonement it falls to his lot by divine intervention to succeed in freeing the Pope in Rome and with him all Christians from the heathens. For a little while the Pope becomes his father confessor and explains to him the meaning of the vision of a tree of candles which he experienced during his travels. On the tree there are bright and dull candles burning, and the Christ-child uses them to carry out a symbolic Last Judgement:

Celes qui vers terre clinoient
Et qui laide flanbe jetoient
Senefïent les outrageuz
Et les *chaitis luxurïeuz*
Qui sunt espris de mavais fu
Dont li pecheor sont perdu. (15,827–32)

(Those leaning towards the ground and producing ugly flames signify the people without self-discipline and *slaves to wantonness*, who are seized with the evil fire through which sinners are brought to perdition.)

In his youth Durmart had come close to being consigned to eternal damnation, since he was indeed leading the life of a *chaitif luxurieus* (slave to wantonness).

[35] This is the view expressed by Southworth, *Etude comparée*, p. 112.

However, his becoming aware of the styles of behaviour appropriate to him as a king's son, which imply abhorrence of sin and vice, and his inclination towards *bonté* (goodness), *prodomie* (nobility) and exemplary chivalry have saved him from the fires of hell. It is therefore inaccurate to claim that there is no meaningful connection between the two episodes involving the tree of candles,[36] or that the Christian element is a mere external dressing.[37] Indeed the first vision includes an explicit forecast of a second one; Durmart's development culminates in his embodying the perfect *Christian* knight. The motif of the tree of candles is closely bound up with the themes and the *sens* of the whole romance.[38] It is a symbol of the danger to which the hero was originally exposing himself but which he is able to overcome by virtue of his *nature*—and because divine grace is on his side. God has been directing his life since the moment of self-awareness, and his repentance makes grace possible. God's intermediary and messenger is the venerable old pilgrim, and the two appearances of the tree of candles constitute the miracle by which God makes known his willingness to be gracious. *Durmart* differs from most of the Arthurian verse romances in its pervasive atmosphere of genuine piety. However, it remains expressly within the framework of the Western Church and, unlike Chrétien's *Perceval* or the prose romances, it does not make use of mythology.[39]

The warning against *perece* and *luxurie* is linked throughout the romance with the didactic intentions of the author. He sketches a picture of a hero who is to serve as a model for the young people of his time.[40] The repeated invocation of the term *filz de roi* brings home the fact that this is a handbook for a prince in the form of an Arthurian romance. In this respect *Durmart* is comparable with *Beaudous*.

In presenting this kind of exemplary hero the author of *Durmart* is simultaneously adopting a stance against another Arthurian hero whose development is familiar to his public: he is conducting a critique of Chrétien's *Erec*. This

[36] Southworth, *Etude comparée*, p. 106; she also postulates a complete absence of allusions to the dissipated life of the first few lines throughout the rest of the romance (p. 104). For more on the Tree of Candles episodes (lines 1501–48 and 15,541–637), see the introduction to Gildea's edition, p. 60ff.

[37] Gaston Paris, 'Romans en vers', p. 145.

[38] This motif also occurs in the Second *Perceval* Continuation, but there, unlike in *Durmart*, it is not integrated into the plot as a symbol.

[39] On the other hand, the purification ethic in *Durmart* is certainly reminiscent of the *Queste del Saint Graal*. The motif of the Perilous Seat is similarly indicative of a relationship with this text, being inserted into *Durmart* as a symbol of the Messianic hopes focused on Durmart himself.

[40] See in particular the direct appeal to the audience at lines 15,911–33, also the numerous exhortational and philosophical interpolations which all relate to the theme of contrasting baseness and laziness with nobility and prowess. Arthur's words at lines 13,928–36 are also relevant.

important aspect of *Durmart* has not previously been considered, but the narrator of this romance reproaches his predecessor for having allowed Erec to commit a fundamental error; unlike Durmart, Erec did not strive to find a partner who was fully his equal by birth:

> ...monsaignor Erec le sage
> Qui nez est *de roial linage.*
> Il prist *une povre pucele,*
> Por ce qu'il le vit jone et bele,
> Et s'est Erec *mout riches hom*
> Et *fiez a roi* de grant renom. (8453–8)

(My lord Erec the wise, born *of royal lineage.* He took *a poor maiden* simply because he saw that she was young and beautiful, and yet Erec was a *man of great standing* and the *son of a king* of great renown.)

The poet of *Durmart* is of the opinion that this false step is the root cause of Erec's crisis and initial failure. If Erec, the son of a king, had married a lady of equal rank instead of the poor daughter of a vavasour he would never have succumbed to *recreantise*.[41] The image of the hero Durmart is then built up in such a way as to contrast with Chrétien's hero. At the beginning of the narrative Durmart is allowed to make the same mistake as Erec, in that he loves the wife of a vavasour, a member of the lower aristocracy, and the relationship is then made to founder. This contrasting outcome is the starting-point for *Durmart* to become an anti-*Erec*. The problem of *recreantise* is aired by the narrator towards the end of the romance (lines 15,367–76) in a conversation between the Queen of Ireland and her mother-in-law, Queen Andelise. The intelligent young woman of royal blood gives an assurance that she will protect her beloved from the dangers of *repos* (idleness), and that she will be able to do so precisely because there is such great love between them. In her view, one has to keep proving oneself even within marriage as the prerequisite for a love that will last. The idea is taken up again soon afterwards in a more lengthy passage of comment by the narrator; the author gives the following report on Durmart:

> Tot adés croist ses pris et vient;
> Durement amoit sa moillier,
> Mais il ne vot onques laissier
> Por li ne por sa compaignie
> Son pris ne sa chevalerie,
> Ains maintenoit bien sa proëce,
> Car il pensoit a grant hautece...
> Mais li Galois n'enpira mie

[41] On this point see Köhler, *Ideal und Wirklichkeit*, pp. 72–3.

De ce qu'il esposa s'amie.
Verités fu que mout l'ama,
Mais ains por li ne sejorna. (15,446–66)

(His reputation continues to grow. He loved his wife passionately but he never had any desire to abandon fame and chivalry for her or her companionship. Rather he maintained his prowess, for his thoughts were set on high deeds... But the Welshman did not deteriorate by marrying his beloved. It was true that he loved her very much but he never stayed at home because of her.)

The author of *Durmart* applies great emphasis to his suggestion that the love between *amie* and *ami* can maintain all its elevating and stimulating power even after entering upon marriage (which is indeed the state that lovers must aim for), as long as the preconditions for such a permanently satisfying union are in place. These preconditions lie in the absolute equality of the couple and especially in their being of equal rank within society, which the author of *Durmart* took to be lacking in *Erec*.[42]

The poet's criticism of the image of marriage represented in *Erec* culminates in a seemingly generalized remark which nevertheless contains a concealed barb directed against Enide and the *parole* she uttered, 'con mar fus' (2503, 'how disastrous for you'). This is yet another indication that on the one hand there is here specific polemic against Chrétien's *Erec*, whilst on the other hand the author of *Durmart* (like the authors of *Meraugis* and *Fergus*) assumes such an intimate knowledge of the earlier work on the part of his audience that his discreet reference is capable of being understood and of evoking a response:

Trop est mavais et vielz et nices,
Cant il por sa moillier enpire
Ne por chose qu'ele puist dire.
Ja qui de bien haut cuer sera
Por sa moillier n'enpirera,
Ains s'avance mout durement
Prodom qui *bone dame prent.* (15,454–60)

(A man is feeble and decrepit and foolish in the extreme if he degenerates because of his wife *or because of anything she may say*. Anyone who is of high courage will certainly not degenerate because of his wife; on the contrary the noble man who *takes a good lady* will be greatly improved by it.)

[42] The poet of *Durmart* implicitly accuses Enide of not being equal to the tasks facing the wife of a member of the higher aristocracy, and this because of her origin and upbringing. The poet thus allows himself to be the spokesman of conservative ranks seeking to protect themselves against the intrusion of foreign elements, and to a greater extent than Chrétien, whose thinking appears to be more open-minded. In the eyes of the upper nobility for whom *Durmart* was intended, Erec's marriage to Enide represents a misalliance.

This analysis has aimed at showing that the author of *Durmart* explicitly reshapes the narrative content (and thereby also the *sens*) supplied by Chrétien as his predecessor in the genre, and that he also develops a distinct outlook of his own which he holds up against Chrétien's and invites the audience of both works to make the comparison. This kind of response to an earlier romance had already been established as a literary procedure by Chrétien himself. *Yvain* is a reaction to *Erec* and illuminates the same basic problem from the other side; *Cligés* takes issue with *Tristan*. The author of *Durmart*, like the author of *Hunbaut*, has looked for a flaw in Chrétien's work and has found it in Erec's marriage to a poor girl of inferior birth. His own romance then corrects Chrétien's approach.

The *sens* of the resultant romance is at no point systematically spelt out, and yet it can be deduced from a multitude of comments by the narrator together with the direction given to the plot. Formulated as a thesis it might read: a good-for-nothing can become an example for all mankind, a perfect knight, lover and Christian, if he behaves in accordance with his *nature* and is led on his way to this goal by his love for a lady of equal rank. The poet of *Durmart* is calling on all people of noble birth to do likewise.

6

Aspects of the response to Chrétien: from plagiarism to nostalgia

CHRETIEN'S WORKS AS A 'SOURCE' FOR LATER ARTHURIAN POETS

A continuation to Labouderie's version of the *Chastoiement d'un père à son fils*[1] contains two substantial passages from older texts; the first derives from *Partonopeus*, whilst the second has been taken from the fragmentary Arthurian romance of *Hunbaut* (lines 2414–640). The author of the *Chastoiement* has incorporated the Arthurian poet's words into his own work with only minor changes and abbreviations. Similarly, extracts from Wace's *Brut*, the *Lai de Narcissus*, the *Lai du conseil*, *Athis et Prophilias*, *Partonopeus*, *Erec*, *Yvain* and *Perceval* reappear in *Cristal et Clarie*, a romance of adventure.[2] Both these works exemplify a technique of composition which by modern standards one might justifiably call plagiarism, but without wishing thereby to vilify the procedure as objectionable and as both legally and morally reprehensible.[3] There are after all certain qualitative distinctions to be observed in the type of such borrowings made by other authors and in their evaluation. It is well known that Jean de Meung incorporates various translations and reworkings of Latin poems into his *Roman de la Rose*. They could always be readily identified as such by his contemporaries, and they were used in pursuit of a more important goal. Jean de Meung makes no claim that the borrowed passages are the products of his own creativity, but this is precisely what the author of the *Chastoiement* does when he works 200 lines of an obscure poem, a largely unknown and moreover incomplete Arthurian romance, into his own text. He may well have hoped that none of his readers would know the Arthurian romance of *Hunbaut* and that no one would be able to identify the description of the *costume du pavillion* (the

[1] This continuation is preserved in BN n.a.fr.7517, for which see Paul Meyer, 'Notice d'un manuscrit appartenant à M. le comte d'Ashburnham', *Bulletin de la SATF* 1887, 82–103. [The section from *Hunbaut* has now been published in Winters' edition of this romance, pp. 118–22.]

[2] See the introduction to Breuer's edition.

[3] A. Hilka, 'Plagiate in altfranzösischen Dichtungen', *ZfSL* 47 (1924), 60ff.

custom of the tent) as deriving from a different work.

As yet no examples of borrowings with such plagiaristic tendencies[4] have been found within the genre of Arthurian verse romance itself, although in the years before the First World War a considerable number of scholars directed their efforts into tracking down plagiarisms, quotations, borrowings and allusions in the thirteenth-century Arthurian romances, and Chrétien's works were always postulated as the source referred to. The increasing number of reliable editions opened up new opportunities for verifying the texts, and in the resulting exuberance it was not unusual for scholars to go way beyond the mark. This is another instance where the naive demand for unlimited poetic originality as a measure of quality in assessing medieval texts inevitably led to false conclusions. The studies by Rohde, Marquardt and Habemann can be taken as representative of this line of research.[5] They would frequently reduce the problem of imitation to cases of verbal or stylistic borrowings that could be established beyond doubt. Much of the material they adduce in evidence does indeed appear to be irrefutable and yet it also seems somehow grotesque. Thus Rohde, *La Vengeance de Raguidel* (translated from p. 2):

> The Hunt of the White Stag. The episode of the hunt, which constitutes the starting-point of the adventures narrated in *Erec*, is also narrated in *La Vengeance de Raguidel*, line 1539ff. Although there are discrepancies of detail, there are nevertheless several points where the wording corresponds, making it probable that the latter text made use of *Erec*. Such similarities can be seen in the following pairs of lines:
>
> *Erec* 278: Ou li rois ot le cerf ataint
> (Where the king had caught up with the stag)
> *VR* 1583: Sempres orent le cerf ataint [Friedwagner 1587]
> (Straightaway they had caught up with the stag)
>
> *Erec* 281: Le blanc cerf ont desfet et pris
> (They have taken and killed the white stag)
> *VR* 1586: Issi ont cil le blanc cerf pris [Friedwagner 1590]
> (In this way they have taken the white stag)
>
> *Erec* 283: Le cerf an portent si s'an vont
> (They carry away the stag and go on their way)
> *VR* 1644: Le cerf ont torsé, si s'en vont [Friedwagner 1648]
> (They have bundled up the stag and go on their way)

[4] Hilka ('Plagiate', 60) sees such borrowings as plundering on a significant scale.

[5] R. Rohde, *La Vengeance de Raguidel. Eine Untersuchung über ihre Beeinflussung durch Christian von Troyes und über ihren Verfasser* (Dissertation, Göttingen, 1903; published, Hanover, 1904); W. Marquardt, *Der Einfluss Kristians von Troyes auf den Roman 'Fergus' des Guillaume le Clerc* (Dissertation, Göttingen, 1905; published, Göttingen, 1906); C. Habemann, 'Die literarische Stellung des *Meraugis de Portlesguez* in der französischen Artusepik' (Dissertation, Göttingen, 1908).

Marquardt, *Der Einfluss Kristians von Troyes* (translated from pp. 7–8):

...a series of parallel structures which allow the use of *Erec* in the composition of *Fergus* to stand out that much more clearly:...

Erec 4427: Traiiez vos la! je vos desfi
(Stand back, I challenge you)
Fergus 159/12: Traiiez en la, je vos desfi
(Stand back, I challenge you)...

Erec 5615: Mes se vos me voliiez croire
(But if you are willing to believe me)
Fergus 77/33: Mes se vos me voliés croire
(But if you are willing to believe me)

Erec 5999: Tant que l'ore de none passe
(Until past three o'clock)
Fergus 147/29: Endroit que l'ore de none passe
(Until past three o'clock)

Habemann, 'Die literarische Stellung des Meraugis' (translated from p. 23):

A number of definitive borrowings from *Perceval* can be demonstrated in *Meraugis*:

Perceval 5981–3: grant fu la joie, que li rois
fist de Perceval le Galois
et la roine et li baron. [Roach 4603–5]

(Great was the rejoicing of the king, the queen and the barons over Perceval the Welshman.)

Meraugis 5070–2: onques li rois n'ot si grant joie
com il ot de son neveu—
grant joie en firent li chevalier.

(The king had never known such great joy as he felt for his nephew—the knights rejoiced greatly over him.)

Perceval 5988–91: ...il virent
une damoisiele ki vient
sor une fauve mule et tint
en sa main destre une escorgiee. [Roach 4610–13]

(They saw a damsel coming on a tawny mule, and she held a whip in her right hand.)

Meraugis 5087–9: ...une dame vint
desus un mul, la dame tint
une escorgiee en sa main destre.

(A lady came on a mule; the lady held a whip in her right hand.)

Correspondences in content or motifs were likewise regarded in principle as testifying to dependence on the donor text. The authors of those studies did not realize that these storylines and motifs represent nothing less than the building blocks of the genre, so that their use in the Arthurian romances is inescapable. Scholars bestowed their greatest admiration on those authors who were supposedly especially skilful in a technique whereby their plagiarisms from Chrétien's works were altered or concealed to such an extent that a researcher could only identify them with difficulty. The more limited the 'imagination' of the dependent author, the more he allegedly had to make up for this deficiency in the technical refinement of the process of compilation that was his working method. This is Rohde's verdict on Raoul de Houdenc:

> From the examples given, the following conclusion can be drawn about the way in which Raoul used Chrétien's romances. The poet did not imitate the main motifs of the epics so much as those many little touches which are less conspicuous at first sight but which Chrétien used to lend life and colour to his narrative. These touches were not derived from his sources but are truly his own, and it was precisely these that Raoul needed to embroider his own poem; his imagination was not very fertile, so this was where he directed his attention.[6]

Now as it happens Raoul de Houdenc is probably not the author of *La Vengeance Raguidel*, as Rohde still supposed, but in any case that other Raoul did not deserve Rohde's critical verdict either. If he had had so little imagination, he would scarcely have been the only one amongst the Arthurian poets of the thirteenth century to hit upon the idea of writing a parody of Gawain, the perfect knight.

The majority of the texts under discussion here do not yield examples of a lack of ability leading to an increasing dependence of the later poets on Chrétien; what they reveal instead is their close relationship to the traditions of the genre as represented by Chrétien's works. However, a clear change of critical approach is already becoming apparent in the work of Klose.[7] Having first of all unearthed cases of verbal and stylistic borrowings from Chrétien, he allocates the majority to the sphere of historical developments in style. Incidentally, he acknowledges that not everything derives from Chrétien; works of the same type from the intervening period, such as the other Arthurian romances but also including the traditional epics, are likewise to be regarded as models.

> It is inherent in the very nature of many of the so-called borrowings that both the plot and the formal side of a work...can be associated with a great diversity

[6] Translated from Rohde, *La Vengeance de Raguidel*, p. 25.

[7] M. Klose, *Der Roman von Claris et Laris in seinen Beziehungen zur altfranzösischen Artusepik des XII. und XIII. Jahrhunderts*, *ZrPh* Beiheft 63 (Halle, 1916).

> of predecessors and cannot be exactly defined as relating only to this or that particular source; the borrowings are not exclusively deliberate imitations, although these can also be found in plenty, but are often merely reminiscences.[8]

However, taking Klose's line even further, it is reasonable to suppose that the language of various authors of Arthurian verse romances reveals such close relationships and similarities because for one thing these poets are writing in the literary language of their time, where a general linguistic norm is common to all of them, and because furthermore they naturally employ the specific forms of expression of their genre.[9] A certain formulaic element in the manner of describing events typical of the genre, circumscribed amongst other things by the verse form, is only to be expected. These events and scenes can be taken to include, for example, the Arthurian romance opening, catalogues of beauty, duels and festivals, as well as a number of stereotypical adventures with young ladies, knights guarding fords, giants, dwarfs and monsters. Thus it is probably not appropriate to assume, as Marquardt does,[10] that the author of *Fergus* borrowed the following comparison from the author of *Erec*:

Erec: Plus ot que n'est la flors de lis
cler et blanc le front et le vis. (427–8)
(Her face and her brow shone whiter than the lily flower.)

Fergus: Le front ot plus blanc et le vis
Que n'est la blance flors de lis. (1551–2)
(Her face and her brow were whiter than the white lily flower.)

In fact the author of *Fergus* is resorting to a formula for descriptions of beauty that is available to all poets and that is in its turn rooted in a European cultural tradition of long standing. An author cannot avoid using the linguistic modes of expression available in his own day, including the formulas, any more than he can relate particular sets of facts without employing the corresponding nouns and verbs. An account of a duel is bound to mention horses, lances, shields, the collision, the bleeding of the wounds and the combatants falling or dismounting. The combat itself proceeds according to strict rules, and the same is true when it is described. The mere fact that another poet has used comparable descriptions on a previous occasion does not justify our assuming direct dependence or a decadent decline in quality. As Klose points out, 'we can only think in terms of

[8] Translated from Klose, *Der Roman von Claris et Laris*, p. 303.

[9] Cormeau, *'Wigalois' und 'Diu Crône'*, [translated from] p. 108: 'The language of courtly romance is subject to...various restrictions typical of the genre. These are determined by the form, the subject matter and the literary tone required by that subject matter.'

[10] Marquardt, *Der Einfluss Kristians von Troyes*, p. 50.

borrowings when word for word agreements go beyond the bounds of whatever the relevant formula may be; but even then it is quite often the case that coincidence still has a hand in it.'[11] The same is true for the actual stylistic features; formulas for specific sequences of events with scarcely any variation constitute the linguistic norm and the common repertoire of the genre.

'QUOTATIONS' FROM CHRETIEN

As was the case in the previous chapter, the following considerations are based on the realization that later authors of Arthurian verse romances not only knew Chrétien's works but were familiar with them on a detailed level. Chrétien formulated the prototypes of the genre and is taken as the norm throughout the entire history of that genre, acting as the point of reference for all subsequent narrators. However, earlier scholarship started from the premiss that the Arthurian poets had wanted as far as possible to draw a veil over such familiarity in the hope that their public would not notice, and it was therefore deemed to be important to adopt scientific methods in revealing the different forms of dependency, from plagiarism to mere echoes. By contrast, if we now review some selected examples from the abundance of possible references, the evidence is available that as a rule the authors introduced quotations from Chrétien's works as a deliberate stylistic device. At the same time, this means that the powerful influence of Chrétien on these later poets is certainly not to be denied, but should merely be seen in a new light.

The effectiveness of a quotation as a stylistic device depends on the receptivity of the public. They are intended to recognize lines directed as signals to audience or reader, yet at the same time the quotation must be integrated smoothly into the new text, whilst nevertheless remaining identifiable for what it is.

> If the quotation is melted down into the new linguistic entity to the point of being unrecognizable, it will then simply lose its specific character and its specific effect. In general it could be said that the charm of the quotation lies in a peculiar tension between assimilation and dissimilation.[12]

Thus the function of any Chrétien quotation is new each time because individual to each situation, since it develops solely from the context of the new narrative. The public for its part must be capable to a certain extent of making associations, or the quotation will lose its proper impact. These considerations necessitate an approach whereby any given quotation is subjected to a comparison in its old

[11] Translated from Klose, *Der Roman von Claris et Laris*, p. 7.

[12] Translated from H. Meyer, *Das Zitat in der Erzählkunst* (Stuttgart, 1961; second edn., 1967), p. 12.

and new contexts. The repetition of individual lines in isolation, which earlier scholars concentrated on, inevitably led them to pronounce a negative verdict of derivativeness resulting from lack of talent, and blinded them to the poets' techniques of literary embellishment.

The following examination is limited to examples of word for word quotation ('wortlautliche Anführung')[13] from Chrétien's romances; allusions to other famous works such as the romances of *Troie* and *Eneas* or the Tristan material (in so far as they can be characterized as quotations at all) will not be considered here. It is also impossible to be certain whether Arthurian poets of the thirteenth century quoted from each other's works. The only reference point that remains constant for all of them, and is thus far also their permanent authority, is the work of Chrétien as the story-teller who created the genre. The examples about to be examined are for the most part 'cryptic' quotations; in other words, the author does not divulge their origin and they can only be recognized by the initiated amongst the public. The whole process is like a game of hide-and-seek: 'The point of the game is to discover the quotation, because that is the only way it can achieve its specific effect.'[14]

Together with Chrétien's other Arthurian romances the story of Erec and Enide had a powerful influence on the composition of Raoul's *Meraugis*; this has already been demonstrated by Friedwagner and Habemann.[15] Like Enide, the heroine Lidoine is a girl whose external beauty is in keeping with her superior inner qualities. In a beauty contest she wins a sparrowhawk. Like Enide she accompanies her knight on a journey of adventure. Both women show cunning in dealing with unwanted suitors, and both are unconditionally faithful. Lidoine is just as inconsolable at Meraugis' supposed death as Enide was over Erec's apparent demise. Both women, each with their *ami*, find themselves having adventures with a close structural similarity; for Meraugis it is the Cité sanz non (City without a name), and for Erec the Joie de la Cort (Joy of the Court). The relationship between the plots of the two romances is so obvious that it cannot be explained by chance or by Raoul's lack of ability. Consequently the parallels were presumably intentional. It is decisive for the effectiveness of *Meraugis* that the public should be able to grasp what is new about Raoul's romance and the ways in which it differs from Chrétien's *Erec*, against the background of its relationship with that earlier work. Where the elements of novelty actually lie was discussed in Chapter 5.

[13] Meyer, *Das Zitat*, p. 15.

[14] Translated from Meyer, *Das Zitat*, p. 13.

[15] See the introduction in Friedwagner's edition, p. LXXff., and Habemann, 'Die literarische Stellung des *Meraugis*', *passim*.

The assumption that Raoul deliberately used a famous earlier work as a foil for his romance is confirmed at the formal level by the fact that clear references to specific elements of the plot peculiar to that earlier text, as well as some actual quotations from *Erec*, have been incorporated into Raoul's own work. Early in the text he describes the preparations for the tournament of Lindesores. The festive proceedings also include a beauty contest, and the author informs his readers of the conditions of the competition:

Sus une lance de sapin
Sera uns esperviers muëz
Qui ja n'iert pris ne remuëz
Devant la que cele le preigne
Qui par veüe lor apreigne
Qu'ele soit plus bele que totes;
Se la robe ert perciee as cotes,
Por tant que ce fust la plus bele,
N'i avra il ja damoisele
Qui ait l'espervier se li non. (176–85)

(On a lance of fir there will be a moulted sparrowhawk that will not be taken or moved until it is claimed by the lady who is visibly the most beautiful of all. *Even if her dress were worn through at the elbows*, as long as she was the most beautiful, no maiden other than her would obtain the sparrowhawk.)

These lines contain a quotation which makes a subtle reference to the romance of *Erec*, namely the allusion to Enide's dress, which was so old 'que as costez estoit perciez' (408 and 1548ff. [1568ff.], 'that it was in holes at the sides').[†] The torn

[†] [*Translator's note*: The form *cotes* (required by the rhyme) at line 182 of *Meraugis* is ambiguous. It could stand for *coutes* (= 'elbows') or *costes* (= 'sides'). This also affects the interpretation of *perciez*, meaning simply 'with holes', either as a result of natural wear (most characteristic of the elbows) or as a result of some accident or deliberate destruction (perhaps more likely at the sides). In *Erec et Enide* the intended meaning is in fact 'worn through at the elbows', but this is not made clear until lines 1548–50: 'Povretez li a fet user / ce blanc chainse tant que as cotes / an sont andeus manches rotes' ('Poverty has caused her to wear out this white shift until both sleeves have holes in the elbows'). At line 408 manuscripts *EPBVA* have *coutes* (or its dialectal equivalent); *H* has *costes* and *C* (used by Roques for his edition) has *costez*, surely intending the meaning 'sides' (as translated above) despite the editor's ingenious note on p. 214. Writing long before the date of any surviving French manuscript Hartmann von Aue describes Enite's dress as 'gezerret begarwe' (325, 'torn to shreds') and refers to the fact that her body (329, 'lîch') is visible through it. It would be a matter of speculation whether this implies an exemplar with *costes*, a misunderstanding of an ambiguous *cotes*, or pure invention by Hartmann himself. Raoul de Houdenc, working not very much later than Hartmann, could have known either tradition, and so could his audience. In her own comments Schmolke-Hasselmann seems to favour 'torn' rather than 'worn' and 'sides' rather than 'elbows', whereas the passage she quotes from Habemann refers unambiguously to 'elbows' but interprets the text of *Meraugis* as meaning that the dress will be cut deliberately as a sign that the lady has been chosen as the most beautiful (which is certainly not correct).]

dress can be seen as a standard attribute of Enide, and it symbolizes her beauty better than could any magnificent robes, playing an important part throughout the whole of the *premerains vers*. Now Raoul informs us that in Lindesores the bird must be claimed by the lady who can prove that she is more beautiful than all the rest. Provided that she really is the most beautiful, nobody will be able to withhold the sparrowhawk from her, even if her dress is torn at the sides (or elbows). The mention of this torn dress remains meaningless as long as the public fails to make the connection with the romance of *Erec*, but in fact Raoul's contemporaries were certainly in a position to do this. Raoul is evoking a literary narrative tradition. In the minds of readers of Arthurian romances the sparrowhawk contest has for decades been inseparably bound up with the figure of Enide. But it is not necessary for Raoul to give her name here. A key word is sufficient to produce the connection with the desired frame of reference. In addition, there is a further aspect to consider. Since the prototype sparrowhawk contest from Chrétien's *Erec* is anchored in the minds of author and public as the literary norm, Raoul can incorporate the traditional outcome into his narrative as well; to a certain extent he expands the custom, adding the rule that a torn dress must not be allowed as grounds for disqualification in a beauty contest. With some humour he gives his sparrowhawk episode a dimension of legal history, where the precedent can be looked up in Chrétien's romance.

A diametrically opposite interpretation of this passage can be found for example in Habemann:

> We have a definite criterion for determining that the sparrowhawk episode in *Meraugis* cannot have been taken from some common source for *Erec* and *Meraugis*, but is a direct derivation from *Erec*: when Enide tries to take the sparrowhawk she is very shabbily dressed, with her shift worn through at the elbows...and despite her shabby clothing, she receives the prize for beauty. When the custom is described in *Meraugis* whereby the most beautiful lady, who is to receive the sparrowhawk, has her dress cut open at the elbows...as a sign that she is the most beautiful, then this is doubtless to be seen as reminiscent of Enide in Chrétien's *Erec*.
>
> The deviation from *Erec* in this episode is therefore to be understood as a deliberate alteration; Raoul, who was struck by the contradiction in *Erec*, has eliminated this in his own work. In my opinion there is no reason to postulate a common source for this episode in the two works, simply in order to be able to claim that *Meraugis* preserved the original version.[16]

On another occasion, however, Raoul uses a quotation from *Erec* placed in a radically altered context. In Chrétien's text the poor vavasour used these words when telling the hero about his daughter:

[16] Translated from Habemann, 'Die literarische Stellung des *Meraugis*', p. 13.

'Quant ge ai delez moi ma fille,
tot le mont ne pris une bille;
c'est mes deduiz, c'est mes deporz,
c'est mes solaz et mes conforz,
c'est mes avoirs et mes tresors,
je n'ain tant rien come son cors.' (541–6)

('When my daughter is beside me I do not give a marble for the whole world. She is my delight, she is my pleasure, she is my solace and my comfort, she is my wealth and my treasure; I love nothing so much as her.')

Such words are also very suitable for a lover, so Raoul allows Meraugis to use them as he thinks of his distant Lidoine:[17]

'... Qu'or la verroie
Volentiers! Se j'en ai envie,
Je n'ai pas tort; car c'est m'amie,
C'est mes deduiz, c'est mes deporz,
C'est ma joie, c'est mes conforz,
C'est quan que j'aim, c'est ma puissance,
C'est ma baniere, c'est ma lance,
C'est mes desirs, c'est ma richece,
C'est mes escuz, c'est ma proece,
C'est ma hautece, c'est mes pris,
C'est *tot li monz*, ce m'est avis,
C'est mes chasteaus, c'est mes *tresors*,
C'est mes douz cuers, c'est mes beaus *cors*,
C'est ma main destre, c'est ma dame,
C'est moi meïsmes, car c'est m'ame,
C'est mes *solaz*, c'est quan que j'ai,
C'est la santé dont je garrai.' (4874–90)

('How I'd like to see her now! And if I want to, I am not in the wrong, for she is my mistress, she is my delight, she is my pleasure, she is my joy, she is my comfort, she is all that I love, she is my strength, she is my banner, she is my lance, she is my desire, she is my wealth, she is my shield, she is my prowess, she is my reputation, she is my fame, she is *my whole world* as I see it, she is my castle, she is my *treasure*, she is my gentle heart, she is my handsome *body*, she is my right hand, she is my lady, she is my own self, for she is my soul, she is my *solace*, she is all that I have, she is health and my cure.')

The function of this passage is now totally different. The structure used to make the association of ideas with *Erec* has undergone considerable amplification, and

[17] A similar quotation is to be found in the Prose *Lancelot*, edited by Alexandre Micha, *TLF* 247, 249, 262, 278, 283, 286, 288, 307 and 315, 9 vols (Geneva, 1978–83), Vol. II, p. 194. The passage is spoken by a woman, about Boorz li Essilliés.

the lines that originally belonged together now appear widely separated. It is difficult to judge whether the fourfold extension of the sequence signifies a deliberate exaggeration in the application of Chrétien's stylistic technique, but that seems entirely possible for Raoul. In any case the words of the vavasour have evolved into something quite different: we have a new speaker, a new context, a new form and a new function.

If Lidoine can be understood in many respects as a parallel and a contrasting figure for Enide, this is nevertheless not the only such point of comparison. Meraugis and Erec are in a similar position. Before his main adventure, which in itself is obviously closely related to the Joie de la Cort episode, Meraugis sees the inhabitants of the Cité sanz non dancing and singing with malicious pleasure because someone has fallen into the trap again. In Chrétien's romance, by contrast, the inhabitants of the town manifest genuine sympathy for Erec. However, Meraugis does not allow himself to be intimidated. In making an ironic comment on the people's behaviour he utters the same words that Erec pronounces when he learns the name of his *aventure*: '...en joie n'a se bien non' (2900, 'there is nothing but good in joy', corresponding to *Erec et Enide*, line 5418). Such examples serve to demonstrate what literary quotations can achieve as structural elements in the context of another work.

The close connections between *Fergus* and Chrétien's *Perceval* have already been discussed at length in Chapter 5. It now remains to complete the picture by showing that Guillaume le Clerc is also a master of the technique of quoting Chrétien, which is typical of the genre. It will occasion no surprise to learn that such quotations originate only from *Perceval* and not from other Chrétien romances. When Arthurian poets of the thirteenth century deliberately link their work to a particular romance by their predecessor Chrétien, this is always carried out on several levels. Citing linguistic nuggets pregnant with meaning from the earlier text can be seen as one of these levels of reference. Guillaume proceeds in a different way from Raoul. He makes his hero Fergus quote from *Perceval* where we least expect it, and where the narrative context is fundamentally different, thereby achieving a distinctly comic effect. The amusement of his public, who can recall the context in *Perceval*, is provoked by his setting up literary contrasts, as the following two examples will show.

In a duel Fergus scalps the back of his opponent's head with his sword. As is his wont, he then quite unconcernedly makes fun of the rascal's predicament:

> 'Foi que do[i] cele clere lune,
> Orendroit resanblés Fortune,
> Qui ens el front [est] chavelue,
> El haterel deriere nue.

Jo avoie tos jors apris
Que on fust chaut devers le vis,
Et vos l'estes par de deriere.'
'Tels en est or[e] la maniere,'
Fait li chevaliers de noviel. (3041–9)

('By the faith I owe to that bright moon, now you look like Fortune, who has hair at the front but who's bald at the back. I had always understood that it was people's foreheads that were hairless, but in your case it's the back.' 'That's the latest fashion,' says the knight in reply.)

At this point Guillaume is making his hero repeat the first words of Chrétien's *hideuse demoisele* in *Perceval*:

Ha! Perchevax, Fortune [est] cauve
Detriers et devant chavelue.
Et dehais ait qui te salue... (4646–8)

(Ah, Perceval! Fortune is bald at the back with hair at the front, and a curse on anyone who greets you...)

In so doing he forges an association with one of the most poignant and impressive scenes of the Grail romance. There the words of the quotation are a bitterly serious admonition, with symbolic force and in a very prominent position, whereas here they are intended merely as a mocking comment, and on an entirely concrete level. Uttered in passing in the course of a secondary episode, they give the quotation a new function, to distance and to amuse.

The second example reveals a similar procedure. A king defeated by Fergus comes to court to submit to Arthur, who ponders whether he should hang him, burn him or drown him. Finally he calls on Gawain's advice, and the latter impresses upon him that he should be more merciful:

Qu'il pardoinst deboin[ai]rement
Au chevalier son mautalent.
S'il l'ocio[i]t que li vauroit?
Ja por cho ne recoverroit
Icels qui estoient ocis.
Les mors as mors, les vis as vis. (3545–50)

(That he should do the noble thing and pardon the knight his ill-will. What good would it do him to kill him? He would not thereby recover those who were dead. *To the dead, the dead; to the living, the living.*)

The contrast is effected here by the fact that Perceval uttered this proverb with the unfeeling attitude of an immature boy as he addressed his cousin who was mourning her beloved (*Perceval*, line 3630). On that occasion the words were hardly suitable as consolation, but here, forming part of Gawain's reasoning as to whether murder should be punished by death, they are entirely appropriate. The quotation evokes the previous context and in so doing recalls an example of the inadequate standard of behaviour so characteristic of Perceval; Fergus, as the new Perceval, is supposed to avoid such behaviour.

Another way of toying with quotations from Chrétien is exemplified in a play on words from *Yvain* which subsequently became famous. The quotations, although sometimes slightly altered, refer back to the unforgettable opening lines of *Yvain*, the Whitsun festival in Carduel:

> a cele feste qui tant coste,
> qu'an doit clamer la Pantecoste. (5–6)
>
> (at that festival which costs so much that it should be called Pentecost.)

This witty rhyme probably already made an impression on *Yvain*'s entire readership, as it certainly did on the thirteenth-century authors of Arthurian romances. After Chrétien the term for Whitsun, which is the festival typically associated with the genre of Arthurian literature (see Chapter 2), can never again be placed at the end of a line without rhyming with 'coste':

> *Gliglois*: Molt y despent et molt li couste.
> Che fu a unne Pentecouste... (91–2)
>
> (He spends a lot on it and it costs him a lot. It was one Pentecost...)

> *Lai du cor*: Une feste ki mout couste
> Un jour de Pentecouste. (7–8)
>
> (A festival that costs a lot, one Pentecost.)

> *Meraugis*: '...il le fera
> Si hautement com il devra
> Chevalier a la Pentecoste.'
> Lidoine ot ce qui mout li coste... (3829–32)
>
> ('...he will make him a knight with all due ceremony at Pentecost.'
> Lidoine hears what costs her dearly...)

> *Escanor*: [Artus] tendra cort a la Pentecouste
> A Carlion, coi qu'ele couste. (11,709–10)
>
> (Arthur will hold court at Caerlion at Pentecost, whatever it costs.)

It appears that before *Yvain* this rhyme and the associated pun were unknown, and even after *Yvain* they hardly ever occur outside Arthurian verse romances. One of the rare exceptions is represented by a couplet in the *Roman de la Rose* by Guillaume de Lorris (Lecoy's edition), which is rendered ironical by the use of the word 'petit':

Chapel de flor, qui petit coste,
ou de rouses a Pentecoste. (2149–50)

(At Pentecost a garland of flowers or roses that does not cost a lot.)

In Wace's *Brut* 'Pentecoste' still rhymes with 'dejoste'. The new level of meaning with which the day of Pentecost is imbued in the *Queste du Saint Graal* has the effect that there too the play on words can be dispensed with. Compare also the *fabliau* of *Auberee*, edited by Christmann, lines 211–12, the *Chastelaine de Vergi*, edited by Stuip, lines 691–2, and the *Roman de Renart*, Branch I, edited by Martin:

'...Conme le jor de pantecoste.'
Mes sa parole, que li coste? (781–2)

('...as on the day of Pentecost.' But what do his words cost him?)

This is the Arthurian rhyme *par excellence*. Although there were always plenty of other possible rhymes for *-oste* readily available, even Froissart cannot resist this insidious compulsion in his Arthurian work *Meliador*:

Droit au jour de la Pentecouste,
Chevaliers sera, quoi qu'il couste. (2518–9)

(He will become a knight on the very day of Pentecost, whatever it costs.)

Pour estre la, quoi qu'il leur couste,
Trois jours devant le Pentecouste... (2564–5)

(To get there, whatever it may cost them, three days before Pentecost...)

The magic of Chrétien's play on words continues to be active for nearly two hundred years, and this indicates once more that throughout the entire development of the genre his work remains an absolute frame of reference.[18]

Examination of the quotations from Chrétien has shown that authors cannot just quote anything and everything. They must necessarily confine themselves to those passages which they can predict without any shadow of doubt will be known to their audience. The procedure is cryptic but not esoteric, and quotations are selected accordingly: Enide's dress, the words of the ugly damsel, the opening lines of *Yvain* and little else. A thirteenth-century author can count on not only a knowledge of such popular passages amongst his readers but also a particular set of expectations; he uses these to achieve contrasting and generally comic effects. This phenomenon begins to confirm Meyer's assertion that 'the humorous romances saw quotations develop for the first time into a truly epic

[18] For more on this subject see F. W. Locke, 'Yvain, "A cele feste qui tant coste qu'an doit clamer la pantecoste"', *Neophilologus* 43 (1959), 288–92.

and aesthetically successful artistic technique'.[19] At the very least, by using Chrétien quotations the Arthurian poets of the thirteenth century drew attention to the literary tradition common to themselves and their public, and consciously secured for their works a place within the development of the genre. Here as always the writers are sharing in the organization of their cultural heritage. Each new work also helps to reinforce that continuity. The art of quotation as demonstrated in the Arthurian romances of the thirteenth century bears witness to 'the more universal phenomenon that literature is nourished by other literature'.[20]

MOTIFS FROM CHRETIEN

Arthurian literature is largely defined by its own particular collection of motifs, yet most of these can be traced back to the more general spheres of myth and fairy-tale. However, the following section is not intended to conduct yet another investigation into the origins of Arthurian motifs. Instead the aim is to view them in the context of the generic development of Arthurian verse romance, in an attempt to determine which of the prototype motifs introduced in Chrétien's romances are retained in the later Arthurian romances, which ones proved to be especially popular in the genre's development and helped to create a tradition, and which ones were subjected to particular changes. These questions are central to a study of the romances.

It rapidly emerges that the only motifs of significance in this discussion are those which are solely characteristic of their own individual Chrétien romance, in other words which can be unambiguously and exclusively allocated to *Erec* or *Yvain*, to *Perceval*, *Cligés* or *Lancelot*. This implies that standard Arthurian motifs such as adventures with fairies, encounters with young ladies, giants, dwarfs and dragons, as well as rescue missions, the ever-recurring festivals at Arthur's court, the messenger scenes, the romantic elements in their generally Arthurian characteristics and much more besides will not be discussed in this context, because right from the start, even in Chrétien's works, they appear with such a breadth of variation, although within standardized types, that they cannot be used to illustrate any diachronic perspectives.

Like the use of quotations, the recurrence of motifs which derive unmistakably from one particular romance and are characteristic of it, such as the adventure at the spring in *Yvain* or the Joie de la Cort in *Erec*, proves to be another phenomenon of the reception of Chrétien's works. The term motif as

[19] Translated from Meyer, *Das Zitat*, p. 16.
[20] Translated from Meyer, *Das Zitat*, p. 22.

used here also includes particular episodes which occur so frequently that they develop the character of motifs. The function of all these recurrences is circumscribed by the fact that the origin of the motif is ever present in the minds of the author and his public, and without exception this origin is envisaged in conjunction with the novel application of the motif. This gives rise to an opportunity for communication on the premiss of a common awareness of a literary tradition. Thus the use of traditional motifs is another way in which the Arthurian verse romances mirror their own development. We have already discussed the fact that the links with the common frame of reference, namely Chrétien's works, are established not merely through a general similarity or comparable motifs, but precisely through explicit references to well-known sequences of events, mentioning of names and quotations. It is not, therefore, a case of plagiarism when motifs from Chrétien's works familiar to both authors and the public are later re-used; on the contrary, this is deliberate duplication of motifs.[21]

Furthermore, it is characteristic of the process that the authors will only use those familiar motifs which they can assume to be clearly imprinted upon the public mind. As a result of this, and having with hindsight established the frequency with which a particular motif was re-used, it is then possible to assess the level of that motif's familiarity and popularity with thirteenth-century readers, and also to draw certain conclusions about literary developments.

The most frequently re-used, and by a considerable margin, are motifs from *Erec*: the stag hunt, the characteristics of Enide and her family, the sparrowhawk episode, the apparent death of the hero, the Joy of the Court adventure, the problems of *recreantise* and the equal rank of partners—all these recur in the verse romances of the thirteenth century, with a variety of modifications and placed within different contexts. Motifs from *Perceval* are in second place, although here it would seem that only the opening section, namely Perceval's *niceté* (naivety), his departure from his mother, the encounter with the knights and his first visit to Arthur's court, managed to establish themselves as lasting memories in the literary consciousness of consumers of Arthurian verse romances. It has already been shown elsewhere in this study that the Grail and its attendant complications are omitted *en bloc* from this genre, and not only the central narrative element but also the motifs associated with it.

From the perspective of a thirteenth-century author the only motifs specific to *Yvain* are the adventure at the spring, the encounter with the wild herdsman and the hero's madness. All three motifs recur in later romances, but not very

[21] Cormeau, *'Wigalois' und 'Diu Crône'*, p. 211, establishes that this is also true of German Arthurian romances.

often.[22] The modern reader is more inclined to see Chrétien's great achievement in terms of his innovations in the spheres of thematic structure and the psychological presentation of characters, and may therefore be surprised to find his romances reduced to just a few particularly memorable scenes. However, this drastic simplification in the reception of Chrétien's romances, often also limited to the opening sections, is likewise found in the pictorial arts of the Middle Ages, in miniatures and the decorative arts. It seems to be characteristic of an essentially more uninhibited attitude towards great works of literature, despite the fact that in this case their outstanding qualities were undoubtedly recognized by Chrétien's contemporaries and immediate successors.[23]

In total contrast to the authors of prose works, the poets of the Arthurian verse romances do not seem to have been particularly fond of *Lancelot* or *Cligés*. Whilst an abduction of the queen does occur once more (*Durmart*, lines 4188–868), the episode bears no resemblance whatsoever to the plot of *Lancelot* apart from the fact of the abduction itself. Villains like Meleagant, who would rather die than repent, can also still be found in later works (e.g. Gornemant and Brien in *Li Chevaliers as deus espees*), and many a hero succumbs to *penser*, sinking into a profound meditation at the thought of his beloved;[24] however, the allusions are too vague for us to be able to speak unhesitatingly of a deliberate reference by the author to the known context of a particular Chrétien romance. Finally, neither the content nor the motifs of *Cligés* attract the attention of later authors, which may mean that this romance played an equally insignificant part in the literary consciousness of that section of the public specifically interested in Arthurian verse romances.[25]

The references to *Erec* are not only the most frequent, but are also, as we shall see, the most revealing in the way that they are modified. It will be remembered that Gawain in *Erec* expresses grave misgivings when he hears that his king is summoning everyone to join in the traditional hunt of the white stag. He is aware that observing this custom must entail far-reaching consequences for the state of harmony amongst the members of the court. In the later romance of *Fergus*, Arthur is similarly intent on hunting the white stag, and the audience will have been surprised to hear Gawain adopting the following attitude:

[22] There is also a wild herdsman in *Aucassin et Nicolette*.

[23] See R. S. Loomis and L. Hibbard Loomis, *Arthurian Legends in Medieval Art* (New York, 1938), especially the cycles of frescoes and the portrayals in ivory, where the narratives of *Perceval* and *Yvain* appear similarly reduced to leave those scenes which also recur in the verse romances.

[24] For example Yder and Durmart; this notion of *penser* may equally well derive from the episode of the blood on the snow.

[25] On the other hand, it is interesting that there is a prose version of *Cligés* [a fifteenth-century adaptation of Chrétien's verse, associated with the court of Philip the Good of Burgundy].

'Sire, tot a vostre talent,'
Fait mesire Gavains au roi,
'Car contre vous aler ne doi.' (56–8)

('Just as you wish, sire,' says my lord Gawain to the king, 'for I must not contradict you.')

The piquancy of this reply can only be appreciated against the background of *Erec*, and with prior knowledge that Gawain traditionally appears as an adviser who criticizes and admonishes the king.

The sparrowhawk episode, which is particularly frequent in its reappearances under new guises,[26] is divested of any claim to a mythological absolutism in both *Meraugis* and *Le Bel Inconnu*. Raoul de Houdenc and Renaut de Beaujeu both feel the need to add their own comments to the fossilized ritual of the beauty contest. Thus when the prize has been awarded Raoul divulges the fact that it has not been a genuine competition. People had already agreed beforehand that a particular lady should be chosen, although in fact she was 'pas si covoitable' (*Meraugis* 328, 'not so attractive'). But because of her general popularity people did not want to offend her. Renaut even goes a step further: the lady who claims the sparrowhawk for herself in *Le Bel Inconnu* is called Rose Espanie ('Rose in bloom', implying 'overblown'), and 'Molt estoit et laide et frencie' (1727, 'she was both very ugly and very wrinkled'). However, her companion regards her as the most beautiful of all, and in his eyes she deserves to win the sparrowhawk:

K'Amors li fait son sens müer.
Mais nus hom ne se puet garder
K'Amors nel face bestorner;
La laide fait biele sanbler,
Tant set de guille et d'encanter. (1731–5)[27]

(For love had turned his brain, but no man can guard against love turning him inside out; it makes the ugly seem beautiful, such is its command of deceit and enchantment.)

The seriousness of the duel for the sparrowhawk in *Erec* has given way to a gently ironic ability to see through the real conditions of the contest. On the other hand, its original function is largely preserved: placed at the beginning of

[26] R. S. Loomis, *Arthurian Tradition and Chrétien de Troyes* (New York, 1949), p. 86, gives a list of all the works that include the sparrowhawk episode.

[27] *Le Chevalier del Papegau*, a thirteenth-century prose romance, also has the motif of the sparrowhawk contest in this variant version with an ugly lady. It is apparent from this that even the transformation of an episode originally appearing in Chrétien's works can itself develop into an Arthurian motif. This prose romance also exhibits further characteristics surprisingly akin to those of the verse romances. Its burlesque features merit renewed attention.

a chain of Arthurian adventures, the sparrowhawk contest establishes the relationship of the amorous couple who are the leading protagonists in that particular romance.

In *Meraugis*, Raoul de Houdenc treats the Joie de la Cort motif in accordance with his principle of reversing the meaning, thus also achieving literary irony in his version of the well-known episode. At first the situation appears to be identical with that in *Erec*. Meraugis, accompanied by Lidoine, enters the town in which there awaits him a mysterious adventure from which he cannot withdraw. In this case the adventure is located on an island (as opposed to the garden in *Erec*), where a lady has dwelt with her knight for seven years. In contrast to *Erec*, it is in the first instance not her *ami* but her husband whom she guards so jealously and shields from any contact with the outside world. The inhabitants of the town are the guards intended to prevent his escape. Magic spells, a wall of air, a horn and threatening rows of stakes with heads impaled on them no longer have any part to play in *Meraugis*. The place has been stripped of any mythical overtones. Every knight who enters the town must fight the husband. One year before Meraugis' arrival Gawain, the perfect knight, had arrived on the scene and had defeated and killed the lady's husband. Since then, as the custom demands, Gawain has had to take the husband's place. Thus in this case, unlike Erec in Chrétien's romance, Gawain did not free the pair of lovers from their self-imposed isolation, and the lady has been neither persuaded of the senselessness of her possessive claim nor converted from the antisocial aspects of her jealousy. Instead the complete reversal of meaning in the adventure lies in the fact that the lady's jealousy and possessiveness are in no way attached to any particular person. Her partners are interchangeable, her relationship with them forced and correspondingly uncourtly. Moreover, the custom even demands that one of the two opponents in the fight must die each time, so that a knight arriving in the town has his choice limited to either his own death or imprisonment without honour or dignity in the lady's tower. This is the grotesque situation in which Gawain finds himself. If he now kills Meraugis, his friend and temporary opponent, he will have to stay on the island even longer; if, on the other hand, Meraugis kills Gawain, he will have to take Gawain's place with the lady. Gawain is deeply depressed, and after a year of constant humiliation he longs for death. He would like to be defeated in the fight and tries to make victory appealing to Meraugis:

> 'Tu seras mestre chastelains
> De ceste tor tote ta vie.' (3186–7)

('You will be the chatelain in charge of this tower all your life.')

Meraugis replies: 'De ce n'ai je pas grant envie' (3188, 'I have no great desire for that'). Only by a cunning trick (see Chapter 5) can he release himself and his friend from this apparently hopeless situation. He encourages Gawain to pretend to be dead after a mock fight. Then the lady is barricaded in her tower, and Gawain and Meraugis flee in women's clothes. Any analogy with *Erec* ceases at this point. The custom has not been abolished, only temporarily impeded in its execution. The lady will take the next opportunity to reassert her claim to power over the world of men; unlike in *Erec*, there are no grounds for joy.

The Joie de la Cort episode sheds light on a different aspect of Erec and Enide's marital problem and thus acquires a definable function within the thematic structure of the romance. Even in Raoul's work, despite all the changes, the episode has still maintained its function as a contrast. It should be borne in mind that the excesses of the Provençal doctrine of love make their appearance with thematic significance in *Meraugis*. In this romance the concept of the lady as sovereign mistress, whose wishes the lover has to comply with, is intentionally exposed in the course of the narrative as false and harmful, a theme illustrated by the changing relationship between Meraugis and Lidoine. If Raoul then transforms Chrétien's Joie de la Cort episode to such an extent that he uses it to present a completely absurd case of female lust for power, then this has its own place within the *sens* of the romance of *Meraugis*, which differs in its points of emphasis from that of *Erec*. At the same time the exaggerated alterations to Chrétien's prototype episode, which remains constantly in the minds of Raoul's public in its own right, have the effect of comic distancing whilst simultaneously directing light-hearted irony at Raoul's own procedure. Raoul is flirting with the idea of his 'dependence' on Chrétien, and his audience join in the literary game. Meanwhile, other variations on the Joie de la Cort episode were incorporated into the romances of *Le Bel Inconnu* and *Li Chevaliers as deus espees*.

In *Meraugis* it is specifically the *chevalier as damoiseles* who lands in the situation of having to languish for a whole year as the prisoner of a woman he does not love. In the mind of the public, encountering the episode against the background of the Gawain romances, this fact strikes an additional humorous note reminiscent of the parodying procedure used by the poet of *La Vengeance Raguidel*.

The problem of *recreantise*, which is recognized as such and given literary treatment for the first time by Chrétien in his *Erec*, must have left a powerful impression on his contemporaries and successors, to judge by its reverberations in the Arthurian verse romances of the thirteenth century. After Chrétien the *recreantise* is admittedly no longer treated as the central motif it represented in *Erec* (although in *Floriant et Florete* for example it appears with a similar function as a structural element), but a warning against sinking into inactivity occurs quite frequently at the end of a thirteenth-century Arthurian romance as a final piece of good advice after the successful completion of a sequence of adventures. This relates to the fact that in most of these romances the union of the lovers represents the final goal of the action and it is only after this union that the problem of *recreantise* as exemplified in *Erec* can become a real threat. Erec's mistake is recalled more or less explicitly in *Durmart* and *Fergus*, and in each case the hero is warned by Gawain (following the precedent set in *Yvain*) that under no circumstances should he do as Erec had done. This warning, which in view of its repeated recurrence can already be termed a new Arthurian motif, has even found its way into the Provençal romance of *Jaufré*, line 10,212–18.

The motifs from the introductory episode of *Perceval* are employed once again in *Fergus*. In fact, this entire romance is to be seen as a variation on *Perceval*, as already described in Chapter 5, but nevertheless the motif of the foolish youth has particular force in *Fergus*. The foolishness is stripped of all mysterious or mythical qualities. *Fergus* is not intended to show a youth trying to redeem the world against all the odds by virtue of his predestined role within an Arthurian concept of salvation; it represents instead a naive youth's progress in divesting himself of that naivety to become through experience a knight and a man.

The author of *Tyolet* creates a short independent lay on the basis of the motif he came across in Chrétien. Tyolet is also an ignorant child, but here his ignorance is seen as a positive ability to confront the corruption of the world with inner strength. It is an expression of an unwaveringly pure heart, and in the eyes of the author this is the only quality that can enable the young Tyolet to be victorious against the despicable machinations of his opponents.

This opening section of *Perceval* is probably matched only by the episode of the blood on the snow in the extent to which it became common knowledge (the latter episode being recalled in *Durmart*, lines 3741–4).

Another scene from *Perceval* that proves to be of structural significance for the majority of later Arthurian romances is Kay's mocking, insulting and at the same time provocative attitude towards a young and still unknown knight, who takes such provocation as the spur to a journey of adventure. The hero of the particular romance has to prove to Kay more than all the rest that he is not the person they first thought him to be, and at the appropriate time he has to avenge himself on Kay by inflicting upon him a humiliating defeat. In essence this scene is already present in *Yvain*, where Kay's mockery of Calogrenant arouses Yvain to the necessity of making good his cousin's defeat. However, not until *Perceval* does Chrétien bring his own initiative to completion in such a way that the need for revenge on Kay becomes a motif running through the entire Perceval narrative. It is in this form that the motif lives on in numerous Arthurian romances of the thirteenth century, where Kay always has a provocative function, unsettling the self-esteem of the young hero to such an extent that the latter can only survive by proving that he did not deserve such mockery. Thus Kay becomes a personification of the hero's motivation.

A further important motif, which apparently also has its debut in *Yvain*, is the fight with Gawain. This episode normally has the structural and thematic function of giving the young hero an opportunity to test his superiority over even the authoritative figures of the Arthurian court, at the end of an arduous quest during which he has hitherto performed only against forces not directly associated with the court. As a rule the fight with Gawain comes as the culmination of a series of encounters with other well-known Arthurian knights whom the hero confronts in the course of a tournament or a battle. The Gawain fight usually ends indecisively or is broken off prematurely. Sometimes the hero is victorious even over Gawain (as in *Yder* or *Durmart*), but this is an unheard-of eventuality and remains the exception. Thus in the lists of knights given by authors before such tournaments Gawain is not just one name amongst many. His appearance always has a specific function. The order of the other knights is arbitrary and the length of the list also varies. Beaudous, for example, unhorses one after another Kay, Erec, Lancelot, Yvain and Calogrenant; at the final tournament in *Le Bel Inconnu* (lines 5455–6104) the roll-call of participants includes amongst others Yvain, the Lait Hardi, Perceval le Galois, Lancelot du Lac, Melian de Lis, Marc de Cornouaille, Gawain (here in his role as the hero Guinglain's father) and Tristan, wearing one of Iseut's sleeves as his favour.

Yvain's adventure at the spring is brought to mind once more in the romance of *Claris et Laris*, but in this work it no longer preserves any structural or thematic function as a motif. Claris and Laris, the two male heroes, have taken two villains prisoner. They learn from a lady who at first remains anonymous that shortly beforehand the two rascals had abducted and incarcerated Yvain. The lady explains:

> 'Ier main mon seigneur Yvein pristrent
> En trop male prison le mistrent;
> Ja iert ce mes tres doz amis
> Et je sui cele, qui a mis
> Mon cors en son comandement
> Pour l'amor du grant hardement,
> Qu'il a toz les jours maintenuz,
> Puis qu'il fu au perron venuz,
> Seur quoi versa de la fontaine,
> Ou assez ot anui et painne

De foudre qu'entor li cheoit
Et des arbres qu'il peceoit,
Si con Crestiens le tesmoine.
Et je sui cele sanz essoine,
Cui la fontaine iert ligement,
Se dieux me doint amendement.' (615–30)

('Yesterday morning they took my lord Yvain and put him in a most vile prison. He was my very dear companion and I gave myself to him for love of the great courage that he has always displayed since he came to the slab on which he poured water from the spring, where he had great trouble and difficulty from the lightning that struck all round him and the trees that it destroyed, just as Chrétien bears witness. And it was to me that the spring belonged, absolutely and without lien. May God give me redress.')

This suggests that the speaker is Laudine herself, and the whole passage represents an interpretation of *Yvain* from the viewpoint of a thirteenth-century Arthurian poet. There is no guilt problem, and no explanation from Laudine as to why she forgot her first husband so quickly; indeed, the fight with the guardian of the spring is not even mentioned. Nor is there any reference to the separation of Yvain and Laudine. Here again we can witness the procedure of a romance being reduced to a few aspects of the plot (in this case the motif of the adventure at the spring), and ones which appear of lesser importance in modern eyes. It seems equally strange to hear a character of Chrétien's own invention calling on this same author as her authority.

When Claris and Laris hear of Yvain's imprisonment they rejoice at the opportunity to release the famous knight:

Doucement les en mercia
Mesire Yveins, puis lor demande... (648–9)

(My lord Yvain thanked them graciously for it, and then asks them...)[28]

Another adventure is thus already set in train. The author of *Claris et Laris*, a romance which is something of a digression from the generic norm, no longer uses the technique of referring to an episode from Chrétien with the same significance as his predecessors had done in the first half of the thirteenth century. At that time, as we have seen, the technique had blossomed into a subtle artistic procedure, but now the author of *Claris et Laris* merely recalls a particular episode of *Yvain*, explicitly rather than cryptically, and without deriving from it any original concepts for his own work. The adventure at the spring is not actually used as a motif here, but is merely inserted to narrate the

[28] See also the episode of the spring in the *Tornoiement Antecrist*.

content of an earlier representative of the genre, and is one amongst innumerable other such insertions characteristic of this late specimen of Arthurian verse romance. It is incidentally also the only text amongst those that cannot actually be counted as Gawain romances where motifs from the Gawain romances are nevertheless used. These include Gawain being ambushed by hostile knights while unarmed. The enchanted forest of Broceliande and Arthur's sister Morgan also make an appearance in *Claris et Laris*, despite having no part to play anywhere else in the verse romances. Alongside the story of the two youths there are also the adventures that befall the eleven heroes (who include Gawain, Yvain, Gaheriet, Brandaliz, Sagremor, Agravain and Kay), but all these are devoid of particular characteristics and therefore interchangeable; they can no longer be regarded as motifs that might have been derived from Chrétien and given renewed vitality via a creative process of reception.[29] On the other hand, we can regard the romance of *Claris et Laris* as a *summa* of all Arthurian motifs. Nevertheless, or perhaps precisely because of that, this enormous backward-looking text fails to keep its readers riveted throughout its 30,000 lines.[30]

The considerations undertaken in this section enable us to realize that it is only episodes from Chrétien's *Perceval*, *Erec* and *Yvain* that recur repeatedly in such a way as to invite discussion of their reception; they are the only ones to share in the literary procedure we have described amongst the authors who succeeded Chrétien. Repetition makes some episodes and scenes into motifs whereas they still occur as isolated examples in Chrétien; such motifs can be counted amongst those defining the genre of Arthurian verse romance. Seen from the standpoint of the genre's development they are part of the repertoire which becomes obligatory as the genre evolves. The degree of popularity and familiarity of the Chrétien motifs specified above seems to have exceeded that of all other episodes and motifs from Chrétien's romances when viewed from the perspective of the genre's evolution. This leads us to suppose that they initiated such powerful reverberations because they could be accepted as the unmistakable products of the imagination of one individual poet, as distinct from so many other Arthurian motifs whose origins in the oral or written

[29] See the postscript in the edition by Johann Alton, *BLVS* 169 (Tübingen, 1884, reprinted Amsterdam, 1966), pp. 817–21.

[30] 'It is particularly characteristic of his working method that from time to time he fuses together elements originating from different works or at least from different episodes of the same source. Moreover he often uses one single motif from his source in varying forms at different points of his own romance; it is in keeping with a certain symmetry in the organization of the whole work when this leads to a related motif being repeated in the first and second half of the romance in almost the same or a slightly revised form.' (Translated from Klose, *Der Roman von Claris et Laris*, p. 303.)

narrative tradition before Chrétien may still have been known to the general public in the thirteenth century. Whatever is special or new amongst the motifs of Chrétien's romances is what attracted attention. The constant revival of such characteristic episodes keeps alive the memory of the romances of *Erec*, *Yvain* and *Perceval* throughout the entire evolution of the genre of Arthurian verse romance, whilst the motifs specific to *Lancelot* and *Cligés* increasingly sink into oblivion within this genre. By contrast, the prose romances exhibit a tendency to include precisely the subject matter and motifs of these latter works.

REFERENCES TO WELL-KNOWN CHARACTERS IN NEW ROMANCES

Jean Froissart, author of the last in this series of Arthurian romances, introduces his story of *Meliador* with an unusual dating of the events of the romance:

> Environ ou .IX. ans ou .X.,
> Avant que li preus Lanselos,
> Melyadus, ne li rois Los,
> Guiron, Tristrans ne Galehaus,
> Gauwains, Yewains, ne Perchevaus,
> Ne chil de la Table Reonde
> Fuissent cogneü en ce monde,
> Ne que de Merlin on euist
> Cognissance, ne c'on seuist
> Nulle riens de ses prophesies,
> Plusieurs belles chevaleries
> Avinrent en la Grant Bretaigne,
> Si com cilz livres nous ensengne... (28–40)

(About nine or ten years before the noble Lancelot, Melyadus or King Lot, Guiron, Tristan or Galehaut, Gawain, Yvain or Perceval or the knights of the Round Table were known in this world, or anyone had knowledge of Merlin or knew anything about his prophecies, many splendid deeds of chivalry were done in Great Britain, as we may learn from this book...)

Froissart thus transfers the events of his romance to a time when the Round Table and its famous knights (including those featured in the prose romances) did not yet exist; even the sorcerer Merlin is still supposed to have been completely unknown at that time, although legend already has him playing a significant role at the birth of King Arthur. Nevertheless, it is Froissart's intention to write an Arthurian romance. He plans to depict *aventures de Bretaigne* (adventures of Britain), with King Arthur and his court given their normal well-known functions. But as the narrative proceeds we come across none of the well-known names any more, apart from Arthur. There may well be rather different reasons for this than those proposed by Micha:

> There are many signs of the poet's familiarity with Arthurian fiction in its later stages, such as references to Guiron and Melyadus and the adoption of the principle of 'entrelacement' on a grand scale. He takes over a few names without change from the Matter of Britain: Loth, Florée, Lionnel, Carlion, Clarence (a broad river in Ireland!); other names he alters slightly: Meriadoc becomes Meliador; Carmelide, Carmelin; Sinaudon, Signandon. The last he identifies with Stirling on the basis of information received there in 1365. One detects the conscientious chronicler in the fact that, having once dated his romance at the beginning of Arthur's reign, he excludes all those heroes later destined to achieve fame, Perceval, Lancelot, and so forth; also in the effort to keep his geography somewhat close to reality.[31]

This suggests that Froissart had unwittingly fallen victim to his own chronicler's habits of giving dates, and that the unusual dating had unfortunately resulted in the eradication of all the well-known names. But then why should he make any such stipulation? Dispensing with the tradition of the Round Table is almost like abandoning the traditions of the genre itself. On the one hand Froissart did clearly recognize that Arthurian characters are a necessary constituent of the genre as such; on the other hand these characters are not allowed to make an appearance in his romance. Is his renunciation intended seriously or is this yet another case of a tongue-in-cheek game with the literary convention? Meanwhile even Froissart cannot avoid at least citing the names of the famous knights, and this catalogue of names at the beginning of every Arthurian romance has a specific function in signalling to the public a particular type of romance, in this case Arthurian (see also Chapter 2). This is precisely what it achieves in *Meliador* as well. Thus Froissart accepts the conditions of the genre whilst at the same time distancing himself from them. What does he achieve in so doing? Does he want to demonstrate that an Arthurian romance can take shape even without constant references to the well-known characters? It is not very likely that Froissart chose this direction because he made a mistake about the basic ingredients of an Arthurian romance; he has certainly not neglected other decisive features, retaining in particular *aventure* as the structural basis, the romantic element, the demeanour of the characters, the function of Arthur's court as both legal arbiter and a moment of calm in the narrative, and the pattern of the hero having to prove himself. However, Froissart is obstinately determined to invent new characters and names instead of letting the familiar characters stay in their traditional spheres. Nowadays it is hard to decide to what

[31] Micha, 'Miscellaneous French Romances', p. 392.

extent these new names are intended to sound comic: is there a humorous intention lying behind the sound and the associations evoked by Camel de Camois, Gobart des Marais, Montgoffin, Madrigais, Balastre, Cobastre, Griffamont and many more? They must have seemed immensely strange to a public very conscious of traditions, but the question is whether Froissart's invention of these literary Arthurian names is to be interpreted as the launch of a parody of the genre, as deliberate alienation or merely as a consequence of the fact that Froissart, writing a good hundred years after *Claris et Laris*, the penultimate Arthurian verse romance, was no longer bound by any rigid generic tradition and was therefore free to take liberties with it. Whatever was it that inspired him to resurrect a long-defunct genre once more? Such questions require a more thorough study than can be achieved within the confines of this chapter.[32]

In dispensing with the traditional Arthurian cast Froissart also renounces all the possibilities of presenting his hero Meliador in the typical situations of the genre, such as comrade-in-arms to Gawain and Yvain, or fighting in a tournament against the acknowledged great names of the Round Table. It is after all precisely and solely the role of the well-known characters to represent the Arthurian court and its claim to quality on official occasions. As a rule the same applies to the other episodes located at the Arthurian court, such as festivals and messenger scenes. The audience can associate with each well-known name a narrative context from another romance which alone can account for these heroes being able to appear as arbiters. The well-known names are the key to the familiar framework. Perhaps Froissart's dispensing with them is to be explained by the inability of his public towards the end of the fourteenth century to make the customary associations any more.

Whilst the characters named rate at least a mention in nearly all the romances, nothing more is heard of Laudine and Lunete, and even the names Enide and Guinevere are rarely heard. These heroines of the earlier romances withdraw behind the undying fame of the knights of the Round Table; in terms of the genre's development their appearance was purely episodic. Thus it is also not surprising that the image of Yvain and Erec surviving in the minds of some authors is not actually that of married men. They now belong to the Round Table as immutable figures, with only the odd very occasional allusion to their individual literary past. The following lines from *Meraugis* are also indicative of this state of affairs:

[32] However, see Part Two. Diverres' research brings out the political references contained in this re-creation of Arthurian names; they were discussed for example in 'The Welsh Adventures in Froissart's *Meliador*' (paper read to the XIIth Congress of the International Arthurian Society in Regensburg on 9 August 1979).

Mes sor totes les autres semble
Lidoine rose et flor de lis.
Fenice, la feme d'Alis
N'ot onques ausi grant beauté. (264–7)

(But Lidoine above all others is like the rose and the lily. Fenice, the wife of Alis, never had such great beauty.)

Once we have rejected the idea that this instance could perhaps have been forced by the rhyme (and Raoul does not otherwise have to resort to such tactics), we are left with the fact that Fenice is named as the wife of Alis, not the mistress of Cligés.

This passage is also remarkable in one further respect, because Arthurian romances otherwise draw exclusively on the female characters of classical antiquity, familiar from the romances of *Troie* and *Eneas*, for their comparisons of beauty. Some rare references to Iseut may be regarded as taking an intermediate position. However, the line about Fenice, using a well-known female figure from the same body of material as a comparison, is an indication of the genre increasingly mirroring itself even in the sphere of citing names. There remains only one solitary further example of this. In *Li Chevaliers as deus espees*, by analogy with Chrétien's *Erec*, lines 6674ff., there is a description of the bride's coronation robe:

S'estoit portrais tous li mantiaus,
Comment Merlins Uter mua
Sa face et comment il sambla
Le conte Gorloys de chiere
Et de vois, et en quel maniere
L'avoit por son seignor tenu
Ygerne, et comme engendres fu
Li boins Artus a Tintaguel,
Et comment ele fist puis duel
Des nouvieles ki la nuit vinrent,
Car son seignor por ocis tinrent
Cil ki de l'estor escaperent,
Comment li baron s'acorderent
De Bretaigne, ke l'espousast
Uter et k'il la coronast,
Et furent ou mantel portrait
Et les proeces et li fait
K'Artus fist dusqu'au ior de lores. (12,180–97)

(The robe portrayed in its entirety how Merlin changed Uther's face and how he resembled Count Gorloys in appearance and in his voice, and how Ygerne

> took him to be her lord, and how the good Arthur was conceived at Tintagel, and how she then mourned over the news that came that night, for those who survived the battle thought her lord had been killed, how the barons of Britain agreed that Uther should marry her and crown her, and on the robe were portrayed the deeds and feats of arms that Arthur had accomplished to that day.)

Whereas Erec's robe had been embroidered with allegories of the arts, in other words with a general pictorial theme, the design of this robe reveals once again the genre contemplating itself and its own origins, which lie long before even Chrétien, in an oral tradition. One may also suspect the direct influence of Wace here, as absorbed by the poet of *Li Chevaliers as deus espees*.[33] This kind of reminiscence and literary influence proves to be extremely important in shaping the genre.[34]

Finally, reference must be made to one special kind of context for mentioning Arthurian heroes, namely lists of works. They can be seen as comparable to the lists of knights mentioned earlier. The poet of *Flamenca* uses just such a list to amplify his description of a festival at court, by enumerating which works the many travelling players recited. After a long list of all the familiar stories and romances taken from antiquity there follows a panorama of Arthurian literature:

> L'us diz de la *Taula Redonda*,
> Que no i venc homs que noil responda
> *Le reis* segon sa conoissensa;
> Anc nuil jorn no i failli valensa.
> L'autre comtava de *Galvain*,
> E *del leo* que fon compain
> Del cavallier qu'estors *Luneta*.
> L'us diz de la piucella breta
> Con tenc *Lancelot* en preiso
> Cant de s'amor li dis de no.
> L'autre comtet de *Persaval*
> Co venc a la cort a caval.
> L'us comtet *d'Erec e d'Enida*,
> L'autre d'Ugonet de Perida.
> L'us comtava de Governail
> Com per Tristan ac grieu trebail.
> L'autre comtava de *Feniza*,
> Con transir la fes sa noirissa.
> L'us dis del *Bel Desconogut*,

33 See Pelan, *L'influence du* Brut *de Wace*, p. 133ff.

34 This series of references might also include the passage from the First Continuation (the episode of the Pucelle de Lis) where a tent is furnished with tapestries depicting Gawain's heroic deeds (see Chapter 4).

E l'autre del vermeil escut
Que l'yras trobet a l'uisset.
L'autres comtava de *Guiflet*.
L'us comtet de Calobrenan,
L'autre dis con retenc un an
Dins sa preison *Quec* senescal
Lo deliez, car li dis mal.
L'autre comtava de *Mordret*.
L'us retrais lo comte Divet,
Con fo per los Ventres faiditz
E per *Rei Pescador* grazitz.
L'us comtet l'astre d'*Ermeli*;
L'autre dis con fan l'Ancessi
Per gein lo Veil de la Montaina... (662–94)[35]

(One told of the *Round Table*, to which no man ever came without receiving from *the king* a suitable reply, and where there was never a day when valour was found wanting. Another told of *Gawain* and *of the lion* that was the companion of the knight who was rescued by *Lunete*. One told of the Breton maid who kept *Lancelot* in prison when he refused her love. Another told of *Perceval* who came into court on his horse. One told *of Erec and Enide*, another of Ugonet de Peride. One told of Governal and how he had suffered hardship for Tristan's sake. Another told of *Fenice*, and how her nurse made her die. One told of the *Fair Unknown*, and another of the red shield that the herald found outside the door. [See *Lancelot* 5536ff.] Another told of *Guiflet* [= Gifflet?], one told of Calobrenan [= Calogrenant?] and another how Deliez kept *Kay* in prison for a year for speaking ill of him. Another told of *Mordred*. One narrated how Count Divet was driven from his land by the Vandals and welcomed by the *Fisher King*. One told of *Ermeli* [= Merlin?] and his star, another told how the Assassins serve the Old Man of the Mountain...)

Comparable lists, almost amounting to a historical survey of the evolution of their own genre, are not found in Arthurian verse romances. They appear predominantly in the non-Arthurian although closely related romances of love and adventure, but also in quite different genres.[36] The audience for such works, perhaps less familiar with the content of specifically Arthurian romances than would be an audience of enthusiasts for the latter genre, were prepared to settle for this kind of at best vague and in terms of detail even misleading evocation of narrative outlines from Arthurian literature, conjured up by means of key

[35] In addition, Cabrefoil, Tintagoil and Ivans are named in lines 600–3 of this text.

[36] See for example the *Roman de Renart*, Branch II; *Roman de la Violette*, line 34ff.; *Richars li Biaus*, line 6ff.; *Miracle d'une none tresoriere*, line 5ff.; *Vies des Pères*, line 33. The texts are quoted in U. Mölk (ed.), *Französische Literarästhetik des 12. und 13. Jahrhunderts*, *SRÜ* 54 (Tübingen, 1969).

words, names, attributes and references to scenes that are often the less important ones.

Towards the end of the thirteenth century the characters of Arthurian romance, once so lively, were reduced even in the courtly circles of northern France to purely superficial cultural allusions; this process is illustrated in the case of the *Roman du Hem* (circa 1278). The author Sarrasin breaks up his factual account of a tournament at the court of the Count of Artois at Le Hem (near Péronne, Somme) with the description of some strange charades which appear to have been inspired by Arthurian literature. After proving his cultural credentials with a lengthy list of works similar to the one in *Flamenca*, he narrates how the host, dressed up as Yvain and accompanied at all times by a lion, attempts to release various *puceles*; the patroness of the tournament appears as Guinevere (line 373). The entire event seems to have been planned as a kind of Arthurian festival, and the account of it frequently reads like stage directions:

Et al tierc jour communalment
I enterront toute le gent,
Qui de lonc i seront venu.
Gardés qu'il n'i ait ja tenu
Postis ne porte a entrer ens
Vers nule maniere de gens
C'aventures i amerront;
Li estrange qui les verront
Les esgarderont volentiers.
Il i verront set chevaliers,
Tous armés, les haubers vestus,
Il aront hiaumes et escus
Et seront tous set d'un samblant.
Sans faire nul felon samblant,
Venront al mengier la roïne
Et li diront tout lor couvine,
Qu'il se metent en sa prison
De par le Varlet au Lyon.
Aprés venra une pucele,
C'uns nains i amenra, et cele
Querra la roïne secours;
Adont verrés venir le cours
Chevaliers pour le secours faire.
Or atournés chi vostre afaire
Que n'en puissiés estre repris,
Que haut afaire avés empris.
Prenés hiraus des mix saçans
Et faites ja crier as chans

A Warenes et a Noyon,
Si haut que par tout l'oie on,
Si com nous avons devisé. (411–41)

(And on the third day everyone who has come from far away will enter together. Make sure that no postern or gate is guarded to prevent the entry of any kind of person whose adventures may bring them there. The strangers who see them will be happy to watch them. Seven knights will come there, fully armed, wearing their hauberks; they will have helmets and shields, and all seven will be dressed alike. Without any trace of discourtesy they will come to the queen's feast and explain their situation to her, that they are to surrender themselves to her mercy by order of the Knight of the Lion. After that a maiden will come, led there by a dwarf, and she will ask the queen for help. Then you will see knights rushing to offer assistance. Now arrange your proceedings so that you cannot be criticized, since you have undertaken a great affair. Take the most knowledgeable heralds and have them proclaim the tournament in Varennes and Noyon, so loudly that they are heard everywhere, as we have described.)

A literary examination of this puzzling text is still lacking, but there is a need to re-examine Jeanroy's verdict that the *Roman du Hem* is of a most inferior standard.[37] What is the role of the Arthurian element in this account of the tournament?[38] In this connection it may also perhaps prove possible to shed light on the question of whether the tournament of 1278 really was organized as an Arthurian festival or whether Sarrasin in his literary chronicle merely stylized the proceedings as such after the event.[39]

CHRONOLOGICAL PARALLELS BETWEEN CHRETIEN'S WORKS AND LATER ROMANCES

Three times in the course of his narrative about Yvain, the Knight with the Lion, Chrétien refers to the plot of his *Lancelot*, whether it be to explain Gawain's absence from Arthur's court or to specify particular periods of time (*Yvain*, lines 3706, 3918 and 4746). In other words, Chrétien intends us to see the events of *Yvain* and *Lancelot* as taking place concurrently. There may be various

[37] A. Jeanroy, review of *Le Roman du Hem*, edited by Albert Henry, *Travaux de la Faculté de Philosophie et Lettres de l'Université de Bruxelles* 9 (Paris, 1939), *Romania* 66 (1940/1), 105.

[38] It seems probable that we have here a poetic account of a tournament in the form of a round table. Entertainments of a similar kind took place in Acre in 1286. A festival of this type is also mentioned by Adam de la Halle (*Jeu de la Feuillée*, lines 722–3). There was also the case of Ulrich von Liechtenstein, who travelled around dressed up as Arthur.

[39] Whatever the answer, it is interesting that an account of a tournament of this kind, cast in poetic form, should have been commissioned. The *Roman du Hem* merits renewed study from this angle.

reasons for this. In the first place it is suggested that Chrétien may have been working on both romances simultaneously; secondly, Arthurian tradition after Wace would have us believe that all the adventures of the knights of the Round Table take place within a limited period of time, namely the twelve years of peace. A third possibility is to regard the technique of placing these two romance narratives in parallel as a literary device introduced by Chrétien, especially as he is also credited with inventing the technique of *entrelacement*, which does not occur in Wace, the *chansons de geste* or the romances of antiquity.[40] Various authors of later Arthurian romances were open to the stimulation of this technique of allusions used for the first time by Chrétien, and they incorporated similar references to those that appear in *Yvain* into the narrative sequences of their own romances. On the basis of what has already been established about the general tendencies of the romances in question, it comes as no surprise to find that the allusions always relate to Chrétien's works alone and not, for example, to any contemporary Arthurian romances by other authors.[41] What is astonishing, however, is that all the corresponding passages turn their attention exclusively to the events of *Perceval*.

Raoul de Houdenc reports in *Meraugis* that at the time Gawain is still searching for the 'espee as estranges renges' (1304, 'sword with the strange belt'), and is therefore absent from Arthur's court. It is then mentioned in lines 5062–4 that Gawain's quest has reached its goal. This means that Raoul is placing the events of *Meraugis* in a chronological relationship with those of *Perceval*. There Gawain has set off to look for the mysterious sword, but because of the limitations imposed by the fragmentary nature of the *Conte du Graal* there is no further information as to whether he succeeds. Raoul now furnishes this

40 In any case this technique features much more prominently in the late verse romances and in the prose romances.

41 The Dame del Gaut Destroit makes her appearance in *La Vengeance Raguidel*, and receives a similar mention in *Hunbaut*, with the same characteristics and still in her role as Gawain's mistress. Are we to see this as an intentional reference to the earlier romance? A reading of the text does indeed give the impression that the reader is already supposed to have knowledge of the background to the action: 'J'ai non "Cele del Gaut Destroit", / Qui vo [ne]veu Gauvain covoit' (3409–10, 'I am known as the lady of the Narrow Wood, and I yearn for your nephew Gawain'). Is this merely a case of a shared motif or is it a deliberate linking of the two romance narratives, which would then be visualized as taking place only a short time apart?

Other such references include the First Continuation recounting the adventure of Caradoc, the hero of the *Lai du cor*. The Second Continuation contains allusions to *Le Bel Inconnu*, and the Yde episode in *Le Chevalier à l'épée* also occurs in *La Vengeance Raguidel*. However, these instances where names are referred to and incidents reintroduced are not to be seen as links in the sense discussed above. See B. Schmolke-Hasselmann, 'L'intégration de quelques récits brefs arthuriens (Cor, Mantel, Espee) dans les romans arthuriens du XIIIe siècle', in *Le récit bref. Actes du Colloque 1979 du Centre d'Etudes Médiévales d'Amiens* (Paris, 1980).

supplementary information in a manner suggesting that we are not dealing with fiction here but with a historical event, and in all probability this would have involved a certain comic effect.[42] Lidoine, the heroine of the romance, is introduced as the daughter of the King of Cavalon (Escavalon!):

> Ce fu li rois de Cavalon
> Qui fu plus beaus que Absalon,
> Si com tesmoigne li Greaus. (37–9)

(He was the King of Cavalon, who was more beautiful than Absalom, as it says in the Grail.)

Lines 37–43 of *Meraugis* correspond to lines 4791–2 of *Perceval*. Is this supposed to imply that Raoul is making Gawain's companion in that well-known episode the heroine of his romance? In that case the word 'vaillant' with which she is sometimes characterized has to be appreciated as a witty reference to her ability to defend herself.

In the romance of *Beaudous* Perceval takes part in a tournament and wears as his insignia a sleeve belonging to the maiden of Belrepaire. Robert de Blois comments that he has previously been unjustifiably reproached for his *folaige* (folly; see lines 3942–55). The poet of *Durmart*, who likewise brings in the knight Perceval as a participant in a tournament, tells of the disappointment of the ladies who had hoped that the victor of the tournament would choose one of them as his wife:

> Mais les dames n'i entendoient
> Ne esperance n'i avoient
> Por la queste del saint Graal;
> Quar il [ert] castes et loial.
> Se ce ne fust, mout bien creüssent
> Que son amor avoir deüssent. (7375–80)

(But the ladies did not expect anything of him nor have any hopes in that direction because of the quest of the Holy Grail; for he was chaste and faithful. Had it not been for this, they would surely have believed that they ought to have his love.)

In *Fergus* there is talk of 'Perceval, / Qui tant pena por le Garal' (13–14, 'Perceval, who endured so much for the Grail'), and in *L'Atre périlleux* he is characterized as the one who took the Red Knight's arms, making it sound as though that day was only a short time ago.

[42] The Dutch *Walwein* is similarly occupied with the unfinished search; in this Gawain romance the public are also informed about the characteristics of the sword; it is to be found in the possession of King Amoris, and anyone who wins it will be helped to victory.

These examples, assembled from five different and important texts, favour the suggestion that the poets were striving to present their narratives as running concurrently with the events of Chrétien's last romance; the romance authors of the thirteenth century also saw this work as the crowning glory of the Arthurian world and Arthurian literature. Because the *Conte du Graal* remained unfinished it lends itself particularly well to such a technique of making connections.

This first survey of the evolution of Arthurian verse romances furnishes us with some convenient criteria for describing them. The genre consists of twenty romances and four fragments of romances. A group of eight shorter texts in verse can be described as a fringe group of the genre, and the *Perceval* Continuations are likewise to be seen as a peripheral grouping. All the works use octosyllabic couplets. They have in common their characters, general types of motifs and the principles of *aventure* and *queste*. The characteristic opening sequence of the romances gives an unmistakable signal as to the type of narrative, and arouses a particular set of expectations. Chrétien's prototype romances set out possibilities for the structural use of Arthurian scenes from which the genre developed a basic pattern with a framework of opening and closing scenes. The crisis is unleashed by the loss of the beloved.

The love story becomes the main narrative element, with marriage and becoming ruler as its goal. The hero of a verse romance seeks and finds sensual fulfilment within this world. The avoidance of any transcendental significance to the narrative is coupled with a morally pragmatic, didactic element, which elevates the figure of the hero to exemplary status once he has blossomed through self-realization to achieve perfect courtliness and humanity. All courtly people are called to follow this example within the secular sphere. The adventures are certain of a happy outcome because conflict is sought in order to be overcome. The general outlook of the Arthurian verse romances, as opposed to the prose romances, is fundamentally optimistic. Nevertheless, the ability to see through the fragility of the Arthurian community's perfection and thereby to exercise self-criticism is fundamental to the genre and inherent in it from the start of its development.

The creator of the first Arthurian romances founded a genre which subsequently made a deliberate policy of continually referring back to his works. This study has attempted to convey a picture of the many possible ways of coming to terms with Chrétien's works, with regard to both poetic techniques and content. Internal echoes are a key characteristic of the genre. In order to build relationships between the works, the narrators use a refined technique of chronological and personal links. Allusions, quotations, motifs stamped by Chrétien's individual poetic gift and echoes in the content combine to achieve a very special kind of generic cohesion and continuity. This literary basis produces a narrative directed at an audience of connoisseurs.

PART TWO

A historical survey of the impact of Arthurian verse romances

7

The popularity of Arthurian verse romances

It is still not possible to say how many Arthurian texts in verse the canon of French literature may once have included in addition to those considered here. Some may still be found in the future, but in total there were probably not many more than have survived today in complete or fragmentary form. An attempt was made by Gaston Paris to infer more lost French originals on the basis of the whole corpus of Arthurian literature in Europe.[1] His procedure is not always convincing; his argumentation is influenced by nationalist thinking which is very much inclined to deny any personal powers of invention to non-French authors in the sphere of Arthurian literature; as far as he is concerned, their necessary dependence on a lost Old French source is beyond question.

The history of French Arthurian literature in verse extends over more than two hundred years, from Wace, Chrétien de Troyes and Marie de France right through to Froissart. It is certainly true that the popularity of the genre was in constant decline during this period, especially in terms of the literary creative process and the popularity of Arthurian material amongst authors. This is confirmed by a glance at the chronological table, although this summary also reveals that a first golden age from approximately 1155 until the composition of Chrétien's *Conte du Graal* was followed by a second creative period during the years 1204 until 1250, which also produced high-quality literary works.

In discussing the public popularity of these texts it is necessary to draw distinctions. It is an established fact that Wace's *Brut* gained very widespread popularity; indeed, the positive reaction to Chrétien's Arthurian romances, their breadth of influence and their literary effect are also beyond question. If Legge casts doubt on this,[2] one can carry the argument further by pointing out that the texts of Chrétien's successors themselves bear witness in the manner that has been described in the first part of this study to the intensive literary response generated by Chrétien's works.

[1] Gaston Paris, 'Romans en vers', *passim*.

[2] M. D. Legge, *Anglo-Norman Literature and its Background* (Oxford, 1963), p. 372.

THE MANUSCRIPT TRADITION

It now remains to ascertain whether the thirteenth-century Arthurian romances achieved equal fame. Is it acceptable to evaluate the relatively large number of texts as an indication of the genre's popularity? In fact caution is advisable here; whilst manuscripts of Chrétien's romances survived for posterity in abundance, the Arthurian works of his successors are generally known in only one manuscript, as shown in the table opposite. In addition, it is a fact that the majority of these unique copies are found together in just a few collective codices. This should be taken as evidence against the texts having been very widespread. The large manuscript that once belonged to the Duke of Aumale, now Chantilly, Musée Condé 472, combines *L'Atre périlleux*, *Le Bel Inconnu*, *Fergus*, *Hunbaut*, *Les Merveilles de Rigomer* and *La Vengeance Raguidel* with three Chrétien romances (*Erec*, *Lancelot* and *Yvain*), a prose Grail romance [in fact part of *Perlesvaus*] and branches of the *Renart*. The collective manuscript Bern, Burgerbibliothek 354 contains a copy of the *Lai du cort mantel* as well as *Le Chevalier à l'épée*, *La mule sans frein* and *Perceval*. The Turin manuscript L.IV.33, severely damaged in the fire of 1904, also included some of the Arthurian romances, namely *Gliglois*, a copy of *Meraugis* and a fragment of *Rigomer*.

Almost all the manuscripts that have been preserved date from no later than the thirteenth century, the same century in which the texts originated. The only exceptions are the manuscript of *Escanor* and one manuscript of *Fergus* (both from the beginning of the fourteenth century), and the Turin Codex mentioned above, which has been dated to around 1400. There are also the two Froissart manuscripts from the end of the fourteenth and the beginning of the fifteenth century; however, these could almost be called contemporary with the text, because *Meliador* was written so late.

The limited number of manuscripts, the collective Arthurian codices and the rarity of fourteenth-century manuscripts all lead to the conclusion that these texts did not enjoy very widespread circulation and that their popularity did not extend much beyond the thirteenth century. However, trying to set up a scale of popularity on the basis of the surviving manuscripts is fraught with problems and sometimes even misleading,[3] as the following examples relating specifically to the Arthurian verse romances themselves will show.

The romance of *Le Bel Inconnu* is the only Arthurian romance in verse apart from the works of Chrétien to be featured in the famous list of literature in *Flamenca*.[4] If it did not enjoy widespread fame, mentioning it in this context

[3] Compare the debate about the popularity of the *Romance of the Rose* in the years before Jean de Meun's continuation.

[4] See Chapter 6, p. 172f.

THE TRANSMISSION OF 13th-CENTURY ARTHURIAN LITERATURE

TEXT	SURVIVING MANUSCRIPTS		
	Number	*Date*	*Location*
Atre périlleux	3	All end of 13th cent.	BN fr. 2168, BN fr. 1433; Chantilly, Musée Condé 472.
Beaudous	1	Third quarter of 13th.	BN fr. 24301.
Le Bel Inconnu	1	End of 13th cent.	Chantilly, Musée Condé 472.
Lai du cor	1	End of 13th cent.	Oxford, Bodleian, Digby 86.
Ch. as deus espees	1	End of 13th cent.	BN fr. 12603.
Ch. à l'épée	1	End of 13th cent.	Bern, Burgerbibliothek 354.
Claris et Laris	1	End of 13th cent.	BN fr. 1447.
Lai du cort mantel	5	13th cent. (except one)	BN fr. 353, 837, 1593, and n.a.fr. 1104; Bern, Burgerbibliothek 354.
Durmart	1 (+fragment)	13th cent.	Bern, Burgerbibliothek 113; Carlisle, Cathedral Library.
Escanor	1	Beginning of 14th.	BN fr. 24374.
Fergus	2	End of 13th cent., beginning of 14th.	Chantilly, Musée Condé 472; BN fr. 1553.
Floriant et Florete	1	14th cent.	formerly Newbattle Abbey, now New York.
Gliglois	1	End of 14th cent. or beginning of 15th.	Turin, L.IV.33 (fire-damaged).
Hunbaut	1	End of 13th cent.	Chantilly, Musée Condé 472.
La Mule sans frein	1	End of 13th cent.	Bern, Burgerbibliothek 354.
Melion	1 (+fragment)	End of 14th cent.	BN fr. 12557; BN n.a.lat. 2374.
Meraugis	3 (+2 fragments)	4 mid-13th cent. 1 end of 14th cent. or beginning of 15th.	Vatican, Reg. 1725; Vienna, Hofibliothek 2599; Turin, L.IV.33; Berlin, gall. qu. 48; Var, Archives départmentales.
Rigomer	1 (+fragment)	1 end of 13th cent., 1 end of 14th cent. or beginning of 15th.	Chantilly, Musée Condé 472; Turin, L.IV.33 (fire-damaged).
Tyolet	1	13th cent.	BN n.a.fr. 1104.
Vengeance Raguidel	2 (+fragment)	Mid-13th cent. and end of 13th cent.	BN n.a.fr. 1263; Chantilly, Condé 472; Nottingham UL, Mi LM 6.
Yder	1	13th cent.	Cambridge UL, Ee. 4.26.

Erec et Enide	7	(+ 4 fragments)	
Cligés	8	(+ 2 fragments)	
Lancelot	7		
Yvain	8	(+ 2 fragments)	
Perceval	15	(+ 2 fragments)	
First Continuation	11		
Second Continuation	11		(*For comparison*)
Manessier	7		
Gerbert	2		
Mort Artu	50		
Queste del S. Graal	39		
Prose *Lancelot*	30 to 40		
Perlesvaus	8		

would seem pointless, because naming a work whose fame had scarcely spread at all could not be expected to evoke much of a response from the audience. It is therefore reasonable to suppose that *Le Bel Inconnu* enjoyed more widespread popularity even in Provençal-speaking territory, despite there being only one manuscript in existence today. Only a fragment remains of *Le Vallet a la cote mautaillie*, but the story must have been very well known because it has been worked into the Prose *Tristan*, whilst the appellation occurs in lists of knights in *Le Bel Inconnu* and *Rigomer*.[5]

Durmart is a similar case. The hero is mentioned as an example of a model lover by Christine de Pisan at the beginning of the fifteenth century in her *Débat des deus amans*, where she gives a kind of résumé of the romance. Jean Froissart alludes to Durmart about thirty years earlier in the same context, both in *Meliador* (where admittedly we could be dealing with an interpolation, but then that in itself would be of interest) and also in his *Paradis d'amour*, where Durmart is mentioned in one breath with Tristan and Perceval. This documentary evidence that the naming of the hero Durmart was employed as a topos in the fourteenth and fifteenth centuries favours the romance being widely known, and yet only two manuscripts have survived.

Evidence for the popularity of the *Lai du cort mantel* and the *Lai du cor* with their burlesque chastity tests can be found in frequent references and in reworkings incorporated into later literary texts, not all of them of French provenance. *La Vengeance Raguidel* is another example of this kind of reception.

Thus the manifold references to characters and narrative elements from the Arthurian pool of subject-matter in later texts, both Arthurian and non-Arthurian, remain sure signs of the popularity of Arthurian literature. There is scarcely a list of literary characters in the Middle Ages that does not contain Arthurian names. On the other hand, the impression is often given that knowledge of these characters for both author and public is limited to the name and a general idea of the plot, and is certainly not based on any more precise knowledge of the texts. Indeed, a comparable situation also applies when Tristan and Iseut or Roland and Oliver receive a mention in medieval literary texts.

POPULARITY AND DISTRIBUTION

The relatively small number of manuscripts known about today is no proof of a lack of popularity. Indeed, many of these storylines that originated in France became very well known in German, Dutch and English adaptations, for example *Wigalois*, *Ferguut*, *Wrake van Raguisel* or *Libeaus Desconneus*, with a

[5] See Chapter 3, p. 65, note 17.

better manuscript tradition than their corresponding French originals. However, this in turn implies that numerous copies of the French originals were widely available for them to be able to find their way into other countries.

Moreover, some of the Arthurian verse romances survive in more than one manuscript: there are five of *Meraugis*, three each of *L'Atre périlleux* and *La Vengeance Raguidel*, and two of *Fergus*. Is it pure coincidence that these are works of high quality? *Gliglois*, *Meraugis* and *Les Merveilles de Rigomer* were copied again as late as 1400; consequently there must have been an audience for them at that time, a hundred and fifty years or more after they were written. Perhaps it is mere chance that other late manuscripts have not been preserved, and just because all the manuscripts of Chrétien's *Erec* go right back to the thirteenth century, no one will try to claim that this romance was therefore no longer read in the fourteenth; the state of transmission of Chrétien's other romances would seem to argue against that. The fact that at the end of the fourteenth century an author like Froissart could still write an Arthurian romance of over thirty thousand lines for a princely patron is highly revealing. The general popularity of Arthurian concepts, both in the thirteenth century and later, is further documented by the numerous round tables (festive tournaments in Arthurian guise) held throughout Europe,[6] as well as the inclusion of Arthur in the ranks of the Nine Worthies around 1310, Arthurian scenes on small French artefacts of the fourteenth century and even murals with Arthurian subjects decorating in particular public buildings. That is sufficient evidence for this material being in favour with a broad section of the public. Nevertheless, it can probably be assumed that the literary associations still enjoying public awareness at that time derive more from the Arthurian prose romances, whose manuscript tradition points to an enormous readership, than from the verse romances—if indeed such associations can still be understood as anything more than general and therefore vague cultural background after the end of the thirteenth century.

Despite the factors just adduced, which could argue for a wider distribution of the verse romances, we incline to the view that these texts were far less well known and popular than the works of Chrétien, the *Perceval* Continuations and the prose romances. The evidence from within the texts—the sophisticated toying with literary allusions and associations—points to these romances having been written for an audience of devotees, necessarily limited in numbers; they were directed at a particular group of recipients with an intimate knowledge of Chrétien's works at their disposal, who had a special interest in Arthurian

[6] See R. S. Loomis, 'Arthurian Influence on Sport and Spectacle', in *ALMA*, pp. 553–9.

literature and who felt a particularly acute need for a representation of the Arthurian world that differed substantially from its image in the prose romances.

For by comparison with the prose romances the genre of the Arthurian verse romance appears largely conservative. The texts record the Arthurian world in much the same condition as it appeared in Chrétien's early works, admittedly with changes of detail since that time but with no fundamental alterations. If one acknowledges the premiss that historical conditions had undergone decisive changes since the composition of *Yvain*, it must become apparent that the genre of verse romance had not undergone any parallel development. In a formal sense, by retaining the metrical form, as well as in terms of content, where they fail to follow the direction suggested by *Perceval* and adopted by the prose romances, the verse romances do not move with the times, but mark time. In striking contrast to the doom-laden atmosphere of the prose romances, the majority of the verse texts still convey the positive image of a good world; the basic tone is optimistic, and the focus is on perfecting knights in this world rather than pointing them towards eternity. If the contemporary prose romances being composed in the thirteenth century and afterwards made a disproportionately greater impact than the verse romances, then we must assume that they were much better designed to meet the needs of a broad spectrum of the public, and that the verse romances appealed only to a small group of enthusiasts.

8

The audience

Sachiez que deus Bretaignes sont,
Et genz diverses i estont.
Li Englois sont en le grigneur,
Mais li Normant en sont signeur;
En le meneur sont li Breton.[1]

THE CHARACTERISTICS OF THE AUDIENCE

On the basis of the considerations that have been assembled so far, we are looking for readers distinguished by the following characteristics: a knowledge of literature, a strong interest in Arthurian material and conservative tendencies. There is evidence for the proposal that such a section of the public is to be found within the territories not of the French kings but of the Angevin kings of England. This suggestion is supported by the dominant role of Anglo-Norman literature in the twelfth century, continuing into the thirteenth,[2] as well as by the political significance of the Arthurian material for the Anglo-Norman aristocracy's claims to legitimacy and sovereignty, and by the social and psychological position of the French-speaking stratum of the population in England, especially after the loss of their hereditary fiefs on the Continent at the beginning of the thirteenth century.

It is not possible at this point to go into detail about the significance and development of those works of French literature which were produced within the social circles of Henry II and his family. We recall the romances of *Thèbes*, *Troie* and *Eneas*, Lambert's *Alexandre*, the authors Wace, Benoît de Sainte-Maure, Marie de France, Walter Map, John of Salisbury, Giraldus Cambrensis, and the troubadours Bertran de Born and Bernart de Ventadorn, to name but a

[1] *Ille et Galeron*, Löseth's edition, lines 135–9, 'You should know that there are two Britains, with different people living there. Greater Britain is inhabited by the English but ruled by the Normans. Lesser Britain is inhabited by the Bretons.'

[2] R. R. Bezzola, *Les origines et la formation de la littérature courtoise en occident 500–1200*, Part III, Vol. I, *La cour d'Angleterre sous les rois Angevins* (Paris, 1967), pp. 1–311; Legge, *Anglo-Norman Literature*; J. Vising, *Anglo-Norman Language and Literature* (London, 1923, repr. Westport, 1970).

few whose connections with the court of the English king or the courts of his wife and sons seem clear. Bezzola's discussion of that subject is for the most part convincing.[3] The focal point of courtly literature in French is to be found here, whereas there is very little evidence that the patriotically political literature of the *chansons de geste* was particularly favoured within the territory of the Angevin rulers;[4] this genre contributed to the self-image of the royal house of France and was at home in its sphere of influence. Nevertheless, the heroic epics were still read and copied in England, witness the Anglo-Norman manuscripts of *Roland, Gormont* and *Willame* as well as the *Pelerinage Charlemagne*. Before 1200 it is in any case difficult to distinguish between works that were produced in the northern part of France and those from the British Isles. The same princes supported poets on both sides of the Channel, and both patrons and poets travelled to and fro between England and France, whilst most authors used the common written language of the twelfth century, the Norman *koiné*.[5] Literary works crossed the sea in both directions, and circulated in both France and England in continental and Anglo-Norman transcriptions.[6]

From the Norman Conquest in 1066 until at least 1200, Anglo-Norman literature, the literary activity of English society under the Angevins, exhibits progressive if not indeed avant-garde tendencies by comparison with any other French literature of the same period.[7] As a rule the poets who looked to those circles for their audience were more creative. If their works differ from those produced within the sphere of influence of the Capets, it is because they were written for a different and often more demanding audience with different interests. The style and purpose of Anglo-Norman texts often diverge from their continental counterparts because different needs have to be satisfied and different fashions taken into account. It would be wrong to classify them as provincial on the basis of such differences.[8] The loss of the crown territories on the Continent under King John was by no means immediately accompanied by the stagnation and retrogression in literary production that has so often been postulated.[9] After 1204 a large number of people from Anjou, Brittany and Normandy moved to

[3] Bezzola, *La cour d'Angleterre*.

[4] See Legge, *Anglo-Norman Literature*, p. 5.

[5] See G. Wacker, *Über das Verhältnis von Dialekt und Schriftsprache im Altfranzösischen* (Halle, 1916), and Legge, *Anglo-Norman Literature*, pp. 3 and 364.

[6] According to Legge (*Anglo-Norman Literature*, p. 366), before 1200 people especially in England were still not conscious of a decisive difference between French as spoken in Britain and any continental dialects. The awareness of the Anglo-Normans that they were speaking an archaic and provincial type of French did not develop until later.

[7] Legge, *Anglo-Norman Literature*, p. 362.

[8] Legge, *Anglo-Norman Literature*, p. 371.

[9] Vising, *Anglo-Norman Language and Literature*, p. 20.

England and settled there, because they did not wish to submit to the new power structures in their homeland. The demands of feudal law forced them to choose between Philip of France and John of England; it was not possible to be a loyal vassal to two masters who were constantly at war with each other. These immigrants brought to England fresh impulses in literature and language. The influx from the Continent continued without interruption throughout the whole of the thirteenth century; under Henry III at least 2,000 vassals from Brittany and from the south of France moved to England with their families and retainers, and they included such large numbers of relatives of Henry's wife, Eleanor of Provence, that it provoked violent reactions amongst the long-established barons of Anglo-Norman descent; they could not forgive the king for entrusting himself to the influence of these 'foreigners', instead of taking advice from his crown vassals.[10] This xenophobic attitude, which finds expression in the Provisions of Oxford (1258)[11] as well as in the writings of Robert Grosseteste and Matthew Paris,[12] is evidence of an established national identity growing from an awareness of being different from the French on the Continent, and of having taken root in the country that they had ruled for two hundred years and with which they increasingly identified.[13]

The consciousness of the barons—and after 1204 also of their eldest sons in particular—that their home was in England, had some considerable influence on the literature of their epoch and their intellectual environment. 'It was not upon the history of the language, as has been assumed, but on the history of the literature that the separation of kingdom and duchy had its effect.'[14] Thus there develops an increased need to prove legitimacy and with it the search for

[10] M. Powicke, *The Thirteenth Century* 1216–1307, *Oxford History of England* (Oxford, 1953), p. 73ff.; Vising, *Anglo-Norman Language and Literature*, p. 18.

[11] Vising, *Anglo-Norman Language and Literature*, p. 19: 'The Provisions insisted upon a clean sweep of the aliens.'

[12] Vising, *Anglo-Norman Language and Literature*, pp. 18–19.

[13] This also explains how Simon de Montfort came to be leader of the party of barons opposed to the rather ineffectual rule of Henry III, because of his territorial connections with England, although he himself had only come to England from southern France in 1233 to claim the earldom of Leicester as his inheritance. As brother-in-law to the king and an earl of the realm Simon had no interest in weakening the monarchy or the ruling dynasty, but for England's sake he took sides with those who were rebelling against misrule. The unjust treatment that Simon had received from the king may have contributed to this. However, Henry enjoyed little sympathy amongst the barons in general; he failed totally to correspond to their fantasy of a chivalrous and courtly king. All hopes were therefore focused on the crown prince Edward, who promised to fulfil this ideal. He joined the barons' party against his father.

[14] Legge, *Anglo-Norman Literature*, p. 5.

fictitious ancestors of the barons' own families within their adopted country.[15] Following the example of the royal household they made use of Arthurian material, as we shall see later, but the romances of *Waldef*, *Boeve de Haumtone*, *Gui de Warewic* and *Fouke Fitzwarin* are also to be included in this group of texts which pursue a political goal of legitimization. They can be termed *romans d'origine lignagère* or ancestral romances;[16] *Guillaume d'Angleterre* provided them with a literary prototype from the twelfth century.

The twelfth and thirteenth centuries produced a rich corpus of Anglo-Norman literature, although it is relevant in this context to mention only the courtly romances of *Amadas et Ydoine* and *Blonde d'Oxfort* (or *Jehan et Blonde*), in which the hero makes frequent journeys to and fro between England and France, plus the *chanson de geste* of *Amis et Amiloun*. Religious writings (saints' lives and plays) enjoyed a golden age. We therefore have good grounds for asserting that Angevin society was extremely interested in literature and was intensely active in contributing to its promotion. Not until the second half of the thirteenth century do we hear increasing calls for the use of the English language in works of literature destined for a readership in England.[17] These demands introduce a development which explains the numerous adaptations into Middle English of works originally written in French. Arthurian literature of the Middle Ages in both French and English is important not least because it plays a decisive role as mediator in this situation.

POLITICAL AND SOCIAL PROBLEMS IN THE ARTHURIAN VERSE ROMANCES

If it is indeed the case that the French Arthurian verse romances were composed predominantly for a French-speaking public in England and were an expression of the interests of that social group, then it is also reasonable to suppose that any political and social problems exercising the minds of the English barons in the thirteenth century will also have left their mark on some of the texts. In fact one can point to a number of striking parallels. In Chapter 3 we were able to show

[15] M. D. Legge, 'The Dedication of *Guillaume d'Angleterre*', in *Mélanges E. Vinaver*, edited by F. Whitehead, A. H. Diverres and F. E. Sutcliffe (Manchester, 1965), pp. 196–205; also *Anglo-Norman Literature*, pp. 4 and 363.

[16] Legge, *Anglo-Norman Literature*, pp. 139–75, and 'The Dedication of *Guillaume d'Angleterre*', pp. 196–7.

[17] References to sources can be found in Vising, *Anglo-Norman Language and Literature*, p. 20ff. See also *Arthour and Merlin*, lines 22–3, quoted from K. H. Göller, *König Arthur in der englischen Literatur des späten Mittelalters*, *Palaestra* 238 (Göttingen, 1963), p. 45: 'Riȝt is, þat Inglische vnderstond, / þat was born in Inglond' ('It is right that anyone born in England should understand English').

that in various Arthurian romances the problem of the need for dangerous adventures, the risks in tournaments and the horrors of war gave rise to discussion. The knights perceptibly succumb to a general reluctance to gamble with their own lives and a lack of readiness to do battle. Similar tendencies are to be found amongst the English barons of the thirteenth century.

From the twelfth century onwards the English kings were already increasingly dependent on paid mercenaries. According to feudal law their barons were under an obligation to give war service, but with increasing frequency they refused to make themselves available to pursue the king's interests for more than the agreed forty days per year. They would arrange for other knights to take their place, or exempt themselves by paying considerable sums of money with which the king could acquire the services of soldiers for an indefinite period. Indeed, the long wars on the Continent made such a standing army necessary. In 1181 Henry II issued regulations about the provision of arms which make it apparent that to equip a knight was an extremely expensive business;[18] many barons were simply not prepared to spend the money on it. After the loss of the fiefs on the Continent they were even less motivated than before to embark on a rather unpromising war for their faithless king. Many of the sons of noble households chose not to be trained as knights any more, as a way of escaping their obligations. This lack of willingness to become involved was particularly noticeable in the early years of the reign of Henry III. The king had to face the worrying possibility that if a dangerous situation arose his barons would no longer be able to defend the country effectively. His reaction to this state of affairs can be seen in an edict of 1234, which instructed the sheriffs of the kingdom to ensure that all incumbents of the so-called *knights' fees* should acquire the equipment necessary for a knight and have themselves knighted without delay.[19] The reluctance to fight which finds expression in the verse romances amongst a number of the Arthurian knights and which is so little in keeping with the stereotype of a romance of chivalry can perhaps be understood as an echo of these historical circumstances.[20]

Criticism of the *meslee*, or tournament using sharp weapons, which occurs repeatedly in Arthurian romances, is probably also to be seen in the context of contemporary discussion of the problem. The popes had already been forbidding tournaments since 1197, and any knights mortally wounded at such events were supposed to be refused a Christian burial. In 1186 Geoffrey of Brittany, the son

[18] D. M. Stenton, *English Society in the Early Middle Ages, The Pelican History of England*, Vol. III, fourth edition (London, 1965; first published 1951), p. 89.
[19] Stenton, *English Society in the Early Middle Ages*, p. 91.
[20] See Stenton, *English Society in the Early Middle Ages*, pp. 99–100.

of Henry II, lost his life at a tournament in France, which is where the English knights went whenever their rulers attempted a consistent enforcement of the papal ban on tournaments throughout their own territories.[21] Richard I was very fond of these fighting games, but nevertheless he did at least formally submit to the Church's prohibition in so far as he attempted to restrain his subjects' passion for tournaments; during his reign they were still allowed, but could be held at only five predetermined places in England; these included the plain between Salisbury and Wilton, which was to rise to literary fame a short time later in *La Mort le Roi Artu*. Furthermore the king tried to capitalize on the drawing power of the fighting games, in that every participant had to pay a particular sum into the royal coffers before they started. Laws were passed to the effect that any kind of combative activity on the way to or from the tournament site would be punished. Henry III was well known for his dislike of tournaments. Only very rarely during his long reign did he make any concessions to the needs of the knights in his entourage; he did, for example, permit the holding of a tournament and festival in honour of the knighting of his younger half-brother William of Valence in 1248.[22]

The more playful fights with blunt weapons, or so-called round tables, met with less criticism than the *meslee*. Writing in 1255, Matthew Paris characterizes them as more noble and less dangerous. Nevertheless he also reports on the manner in which such a round table in Walden was misused to settle private feuds: one knight killed another, who had wronged him a long time previously, by deliberately using a sharp lance.[23] If the Arthurian romances of the thirteenth century lash out at the senseless shedding of blood at tournaments, then this is probably a reflection of the fact that many story-tellers were clerics, with their attitudes shaped by the Church.

A further important problem for the barons during the years when Richard and John were on the throne was the sovereign's traditional right to give the widows and single ladies of the land husbands in accordance with his own political and economic interests, and without regard to their personal desires. Even in the romances it is always Arthur who has to give his formal agreement to the marriage of the protagonists and at whose court or alternatively in whose presence the wedding takes place. However, the king's right to a free hand in this matter was abused all too often by the sons of Henry II. Aristocratic ladies had to pay large sums of money to buy their immunity from the exercise of the

[21] Increasing xenophobia in England and the constant emigration of Frenchmen from the Continent also led to tournaments becoming battles between Englishmen and Frenchmen at which much blood was shed.

[22] Stenton, *English Society in the Early Middle Ages*, p. 87.

[23] Stenton, *English Society in the Early Middle Ages*, p. 88.

crown's influence, as can be deduced from a fine roll of 1199.[24] The barons therefore demanded in Magna Carta that the king make some concessions in this regard, and he thus had to promise[25] not to marry any heirs or heiresses (who even now continued to be in his power) against their will to someone of lesser rank ('disparagement').[26] In the light of this historic demand by the barons it is easier to understand why in the Arthurian romances of that same period, in *Meraugis*, *Fergus*, *Yder* and especially *Durmart*, there is such importance attached to the equality of the couple and especially to their being of the same rank. There is a particularly fine example to be found in *Fergus*, where Galiene wants Arthur to provide her with a husband:

> Si li requesist et proiast
> Qu'a son talent le marïast
> A tel u bien fust enploié
> Et que ne fust *desparagié*. (6359–62)

(And she should request and beg him to marry her as he pleased, to a man with whom she would be well placed and not marrying beneath her.)

The social self-image of the English barons finds expression in these romances[27] with their representation of and demand for a liaison appropriate to one's rank, which they see as an indispensable prerequisite for a happy union that will be advantageous to both the individual and society. In this situation the Arthurian verse romances take on the character of ideological campaign literature in the power struggle between the English magnates and their king.

The basic aim being pursued in Magna Carta was to force the king back into the confines of traditional customs. The barons were defending themselves against arbitrary contraventions of the established customs under feudal law. They wanted to restore the conditions they believed had existed under Henry I, and in so doing idealized a past that had not been nearly as perfect as they chose to envisage it at the beginning of the thirteenth century.[28] The striking insistence on examples of customs, which the knights exhibit in opposition to the king in many Arthurian romances, is to be viewed in connection with baronial interests, as Köhler has already brought to light. The image of a model king, who regards himself as being under an obligation to the customs of his ancestors,[29] still

[24] J. C. Holt, *Magna Carta* (Cambridge, 1965), p. 46.
[25] Chapter 6 of the charter.
[26] Stenton, *English Society in the Early Middle Ages*, p. 77; Holt, *Magna Carta*, p. 47.
[27] See also in particular the problems arising from the difference in rank in the Anglo-Norman romance of *Amadas et Ydoine*, which the editor suggests was written around 1190–1220.
[28] Holt, *Magna Carta*, p. 99: 'The "good old times" of Henry I were an invention.'
[29] See above p. 88, and compare *La Vengeance Raguidel*, line 18ff.

corresponded to the perceived ideals of the barons even in the thirteenth century, as it had already in Chrétien's time. Magna Carta is the document which testifies to the victory of the royal vassals over the aspirations to power of their feudal lord.[30] It is therefore understandable if scholars evaluate Magna Carta not only as a pointer to the future but also as a reactionary document, being an expression of the barons' conservatism.[31]

THE COMMISSIONING OF CHRETIEN'S *EREC ET ENIDE*

In his description of Erec and Enide's coronation Chrétien has included some lines which invite closer scrutiny in the light of the political background currently under discussion:

> ne je n'an voel ore plus dire,
> car vers la gent li cuers me tire
> qui la estoit tote asanblee
> de mainte diverse contree.
> Asez i ot contes et rois,
> Normanz, Bretons, Escoz, Einglois,
> d'Eingleterre et de Cornoaille;
> i ot molt riche baronaille,
> car des Gales jusqu'an Anjo,
> n'an Alemaigne, n'an Peito,
> n'ot chevalier de grant afeire
> ne gentil dame de bon eire,
> don les meillors et les plus gentes
> ne fussent a la cort de Nentes,
> que li rois les ot toz mandez. (6581–95) [6641–55]

(I wish to say no more about this now, for my heart draws me towards the people who were all assembled there from a number of different countries. There were numerous counts and kings, Normans, Bretons, Scots and English, from England and Cornwall. There were many powerful barons, for from Wales to Anjou, Germany or Poitou there was no knight of importance nor any noble lady of high birth of whom the best and the fairest were not in the court at Nantes, for the king had summoned them all.)

30 Holt, *Magna Carta*, Chapter 4, 'Custom and law', pp. 63–104.

31 C. Brooke, *From Alfred to Henry III 871–1272, A History of England*, Vol. II (Edinburgh, 1961; third impression, London, 1969), p. 222. In the context of these deliberations there is a need to reassess Köhler's view that the Arthurian romances are generally influenced by the lower orders of chivalry who had been robbed of their *raison d'être*. This is not the case, at least not for the thirteenth-century Arthurian verse romances written in or for England. The results of our audience analysis contradict his theory, as does the fact that from the beginning of the thirteenth century England was in a permanent state of war, both at home and abroad, which undermines the theory of the knights having lost their role in life.

This passage has repeatedly given rise to speculation that in his first Arthurian romance (which is also the first example of the entire genre) Chrétien was seeking to appeal to an audience at the court of Henry II of England,[32] as Wace, his most important precursor, had already done. It is indeed the case that the names of territories included here as well as other place-names in *Erec et Enide* (Tintagel, Finisterre, Limoges, Gascony) correspond to the territory ruled by the Angevin kings at the time when their empire was at its most extensive. Moreover it has attracted very little notice hitherto, but amongst the barons to whom Chrétien's heart is drawn (according to lines 6581–4) there is a total absence of any from France as it was then, and on the sole occasion when the kingdom of France is explicitly referred to, it serves only to illustrate the proposition that the fortress of Brandigan (the scene of the Joy of the Court adventure) could not be captured by 'France et la rëautez tote' (5344 [5392], 'France and all her royal power'). France is seen here as a potentially hostile power. What sort of audience does Chrétien presuppose for this text, and to whom is he seeking to appear so openly sympathetic in his writing? In both cases we may assume that he cannot be envisaging either the French royal family or vassals of the French crown.

When Chrétien turned to Arthurian material he cannot have failed to be aware that for years the English royal family had shown a particular interest in the figure of Arthur and his ideological potential. Thus Chrétien's first Arthurian romance could not have found a friendlier reception anywhere else, nor could he have found any greater gratitude for his poetic talent than in the entourage of Henry II, who was increasingly cultivating his image as legitimate successor to the British King Arthur.

The arguments adduced in previous studies tend as a rule to endorse the hypothesis thus implied about how the work originated. In order to undermine the theory one would have to find equally weighty reasons to support an initial target audience for *Erec et Enide* within the territories of the French Capetian kings. Meanwhile, however, there are some further considerations to be raised for discussion, and ones which can lend added plausibility to the notion that Chrétien's *Erec* was composed for an audience at the court of the English king.

The description in *Erec et Enide* of King Arthur's magnificent Christmas festival at the court in Nantes can serve as a starting-point for this line of argument. Henry II also held a Christmas court at Nantes in 1169. This fact is well known and has repeatedly been associated with the origins of the romance. More recent attempts at dating still take it into account.[33] Henry's choice of place

[32] R. Pernoud, *Aliénor d'Aquitaine* (Paris, 1965), p. 161; Legge, *Anglo-Norman Literature*, p. 74; Bezzola, *La cour d'Angleterre*, p. 306ff.

[33] A. Fourrier, 'Encore la chronologie des oeuvres de Chrétien de Troyes', *BBSIA* 2 (1950), 70–4.

was not arbitrary, but was dictated by his intention to betroth his third son Geoffrey (born in 1158) to the daughter of Duke Conan IV of Brittany, who was also his vassal as Earl of Richmond. Following the example of the Capetian kings, who had long been accustomed to providing their sons with fiefs or even crowning them in their own lifetime to ensure the continuity of their line and the obedience of the barons, Henry had conducted three campaigns (1166, 1167 and 1168) in an attempt to force the Breton barons to accept his son as the future legitimate successor to the duke and as their feudal overlord.[34] Now, at Christmas 1169 in Nantes, his long-standing desire was fulfilled, when all the barons did homage to the young Geoffrey, then only eleven years old.[35] His engagement to the young Constance had already been prepared in 1166. The investiture of Prince Geoffrey was celebrated in style, in the presence of guests from all Henry's territories. The old duke died just over a year later and Geoffrey was finally able to take possession of Brittany as his father's representative.

The analogies with the description in *Erec* are obvious: the place, the date and the circumstances are identical, whilst the purpose of the occasion, investing a princely couple with their territorial rights, is comparable. Pernoud advances the view that until 1173 Chrétien belonged to the entourage of Eleanor and her sons in Poitiers, which was the focus of literary activity during those years, and that only in that year, after Eleanor had fallen out of favour, did he transfer his services to her daughter Marie in Troyes.[36] This is not to claim that Chrétien composed his work for the 1169 festival and recited it there. Rather we can assume that while he was in Nantes he was inspired or perhaps commissioned to produce an Arthurian work which would clearly bring out the connections between Geoffrey and Arthur, the legendary ruler of Brittany. The success of Wace's *Brut* a few years earlier had shown that this kind of political legitimization, which Henry urgently needed for his son Geoffrey in Brittany, could be effectively supported with the help of literature.[37] It is therefore not too far-fetched to consider the possibility that *Erec et Enide* has a similar function. Thus the description of the Arthurian court festival at Nantes as a reminiscence of the great festival of 1169 can be perceived as a very elegant mark of respect addressed to the English royal family and in particular to the young Duke of Brittany.

[34] Shortly after this Henry II also nominally made over the most important royal fiefs to his second son Richard as well as to Henry, the Young King. However, he did not allocate to them any real entitlement to wield power.

[35] Pernoud, *Aliénor d'Aquitaine*, p. 154.

[36] Pernoud, *Aliénor d'Aquitaine*, p. 161.

[37] As in the case of Edward I later on, so too in this instance perceptible efforts are already being made to exploit the legendary tradition of the Welsh and Bretons against their own interests and to make it serve instead the interests of the English crown.

In order to add plausibility to the involvement of Henry II in the inception of *Erec* it is necessary to look further afield. The son of the Duke of Anjou and the daughter of Henry I had spent some crucial years of his youth (from the age of nine to thirteen) under the guardianship of his uncle Robert of Gloucester in England. Robert was the addressee of Geoffrey of Monmouth's *Historia* together with Waleran, Earl of Meulan in the first version, with King Stephen of Blois in the second version and finally as sole addressee in the third version. The *Historia* is one of the first works of its kind, and no longer presented a history of the English but specifically that of the English kings. William of Malmesbury had also dedicated his *Gesta Regum Anglorum* and his *Historia Novella* to Robert, who was a kind of 'beauclerc' like his father Henry I and who exerted an important influence on the literary education of his nephew. As half-brother to the Empress Matilda he adopted her cause and represented her claim to the throne in England against Stephen of Blois. Thus it was with Robert, who acted as a kind of vassal king in the west of England and in the Welsh Marches,[38] that Henry II first came into contact with Arthur and his fictitious history. The political tendencies of Arthurian fiction were of advantage to no one more so than to himself, whom the addressee of the *Historia* wanted to make the future ruler of England. Henry was probably already familiar from his boyhood with legends and stories about the ancient British king; he would be able to hear them while staying with his uncle in the Welsh Marches at a time when this narrative material was still completely unknown in the territories of the French king. Thus it is only logical if a few years later, when Henry had come to power in England, the poet Wace should dedicate to the king a French language version of Geoffrey's *Historia*, making it now also accessible to a lay public knowing no Latin, and especially to the native aristocracy. In this version it is precisely the Arthurian part, the one directly affecting and interesting the king, that is presented in a greatly amplified form. Wace's commission to 'translate' the work can be seen as a successful attempt at popularization.

The desire to legitimize their sovereignty, which found particular expression in works of literature, had been a prime concern for the kings of England since the Norman Conquest of 1066; the vital need for it was obvious. William I had already made efforts to prove that he himself and not Harold was the legitimate heir to Edward the Confessor. Henry I pursued these efforts by marrying the great-granddaughter of Edmund Ironside a few months after his accession to the throne in 1100.[39] Messianic hopes were placed in their son William (1103–20), who was the first to unite in his veins the blood of both royal lines, the old English

[38] J. L. Weston, 'Who Was Brian des Illes?', *MPh* 22 (1924/5), 405–11.

[39] Legge, 'The Dedication of *Guillaume d'Angleterre*', p. 196ff.

and the new Norman.[40] His early death destroyed the legitimacy by blood that had been won with such effort. It is also probable that Henry I began to do healings by touch, in imitation of the French kings; the healings were supposed to lend the English monarchy just as great an aura of sanctity as that possessed by the French rulers. However, the principal cause of envy was the anointing of the French kings with chrism, which had been carried out from the time of Philip I at the latest, but could not be introduced into England until the reign of Henry IV.[41] What the English kings also lacked in the twelfth century in order to be able to compete with their rivals on the Continent was a heroic figure amongst their ancestors such as was represented by Charlemagne. Edward the Confessor was not at first in a position to fulfil this function; his death was too recent. Nevertheless, although he had died in 1066 without any indication of saintly characteristics, a cult was at once initiated, cleverly manipulated by the Westminster monks.[42] The *Vita* of around 1093–1120 contains invented prophecies by Edward concerning the future of the country and its kings, along the lines of the later *Prophetiae Merlini*. William of Malmesbury alludes to them in his *Gesta regum anglorum*, dated 1125. He also mentions Edward's healing powers, though these are said to derive not from his sanctity but 'ex regalis prosapiae haereditate' (col. 1203, 'from the heredity of a royal lineage'), an important factor for the English rulers who similarly claimed healing powers by virtue of their descent from Edward. In 1160 Aelred of Rievaulx wrote the official Life, and in 1161, under Henry II, Edward was canonized.[43]

The English monarchy now had a saintly ancestor (which the French did not yet possess), healing powers and, not least, more power and wealth than the French king. The life and deeds of the great British forefather Arthur had meanwhile become accessible to all men of letters, and in addition a wider public could read his story in Wace. Arthur had lived much earlier than Charlemagne, and allegedly, as was already reported in the *Historia Regum Britanniae*, the kings of the Continent had bowed before him, whilst even the emperor of Rome had been his subject. He represents the ultimate in ancestors, able to put Charlemagne himself in the shade. Geoffrey goes so far as to number the Twelve Peers of France amongst Arthur's vassals, a politically explosive notion and an ideological challenge to the rulers of France.[44] However, whereas there had

[40] G. H. Gerould, 'King Arthur and Politics', *Speculum* 2 (1927), 42–3.

[41] M. Bloch, 'Les Rois Thaumaturges', *Publications de la Faculté des Lettres de Strasbourg* 19 (1924), 29ff.

[42] Gerould, 'King Arthur and Politics', p. 42ff.

[43] Henry II also promoted a cult of Alfred the Great. Charlemagne was pronounced a saint by the Anti-Pope Pascal III in 1165, but in the official church he is merely venerated as blessed.

[44] Gerould, 'King Arthur and Politics', p. 49.

grown up in France from the eleventh century onwards an abundant literature (also accessible and widely read in England) about Charlemagne and his Twelve Peers, which served as propaganda material for the French crown, the Anglo-Norman counterpart, a body of literature with Arthur at its centre and the deeds of his knights as its subject matter, was still lacking. At this point it was inevitable that the interests of Henry II, highly literate as he was, would intervene, and the history of ideas suggests a possible connection here between the English king and the origins of *Erec et Enide.*

Someone by the name of Chrétien wrote the ancestral romance of *Guillaume d'Angleterre*. The work is an adaptation of the Eustachius legend and Apollonius of Tyre in the style of the Hellenistic romances, but the subject-matter and the numerous English names indicate a specifically insular audience. Legge and Francis make a convincing case for the hypothesis that it was composed for the Lovels of Minster and Southmere.[45] William Lovel, mentioned before 1191 as a knight of the abbot of Bury St. Edmunds, went on crusade with Philip of Flanders, Chrétien de Troyes' last patron. It is not crucial whether Chrétien really found his source in Bury St. Edmunds as he claims, or indeed whether he was ever there at all. It is the assertion in itself that is decisive and indicative, together with everything it implies about the pretensions of the author and the preconceptions of his audience. An identification of Chrétien de Troyes with the Chrétien of this romance has been repeatedly rejected on the grounds that there is no recognizable trace of the mentality and style of the author of *Lancelot*, *Yvain* and *Perceval* in this story of the English King William and his family.[46] This argument is not a very powerful one; someone like Chrétien de Troyes could surely have changed and progressed as an author. After all, would his adaptations of Ovid be immediately recognizable as the work of the author of *Erec et Enide* and *Perceval*? It is not inconceivable that one early work, and especially one belonging to a different genre, might differ fundamentally from the compositions of the mature author, who is then able to restrict himself to material he finds congenial after trying out various different forms in his youth. To modern eyes even *Cligés* and *Lancelot* appear surprisingly different from the

[45] Legge, *Anglo-Norman Literature*, p. 141: 'the setting and story could only have appealed originally to an English patron'.

[46] J. Frappier, 'Chrétien de Troyes', in *ALMA*, pp. 157–91, is one example amongst many: 'Though the name Chrétien appears in the first line as that of the author, I confess that I cannot recognize in the poem the turn of mind and the style of the author of *Lancelot*, *Yvain*, and *Perceval*' (p. 159). Stefenelli has recently argued for identifying the author with Chrétien de Troyes (A. Stefenelli, 'Die Autorfrage des *Guillaume d'Angleterre* in lexikalischer Sicht', in *Verba et Vocabula. Festschrift E. Gamillscheg*, edited by H. Stimm and J. Wilhelm [Munich, 1968], pp. 579–91), whilst Brand (*Chrétien de Troyes*, pp. 201–12) rejects the evidence unearthed by Stefenelli and presents arguments against identifying the two authors with each other.

three other Arthurian romances by the same author. Unless substantial additional reasons are found for not identifying the author of *Guillaume d'Angleterre* with the Chrétien of the Arthurian romances, the one argument just reviewed can safely be ignored. In the present context, on the other hand, it does seem well worth considering the possibility that Chrétien worked for English patrons even before *Erec*. One would then have to trace his route from the Lovels to Henry II, Eleanor, Marie de Champagne and Philip of Flanders.

However, at this point there is yet another argument to be adduced in favour of Henry II as the addressee of *Erec*. During the years of his youth that he had spent with Robert of Gloucester the young Henry had a companion called Brian, a natural son of Alan Fergant, Count of Brittany.[47] Although significantly older than the young claimant to the throne, Brian became his best friend, and after the death of Robert he adopted the role of political spokesman for Matilda and her son in England. It was he who brought Henry and Eleanor to England in 1153, when the prospects for his protégé's ascent to the throne became favourable in the light of Stephen's illness and approaching death.[48] Similarly, more than twenty years previously it was he who had conducted the widowed empress to her marriage with Geoffrey of Anjou and later repeatedly granted her refuge and protection in his castle at Wallingford, especially after her imprisonment in Oxford. Like his friends he himself was also a man of letters, and had even composed a treatise about the empress' claims to the throne; the letters he exchanged with the Bishop of Winchester have survived.[49] He was married to the heiress of Wallingford, and in the year 1130 possessed land in twelve counties and was already constantly favoured by Henry I. His whole life was devoted to the service of one goal, placing his friend the grandson of Henry I on the throne of England as Henry II.

In a hitherto largely neglected study dating from 1924, and one which certainly merits greater attention, Weston was already able to make an absolutely confident identification of the Arthurian figure Brian des Illes with this Brian of Wallingford, named in documents as Brian Fitz Count, Brian de Insula or Brian

[47] The *Lai de Tydorel*, which survives in the same manuscript as *Tyolet*, contains an indication that from an early stage Breton poetry could be put to use for the glorification of a dynasty, and that at the time when *Erec et Enide* was composed this process was already something of a tradition in Brittany. In the lay, Alan Fergant and his son Conan III (as well as the wife of Geoffrey of Brittany) are supposed to be descended from Tydorel's sister: 'De ceus istra li quens Alains, / Et puis après ses filz Conains' (147–8, 'Of this line was born Count Alan, and afterwards his son Conan'). See also the edition of *Tydorel* by Gaston Paris, 'Lais inédits de *Tyolet*, de *Guingamor*, de *Doan*, du *Lecheor* et de *Tydorel*', *Romania* 8 (1879), 66.

[48] A. L. Poole, *From Domesday Book to Magna Carta* 1087–1216, *Oxford History of England*, second edition (Oxford, 1955; first published 1951), p. 163.

[49] Weston, 'Who Was Brian des Illes?', p. 406ff.

de l'Isle: 'For the first time we can point to an unmistakably historic character figuring in Arthurian romance.'[50] The name Brian de Insula is mentioned in the chronicle of Abergavenny (where Brian of Wallingford was lord of the castle and the monastery) and also in Giraldus Cambrensis. As the king's representative in Wales he was shunned by the Welsh, which according to Weston explains the unique instance where he appears with a negative image, namely in *Perlesvaus*, which may perhaps have been written by a Glastonbury monk of Welsh descent. In other later romances, in which Brian des Illes is more often named as a peripheral character, he is always presented in a positive light as a friend of King Arthur and his knights.

Brian des Illes' first appearance as a character in an Arthurian romance occurs in *Erec et Enide*. On the occasion of the coronation of the hero and heroine in Nantes the poet informs us that in the banqueting hall two magnificent ivory thrones have been put ready for Arthur and the queen:

> En la sale ot deus faudestués
> d'ivoire, blans, et biax et nués,
> d'une meniere et d'une taille.
> Cil qui les fist, sanz nule faille,
> fu molt soutix et angigneus,
> car *si les fist sanblanz andeus*
> d'un haut, d'un lonc, et d'un ator,
> ja tant n'esgardessiez an tor
> por l'un de l'autre dessevrer
> que ja i poïssiez trover
> an l'un qui an l'autre ne fust.
> N'i avoit nule rien de fust,
> se d'or non, et d'ivoire fin;
> antaillé furent de grant fin,
> car li dui manbre d'une part
> orent sanblance de liepart,
> li autre dui de corquatrilles.
> *Uns chevaliers, Bruianz des Illes,*
> *en avoit fet don et seisine*
> le roi Artus et la reïne. (6651–70) [6713–32]

(In the hall there were two beautiful new white thrones, made of ivory and identical in size and appearance. The man who made them was without doubt most subtle and skilful, for *he made them both so much alike*, the same in height and length, and with the same decoration, that however much you looked all round to distinguish one from the other you would never be able to find anything in the one that was not in the other. There was nothing in them made

[50] Weston, 'Who Was Brian des Illes?', p. 410.

of wood; everything was of gold or fine ivory; they were carved with great finesse, for on each throne one side was like a leopard and the other like a crocodile. *A knight, Bruiant of the Isles, had given them as a present* to King Arthur and the queen.)

In *Erec* the name of Brian des Illes occurs only at this point. It is meant to be a compliment, and Chrétien's intention in this reference, barely disguised for his contemporary audience, is to point out the merits of Brian of Wallingford, who put Henry II and his queen Eleanor on the thrones of England: 'Cil qui les fist, sanz nule faille / fu mout soutix et angigneus'. A veiled homage to Henry II lies in the description of the thrones: on the side-pieces of the thrones are two carved leopards, but leopards (synonymous with lions, differentiated only by the position of the head) are the heraldic beasts of the English king. Chrétien has thus introduced an element of heraldic flattery here. Brault gives various examples of the flattering transfer of the royal arms to fictitious characters; thus Thomas' Tristan likewise bears the colours of King Henry II of England.[51]

The characteristics of the two identical thrones are a striking reminder of Chrétien's words about the innate equality of Erec and Enide:

Si estoient d'une meniere,
d'unes mors et d'une matiere,
que nus qui le voir volsist dire
n'an poïst le meillor eslire
ne le plus bel ne le plus sage.
Molt estoient d'igal corage
et molt avenoient ansanble... (1487–93) [1507–13]

(And they were so much alike in conduct and character, that no one who wished to tell the truth could have said which was the better, the fairer or the wiser. They were very much equals in spirit and suited each other very well...)

Reviving this idea in the description of the thrones could be a reference to the exemplary equality and the abundance of harmony which characterized the

[51] G. J. Brault, *Early Blazon* (Oxford, 1972), especially pp. 20 and 53. There is no surviving concrete evidence of the royal arms in England before 1198, but there can be no doubt that Henry II had one or two lions (or leopards) in his arms. His son Richard I had three golden leopards on a red ground (p. 21: 'gules, three leopards or'). In *Durmart* both the hero and his father, who is closely related to Arthur, carry the royal arms: 'gules, two leopards or crowned argent'. This fact alone is mentioned nineteen times in the romance. In his *Chronique des ducs de Normandie* Benoît de Sainte-Maure has William the Conqueror carrying the colours of Henry II. Manuscript *K* of the Second Continuation (from the second half of the thirteenth century) ascribes to King Arthur the English royal arms that have now become firmly established: 'three leopards passant or'. See Brault, *Early Blazon*, p. 22: 'There seems little doubt here that the inventor of these arms wished to link the then reigning monarch (Edward I, in view of his known Arthurianism, strikes us as being a logical candidate) to his fabled ancestor, King Arthur.'

relationship of Henry II and Eleanor before the rift in the 1170s, and which had made the kingdom of England into what it was at the time *Erec* was written—the greatest power in western Europe. The passage cited at the beginning of this section, describing the coronation guests (lines 6581–95), can be seen to contain a subtle kind of homage, hardly perceptible any more to the modern reader. However, the leopards and the name Brian des Illes are substantial arguments in favour of Henry II having had a hand in the inception of Chrétien's *Erec*.

The poet's way of working compliments to his patrons into his text, in a more subtle and elegant fashion than is achieved by most of his contemporaries, is also familiar from *Lancelot* and *Perceval*. So why does *Cligés* contain no reference to a patron? Perhaps he was the same as the patron for *Erec*, or at least belonged to the same family. Chaytor[52] sees the tournament of Wallingford (*Cligés,* line 4629ff.) as an echo of the gathering of Henry II and his barons in Wallingford on 10 April 1155.[53] The king bestowed rich privileges on the town as a reward for its loyal services during his struggle for the throne.[54] Who apart from the families of Henry II or Brian of Wallingford could have an interest in a description of the non-Arthurian tournament site of Gualingefort? The precise description of Windsor, as well as the drying up of the Thames, which had in fact been recorded in 1113–14 and 1157, also merit renewed attention in this context.[55]

Geoffrey of Brittany, the son of Henry II and a possible addressee of Chrétien's *Erec*, received a solid literary education and developed over the years into a promoter and benefactor of numerous poets. Like his brother Richard (the troubadour) he was one of the main links between the literary currents of Languedoc and the north.[56] He even emerged as a poet himself. Some *jeus partis* written by him with Gace Brulé and Gaucelm Faidit have survived. Bertran de Born was a friend of his (calling him Rassa) and dedicated various poems to him.[57] Both cultivated a lively exchange of ideas. In the context of the present discussion the *sirventes* which Bertran dedicated to Geoffrey are significant because they contain repeated references to Arthurian material. On one occasion the poet addresses him as 'coms Jaufres, cui es Bresilianda' ('Count Geoffrey to whom Broceliande belongs', Appel's edition, number 14 stanza 5) and expresses the wish that he were the king's oldest son so that he could claim the king's

52 H. J. Chaytor, *The Troubadours and England* (Cambridge, 1923).

53 W. Meyer-Lübke, 'Crestien von Troyes Erec und Enide', *ZfSL* 44 (1917), 162.

54 Poole, *From Domesday Book to Magna Carta*, pp. 75, 164, 165 and 212.

55 Rickard, *Britain in Medieval French Literature*, p. 111.

56 Bezzola, *La cour d'Angleterre*, p. 234.

57 Poems by Giraut de Calanson and Peire Vidal, and the *Ensenhamen du jongleur* (Abrils issia), contain references to the young Prince Geoffrey. See J. Anglade, *Les troubadours et les Bretons* (Montpellier, 1928, reprinted Geneva, 1973).

entire inheritance. This may be an indication that the Duke of Brittany saw himself as the heir to Arthur. A second quotation supports this hypothesis:

S'Artus, lo senher de Cardolh,
Cui Breton atendon e mai,
Agues poder que tornes sai,
Breton i aurian perdut
E nostre senher gazanhat.
Si lor i tornava Galvanh,
Non lor auria esmendat
Qe mais non lur agues tolgut. (number 25 stanza 5)

(If Arthur, the lord of Carduel, whom the Bretons expect in May [= in vain?], had the power to return to this world the Bretons would have lost and Our Lord would have gained. Even if Gawain returned to them [as well?] the compensation would still not match what He had taken from them.)

This poem is an expression of Bertran's mourning for Geoffrey's early death in 1186.[58] The quotations are grounds for supposing that Geoffrey of Brittany felt a close connection between himself and the Arthurian sphere; perhaps this inclination derives not only from his authority over a territory in which the Arthurian saga was still alive amongst the people, but also from the fact that his installation as ruler of Brittany had been glorified and immortalized in the first famous Arthurian romance. His only son, born posthumously, was christened Arthur by his widow, thus giving expression to an intensified ideological claim, whose consequences will be discussed again later.

The predominance of place-names from Angevin territories has already provoked suggestions of connections between the inception of *Erec et Enide* and the English ruling dynasty.[59] This opportunity for a methodological approach will now be pursued, testing Chrétien's other works and the remaining verse

[58] The abundant references in Bezzola, *La cour d'Angleterre*, p. 227ff. have yet to be fully exploited in the context of Chrétien's *Erec*.

[59] Further possible examples of topical associations can be found in a number of names in *Erec*: *Cork*—The Irish town fell to Henry II in May 1169, and he introduced a new legal code there; *Caradigan*—From 1157 Henry II was waging war against Owein Gwynedd; from 1171 the town was finally in the possession of Rhys ap Gryffydd, who now became a close ally of Henry after a period of hostilities (Poole, *From Domesday Book to Magna Carta*, p. 293ff.); *Gavoie*—'li larges rois de Gavoie' (6755, 'the generous king of Galloway'); the ruler of Galloway, Uhtred (1160–74), was cousin to Henry II via a half-sister of his mother and also his vassal; *Bishops of Canterbury and Nantes*—Perhaps an echo of the circumstances surrounding the coronation of Henry's son in 1170 by the Archbishop of York instead of the Archbishop of Canterbury, the only person entitled to perform it (1982: *si com il doit*, 'as he should do'); Henry's action was intended as an affront to Thomas Becket (died 1170); to begin with Erec and Enide are married by the Archbishop of Canterbury (line 1980) but their coronation is performed by the Bishop of Nantes.

romances on this point. *Cligés* is comparable with *Erec* in its use of place-names, whereas English place-names are almost entirely absent from *Yvain*, as they are from *Lancelot* and *Perceval*, which we know were not written primarily for an Anglo-Norman audience. *Guillaume d'Angleterre*, whether composed by Chrétien de Troyes or not, was undoubtedly composed for an English readership. It would therefore seem that the nomenclature of the romances can be viewed as an indication of their sphere of influence and as a clue to their target audience. An evaluation of the indexes of names in the editions of the thirteenth-century Arthurian romances produces results as follows.

Numerous texts (*Yder*, *La Vengeance Raguidel*, *Durmart*, *Le Lai du cort mantel*, *Li Chevaliers as deus espees* and *Fergus*) contain not one single name from the French mainland, but instead a detailed list of English and Scottish places going far beyond the usual naming of the classic Arthurian locations (Avalon, Carlion, Carduel, Castel as Puceles, Gales, Londres, Bretaigne, Orcanie, Escoce, Cornouaille),[60] as can be seen from the following examples:

Durmart — Glastonbury, Galloway, Arundel, Bangor, Benwick, Limerick, Dublin, Winchester, Rushwick.

Meraugis — Canterbury, Gloucester, Cirencester, Dublin, Stirling, Galloway, Handiton, Lammermore, Leicester.

Yder — Warwick, Caerwent, Great Malvern, Pomfret, Gloucestershire, River Severn, Winchester.

Fergus — Cumberland, Dunottar, Dunfermline, Jedburgh (Jedworth), Glasgow, Lammermore, Liddel, Lothian, Melrose, Queensferry, Roxburgh and the Scottish saint, Mungo.

There is no longer any question of this being the traditional setting of Arthurian literature.[61]

Other works contain French place-names, but here we have to distinguish them according to whether they were in territory subject to the French or the

[60] Loomis, *Arthurian Tradition and Chrétien de Troyes*, p. 30, believes that these place-names worked their way into the *matière de Bretagne* via Breton *conteurs* travelling around England. The forms of the names are Anglo-Norman, not Celtic, whilst the Welsh, for example, had other names for their towns: 'Kardoel is an Anglo-Norman form which could only have become known to the Bretons after the Norman Conquest' (p. 29).

[61] Köhler, *Ideal und Wirklichkeit*, speaks of the vagueness of Arthurian romance geography as a poetic symbol of a courtly and idealized feudal realm: 'For that reason a world shaped by the notion of courtly chivalry with its moralizing demands on life-style and leadership can only continue to exist in the fantasy landscape of a fairy-tale poem, in which the new bourgeois reality is made to retreat to the farthest extremities, the real monarchy is ignored and animosities within the ranks are projected into a fantasy "other world", demonic and threatening but avoidable' (translated from p. 32). In the Arthurian romances of the thirteenth century, however, just as the demonization of the outside world is very largely reduced, so too it is no longer generally possible to speak of a lack of real locations.

English kings. By far the largest number of names relate to Eleanor's inheritance, for example Gascony in *L'Atre périlleux*, *Claris et Laris* and *Hunbaut*, or to the former ancestral home of the English kings, Normandy, in *L'Atre périlleux*, *Le Bel Inconnu*, *Claris et Laris*, *Les Merveilles de Rigomer* and *Escanor*. Brittany features in *Le Lai du cor*, *Li Chevaliers as deus espees*, *Claris et Laris*, *Escanor* and *La Vengeance Raguidel*, as well as the towns of Nantes, Esparlot and Carahés in Brittany. Other French names such as Sens, Senlis, Paris, Lyon, France and François are cited in set phrases like 'dusqu'a Paris' ('as far as Paris'), in the rhyme position, or as the place of origin of horses, weapons or armour. Similarly characteristic of the use of French names are expressions like 'jusqu'en France' ('as far as France'), 'a la maniere des François' ('in the French way') and 'ces armes de François' ('these French arms'), all from *Les Merveilles de Rigomer*, or 'des François y avoit Flores' ('Flores was there from amongst the French'), from a list of knights in *Le Bel Inconnu*. In all these expressions we are given to understand that France is felt to be some distance away and different from the narrator's own home territory, or at least from the fictional location and cultural background of his plot.[62]

GLASTONBURY AND BRITISH ARTHURIAN LITERATURE

From the time when *Perceval* was written until around 1200 there is no clear evidence of any Arthurian work in the form of a romance, with the exception of the First and Second Continuations. Is there a connection with the political turmoil in the Angevin Empire during this period, which had an unfavourable effect on the leisurely pursuit and promotion of literature? The great patrons Henry II, Geoffrey of Brittany and Henry the Young King were no longer alive. It was only with the 'discovery' of the graves of Arthur and Guinevere in Glastonbury in 1191 that interest in Arthurian material revived. Henry II had already commissioned the monks of the abbey to search for these graves. After the fire of 1184 the church buildings were completely rebuilt, with generous financial support from the king. But it was only after his death that a systematic search for the bones of the legendary king was undertaken during the work of rebuilding. In the presence of Richard I the precious remains that they had found were then given a dignified burial in a magnificent tomb, as Giraldus Cambrensis reports in his chronicle.[63] There had been knowledge of a connection between Arthur and Glastonbury since about 1150 when, in his *Life of Gildas*, Caradoc of Llancarfan reported the abduction of the queen to Glastonbury; according to

[62] See also *L'Atre périlleux*, lines 3092 and 3992.
[63] G. Ashe, *The Quest for Arthur's Britain*, second edition (London, 1971; first published 1968), p. 99.

the legend the monks of the abbey had played a decisive role in returning Guinevere to her royal spouse. The identification of Avalon with Glastonbury also dates from the time when the bones were discovered. Whether genuine or a fake, the cross which it was claimed had been found in Arthur's grave bore the inscription: HIC IACET SEPULTUS INCLITUS REX ARTURIUS IN INSULA AVALONIA (Here lies buried the famous king Arthur in the isle of Avalon).[64]

The discovery and reinterment of the venerable bones were of great importance for the history of Glastonbury Abbey. The monks had realized the economic significance of this discovery, which would inevitably be followed by an increased influx of pilgrims. However, there was still more significance in the political aspects of the fact that Glastonbury was host to the remains of the greatest king of Britain. Only with the proof that Arthur really was dead and could not return, as the Bretons and Welsh believed, did the ruling dynasty have the means at its disposal for putting pressure on those persistently rebellious sections of the population. After 1191 the favour of the Angevin kings allowed the monastery to function as an imperial abbey comparable with Saint Denis.[65] The associated propaganda makes its mark on the Arthurian literature of the thirteenth century.

Richard I, known to be a highly educated man of letters, continued to show interest in King Arthur as his father had done. Although he was only in England for a total of a few weeks during his whole reign, he still travelled to Glastonbury especially for the reinterment.[66] The crusade and the king's absence and captivity prevented any intensive promotion of Anglo-Norman literature and especially of Arthurian literature on the part of the royal court. However, it may be counted as certain that Richard I identified himself with the claim of his family on Arthur and with the related ideology concerning the legitimization of his dynasty. During the crusade in 1191 he presented Tancred, the ruler of Sicily, with the gift of a sword that he named Excalibur and that he claimed had been found in Glastonbury beside Arthur's skeleton.[67] Only a few years later Ulrich von Zatzikhoven received from Richard's retainer Hugh de Morville a book on an Arthurian topic which he used as the source for his *Lanzelet*.[68]

King John, Richard's brother, had virtually no interest in literature, but he did perceive the dangers that might arise for him from certain aspects of the cult of

[64] Ashe, *The Quest for Arthur's Britain*, pp. 100–1.
[65] After his conflict with the Archbishop of Canterbury, Henry II had been striving to deprive that see of some of its powers, which benefited Glastonbury amongst others. His successors continued to cultivate good relations with the abbey.
[66] Alternatively, perhaps the monks delayed the discovery until Richard was able to visit the abbey.
[67] Ashe, *The Quest for Arthur's Britain*, p. 7.
[68] H. Sparnaay, 'Hartmann von Aue and His Successors', in *ALMA*, pp. 436–9.

Arthur. Mention has already been made of the fact that the son born in 1187 to his brother Geoffrey and Constance of Brittany had been christened Arthur. This Arthur of Brittany was seen as a claimant to the throne: indeed in 1190 Richard had officially named him heir to the throne instead of John. With some justification his supporters had visions of him on the English throne as the future Arthur II. Messianic hopes became attached to him, and the Bretons thought that their Arthur had come back to life.[69] However, John had him murdered in 1203. This provoked bitter reactions from the Bretons and Welsh against the despotic king, resulting in the rebellion and loss of Brittany.[70]

During John's reign the abbey of Glastonbury preserved the Arthurian interests of the kingdom by means of literary propaganda, and we can assume that the audience for this will have included not least the adherents of the murdered Arthur of Brittany as well as all those barons in England who were extremely dissatisfied with John's character and style of government. It has already been pointed out that after 1190 the promoters of Arthurian literature (as indeed of literature in general) were no longer to be found at the royal court. In England the principal centres of literary activity apart from the royal household had always been the barons' castles all over the country, and sometimes they were even more important than the royal court.[71] Gaimar can be taken as the earliest example. He wrote the first chronicle in French (which is at the same time the earliest surviving work in octosyllabic couplets) for the wife of an English landed nobleman.[72] The Lovel family has already been mentioned in connection with *Guillaume d'Angleterre*. Hue de Rotelant wrote *Ipomedon* and *Prothesilaus* for Gilbert Fitz Baderon, lord of Monmouth (1176/7 to 1190/1). On the evidence of Hue this Gilbert possessed a library of Latin and French books. The earls of Warwick, the Beauchamp family, were traditional promoters of literature, and the Anglo-Norman romance *Gui de Warewic* was written for the glorification of their family (1232–42).[73] A deed of gift from the year 1305 survives,

[69] Ashe, *The Quest for Arthur's Britain*, pp. 6 and 109. Peire Vidal speaks twice in hopeful terms of the young prince (XXIII,29 and XXVIII,48–9 in Anglade's edition).

[70] The story of the murder can be read in the *Vida* of Bertran de Born (and elsewhere).

[71] Legge, *Anglo-Norman Literature*, pp. 35 and 85.

[72] Legge, *Anglo-Norman Literature*, p. 35.

[73] Holmes, *A History of Old French Literature*, p. 273. Research by A. Roncaglia ('Préhistoire d'O', paper read at the VIIIth International Congress of the Société Rencesvals, Santiago de Compostela, 22 August 1978) and by de Mandach (A. de Mandach, *Naissance et développement de la Chanson de Geste en Europe*, Vol. III, *Chanson d'Aspremont* [Geneva, 1975]) shows that the history of the origins of the most important manuscripts of the *Chanson de Roland* and of the *Chanson d'Aspremont* must be viewed in close conjunction with English abbeys and the courts of the higher aristocracy. Only from the end of the twelfth century does there seem to have emerged a clear divergence of interests accompanied by political and ideological opposition between the two great genres of Arthurian romances and *chansons de geste*.

testifying that another Guy of Warwick made over to the Cistercian Bordesley Abbey in Worcestershire a bequest of forty books, including 'le premer livere de Launcelot', the 'Romaunce Iosep ab Arimathie, e deu Seint Grael', the 'Romaunce deu Brut' and 'Un Volum de la Mort ly Roy Arthur, e de Mordret'.[74] Perhaps the occurrence of the name Warwick in *Yder* is also to be seen in connection with this aristocratic dynasty. The dukes of Wallingford, successors to the famous Brian des Illes, were also well known as promoters and addressees of literary works. Thus the barons of England and Scotland may have included many more promoters of literature, and moreover a number of them will have been particularly interested in encouraging Arthurian literature. The more hostile the higher aristocracy became in their opposition to King John, the more susceptible they must have been to the image of a king with the characteristics of King Arthur: noble, just, courtly, chivalrous and looking to the advice of his barons. The young Arthur of Brittany could have become such a king, but not until Edward I, son of Henry III, was this ideal eventually to be fulfilled.

Thus the concept of Arthur was turned for a while against those who would normally have been its chief promoters, namely the kings, in order to express indirect criticism of their style of government. King John appeared to his contemporaries as treacherous, unjust and arbitrary.[75] With the concessions they won from him in Magna Carta after their rebellion they tried to keep him in check. As a rule Henry II and Richard I had kept to the accepted practices of the traditional feudal law, but not John. He reveals characteristics which we find reflected in the negatively portrayed Arthur figure in *Yder* and in *Le Vallet a la cote mautaillie*. Is it pure coincidence that *Yder*, written during John's reign, portrays such a degenerate image of a ruler, which has very little in common with the portrayal of Arthur in romances before 1190 and after 1220? The short satirical poems such as *Le Lai du cor* and *Le Lai du cort mantel* also date from this period. In *Yder* the knights and the few members of the court who are not on Arthur's side receive correspondingly positive treatment. Kay in his role as an adviser is made to take the blame for the whole misfortune. All this is scarcely surprising in a work giving voice to the interests of the barons who are protesting against their king's misrule.

There was to be a committee of twenty-five barons which would meet to pass judgement if King John should happen to break the promises given in Magna Carta. However, the barons' aggression had other causes in addition to the injustices of John's reign: by his incompetence he had brought about the loss of

[74] M. Blaess, 'L'abbaye de Bordesley et les livres de Guy de Beauchamp', *Romania* 78 (1957), 512–13.

[75] There is now some dispute as to what he was really like: see Brooke, *From Alfred to Henry III*, p. 216, and Stenton, *English Society in the Early Middle Ages*, p. 46ff.

territories on the Continent after 1204. This affected the barons personally more than the king; it was not only that the loss of Brittany and Normandy severed the last ties between the vassals of the English crown and their ancestral home, but it also deprived the barons' eldest sons of their traditional inheritance. Their reaction bred the type of conservatism combined with hatred that can be characteristic of exiles. This attitude also included a hankering for traditional forms of literature.

The Church for its part was obliged to see the king as an enemy of religion. Until 1214 England languished under a papal interdict, which meant that for years no mass could be held and the clergy were forbidden any kind of sacred activity apart from baptisms and funerals. Thus it is hardly surprising that at the same time a work like *Yder* with its negative image of the ruler should find a home amongst the literary propaganda from Glastonbury.[76] The hero Yder fils Nuth is already mentioned in connection with the abbey by William of Malmesbury in *De antiquitate glastoniensis ecclesiae*.[77] Yder is supposed to have been buried in Glastonbury and the monastery founded in his honour, according to abbey tradition.[78] The romance of *Durmart* is similarly in the service of Glastonbury propaganda, witness not only the occurrences of the names Glastonbury (seven times) and Avalon (three times), but also the fact that it appears in the Bern manuscript (Burgerbibliothek MS 113) in the company of the prose romance of *Perlesvaus*, which can be proved to have originated within the abbey's sphere of influence. Moreover, *Yder* too exhibits some affinity with *Perlesvaus*: both romances depict Kay as an evil scoundrel. *Perlesvaus* can also be shown to have influenced *Li Chevaliers as deus espees*, as in the following remark:

> Et Perceval le fil Alain,
> Le gros Desvaus [=des Vaus] de Kamelot... (2604–5)

(And Perceval the son of Alain le Gros from the Vales of Camelot...)

These words could have been written only by someone who knew *Perlesvaus*, and understood only by a specific section of the public. *Durmart* and *Yder* are the only thirteenth-century verse romances with a strongly religious bias, and appear to be part of a revival movement. With their striking emphasis on

[76] John had allied himself to Bishop Savary (died 1205), who claimed Glastonbury as his and seized it after an armed siege. The monks turned to Rome and were able to prevail against Savary and the king: see G. Ashe, *King Arthur's Avalon. The Story of Glastonbury* (London, 1957), p. 283ff.

[77] *PL* 179, column 1701, 'De illustri Arturo'.

[78] According to R. H. Fletcher, *The Arthurian Material in the Chronicles*, second edition, expanded by R. S. Loomis (New York, 1966), Appendix, p. 326, the section of William of Malmesbury's text that refers to Yder is an interpolation undertaken in the interests of Glastonbury.

religion they could be regarded as links between the verse romances and the prose romances.

At this time, the beginning of the thirteenth century, Glastonbury Abbey was especially active in the particular sphere of Arthurian literature. Apart from *Perlesvaus*, of which the author maintains that he found the book containing his source 'at the monastery in Avalon', it is also possible that Robert de Boron's *Joseph d'Arimathie* and *Merlin* were written there during that period.[79] Robert likewise appears to identify Avalon with Glastonbury and takes upon himself the task of reporting how Joseph of Arimathea brought the Grail to England. In so doing he traces a way of salvation to the West (Britain?) and closes the last gap between the Arthurian world and Christianity.

In the context of the significant role as promoters of Arthurian literature played in the twelfth century by the English royal family it is also hardly surprising if, in the thirteenth century, the prose romances of the Lancelot/Grail cycle were still being wrongly ascribed to the author Walter Map with Henry II as their patron. Scholars and editors generally give this fact short shrift or no mention at all, but its importance for tracing the reception of Arthurian literature in England should not be underestimated. For thirteenth-century audiences it was probably almost unthinkable that any item of Arthurian literature would not be directly or indirectly connected with England, its ruling dynasty and its barons.

If the Angevin rulers from Henry II onwards were trying to see themselves as successors to King Arthur, making political capital out of this idea in order to suppress the Welsh or the Bretons and lay claim to sovereignty over Scotland (hence the striking northward shift in the locations of the action in Arthurian romances of the thirteenth century),[80] then it is only logical that their barons should regard themselves as the successors to the Arthurian knights. The psychological state of the barons after the loss of the continental territories gives rise to their craving for family sagas, each of which places in the role of ancestor to their own dynasty one of the famous Arthurian knights, or rather a knight who only becomes famous when he is presented as such in the text itself. The romances of *Durmart*, *Hunbaut*, *Beaudous* and *Li Chevaliers as deus espees* are possibly to be included in this group of texts, and in all probability so is *Fergus*.

Consequently we can distinguish between two interest groups, both ready to promote Arthurian literature: the ruling household and the barons. At times

[79] P. Le Gentil argues for this in 'The Work of Robert de Boron and the *Didot Perceval*', in *ALMA*, p. 253, as does Ashe, *King Arthur's Avalon*, p. 251. It is disputed by R. S. Loomis, 'The Origin of the Grail Legends', in *ALMA*, p. 286.

[80] This view is represented by Ashe, *The Quest for Arthur's Britain*, pp. 109–10, and can be broadly accepted subject to the additional details discussed in this study.

their aims are identical, but they diverge when there is a temporary lack of general consensus between the groups.[81] Both camps make use of propaganda from Glastonbury Abbey, which for its part is not only interested in the aims of the kings and in national concerns but also has an eye to its own economic and ideological interests. This is not to say that the authors of Arthurian romances were fundamentally dependent on the royal court, the abbey or the courts of the higher nobility; it is likely that not all the Arthurian romances of the thirteenth century are straightforward commissions. On the other hand the poets, including particularly those from the Continent, could reasonably expect at any time to find a positive reception for their compositions in England, especially if they incorporated more or less obvious references and allusions to their current addressee's historical links with the characters and locations of their romances. Turning to England was rendered an even more attractive option by the French kings' well-known dislike of Arthurian material.[82] This by no means excludes the possibility that these poems were also read on the Continent. However, it is likely that after the loss of the territories in northern France to Philip Augustus, any potential continental audience for Arthurian literature, which so extensively reflected the ideological goals of the English kings and their barons, would increasingly lose interest. Only in the south-west of France, in Gascony and the neighbouring territories, which continued to be under English influence, may such interest have lasted rather longer. The composition of *Jaufré*, as well as the fact that Froissart read his *Meliador* in person at the court of Gaston Phoebus in Orthez and was greatly respected for it, should perhaps be seen in this context.[83]

There are good surviving examples amongst the thirteenth-century Arthurian romances for both the interest groups already mentioned, with grounds for a particular involvement in Arthurian literature in verse. However, since it is not possible to examine in equal depth the social and political backgrounds of all the verse romances under discussion here, the following investigation will be restricted to three characteristic texts which at the same time offer the advantage

[81] Köhler, *Ideal und Wirklichkeit*, p. 22, draws attention to the role of the aristocratic families opposed to the French monarchy in the promotion of Arthurian literature.

[82] Köhler, *Ideal und Wirklichkeit*, p. 22.

[83] Given the way in which Geoffrey of Brittany (= Jaufre de Bresilianda) and his mother Eleanor functioned as intermediaries between Provençal and northern French literature, it is worth considering whether there might not be a historical link between the circumstances leading to the composition of the only Provençal Arthurian romance and the figure of the ruler of Brittany, who had become famous because of *Erec et Enide*. It could be a case of reminiscence. Jaime of Aragon was a cousin of Henry III's wife, and the link with England persisted even after that: in 1287 Edward I married his daughter to Alfonso III of Aragon, and in honour of the bridal couple he arranged for a round table to be held.

that they present a particularly clear picture of the ideological intervention of Arthurian literature in England's political affairs.

FERGUS

The text of *Fergus* was first edited by Michel using manuscript P (BN fr. 1553).[84] In 1871 there followed another edition, this time by Martin and using the older manuscript A (Chantilly, Musée Condé MS 472).[85] Since then it has been generally accepted that the romance was composed at the behest of Alan, lord of Galloway. Alan was the great-grandson of a historical Lord Fergus who was of Gaelic and Norse descent and had received the territory of Galloway as a fief from David I of Scotland.[86]

The aim of the romance would thus be the glorification of this Fergus, the ancestor of the patron. Legge supports Martin's theory and proposes a date for the work of around 1209,[87] the year in which Alan married Margaret, a niece of the Scottish king;[88] at that time it may well have seemed to him desirable to make his own socially inferior family descend from an Arthurian knight. As a perfect knight the hero Fergus would make a very respectable forefather for Alan, who also held the post of a constable of Scotland. Legge has shown that all the place-names making their appearance in the romance can be found to have associations with the family's various territories in Scotland.

The author of the romance, one Guillaume le Clerc for whom no further identification has yet been found, demonstrates a good knowledge of the

[84] The editing of the text was commissioned by the Abbotsford Club in Edinburgh; they took a particular interest in the romance because the action is located entirely in Scotland and northern England.

[85] Both editions are still very inadequate (Martin is lacking in sufficient critical apparatus and an index of names, the lines are not numbered continuously and notes on the content are needed), but a new edition has yet to appear, although one was announced in the 1950s by W. L. Frescoln in M. D. Legge, 'Some Notes on the *Roman de Fergus*', *Reprint from Transactions of the Dumfriesshire and Galloway Natural History and Antiquarian Society* 27 (1950), 163. [This eventually appeared in 1983, and has been used for the quotations in this translation.] Michel suspected that there was a third manuscript in the Vatican Library, 'cod. membr. Vat. 6966' [Michel p. vi, quoting Carl Greith, *Spicilegium Vaticanum*, p. 85; Frescoln dismisses this hypothesis on p. 7 of his edition].

[86] Malcolm IV of Scotland had conquered Galloway, until then independent, in 1160. In 1185 Fergus' son Gilbert had to do homage in the same way to the English king as feudal lord of the Scottish king.

[87] See M. D. Legge, 'Sur la genèse du *Roman de Fergus*', in *Mélanges M. Delbouille*, edited by J. Renson (Vol. I) and M. Tyssens (Vol. II), 2 vols (Gembloux, 1964), Vol. II, pp. 399–408, 'Some Notes on the *Roman de Fergus*', and *Anglo-Norman Literature*, p. 161.

[88] In a letter to the author dated 12.12.77 the Scottish historian A. A. M. Duncan expressed the view that the wedding had already taken place a few years earlier.

topography of Scotland and northern England. Legge and Schlauch believe that he was actually in Galloway at the time the romance was written.[89] However, it is precisely in connection with this area that the text contains suspicious contradictions and inaccuracies, which will be discussed again later. In any case an author's knowledge of the area or the fact that he was staying at the scene where his romance was located does not in itself justify the use of such exact geographical details in a genre which generally distinguishes itself by its great vagueness in precisely this aspect of presentation.

To give an impression of how Guillaume le Clerc deals with the problem of place-names, we will take another look at the two journeys described in the romance, firstly the stages of the king's hunt for the white stag and then later the hero's quest.[90]

1. *The hunt*
King Arthur is celebrating St. John's Day in Karadigan (= Cardigan in Wales).[91] He decides to hunt the white stag in 'la forest de Gorriënde lés Cardol' (= Carlisle in northern England). After a long chase the stag escapes in the forest of Gedeorde (= Jedworth, now Jedburgh, in southern Scotland), then leaps through the 'contree de Landemore' (= Lammermuir) and the forest of Glascou (= Glasgow), runs through Aroie[92] and is finally overcome in Ingeval/Indegaus (= Innse Gall, latinized as *Insulae Gallorum*, i.e. the Hebrides and the part of the mainland belonging to the same domain). On the following day the hunting party rides back to Cardoel through Corbrelande (= Cumberland, see line 6147), past the castle of a 'vilain de Pelande' (= from Pentland or Pictland) which lies on the way out of Ingeval. It belongs to Soumilloit, the father of the young Fergus, and the latter decides to ride after the huntsmen.

2. *Fergus' quest*
Fergus finds the king at 'Carduel en Gales' (where 'Gales' does not mean Wales here, but is used in its original sense for all the territory occupied by the Celts or *Kymri*). There he is received by two squires from Loënois (= Loðene,

[89] Legge, 'Sur la genèse du *Roman de Fergus*', and M. Schlauch, 'The Historical Background of *Fergus and Galiene*', *PMLA* 44 (1929), 360–76.

[90] The forms of the names in the two edited manuscripts differ in details of spelling and pronunciation (e.g. MS *A*: Pelande; MS *P*: Pullande); however, they are recognizable as representing the same names. There are greater differences to be observed in the saints invoked by the active characters.

[91] The fact that the romance begins in Cardigan, although this place receives no mention thereafter, has provoked some surprise. In all probability the only reason for it is that the author had Chrétien's *Erec* in front of him when he needed a rhyme for 'Saint Jehan'. See also note 110.

[92] Until now Aroie has been identified with Ayr or Ayrshire in Galloway. However, the internal geography of the text favours Argyll (stress on the second syllable) as the more probable. The phonetic development of Argyll > Aroie would also raise fewer objections.

> 'Laudoniensis provincia' > Loonois).[93] He is sent out to undertake an adventure in 'la Nouquetren', or in manuscript P 'Noquestan', in the Black Mountains.[94] On the way there he comes to Lidel (= Liddel Castle).[95] Later he proceeds to Dunostre (= Dunottar, a castle near Stonehaven) in order to capture the shining shield there. His route leads through Lodien (Lothian)[96] past the 'Castiel as Puceles' ('Castle of Maidens' = Edinburgh, recorded in documents after 1142 as *castellum puellarum*), Port la Roïne (= Queensferry near Edinburgh) and Dunfermline (an abbey and castle belonging to the Scottish kings). He then returns to Lodien, the territory ruled by his *amie* Galiene. He captures the castle of Malreus or Mont Dolerous (= the castle and monastery of Melrose, also appearing in documents as *Mons Dolorosus*) not far from Rocebourc (= Roxburgh, the most important of the five main royal castles in Scotland), the hereditary seat of his *amie*, who is being besieged there by a hostile king. After her release Fergus is victorious in the tournament at Gedeorde (= Jedworth, a castle near Roxburgh, now Jedburgh) and wins the hand of Galiene. At Fergus' insistence the wedding and coronation take place in Roxburgh. In addition to Lothian Arthur gives Fergus Tudiele (= Tweeddale?).

There are no vague fairy-tale features in this Arthurian geography. It would not be impossible to cover each of the specified stages in a day on horseback. What is the author's purpose in naming these places? He was probably making use of their value as concrete images and their inherent scope for associations to convey some particular message. It is immediately striking that Galloway is not named, a strange state of affairs if the romance really was supposed to have been written for Alan of Galloway and intended to glorify the first historical ruler of the territory. Somewhere called 'Galvoie' is named in lines 5433 and 5442; Gawain has gone there in order to look for Fergus, and in the same context we are told in MS *P* that Gawain went 'tot droitement parmi irlande' ('straight across Ireland';

93 See R. L. Graeme Ritchie, *Chrétien de Troyes and Scotland* (Zaharoff Lecture for 1952; Oxford, 1952), p. 5.

94 According to Legge, 'Sur la genèse du *Roman de Fergus*', p. 403, Noquestan represents Tinto, an isolated peak south of Lanark, but it seems more likely that it refers to one of the numerous mountains of southern Scotland with names ending in -stane (= stone).

95 In the thirteenth century Liddel Castle was in the possession of the de Soules family, butlers to the Scottish kings. The castle was destroyed around 1300: see A. A. M. Duncan, *Scotland. The Making of the Kingdom* (Edinburgh, 1975), pp. 434–5. Guillaume le Clerc gives an exact description of its fortified position above the river, Liddel Water. The castle was probably extended in the 1230s and 1240s. The construction of a second fortress for the de Soules family not far away at Hermitage Water led to friction with England, because it was all too obvious that these buildings lying directly on the border were designed for defence.

96 The similarity in sound led to the identification of Lothian with the kingdom of the Arthurian King Lot. Something similar has taken place when William of Malmesbury informs us that Walwen (Gawain) rules over Walweitha (Galloway).

compare line 5393, 'par une lande'). The contradiction is solved if we accept that Galvoie represents the town of Galway in Ireland.[97]

As early as 1951 Greenberg voiced grave doubts over the theory that *Fergus* was commissioned by Alan of Galloway.[98] The objections are worth restating here for they have remained largely ignored in subsequent *Fergus* scholarship:[99]

> Historically Somerled and Fergus were not father and son as in the romance, but only distantly connected by marriage. Alan must have known this.
>
> Guillaume le Clerc confuses Ingeval and Galloway, and thus cannot have been resident there.
>
> The hero Fergus is naive and awkward. The historical Fergus was unscrupulous and had a craving for power. He had received a courtly training and was possibly brought up at the English court. He certainly did not tend his father's cattle in his youth. The identification with the hero of the romance does him no favours.
>
> The characterization of Fergus' father Soumilloit as a *vilain* is no compliment to his descendant Alan, especially since the historical Somerled was a rich and powerful lord. The Soumilloit of the romance behaves in a very uncourtly fashion and the author makes fun of him. Such a portrait of a direct ancestor was hardly designed to flatter a medieval nobleman.

There are still more objections that can be added to these:

> Why should Alan choose to arrange the glorification of that particular ancestor whose rule had seen the loss of Galloway's independence?
>
> The author of the romance repeats the negative cliché, common currency in the Middle Ages, that the inhabitants of Ingeval (Galloway?) are unchristian, 'niches et bestïaus' (199, 'ignorant and bestial'); it would be extremely unusual for a poet to represent the subjects of the ruler he was supposed to be glorifying, and of the ruler who had commissioned the work, in such an insulting fashion. However, it is in any case unconvincing that Guillaume should have thought that Ingeval was to be identified with Galloway, any more than Aroie can be identified with Ayr. If the inhabitants of Ingeval can be represented by a negative stereotype, then this is because they are Celts like the people in Galloway and in Wales, who are traditionally assigned comparable attributes.[100]
>
> Why should the Fergus of the romance be married off to Galiene, mistress of Lothian, when after all he was in fact married to a lady of more elevated descent, a natural daughter of King Henry I of England?

If we adopt the dating of Legge (1209) or Schlauch (1216) we observe that at the time the romance is supposed to have been composed the historical Fergus (who

[97] Rickard, *Britain in Medieval French Literature*, p. 115.

[98] J. Greenberg, 'Guillaume le Clerc and Alan of Galloway', *PMLA* 66 (1951), 524–33.

[99] Legge, *passim*; Southworth, *Etude comparée*.

[100] There are further derogatory comments quoted in Greenberg, 'Guillaume le Clerc and Alan of Galloway', and Poole, *From Domesday Book to Magna Carta*, p. 271.

died as a monk at Holyrood in 1161) had been dead for only about fifty years. This is astonishingly early for a myth-making representation which furthermore is inaccurate in decisive aspects. It is also in contradiction with the final words of the text, which read:

Guillaumes li clers trait a fin
De sa matere et de sa trove.
Car en nule terre ne trove
Nul homme qui tant ait vescu
Del chevalier au biel escu [Fergus]
Plus en avant conter l'en sace. (7004–9)

(Guillaume le Clerc comes to the end of his story and of his poem, for there is no one to be found in any land who has lived long enough to be able to relate anything further about the knight with the splendid shield [Fergus].)

If these words, prominently placed as they are, referred to the historical Fergus they would make no sense. At a time when it was a part of daily life to be fighting inheritance claims, genealogical accuracy was extremely significant, and not only Alan of Galloway but also the other families in the country would surely have retained a very clear memory of the powerful Fergus of Galloway. Furthermore, at the specified dates the sons of the historical Somerled, who died in 1164, were still alive, Reginald or Ranald until at least 1230; no doubt they would have taken decisive steps to prevent their father being stigmatized as a *vilain* and their own positions as his sons usurped by some obscure Fergus. There was no further very close connection between the families of Fergus and Somerled until about 1223 when Alan's illegitimate son Thomas married Somerled's granddaughter.

Two very important textual references have been totally overlooked until now, although they occur in both manuscripts. According to line 322 the Soumilloit of the romance is supposed to have been justiciar for his area. This was a high administrative office of the Scottish and English crowns,[101] and Guillaume explains:

Del vilain mentir ne vos quier
Que il avoit a justicier
Tot le païs et la baillie,
Et si l'avoit d'anchiserie
Que nus tolir ne li pooit.
Li vilains ot non Soumilloit. (321–6)

[101] Stenton, *English Society in the Early Middle Ages*, p. 41: 'The Justiciar was the man who took the king's place in his absence, who acted, in fact, as an extension of the person of the king. He was the second man in the kingdom.'

(I do not want to lie to you about this peasant, when I tell you that the whole country was in his possession and subject to his justice, and he held it from his ancestors so no one could deprive him of it. The peasant's name was Soumilloit.) [*Translator's note*: This translation is in accordance with Schmolke-Hasselmann's interpretation, though it is not certain that the verb *justicier* implies formal office, nor that 'd'anchiserie' means more than 'for a long time'.]

Thus Guillaume is eager to inform us not only of the office itself but also of the fact that the *vilain* inherited it from his ancestors so that it cannot be taken away from him. What is the significance of this? It is in keeping with the office that Soumilloit, because of his great wealth, was able to marry a wife of noble descent, 'de molt grant noblece' (328, 'of very great nobility'). It is from this marital connection that Fergus has derived his noble blood. Upon his marriage to the mistress of Lothian Arthur makes Fergus justiciar of Lothian (line 6864). To what claims, wishes or hopes is Guillaume lending poetic expression with these references?

In the romance Fergus becomes the ruler of Lothian, which is the richer and politically more important half of Scotland, with Roxburgh as one of the main castles. How could Alan of Galloway have allowed himself such presumptuous claims for his great-grandfather, especially since everyone in fact knew that his ancestor Fergus had not settled in Galloway until 1100 and that the family had only gradually built up additional power and respect. Only one solution dispenses with this whole series of discrepancies: the Fergus of the romance is not intended to be seen as the historical Fergus, and Alan of Galloway did not commission the work. The intention of the romance is not the glorification of the lord of Galloway, past or present, but a poetically embellished expression of hope that some member of the family will achieve fame in the future. Against this background there is increased significance in the prophecy of the dwarf, which comes approximately in the middle of the poem:

Atant fors de la capiele ist
Li nains. Si l'a reconneü,
Et dist: 'Vasal, bien aies tu,
Li fius au vilain de Pelande!
Joie et baudors et honors grande
T'est aprestee, bien le di.
Je te connois mius que tu mi...' (3736–42)

(Then the dwarf comes out of the chapel, and having recognized him he said: 'May you have good fortune, noble son of the peasant of Pelande! I can see clearly that joy and gladness and great honour await you. I know you better than you know me...')

We are told that this dwarf guesses everything that is to happen in the future and does not tell lies.

Greenberg rules out Alan of Galloway as either addressee or patron. However she offers no alternative, but believes the work was not written for any particular addressee. However, this is almost unthinkable in view of the fact that the hero bears an unusual name typical of that time and place, whilst the work is characterized by exact topography. It is therefore reasonable to suggest that the romance of *Fergus* was composed at the behest of Dervorguilla of Galloway and her husband John de Balliol to highlight the claim of their sons to the Scottish throne. The prophecy of the dwarf is to be seen in this light.

When Alan of Galloway died in 1234 he left three daughters from his marriage to Margaret of Huntingdon as well as the natural son Thomas already mentioned. Galloway together with extensive territory of the Morvilles, which had been in the family's possession for about forty years, was divided according to the prevailing laws of inheritance between the three daughters, who all married powerful English barons. Their half-brother Thomas, whom the people of Galloway would have preferred as their lord, was for decades after Alan's death kept prisoner by John de Balliol, the most powerful of Alan's sons-in-law, at his ancestral home of Barnard Castle, precisely in order to prevent Thomas' accession.

Alan had been forced by King John of England to send his daughters to England as surety for his good behaviour. As a result, Dervorguilla grew up with her grandfather, David, Earl of Huntingdon, where in all probability she received a thorough literary and courtly education. Her grandfather, who died in 1219, was a younger brother of the Scottish kings Malcolm IV and William I. Dervorguilla's marriage to John de Balliol around 1223 made him one of the richest barons of his day.[102]

The possibilities for laying hereditary claim to the Scottish throne which opened up for the male successors to Dervorguilla and John de Balliol must have been clear to that ambitious couple from the start. If Alexander II of Scotland had had no children (his long-awaited son was not born until 1241) the succession would already have seemed probable for Dervorguilla's eldest son Hugh de Balliol from 1237.[103] The birth of the heir to the Scottish throne and his long

[102] See the *Dictionary of National Biography* under 'Baliol, John de (1249–1315)', Vol. III, pp. 66–70 (Vol. I, pp. 986–90, of the reissue). His ancestors probably came to England with William the Conqueror from Picardy and Normandy; they received Bywell in Northumberland as a fief from William Rufus, as well as the forests of Teesdale and Charwood and lordship over Middleton in Teesdale and Ganisford. Bernard de Balliol built the family seat of Barnard Castle on the Tees.

[103] John, Earl of Huntingdon and Chester, died in that year. The claim then bypassed Dervorguilla and her sisters to the next male heir.

reign (1249–86) made the hopes of the Balliols much more distant. Nevertheless they continued to have some justification, witness the fact that on 6 November 1292 Dervorguilla's last surviving son, John de Balliol, was declared the rightful heir of the late Alexander III by a tribunal consisting of eighty Scottish and twenty-four English barons presided over by Edward I; there were twelve candidates but no dissenting voices, and John was crowned King of Scotland in Scone on 30 November of that year.[104] He was the grandson of Alan of Galloway, but his claim to the throne derived from Alan's wife Margaret, niece of the Scottish king.

However, it is now relevant to recall that the Scottish royal family was descended from Fergus Mor Mac Eirc, a historical chieftain-king who died in the year 501, after he had led the Scots from Ireland to Dalriada (Argyll). This line of succession is 'one of the safest genealogies which have come down to us',[105] and survives in numerous medieval genealogies.[106] John de Balliol's claim to the Scottish throne is therefore ultimately based on his descent from Fergus Mor.[107]

Thus the name of the romance hero Fergus in the thirteenth century evokes in the first instance the famous Fergus Mor, founder of the line of the Scottish kings, who lived at much the same time as Arthur and came from Ireland to Argyll (Aroie!) at that period. For this reason Guillaume le Clerc is able to declare that the hero has been dead for so long that no one can tell us any more about him. However, the romance is intended to be not so much the story of Fergus Mor as that of one of his descendants, a fictitious member of the family called Fergus, with a father called Somerled, for the genealogical tree of Fergus Mor contains another surprise: the historical Somerled is also a direct descendant. Thus Somerled and the historical Fergus of Galloway had been directly related in the male line in the distant past, a similar situation to that represented in the romance.[108] From this kinship with its set traditions for allocating names it is easy to construct a fictitious father/son relationship. The hero Fergus, presented as living in Arthurian times, may well have been seen in the thirteenth

[104] For details see Powicke, *The Thirteenth Century*, pp. 601–15, and G. Neilson, 'Bruce vs. Balliol, 1291–1292. The Model for Edward I's Tribunal', *Scottish Historical Review* 16 (1918), No. 61, 1–14.

[105] Chadwick, *Early Scotland*, p. 132, quoted in A. R. Wagner, *English Genealogy* (Oxford, 1960), p. 26.

[106] W. D. H. Sellar, 'The origins and ancestry of Somerled', *Scottish Historical Review* 45,2 (1966), 125ff. The direct male line from Fergus Mor ended with the death of Malcolm II in 1034, but the succession continued via the female line until the death of Alexander III in 1286.

[107] Wagner, *English Genealogy*, p. 26: 'The succeęding Scottish dynasties, Balliol, Bruce and Stewart were by paternal origin Picard, Norman and Breton respectively, though their claim to the throne came by descent from Fergus Mor.'

[108] Sellar, 'The origins and ancestry of Somerled', 137.

century as indeed the son of a *vilain*[109] because he had not yet been integrated into the feudal system and could not be described as *noble* in the Norman sense. In the thirteenth century the inhabitants of the Celtic northern territories were still regarded as coarse and lacking polish, because the Normans had exercised only minimal cultural influence in their territory. In the romance Somerled is a rich and powerful man but does not yet belong to proper society. His three sons have to tend their father's cattle and plough his fields instead of learning the art of weapons. However:

> Se il fuissent fil a un roi,
> Si fuissent il molt biel, je croi,
> Et chevalier peüssent estre. (331–3)

(If they had been the sons of a king, I believe they would have looked the part well and could have been knights.)

So the sons possess noble, even royal qualities, and the narrator toys with the idea of what might happen if their father were king. This remark is also connected with the first prophecy of a great future for the eldest son; it is significant that this is pronounced by his own mother: 'Encor puet a grant pris venir' (512, 'He may well achieve great fame'). There is more behind this remark than a prediction of the hero's rise to fame that is already in the past: only a projection of the narrative into the historical future makes the saying really meaningful.[110] However, the search for historical analogies should not be taken

[109] As Legge in 'Sur la genèse du *Roman de Fergus*' rightly supposes, this means a *yeoman*, a free man who farms his own land; *vilain* is an attempted translation.

[110] There are yet further grounds for suggesting that the romance of *Fergus* was promoted by Dervorguilla and John de Balliol. In the context of this study, which has other ends in view, it has not been possible to research in full detail how the romance came into being, and much work remains to be done on that subject. However, there are a few further points to bring out here:

1. John de Balliol and his wife founded Balliol College, Oxford; see H. W. C. Davis, *A History of Balliol College* (Oxford, 1963). In 1660 the Master, Henry Savage, composed a history of the institution, gave it the title *Ballio-Fergus* and in so doing became the founder of the art of writing college history. The author's hand-written notes, in an address to the reader not included in the printed version, explain his choice of title (MS Balliol College 255):

To the Reader

Good Reader, the reason why I style this History *Ballio=fergus* is because that albeit the loyall Balliol in his life time, provided a dwelling for his scholars, and allowed them maintenance: yet they by reason of the civil wars, not endowed by him with Lands, continued as his Pensioners till his death. After wich, his Relict Dervorgilla, in performance of the Trust reposed in Her, made it perpetuall; and, at her own charge, bought another place, nere the former, for their mansion, endowing it with revenues, mostly upon her Husbond's account, but partly upon her own. The which Mansion and Revenues were afterwards confirmed by her son John de Balliol, and her Grandchild Edward, both Scotish Kings successively: who, *by their mother Dervorgilla* (whom we have ever owned as Co=foundresse) *descended from*

to extremes. In *Fergus* what we are dealing with is a courtly romance; the genre of romance and the use of the vernacular and of rhymes are a clear enough indication that not everything stated here has to be taken seriously and literally. The aim, as in other ancestral romances, is to flatter the family by means of hidden allusions to a glorious future or past.[111] Arthurian romances occupy the middle ground between purely fictitious and pseudo-historical texts, and *Fergus* is only one example amongst many. To illustrate this proposition we will look again in more detail at the problem of Lothian/Northumberland, which has a part to play in numerous Arthurian verse romances.

---

two Fergus's; the one the first King of Scotland, and the other the first Prince & Lord of Galloway that we read of, as two great heads of one River, wich afterwards received into it both the *streame and name of Balliol...*

Thus even in the seventeenth century the name Balliol was still seen as connected in history and genealogy with Fergus of Galloway and especially with Fergus Mor. 'Fergus' as used here seems to have become a concept analogous to the term 'Brut', which from the thirteenth century could be freely used as the generic term for any presentation of English history. Savage gives the following interpretation of Dervorguilla's surviving seal (which is illustrated in Davis, *A History of Balliol College*): 'In Dervorgilla's seal: a thistle in bud only: to shew haply *the possibility in her line*, not the possession of the Crown in her self' (Henry Savage, *Ballio-Fergus*, 1664 edition, p. 4).

2. There is a place-name in the romance which may contain a further important reference. As mentioned above, Fergus receives Tudiele (variant: Tudale) as a wedding present from Arthur. It has been assumed until now (Martin's edition, p. XXII; Legge, 'Sur la genèse du *Roman de Fergus*') that the name hiding behind this French form is either Thevidale or Tweeddale. However, it probably represents Teesdale, one of the areas the Balliols received as a new fief from the English king in the eleventh century and where their family seat of Barnard Castle lies. If Fergus receives Lothian *and* Tudiele, it follows that the latter must be outside Lothian, and Teesdale as opposed to the other suggestions fulfils this requirement.

3. The action of Fergus begins on St. John's Day and ends on the same day two years later. Now St. John's Day is not a major church festival and does not occur in any other Arthurian romance as the date given for the first and/or last Arthurian scene, appearing only in *Beaudous* at a stage where the function is different. The Arthurian festivals are Whitsun, Easter, Christmas and Ascension Day. So if Guillaume le Clerc now chooses St. John's Day and mentions it twice in prominent positions (at line 1 and as Fergus' coronation day), this may be intended as an allusion to the feast of the saint whose name is also that of his patron (who regularly appears in documents as Jehan de Baylleul). This kind of homage via an obvious allusion would not be unusual.

There are other questions which must for the moment remain unanswered: What is the significance of Fergus becoming justiciar of Lothian? At the time the romance was written the post was held by one David Lindsay. Does he have any connection with it? Why can the dwarf's prophecy be fulfilled only after Fergus has won the shield of Dunostre? What associations or symbolic value does the naming of Dunottar have for thirteenth-century readers? Why is there such striking emphasis on the fact that Soumilloit's armour and weapons were last used *thirty-two* years ago? Solving this problem could lead to a more exact dating. Can the figure of Galiene's uncle, the lord of Liddel Castle, be more closely identified?

[111] Legge, 'The Dedication of *Guillaume d'Angleterre*', pp. 196–7; however Gerould, 'King Arthur and Politics', 49, also describes it as 'a kind of fiction cultivated by story-tellers perfectly conscious of what they were doing'.

Fergus wins the lordship of Lothian, then becomes king and the chief law officer of the land. Lothian is a *pars pro toto* for the kingdom of Scotland. In the romance the term *Escoce* represents only the territory north of the Firth of Forth, the *alta Scotia*; this emerges beyond doubt in the following lines:

> ...le Port la Roïne.
> Iluecques Lodïen define,
> Et Escoche est de l'autre part;
> La mers ces deus terres depart. (3937–40)

(...Queensferry; that is where Lothian ends, and on the other side is Scotland, with the sea separating these two lands.)

However, in the context of *Fergus* Lothian also means part of an area that together with Northumberland forms one cultural unit; the Anglo-Saxon kingdom of Northumbria stretched from the Humber to the Firth of Forth, and the old Bernicia was of similar dimensions. Bede understands Northumbria to mean any territory north of the Humber colonized by the English.[112] In the twelfth and thirteenth centuries it was primarily ruled by former Norman barons who had been entering the territory since the time of David I: Bruce, Morville, Fitz-Alan, de Soules and others. Unlike northern Scotland (Scotia), Lothian was completely feudalized. Scottish kings from David I onwards had never ceased to lay claim to Northumberland as theirs, although it now belonged to England.[113] Meanwhile England also claimed the Scottish territory of Lothian at regular intervals. It is possible that Malcolm IV already did homage to Henry II at Chester in 1157 for Lothian. William I had to accept the whole of Scotland as a fief from Henry when he became a prisoner of the English king in 1174 after an invasion of northern England by the Scots. At that time the five principal castles of Scotland, which play a role in *Fergus*, also came under Henry's control, namely Roxburgh, Berwick, Jedburgh, Edinburgh and Stirling.[114] Not for another hundred years, until John de Balliol, a compliant tool in the hands of Edward I, had ascended to the Scottish throne, did the English kings achieve comparable influence in Scotland again.

From the English point of view the years 1174–89 must have counted in retrospect as a golden age in the relationship between the two countries. The romance of *Fergus* reflects this ideal state of affairs in a poetically embellished form. Guillaume le Clerc (and through him his patron) attaches great importance

[112] See the article on 'Northumbria' in the 1970 edition of *Encyclopaedia Britannica*.

[113] Poole, *From Domesday Book to Magna Carta*, p. 269. David had inherited the claim via his wife, the granddaughter of Siward, the last earl of Northumbria.

[114] Roxburgh, Berwick and Edinburgh were returned by Richard I in 1189, in exchange for financial support for his crusade.

to a clarification of the entitlement of Arthur (= the English king) to reside in Carlisle and to exercise his hunting rights unhindered throughout the whole of southern Scotland as far as Argyll and the Hebrides. He is overlord of Lothian and thus has control over the marriage of the heiress of Roxburgh,[115] as well as being able to proclaim the tournament of Jedworth and install Fergus as lord of that territory. Carlisle was the gateway to Scotland, and therefore of strategic as well as economic significance. It had been Scottish from 1136 until 1157,[116] and was won from the English again from 1215 until 1217, but thereafter it remained permanently on the English side of the border.

As Carduel, chief residence of King Arthur, the town plays a significant role in the romances. This can be traced not least to the geographical and political situation mentioned above, as well as to the close personal ties between Carlisle and Henry II. This is where he had been knighted in 1149, at a time when the Scottish king had supported his claim to the throne.[117] This is where he held court in 1185 and forced various princes to do homage to him, including Gilbert, the son of Fergus of Galloway. In 1237 the Scottish kings officially renounced the territories south of a line from the Tweed to the Solway,[118] and the English kings subsequently strengthened their claim to the overlordship of Scotland. The Arthurian romances in French become vehicles, half in earnest, half in jest, for their territorial fantasies, and are poetic expressions of their struggles for power. The romances of the twelfth and thirteenth centuries constantly and repeatedly emphasize the English monarchy's claim to Carlisle and Lothian, or to Northumberland in its historical dimensions as Northumbria.

Why should the romance of *Fergus*, a mouthpiece for family and baronial interests, simultaneously pursue the cause of the English royal family? John de Balliol was one of the most powerful noblemen in England, and his ancestral home was in Northumberland. His future prospects were totally dependent on Henry III, and he needed to make the ever suspicious and fickle king favourably disposed towards him. The king's interests were also his own. It would have been a misfortune for him if Northumberland had fallen to Scotland, for he was an Anglo-Norman baron through and through. Both the patron and the author of *Fergus* therefore identify with England: even the phrase '(le regne d')

[115] Powicke, *The Thirteenth Century*, p. 579; a branch of the Balliol family had already settled at an early stage at Cavers in Roxburghshire.

[116] In his Sirventes 14, Bertran de Born makes a similar allusion to the battles for Carlisle and Cumberland: 'Ja per dormir non er de Coberlanda / Reis dels Engles ni conquerra Yrlanda' (17–18, 'Sleeping will never get Cumberland for the King of England nor will he conquer Ireland').

[117] Poole, *From Domesday Book to Magna Carta*, pp. 273 and 275.

[118] G. W. S. Barrow, 'The Anglo-Scottish Border', *Northern History* 1 (1966), 21–43, and Poole, *From Domesday Book to Magna Carta*, p. 283.

Angleterre' ('[the kingdom of] England') is used eight times in significant expressions as the essence of all that is good, refined and elegant; apart from two indications of distance in manuscript P, the name France does not occur at all. Only good relations with the royal family could help the sons of the Balliols if it came to a fight for the Scottish throne. For his part Henry III was interested in finding a peaceful means of annexing Scotland. He married his daughter Margaret to the Scottish heir to the throne and from 1249 he installed John de Balliol and Robert de Ros as guardians in Scotland. These soon began to represent Scottish and personal interests against their master, and in a quite disgraceful fashion oppressed the royal couple, who were still only children.[119] John de Balliol may also have been promoting his own very particular interests; thus the young couple were prevented from living together as man and wife, and this was undoubtedly done to prevent the arrival of any heirs in order not to upset the plans of other claimants. In August 1254 Henry III recalled his appointees and punished them for their misdeeds. John de Balliol was put in prison and his lands confiscated. Not until the end of the decade, when he supported the king against Simon de Montfort and the rebellious barons, was he restored to favour and given back his fief. He then remained the king's most loyal servant until his death in 1269. Were it not for chronological objections the crisis in the relationship between king and baron could be illustrated by some lines from *Fergus* which are abruptly introduced into the text and make no sense in their narrative context; it may be a case of interpolation. Fergus asks a robber knight the way to Carduel and says he wants to become an adviser to the king there. The robber knight replies with unexpected vehemence:

'Ce soit el non del vif dÿable,
Fait li leres, fils a putain!
Ja certes ne verrés demain,
Non le vespre, mon ensïent.
Je sai bien que vostre parent
Furent trestot mort desconfés
De consillier en son palés
Le roi Artu et sa mainnie.' (666–73)

('In the name of the living devil, you will', says the thief, 'you son of a whore! You'll certainly never live to see tomorrow or this evening if you ask me. I'm well aware that your relatives all met their deaths unshriven through counselling King Arthur and his household in his palace.')

However, we would suggest that the romance dates from before 1254, even if significantly later than previously supposed. If the attribution to John and

[119] Duncan, *Scotland. The Making of the Kingdom*, p. 563.

Dervorguilla is correct, the year when their oldest son Hugh was born, around 1234, can be seen as a *terminus post quem*, whilst the latest date is probably 1241, the year in which the Scottish heir to the throne, Alexander III, was born. A date between 1237 and 1241 is the most likely. During these years the Balliols had to defend themselves against their cousin Robert Bruce, who had apparently been recognized by Alexander II as heir presumptive. Legally speaking, however, their own descendants had the same rights. Robert Bruce later ascended to the Scottish throne as successor to John de Balliol.[120]

The two surviving manuscripts of *Fergus* show different dialect characteristics. Manuscript A has a strong Picard colouring with French elements, whereas P is less markedly Picard. Jordan thought the author was a Walloon.[121] Legge makes the apt comment that it is difficult to make a definitive pronouncement on Guillaume's dialect.[122] It is possible that the surviving manuscripts may already be continental transformations of an originally insular text. Based on the dating suggested above, manuscript A would have been written about fifty years after the composition of the poem. Legge does not rule out the possibility that the romance was brought to the Continent by Dervorguilla's sister Christina and her husband, the Duke of Aumale.[123] It should be added that manuscript A is in fact Chantilly 472, the famous collective Arthurian manuscript, which in the nineteenth century was (still?) in the possession of the Duke of Aumale.[†]

[120] See Duncan, *Scotland. The Making of the Kingdom*, p. 534. The name Fergus for an Arthurian knight occurs in the Prose *Tristan*, the *Prophecies de Merlin* and *Perceforest*, which are all to be dated as later works. See L.-F. Flutre, *Table des noms propres...dans les romans du moyen âge* (Poitiers, 1962). It has not been possible to clarify which of the countless clerics called William around during those years could be considered as a possible author for *Fergus*. He may perhaps be identified with the Prior of Traill, as Legge suggests ('Sur la genèse du *Roman de Fergus*', p. 406); this was the beloved and trusted cleric who was sent to the court of Henry III in 1220 by Alan of Galloway and who may have entered the service of Alan's daughter Dervorguilla after the death of his master. The author was certainly an experienced poet; *Fergus* is not the work of a beginner. He must have possessed an outstanding knowledge of the French literature of his day and also had access to a rich library, which could well have been provided by the Balliols. The same or another cleric called William is named in a document of 15 August 1265, one of the few documents relating to John de Balliol that is in French. In it he claims a considerable sum of money from Thomas of Musgrave as compensation for his 'mestre Willm' de Genellestone' having been held prisoner by Thomas; see H. E. Salter (ed.), *The Oxford Deeds of Balliol College* (Oxford, 1913), pp. 325–6.

[121] Jordan, 'Zum altfranzösischen Fergusroman', 159.

[122] Legge, 'Sur la genèse du *Roman de Fergus*', p. 405.

[123] Legge, 'Sur la genèse du *Roman de Fergus*', p. 405.

[†] [*Translator's note*: This interesting speculation is probably without future. The nineteenth-century Duc d'Aumale, Henri d'Orléans, a younger son of King Louis-Philippe, had acquired the manuscript with the rest of the Chantilly collection in 1830 from his uncle Louis-Henri-Joseph de Bourbon-Condé. The manuscript had been in the Condé family for generations, and neither they nor the newly created Duc d'Aumale had any connection with the medieval family of Aumale.]

However, it is also possible that Guillaume le Clerc really was a Picard and was brought over to England by the Balliol family which originally had its home in Picardy.

In that case, how did the Balliols come to order an Arthurian romance at all? Various possible reasons can be considered. In the first place, from its very beginnings in *Erec et Enide* the Arthurian romance was a suitable literary means of defending territorial claims and illustrating the need for legitimization. Secondly, it was the instrument of the kings (primarily of the ruling English dynasty, but looking to the future also of the eventual Scottish kings). Thirdly, Dervorguilla's family was related to the English royal family via Fergus of Galloway's wife, a half-sister to the Empress Mathilda, and was familiar with their propaganda methods, whilst John de Balliol, acting as regent for Henry III in Scotland, was thoroughly versed in the expansionist ideas of the English crown as conveyed by literature.

Fergus is like no other Arthurian romance in being the story of a social ascent. Certain analogies to the rise of the Balliol family are unmistakable. They were bitterly in need of legitimization in Scotland, because unlike their rivals in the struggle for the throne they had no real roots there. It is only after the union with Dervorguilla that the family acquires more power and prestige as well as Scottish territories; one of their sons then ascends to the throne of Scotland. It is not pure chance, as Legge asserts, that the prophecy of the dwarf in *Fergus* is fulfilled decades later.[124] The clever dwarf predicts 'tot sans mentir' (3707, 'without a word of a lie') exactly what lies at the heart of the Balliols' aspirations: the meteoric rise of their family fortunes in the near future. Thus, if our suppositions are correct, Dervorguilla and John commissioned a romance which lent expression to the hopes of their eldest son Hugh with respect to the Scottish throne, and did this in poetic form, though only thinly disguised for the implied and initiated reader:

> Fortune le veult ellever
> Si haut com le porra monter. (3695–6)

(Fortune wishes to lift him up as high as she can raise him.)

The image of Fortune and her wheel, which occurs only at this point in *Fergus* and is rare elsewhere in Arthurian romance,[125] evokes in an extremely graphic form the hero's rise to the monarchy: *regnabo*.

[124] Legge, 'Sur la genèse du *Roman de Fergus*': 'Guillaume could not have anticipated the illustrious destiny that awaited the family's descendants' (translated from p. 404).

[125] There is an instance of Fortune's wheel in *Wigalois*, line 1036ff.

The romance of *Fergus* can be read at different levels in accordance with different intended meanings. At the literal level the text narrates the story of a pseudo-historical hero named Fergus who is supposed to have lived in King Arthur's time. He becomes king of Lothian, where Lothian is taken to represent Scotland. The name of the hero recalls the past in evoking the progenitor of the Scottish kings, Fergus Mor, with whose family he is associated because of his name. Reflecting concerns of the present it is at the same time indicated, though not given equal emphasis, that Fergus is also the eldest son of a lady 'de molt grant noblece' (328, 'of very great nobility'), Dervorguilla, from the family of Fergus Mor and Fergus of Galloway, and is to rise to the highest of honours. The prophecies already mentioned are the means of relating what became 'reality' in the admittedly fictional past with what is supposed to come true in the real future: the son will ascend to the throne of Scotland. The projection of the past into the future has the effect of foreshadowing it via the prototype of Fergus the romance hero; his life-story with the characteristic rise in his fortunes is intended to be repeated and brought to magnificent fulfilment in Hugh de Balliol. The antitype is already living and the hopes have taken concrete form. Thus the Arthurian romance can be seen as narrating a secular version of the path to salvation.

The numerous subtle references to Chrétien's romances and especially to *Perceval* (see Chapter 5) undoubtedly presuppose a highly educated, courtly and initiated public, whilst the political and historical references point to a highly aristocratic class of readership with clearly defined interests. Dervorguilla, John, their relatives and with them a circle at the English court fulfil the criteria for such a closely defined audience of enthusiasts. On the other hand, the literary quality of the romance and its references to Chrétien's works also render it of interest to a readership unfamiliar with the state of affairs in Britain. Legge observes that the romance has left behind no trace of influence in England or Scotland.[126] This is probably attributable to the hated reign of John de Balliol (1292–6), who in just a few years led Scotland to the brink of political ruin and was therefore deposed by Edward I.[127] Thereafter the romance became somewhat inappropriate reading in England and Scotland for anyone apart from immediate members of the family. The king, who lived for another two decades in exile in Normandy, could have circulated the romance on the Continent himself just as easily as could his aunt Christina, Duchess of Aumale. The Flemish adaptation

[126] Legge, 'Some Notes on the *Roman de Fergus*', p. 164.

[127] *DNB*, III, 70, col. 1 (I, 990, col. 1, of the reissue). After that no Scottish king was ever again allowed to bear the name John; John, Earl of Carrick took the name Robert III. The surname Balliol evoked such unpleasant memories in Scotland that subsequent generations changed it to Baillie.

Ferguut, preserved in two versions, eradicates or changes the topographical references, since they would not be understood in this new social circle, nor would they fulfil any purpose outside England; thus *Ferguut*, having divested itself of the original purpose of *Fergus*, was able to find an audience in the wake of other Arthurian works in Germanic languages that were becoming ever more popular.

ESCANOR

It seems as though the Arthurian embellishment of contemporary historical concerns may be a characteristic that is typical of the genre under investigation, since it features in another romance besides *Fergus*, and one which can be traced with equal certainty to an English patron.

Girart d'Amiens dedicated his romance of *Escanor* to Eleanor of Castille, her husband Edward I of England and their children (as indicated in the prologue and epilogue). Eleanor was a half-sister of Alfonso the Wise (1252–84), who as a descendant of Henry II and relative of Arthur of Brittany had laid claim to Gascony.[128] The queen may already have had a certain interest in Arthurian literature on these grounds; moreover she had already come to England as a child. On the other hand we have certain knowledge that her husband had developed a love for all things Arthurian from his earliest youth.[129] From 1259 the young men of the land possessed in him a leader whom they could expect to elevate the monarchy to new splendours in accordance with the ideal of Arthur's court and the royal virtues of prowess, generosity and loyalty.[130] Edward gave particular encouragement to their favourite pastime, tournaments in the form of a round table. He arranged for festivities of this kind on all major political occasions and took an active part in the preparations. The round tables always served to make a political point as well. After his first partial victory over Wales Edward had already employed the Arthurian legend against the subjugated Welsh. In 1278 he went with Queen Eleanor to Glastonbury where he had the bones which had lain undisturbed since the time of Richard I exhumed, put on show and then buried again wrapped in expensive cloth.[131] This was all done to point out to the Welsh once more and very emphatically that Arthur was dead and could no longer defend them as they still hoped against the English kings; rather it was the reigning king who was the legitimate successor to Arthur in

[128] Powicke, *The Thirteenth Century*, p. 116.
[129] R. S. Loomis, 'Edward I, Arthurian Enthusiast', *Speculum* 28 (1953), 114–27.
[130] Brooke, *From Alfred to Henry III*, p. 232.
[131] W. A. Nitze, 'The Exhumation of King Arthur at Glastonbury', *Speculum* 9 (1934), 353–61.

ruling over the Welsh. In 1284, after their definitive defeat, Edward organized a round table at Nefyn in Wales, and on this occasion he also had the sacred possession of the Welsh, King Arthur's crown, placed on his head.[132] Later Edward based his claim to Scotland on the account in Wace's *Brut* of the conquest of that territory by Brutus. At the wedding festivities, on the occasion of his marriage to Marie of Brabant in 1299, the pauses in the round table were used to stage representations of Edward's victories over the Welsh, the Scots and the English barons.[133] In the year 1306 he had his son Edward, the heir to the throne, knighted with great pomp and in the company of nearly three hundred young squires from all over the country. The investiture was combined with a 'swan festival';[134] the elderly Edward swore an oath before God and the swans that he would not accept the illegal rule of the new Scottish king,[135] and his son swore from then on never to stay longer than one night in the same place until he had reached Scotland.[136] It is obvious that they were modelling themselves on Arthurian knights.

It does not seem very likely that an Arthurian verse romance dedicated to Edward I and his household, and probably commissioned by him, should have managed to stay aloof from the political objectives which the king had attached to the Arthurian legend. This can now be assessed by studying the place-names and the course of the action in *Escanor* as has already been undertaken for *Fergus* and *Erec et Enide*.

The place-names are predominantly indicative of English or Scottish topography, with the addition of the former Angevin holdings on the Continent; in the first part of the romance there is an account of a rebellion in Brittany. Gawain crushes it, and the Bretons have to promise never again to undertake any action against Arthur. This is obviously wishful thinking on the part of the English monarchy, because in reality Brittany had already been lost for more than sixty years. It would seem, therefore, that the turmoil of the

[132] Powicke, *The Thirteenth Century*, p. 516: 'He doubtless believed in the story of Arthur, and had opened the tomb at Glastonbury in all good faith. He saw more than a symbol in his Welsh trophy, the crown of Arthur, just as he did in the cross of Neath or later in the stone of Scone... Yet Edward was a political realist. He lived in an age of historical propaganda and knew the value of it.' See also Loomis, 'Sport and Spectacle', p. 554, and Powicke, *Thirteenth Century*, p. 429.

[133] Loomis, 'Sport and Spectacle', pp. 558–9.

[134] An echo of *Le Chevalier au Cygne* which may have been circulated in England via Edward I's second wife, a princess from Brabant; the author of the romance shows a precise knowledge of English topography. The hero Eustache becomes cup-bearer to the King of England. There is guaranteed evidence of a visit to England by the historical Eustache after the first crusade, and he also possessed territories in Britain.

[135] Robert Bruce, successor to John de Balliol, crowned on 25 March 1306.

[136] Powicke, *The Thirteenth Century*, p. 515.

period after 1204 has found its literary echo here in *Escanor*.[137] Girart also mentions the county of Ponthieu (line 18,882, 'Pontiu'), which had only come into the possession of his patroness, Eleanor of Castille, by inheritance in 1279, in other words around the time when the romance was written, making this an extremely topical historical reference. Girart may have entered the service of the queen during the negotiations with her new feudal lord, the King of France, in Amiens in 1279, which were followed by the Treaty of Amiens at Whitsun of the same year.[138] Girart probably then followed the queen to the English court.[139]

One other passage of the text that has a direct bearing on the history of the time is the section of heraldic references to the kings of Scotland and Wales (lines 3692–977), which has been studied by Brault. The first coat of arms described points to Alexander III of Scotland, who died in 1286, and the second to Llywelyn ap Gryffydd, who died in 1284. Everyone at Edward's court was in a position to decipher these references. We can accept Brault's dating of *Escanor* as before 1282, the year in which Llywelyn rebelled against Edward once again. However, what we see in these lines of text is no naive heraldic flattery; in the first few years after 1278 the peace with Wales is far too unstable for such to be permitted. The heraldic reference also serves as a warning. The emphasis lies in the fact that in this Arthurian romance both kings fall from their horses, through which Girart perhaps wants to indicate that they should at all times be aware of their potential defeat by Arthurian knights (=English barons).

Although it is not possible to go into the same amount of detail with *Escanor* as with *Fergus*,[140] a brief survey of the events of the romance is helpful for an understanding of its political intentions.

> Cador, King of 'Norhombrelande', would like to marry his only daughter to a worthy knight, and to this end he arranges a tournament in his capital Bauborc. The best knights from all the countries of northern Europe take part, but Kay carries the day. The Princess Andriuete[141] falls in love with him and he with her, but through a misunderstanding and a forged letter the couple are separated. Ayglin, who wants to seize power for himself after the death of

[137] There is another example of how a historical event or character can find its way into literature in the space of a few years in the romance *Wistasse [Eustache] le Moine*, which shows a character changing sides between England and France in the years up to 1216. The hero of the romance is historical and died in 1217; see Rickard, *Britain in Medieval French Literature*, pp. 134–6.

[138] Powicke, *The Thirteenth Century*, p. 235; G. J. Brault, 'Arthurian Heraldry and the Date of *Escanor*', *BBSIA* 11 (1959), 81–8.

[139] Brault, 'Arthurian Heraldry and the Date of *Escanor*': a poet only names himself after his birthplace when he is no longer there.

[140] Apart from G. J. Brault, 'A Study of the Works of Girart d'Amiens' (Dissertation, Philadelphia, 1958), no relevant preliminary studies of this romance have yet been carried out.

[141] The name comes from the *Lai du cor*, where she is likewise designated as Kay's *amie*.

> Cador, would like to prevent his niece's marriage to Kay, because it would make the country a fiefdom of Arthur's. Vigorous in his support for Kay's plans in Norhombrelande, Arthur sets out with an army to free Andriuete who is being besieged in Bauborc by Ayglin. The inhabitants of the town are on his side, but the princess escapes before Arthur arrives, and flees to Arthur's court where the marriage is celebrated. Ayglin is subjugated and has to do homage to Arthur, whilst Kay and his bride accept Norhombrelande as a fief from Arthur.
>
> A second strand of the plot, closely interwoven with the first, depicts the adventures of Gawain and his brother Girfflet. Without recognizing him, Girfflet has attacked and almost killed Escanor the Fair, nephew of Escanor the Great; in so doing he has brought the enmity of that clan upon his family. Escanor the Great puts the blame for the deed on Gawain and challenges him to a duel. After some complications Arthur brings about a reconciliation, and Escanor has to do homage to him. Girfflet marries the Queen of Traverses. Escanor the Fair learns of the death of his wife, becomes a hermit and dies. Girfflet and his wife erect an expensive tomb for the dead couple and remain nearby. When the Queen of Traverses also dies, Girfflet returns to Arthur's court.

In his edition of the text (p. xxi) Michelant comments on the lack of an ultimate goal. It is a fact that the romance does not have a main plot of the type that is traditional to the genre. It begins and ends differently from other texts in the sequence, and in many respects, but especially in the matter of the atmosphere, it is more reminiscent of the prose romances. The structure remains obscure (see Chapter 2). Michelant probably also made a mistake in adopting a title out of the manuscript which had been added by a later hand, as Escanor is definitely not intended as the hero of the romance. On the basis of analogous structures it would seem that the love-story and Kay's quest form the actual nucleus of the text, although this is the only example in the whole of Arthurian romance where Kay is made the protagonist of the main plot; however, since the work also exhibits numerous other deviations from the typical generic characteristics, this phenomenon becomes more understandable.

Girart d'Amiens is not one of the great writers of Arthurian works, and thus by comparison with Guillaume le Clerc he has also failed to master the art of limiting himself to one central concern that is then clearly worked through. Some of these inadequacies may derive from the fact that this romance is probably a case of a genuinely commissioned work. The poet makes the Queen of England, his patroness, responsible for the content of his romance:

> car il en a conmandement
> de dame noble, bele et sage...
> car li contes est bonz et biauz
> et plainz d'armes et de cembiauz,

d'amours, de joie et [de] deduit:
car cele n'a pas le cuer duit
de qui li contes est venus...
et gart ceuz et celes de honte
c'uimais entenderont le conte
que la gentiex dame m'a dit. (8–49)

(For he has been commanded to do it by a noble lady, fair and wise...for the story is fine and good, full of arms and combats, of love, joy and delight: for she who provided the story does not have a cunning heart [?]...and may [God] preserve from shame all those who will now hear the story that the noble lady has told me.)[142]

Girart places the events of his romance during the time when Northumbria was still a single political entity, as is clearly indicated by the choice of the capital Bauborc (= Bamburgh). This town was the political centre of the old kingdom of Bernicia and also played a significant role in the Anglo-Saxon kingdom of Northumbria. In other words, we have yet another recollection of a golden age in England's territorial history.[143] In the reign of Edward I Bamburgh lay south of the Tweed/Solway line, and thus belonged unequivocally to the English side. In the romance of *Escanor* King Cador is envisaged as King of Bernicia or of the Anglo-Saxon territory. Here as in *Fergus*, with its references to Fergus Mor, the historical aspects are handled more deliberately and less naively than in the early texts of the genre. The marriage of the Princess Andriuete with the highest court official of the English king brings Northumbria to Arthur as feudal overlord, and this after the action has been chronologically located in the era when the territory was at its most extensive and included the whole of southern Scotland. Not content with this, the romance also shows how Escanor de la Blanche (or Grande) Montagne, an area north of the Firth of Forth (probably Albanie or Albaine, the kingdom of the Albanac according to Wace's *Brut*), is forced to accept his land as a fief from Arthur. Thus at the end of the romance Arthur rules over the whole island and all other powerful leaders are his vassal kings. The enemy in the romance is embodied in Ayglin, who is not to be identified with 'Aguises' (4556), the 'bonz rois d'Escoce' (3210, 'good king of Scotland'). Could the sound of his name evoke that of the King of Ireland, father of Iseut,

142 This is not the place to discuss how far this is to be understood literally; suffice it to refer to the argument about Chrétien's patroness Marie de Champagne and the quality of his *Lancelot*. Girart d'Amiens also worked for Charles of Anjou, brother of the French king (on a compilation of *chansons de geste*), and composed a very derivative reworking of *Cleomades*. The question was already posed by Michelant as to how a poet of such poor ability could have had such success at the great princely courts.

143 However, it lies fundamentally further back into the past than the equivalent in *Fergus*.

who is traditionally called Anguin?[144] Or it could it refer to Anguis, a Saxon king who according to legend was killed by Arthur's father Uther. The associative function of this name for a thirteenth-century audience has yet to be clarified.

Despite all the allusions, Edward I's claim to Northumberland is given only restrained expression in *Escanor*. This may reflect Edward's policy of marriage and peace-making towards Scotland. However, after 1278, when the romance was commissioned, the English king had once again begun, if cautiously, to stress his feudal superiority over the Scottish king.[145] Alexander III resisted, and at first the English king let the matter rest since he had an interest in good and peaceful relations with his brother-in-law. Nevertheless, he was convinced of the legality of his concern and never forgot his claim.[146] This is the context in which we can place the origin of the Arthurian romance of *Escanor*.[147]

Edward negotiated the marriage of the heir to the Scottish throne with the daughter of one of his closest allies, Count Guy of Flanders.[148] It is possible that *Escanor* also contains a small element of propaganda for this particular dynastic union, which came into effect in 1281. However, the overall mood of Escanor is conciliatory with respect to relationships with neighbouring countries. It originated during the brief interval of just a few years when Edward I was on good terms with both the Welsh and the Scots, whose kings, the 'roi de Gales' and the 'roi d'Escoce', are represented in the romance as noble, brave and loyally submissive to King Arthur. Nevertheless the old claim to southern Scotland is still voiced in a pseudo-historical form, for championing the claim to feudal overlordship over this territory and over the whole of Scotland has already become a topos in Arthurian verse romance.

MELIADOR

The pioneering studies by Diverres on aspects of politics and of cultural development in *Meliador* allow us to see this work in similar terms as one of those Arthurian romances which to a large extent fulfils its function as a vehicle for the territorial and political interests of the ruling dynasty, a function which

[144] There was unrest in Ireland in the years 1276–7.

[145] Duncan, *Scotland. The Making of the Kingdom*, p. 593.

[146] Powicke, *The Thirteenth Century*, pp. 594–6: 'Everybody in England, and many people in Scotland, approved his obstinacy. His reputation throughout the west would have suffered if he had given way' (p. 596).

[147] Alexander III nevertheless granted him the right, normally that of a feudal lord, to arrange the marriage of the Scottish heir to the throne, the Lord Alexander. See Duncan, *Scotland. The Making of the Kingdom*, p. 592, and Powicke, *The Thirteenth Century*, p. 623.

[148] Powicke, *The Thirteenth Century*, p. 623.

is also an important characteristic of the genre.[149] The next step is to place Diverres' findings, which can be accepted without reservation, in the overlapping context of the genre's development.

In the 1360s Froissart held the office of *clerc de la chambre* in the service of Philippa of Hainaut, wife of Edward III of England. Like his forefathers on the English throne, this monarch had a considerable interest in the propaganda potential of Arthurian literature, and like them he had to spend a considerable portion of his reign dealing with the 'Scottish problem'. As a result of his stay at the English court Froissart became familiar with the dispute about the Plantagenet succession in Scotland which can be regarded as Edward III's main goal, and in essence the poet seems to have identified with the aspirations of his employer.[150] The first version of *Meliador* originated in all probability at the English court of the 1360s. Just as in the other romances discussed here, Froissart's narrative also takes as its overriding theme the marriage of the hero to the heiress of Scotland, which then entails the peaceful annexation of this territory by the British King Arthur. Only four short fragments remain of the first version,[151] and the romance now survives only in the second version, written at some time before 1383, that is no longer aimed at a primarily English audience. This amended version (preserved in MS BN fr. 12557), although it already comprises around 30,000 lines, is likewise fragmentary, and it is not possible to estimate even to an approximation how many more lines Froissart had planned in order that his narrative should cover for example the love-story of Sagremor (exiled son of the Irish king) and the recovery of his sovereignty over Ireland, which is to be brought about by virtue of his transformation from an uncouth Irish lad into a perfectly courtly knight in the English mould. Nevertheless the form of *Meliador*, in the version to which we now have access, permits extensive deductions to be made about the first version, since the basic arrangement of the romance as a whole seems to have remained unchanged despite its being aimed at a different audience.

The framework of the plot reveals a considerable similarity to that of *Escanor*. Several narrative strands are linked together, covering the stories of Meliador,

[149] A. H. Diverres, 'The Geography of Britain in Froissart's *Meliador*', in *Mélanges E. Vinaver*, edited by F. Whitehead, A. H. Diverres and F. E. Sutcliffe (Manchester, 1965), pp. 97–112, 'Froissart's *Meliador* and Edward III's policy towards Scotland', in *Mélanges R. Lejeune*, edited by F. Dethier, 2 vols (Gembloux, 1969), Vol. II, pp. 1399–1409, and 'The Irish Adventures in Froissart's *Meliador*', in *Mélanges J. Frappier*, edited by J.-C. Payen and C. Régnier, 2 vols (Geneva, 1970), Vol. I, pp. 235–51.

[150] Nevertheless, after a prolonged encounter with King David II of Scotland he felt attached to the latter by his high personal opinion of him, as is clear from the chronicles.

[151] Preserved in MS BN n.a.fr. 2334, printed in Longnon's edition of *Meliador*.

Sagremor and Camel. However, Meliador's quest is central with his striving for the hand of Hermondine, daughter of the King of Scotland. The hero, son of the Duke of Cornwall, is competing against Camel of Camois for lordship over Scotland. Camel, who defines his goal with the words 'Je serai encore, je le di, / Rois d'Escoce' (2425–6, 'I tell you I shall yet be king of Scotland'), is besieged and killed by Meliador. Diverres proposes convincingly that for the English court in the 1360s 'Cornwall' would evoke the title of Edward, heir to the English throne and Duke of Cornwall since 1337, whilst Camel of Camois, to judge by heraldic and geographical references, stands for the ruling Bruce family in Scotland.[152] Since we can be certain that the writing of the romance extended over several years, the text also reflects the personal relationships involved in the king's Scottish policy and the way in which they changed in the course of time, for at first Edward III had envisaged his eldest son as successor to the Scottish throne, whilst some time later his second son Lionel of Clarence seemed better suited. The Scots themselves suggested the third son John of Gaunt as a compromise solution. In view of this situation, Froissart's reference to the Irish sea as the river Clarense does not merely indicate that in this Arthurian romance England and Ireland are seen as a single geographical unit, since the border between them merely follows the course of a river that can easily be crossed, but the name of the river, Clarense, also contains a blatant reference to Prince Lionel, who was lieutenant and governor for his father in Ireland in the years 1361–6. His title 'Duke of Clarence' was a new ad hoc invention in 1363 and derived from Clare, the family name of his wife.[153]

Similarly, the choice of Roxburgh as the site of the tournament where Meliador with Arthur's agreement is proclaimed the future King of Scotland represents a clear allusion to an event in 1356 when Edward III had had himself crowned King of Scotland by his courtiers in that same place (which after *Fergus* was also an Arthurian location), in order to strengthen his claims to hegemony.[154] King David of Scotland had already been held prisoner in England since 1346. Edward had planned to keep the son of King John de Balliol, another Edward, on the Scottish throne in the role of rival king as well as compliant vassal to himself, but by this time that plan had already failed.

[152] This is perhaps an indirect reference to Robert the High Steward, regent of the country during the minority and imprisonment of the Scottish king.

[153] Diverres, 'The Irish Adventures in Froissart's *Meliador*', p. 247. It is true that the name 'Duke of Clarence' already occurs in the Prose *Lancelot*; see Micha's edition, Vol. II, p. 116 (=XLIII,19).

[154] Diverres, 'Froissart's *Meliador* and Edward III's policy towards Scotland', p. 1404: 'Hence, in the eyes of an English court public in the 1360s, Froissart's choice of Roxburgh for the culminating scene of the romance, in which the future king of Scotland is effectively chosen with Arthur's blessing, would no doubt imply the latter's suzerainty.'

Diverres rightly suspects that the fictitious figure of Meliador stands not for one particular representative of the English royal family but for the Plantagenet family as a whole; it was the wish of Edward III that they should take over from the Bruces in Scotland:[155]

> En lui sera bien li royaumes
> D'Escoce emploiiés grandement. (29,393–4)

(In him the kingdom of Scotland will be nobly used.)

The heraldic symbolism of the romance also points to the Plantagenets, whilst the crown in Camel of Camois' coat of arms is intended to indicate that he belongs to a ruling dynasty, namely that of the current rulers of Scotland.[156] The technique of presentation in this romance is thus similar to the procedure in *Fergus*; a political aspiration is narrated in the past and in the Arthurian mould, whilst also projected into the future by means of hidden or open allusions. In the fictional version a vassal of King Arthur takes over power in Scotland, whilst it is the desire of the English king that a Plantagenet should take over power from the Bruces in the near future. Admittedly the political aims presented in a literary guise in the romance of *Meliador* differ from the concerns represented in *Fergus*, in that they could not be fulfilled in the real world.

It has been possible to show that Froissart was no less skilful than his predecessors Chrétien de Troyes, Guillaume le Clerc and Girart d'Amiens in his mastery of the technique of hidden allusions to contemporary political events disguised as pseudo-historical literary fiction. However, whilst those predecessors still brought the entire armoury of the genre into play, Froissart consciously dispenses with many of the opportunities it offers, and thus in particular he reduces the genre's typical cast list to the necessary minimum. This helps him to achieve a strictly functional tone in his romance, because he preserves only what he needs to emphasize his ideological goal: a King Arthur whose function is to represent Edward III, a hero representing the Plantagenets and a princess standing for Scotland, an opponent symbolizing the hostile power of the Bruces and a second hero whose personality and experiences can illustrate the cultural and political aspects of the Anglo-Irish relationship, in other words contempt for everything Irish and therefore non-courtly. In this context Kay, Gawain and Guinevere become superfluous, since their firmly established roles can only disrupt the thought patterns constructed here. Because Froissart is writing

[155] Diverres, 'Froissart's *Meliador* and Edward III's policy towards Scotland', p. 1406.

[156] Diverres, 'Froissart's *Meliador* and Edward III's policy towards Scotland', p. 1408. In the years before 1376 there appeared John Barbour's *Bruce*, the history of Scotland from 1286 to 1332 written to glorify the Bruce family.

almost a hundred years after Girart d'Amiens, he finds himself in a completely different literary situation. The purely Arthurian tradition is crumbling and he can make use of it as he pleases, omitting much that was still seen as obligatory for an Arthurian romance at the end of the thirteenth century. As a final and watered down specimen of the genre Froissart's *Meliador* also shows very clearly that in the eyes of patrons literary quality was merely an agreeable accessory but could not be allowed to gain the upper hand at the expense of the real object of the exercise, the ideology; indeed, the reverse was more acceptable.

Meliador is also a graphic pointer to the fact that an Arthurian romance originally written for a limited audience at the English court was also of interest to continental audiences such as those at the courts of Wenceslas of Brabant or Gaston Phoebus; it merely required a slightly amended form and the sacrifice of any attempt to convey the specifically insular network of allusions. The enforced functionality necessary to achieve the intended effect on the initial target audience can now fade into the background and give way to a more general literary approach which succeeds in its own kind of effect on a secondary audience. It remains to be seen whether other Arthurian verse romances in French may originally have contained English references similar to those in *Erec et Enide*, *Fergus*, *Escanor* and *Meliador*, references which have been largely obscured in the continental versions that survive today and are therefore difficult to recognize.

As an afterthought in the genre initiated by Chrétien, *Meliador* leaves much to be desired in terms of quality (see Chapter 2). Nevertheless, in the choice of Froissart Queen Philippa made a more felicitous move than did Queen Eleanor with the author of *Escanor*. In view of the way both the genre and the audience developed, it is in any case no longer surprising that another Arthurian verse romance could still be composed towards the end of the fourteenth century. Once we have grasped the fact that *Meliador* was largely a commissioned work, and that the needs of the English crown were the intellectual driving force behind the ideology of the text, it is easy to see that Froissart could choose no other genre than the one that had served as a vehicle for the claims of the English monarchy to territorial and political hegemony for almost two hundred years, from the first text in the sequence, *Erec et Enide*, until it ends with *Meliador*. Thus in this respect at least Froissart's Arthurian romance stands in a firmly constructed literary tradition: the themes, the setting and the execution of the romance go back to illustrious predecessors, which had also been politically effective in their day. For this reason the English kings repeatedly hark back to the genre, even though as a literary form the Arthurian verse romance had long been supplanted. A fundamentally conservative attitude can be detected in the majority of the verse romances, but given that they were supported by the monarchy and the higher nobility this is in retrospect quite understandable.

Froissart's romance is the last in the sequence of texts in French. However, in the fourteenth and fifteenth centuries these were superseded by Arthurian verse romances in English, which similarly advocate political objectives. After the Hundred Years' War the French language in England was reduced to an archaism even at court, and after the final resolution of the Scottish question there was in any case no further need for Arthurian romances endeavouring to prevail by poetic means in the Anglo-Scottish conflict and conclude it in favour of the English crown.

DIALECT PROBLEMS

This study has revealed that a considerable number of Arthurian verse romances were definitely written for a French-speaking public in England. As can be seen from these examples, the Franco-Picard dialect in which almost all thirteenth-century Arthurian romances were composed did not prevent their being accepted and circulated in Anglo-Norman territory. This *koiné* was common to everyone having a literary education within the sphere of French cultural influence. Translation into their own dialects, whether while reading aloud or while copying (which as a rule involved a kind of memorizing and repeating under the breath), should not have presented any difficulties. Moreover in aristocratic circles efforts were constantly made to speak 'françois de France' ('French of [the Ile de] France'), which was more prestigious. We can therefore assume that, as in the case of *Fergus*, *Escanor* and *Meliador*, the other Arthurian romances could also be received in England without any problem. This is true even of *Jaufré*; the numerous relatives of the royal family from the south of France and the barons of Gascony who often stayed in England were in a position to read this romance, belonging as it did to a literary genre which was cultivated so intensely within the empire of their sovereign. Both old and new editions generally pose the question of the authors' geographical origins; yet where the spread of the texts and the nature of their audience are concerned, the level of the poets' education, the time and the genre in which they wrote and the areas where they stayed, as well as the tastes of their patrons are more important; from the middle of the twelfth century onwards it is the dependence of a poet on the English court or the French court that determines his language.[157]

[157] See A. Långfors, review of Wacker, *Dialekt und Schriftsprache* (*q.v.*), *Romania* 51 (1925), 295–302. On 'Français de France' see R. L. Wagner, *L'ancien français, points de vue, programmes* (Paris, 1974), p. 48ff.

It has in any case already been stated that the same texts were read and copied on both sides of the Channel. Thus the romance of *Yder* is preserved only in an Anglo-Norman copy of a text originally in continental French. This unique manuscript of *Yder* has been in England since the sixteenth century at the latest.[158] There is also an Anglo-Norman copy of *Meraugis* (Berlin mss. gall. qu. 48). The earlier *Lai du cor*, probably first composed in Norman dialect, is likewise preserved only in an Anglo-Norman manuscript (Oxford, Bodleian Library MS Digby 86).

Consequently it can be demonstrated that there was an audience in England for these three texts as well. The production of Anglo-Norman copies can lead us to the conclusion that specifically in England there was a desire for wider circulation of the Arthurian verse romances, and this is a further argument for the proposition that there was a potential audience there which had a very particular interest in Arthurian literature. Mention has already been made of those romances whose origins can be located within the sphere of Glastonbury propaganda, and which therefore inevitably found little response in France.

EXPLICIT REFERENCES BY ARTHURIAN POETS TO THEIR INTENDED AUDIENCE

The results of our audience analysis can be summarized once more as follows:

The primary audience for the Arthurian verse romances composed in French is to be found in England and the English feudal holdings. The works also enjoyed considerable success within the sphere of influence of the French crown; however, this success did not rest on the ideological and political content of the romances, but can be registered as proportional to the literary quality of the works. There is furthermore a third area of influence, opened up via adaptations into other linguistic and cultural spheres. The transmission is effected at least in part via England, as in the cases of *Lanzelet*, *Palamedes* and Eilhart's *Tristrant*. The original political intentions of works like *Fergus* and *Meliador* appear only in reduced form or are totally eradicated in these adaptations.

Patrons and intended audiences belong to the English royal family, the higher nobility and the upper ranks of the clergy (as in Glastonbury). Depending on how far the interests of these different groups converge, the works testify to different objectives in the presentation of the Arthurian material, and especially of its main protagonists, the sovereign figure of Arthur and his barons. Political, didactic and ideological functions take precedence over literary quality. The ideological content is packaged in an entertaining fictional narrative and is only revealed by a network of allusions which the target audience is able and expected

[158] See the introduction to the printed edition.

to decipher. Authors from the Continent, able to write in a language of greater prestige than that enjoyed by Anglo-Norman, were favoured in the commissioning of the romances by a group of rich benefactors.

The social circle at which the texts were principally aimed is more limited in numbers than that of the prose romances, although the two certainly overlap. The adherents are distinguished not only by a keen interest in politics but also by a high degree of literary knowledge. They are in a position to recognize and understand quotations and allusions to other literary works in French, and they are familiar with Chrétien's romances in detail. The patrons and the public are equally conservative in both politics and literature. This conservative attitude emerges not only in the ideology of sovereignty in the works but also in their clinging to a genre that was in literary terms already outmoded, and doing so as late as the fourteenth century; indeed its survival extended into the fifteenth century in its English-language form.

The question remains as to how far these conclusions can be made to correspond to the indications given in the texts by the poets themselves about their intended audience. There are three types of romance that can be distinguished. The first has no prologue or epilogue, where such references are normally contained, but follow the pattern of *Yvain* and plunge straight into the action. The second type has a prologue containing statements by the author about a particular person for whom the romance was written; *Escanor* refers to the wife of the king of England, and there are other examples in *Le Bel Inconnu*: 'Por celi c'aim outre mesure / Vos vel l'istoire comencier' (6–7, 'For the sake of the one I love beyond measure I wish to begin the story for you', a double reference to the addressee and the general public), in *Beaudous*: 'A un de mes millors amis...Vuel je cest livre presenter...En la fin del livre savrez / Par kel nom il est apelez' (219, 222 and 251–2, 'I want to present this book to one of my best friends, and at the end of the book you will know by what name he is called'), and in *L'Atre périlleux*: 'Ma dame...' (1, 'My lady...'). References of this type are found in conjunction with eulogies of the addressee in question, whose high degree of *cortoisie* is particularly emphasized. In all cases they are members of the higher nobility.

The third type contains significant references to the general audience for the romances; here too it is a decidedly courtly public that is being targeted and addressed, and the quotations that follow are very revealing. The author of *Meraugis* in his prologue characterizes his work in these words:

> Mes s'au conter ne vos mescont,
> Il n'i a mot de vilainie,
> Ainz est *contes de cortoisie*

Et de beaus moz et de plesanz.
Nus, s'il n'est cortois et vaillanz,
N'est dignes dou conte escouter
Dont je vos vueil les moz conter. (26–32)

(But unless I deceive you in the telling, there is not a word of baseness in it, but rather it is *a tale of courtliness* whose words are fair and pleasing. *No one who is not courtly and valiant is worthy of listening to the story* whose words I shall now narrate to you.)

The author of *Durmart* speaks in similar terms:

Je ne di pas qu'a totes gens
Doive li hom mostrer son sens...
Por chu me plaist que cil m'entende
Ki bien reprent et bien amende. (5–12)

(*I do not say that* the man should display his knowledge *to all*... For this reason I wish my listener to be someone who criticizes and reforms to good effect.)

The words of the epilogue make clear whom the author is thinking of here; there he harangues his listeners directly:

Or entendés a ma raison,
Roi et duc et conte et baron,
Vos qui les grans terres tenés
Et qui povre vie menés:
Menbre vos des bons ancïens
Qui jadis fisent les grans biens
Dont il les grans honors conquisent.
Faites ausi comme cil fisent
Dont li grant bien sont raconté...
Li roi et li duc et li conte. (15,957–79)

(Now pay attention to what I say, you *kings and dukes and counts and barons,* who hold the great fiefs but live a degenerate life: remember the noble men of long ago who once upon a time did the great deeds through which they won their great domains. Do as they did whose great achievements are still narrated...*the kings, dukes and counts.*)

The author of *Yder* also states with total clarity that his work is intended only for members of the most elevated social group. The last lines of his romance read thus:

Cest livre falt ici et fine,
Por rei fu feit e por rëine
E por clers et por chevaliers
Qui bials diz öent volentiers,

Por dames e por damaiseles
Qui mult sunt *cortaises* e beles
E nïent pas por altre gent
Ne fu fait le livre naient. (6762–9)

(This book finishes here and comes to an end. *It was written for king and queen, for clerics and knights* who are keen to hear fine tales, *for ladies and maidens* of great *courtesy* and great beauty, and the book was *most certainly not* written *for people of any other type*, absolutely not.)

Finally Jehan, author of *Les Merveilles de Rigomer*, also hopes to be addressing kings and counts in his work: 'Or entendés, et *roi et conte*' (6429, 'Now listen, both *kings and counts*').[159]

There is a high degree of homogeneity to be observed in these statements; the audience is to be a select and courtly one, and these works are not intended for anyone and everyone else. Kings and queens are always mentioned with particular emphasis. The authors are agreed amongst themselves that only an audience able to meet the stated criteria will be capable of understanding the nature and the message of the works, and, as the poet of *Durmart* emphasizes, recognize their didactic character and appreciate the teachings they convey. If the audience behave like the heroes of the romances, people will likewise be able to speak well of them in the future:

Por ce sont de lui raconté
Li bien fait qu'il fist a son tans.
Cant li hom est *haus* et *poissans*,
Il doit tant en sa vie faire
C'on puist aprés sa mort retraire
Chose dont il face a loër
Et par coi ses nons puist durer...
Chascuns *hauz hom* se doit pener
Qu'il puist en tel guise finer
C'on doive son non retenir. (15,932–53)

(For this reason the story of the fine deeds that he performed in his time is told of him. When a man is *high born* and *powerful* he should do in his life such deeds that after his death one can tell the story of what he did that was praiseworthy, so that his name may endure... Each *man of high birth* must make an effort to conclude his life in such a state [of honour] that his name will be remembered.)

[159] See also *Erec et Enide*, line 20.

9

Arthurian literature in French and its significance for England

THE RELATIONSHIP BETWEEN ENGLAND, SCOTLAND AND FRANCE IN NON-ARTHURIAN LITERATURE

The above findings relating to the Arthurian verse romances must now be put into a wider context, since it is by no means the case that the Arthurian romances are the only genre to be thus politically oriented towards England. There is also evidence of an equally strong sympathy for the cause of England and the English crown to be detected in a whole series of non-Arthurian texts, both courtly romances and non-courtly genres such as political propaganda, to such an extent that they have to be assessed not so much as examples of French literature but as literary products of the English territories written in French. Rickard deals with a considerable number of these works,[1] and repeatedly expresses his astonishment that Frenchmen could identify to that extent with the interests of England; in so doing he fails to recognize the fact that from the eleventh to the fourteenth century the term 'Frenchman' was of a thoroughly heterogeneous nature, and that a large number of those who were born and lived on the Continent and spoke continental French felt themselves to be part of the Anglo-Norman community because of the feudal situation and the automatic assumption under the feudal system that loyalty to one's lord was an overriding principle. Since the upper echelons of the English nobility in their entirety not only spoke French but also differed only very slightly in their lifestyle from the French in 'France', it was probably not very arduous for Bretons, Normans, Gascons and Picards, i.e. authors speaking and writing continental French, when looking for rich patrons, to identify with the concerns of their feudal lord and the potential source of their livelihood, especially as they found the conditions at the courts of English vassals and allies to be excellent for their literary work,

[1] Rickard, *Britain in Medieval French Literature*, *passim.*

even after the loosening of feudal relationships in England from the beginning of the thirteenth century.[2]

Around 1225 the author of *Galeran de Bretagne* (possibly Jean Renart), whose work shows a predominance of influences from Anglo-Norman literature,[3] tells of a hero who is cousin and vassal to the English king. *Joufrois de Poitiers* (mid-thirteenth century) takes as its theme the disputes between England and Scotland; the Scots invade northern England and besiege Lincoln. The hero fights for England against Ireland. The figures of the rulers in this romance can be identified on the basis of clear references as Henry I and his queen. Although the plot thus takes us back about a hundred years into the past, the romance dispenses with any pseudo-historical Arthurian trappings for the events. It is almost inconceivable that this romance could enjoy much success within the territories of the French crown. The French idea of what a text should be like is illustrated by the *Tornoiement Antecrist*: Huon de Mery ropes in Arthur on the side of the inhabitants of the Ile de France, in other words he claims him for France, whilst he knows only contempt for people from Poitou, Brittany, Normandy, Picardy, Burgundy, the south of France, England and Scotland, and includes them in the hostile army.[4] In the romance *Sone de Nansai* (second half of the thirteenth century), which is predominantly located in the British Isles, the Scots are depicted in an unusually negative manner; the author takes pleasure in describing their lack of good breeding. They are represented as barbarians, although the Scottish court in the thirteenth century was just as much under the influence of French and Norman attention to manners as was the English court. The fictional embellishment of reality for ideological purposes is particularly obvious in this work and can probably only be explained as being from an English standpoint. In this text the Scots are allies of Ireland, which gives an additional dimension to their enmity with England. The romance is apparently strongly influenced by Arthurian literature, especially Chrétien. The author probably originated from Burgundy, a territory which at the time the text was composed had friendly relations with England.

The works of Philippe de Beaumanoir, written between 1270 and 1280, are particularly interesting in this context. The author, a nobleman himself, was at one time Seneschal of Poitou and therefore in the service of the English. His romance *Blonde d'Oxfort* is set in Oxford and Normandy. There is support for

[2] As far as the facts are concerned, the following exposition is based in essence on Rickard, *Britain in Medieval French Literature*.

[3] *Le Fresne* by Marie de France, *Boeve de Hantone*, *Le Roman de Thebes* and *Le Roman de Troie*. See Rickard, *Britain in Medieval French Literature*, p. 121, and Holmes, *A History of Old French Literature*, p. 271.

[4] See Göller, *König Arthur in der englischen Literatur des späten Mittelalters*, p. 142, note 106.

the belief that this is a family romance relating to the Earl of Oxford; his family is blessed with every positive characteristic, whilst the Earl of Gloucester is degraded to a figure of fun. The latter's barely intelligible French is amply illustrated and is made the butt of ridicule, whilst we are informed in the case of the beautiful Blonde that it is hardly noticeable that she is not from Pontoise. In fact she also receives language lessons from Jehan to eradicate the last traces of her insular accent. The hero is from the Continent and has to cross the Channel frequently. In the end he enters into the inheritance of the Earl of Oxford. This romance is worth reading not only for its literary quality but in particular because it furnishes a memorable account of the problems facing an Anglo-Norman nobleman of the thirteenth century with interests on both sides of the Channel.

The romance of *La Manekine* is set further back in history and is moreover from a different genre. In it Philippe de Beaumanoir has combined and reworked two English legends, in a manner not unlike that of the author of *Guillaume d'Angleterre*.[5] The narrative is located in northern England and Scotland, and betrays a really good knowledge of the area. It is known that the author stayed in England, but it is probably wide of the mark to suppose, as Rickard does,[6] that he simply imported his material from there into France. It is more likely that he composed his works as an English vassal of French origin and in so doing recorded his allegiance to this political and cultural circle. The same is true for the author of the biography *Guillaume le Maréchal*. William Marshall was at the peak of his career in the years 1216–19 when he was Regent of England. His son commissioned a talented French writer from the Continent to give his life story poetic form. The stance of this Frenchman is totally on the side of England and certainly not just as a favour to his patron. He praises Henry II as well as his sons (with restrained criticism only of King John), and makes the French king with his lust for power responsible for the death of that exemplary ruler. The biography also contains a prophecy by Merlin predicting the return to English rule of all former Angevin territories on the Continent. Merlin's prophecies in this and other texts merit our particular attention,[7] because they were used by both sides as political ammunition. Whilst the *Bataille des Trente* (after 1351) predicts an English victory in the Anglo-French disputes, the pro-French text *La Paix aux Anglais* contains only prophecies directed against England. Eustache Deschamps proceeds in a particularly cunning manner in making Merlin predict the destruction of England, and substantiating this from English sources such as

[5] It is thus not particularly unusual for a 'Frenchman' to adopt and work on such material.

[6] Rickard, *Britain in Medieval French Literature*, p. 240.

[7] See Rickard, *Britain in Medieval French Literature*, p. 118ff., and R. Taylor, *The Political Prophecy in England* (New York, 1911).

Wace and Bede.[8] Even without Merlin's efforts, political antagonisms throve in the medium of literature. Before 1206 André de Coutances composed a satire directed against France and entitled *Le Roman des François*; the *Voeu du heron* is a political poem the content of which was intended to goad Edward III into active hostilities against France.

To judge from the wealth of examples, it would seem to be the exception rather than the rule in the thirteenth and fourteenth centuries for a literary text completely to ignore political themes. However, in contrast to the political propaganda just mentioned, the Arthurian romances never take issue with France. The literature surrounding the national hero of the Celts is used as a weapon directed against the Celts themselves, and challenging all who oppose the expanding political influence of the English monarchy: Bretons, Welsh, Irish and Scots. From the beginning of the thirteenth century the Scots are the main opponents, and the romances of *Fergus*, *Escanor* and *Meliador* are deployed for the purpose of putting them in their place. However, with the growing autonomy of Scotland from the reign of the Bruces onwards the mood changes; the Scots for their part also begin to defend themselves by literary means, and they use the same weapon, Arthurian literature. Whilst England begins to produce vernacular chronicles and ballads, which present a uniformly glorified picture of the monarch and a very pronounced patriotism,[9] in the northern part of the island a type of Arthurian literature evolves which develops a negative image of Arthur, perhaps reverting to the tendencies already mapped out in French-language Arthurian romances such as *Yder*.

SCOTTISH ARTHURIAN LITERATURE AS A REACTION TO THE FRENCH VERSE ROMANCES

The Scottish national chronicles[10] all pursue the common aim of devaluing Arthur and of elevating their own nation at the same time as putting the English in their place. *Scotichronicon*, the belated counterpart to Geoffrey's *Historia Regum Britanniae*, develops a rich ancestry for the Scottish royal family[11] and demonstrates that it is the oldest in Europe, a late attempt at outdoing their opponents which can be seen as analogous to Anglo-Norman efforts to outshine the French kings. The argument directed against Arthur in the chronicles is

8 Rickard, *Britain in Medieval French Literature*, p. 119.

9 K. H. Göller, 'König Arthur in den schottischen Chroniken', *Anglia* 80 (1962), 390–404; see also Göller, *König Arthur in der englischen Literatur des späten Mittelalters*, *passim*.

10 For example Fordun's *Scotichronicon* or W. Steward's *Buik of the Chronicles of Scotland*; see Göller, 'König Arthur in den schottischen Chroniken'.

11 Göller, 'König Arthur in den schottischen Chroniken', 390–1.

based above all on the repeatedly stressed illegitimacy of the succession; Arthur was conceived out of wedlock, a bastard who is not to be regarded as a legitimate ruler. The reaction to centuries of English claims to hegemony is manifested in the reconstruction of a legal claim by the Scots to the English throne; it was not Arthur but the Scottish kings who at that time should have succeeded to sovereignty over the island. This kind of powerless attempt at revenge by literary means did at least succeed in strengthening the national self-confidence of the Scots from the end of the fourteenth century, but remains completely without political significance internationally. Reverting to legalistic arguments cannot turn back the wheel of history. Boece, the sixteenth-century continuator of *Scotichronicon*, presents Arthur as faithless and unjust, but as a precaution assures us that he does not wish to diminish the fame of a British king or to criticize earlier authors; he is well aware that he cannot make any impression on the positive image of Arthur in the neighbouring country—or indeed in the minds of many Scots who were favourably disposed towards England. W. Steward puts far greater emphasis than Boece on Arthur's bad characteristics.[12]

The same is true for the Scottish chronicles as has already been said of the Arthurian romances in French: 'To the nationalist camp in Scotland Arthur

[12] Göller observes a more conciliatory tendency in the chronicle of John Major, which is less dependent on traditions ('König Arthur in den schottischen Chroniken', 402). However, the overall ideological direction suggests that it is less a case of conciliation than of English interests. It is in fact clear that Major is on the English side, and in the last resort the unification of the island nations under one ruler modelled on King Arthur only benefits the stronger. In time-honoured fashion Major employs the usual images of Arthur's behaviour towards the Scots as found in the French verse romances: 'He remarks with satisfaction that Arthur drove the Saxons from the island and was victorious over all the native populations, including the Picts and Scots... At least, he reports Arthur's resolve to kill all the Scots without a word of protest... However, Major says that the people finally submitted to Arthur and were thus saved. Quite by the way and apparently unintentionally Major does at least work in a reference to Arthur's seat of power being at Edinburgh...' (translated from Göller, 'König Arthur in den schottischen Chroniken', 400–1). 'Major finds it hard to understand that Mordred could assemble such a large army against Arthur; he even states expressly that the King of Scotland loved Arthur for his uprightness and honesty. Thus as far as Major is concerned there is only one possible explanation: Mordred bribed the Scots with money, and they were prepared to commit the most shameful acts for money, even to fighting against their feudal lord, to whom they had promised everlasting fidelity... However, Major distances himself from any such expectation [concerning Arthur's return], calling it senseless and born of excessive attachment to the king' (translated from Göller, 'König Arthur in den schottischen Chroniken', 402). This is not a conciliatory tone. It is interesting to observe how the Scots even make use of the figure of Charlemagne to strengthen the negative image of Arthur. In a very varied sequence of Middle English Charlemagne romances composed north of the border, the exemplary qualities of Charlemagne are emphasized and given thematic importance; this can probably be seen as an additional dimension to the rejection of the figure of Arthur. On this topic see T. F. Henderson, *Scottish Vernacular Literature* (Edinburgh, 1910), and D. Mehl, *The Middle English Romances of The Thirteenth and Fourteenth Centuries* (London, 1968).

represented every English ruler who made claims to power in Scotland, whereas for the minority who thought of themselves as British he was a symbol for reconciliation and the unification of all the island races.'[13]

The Scots had been oppressed for a long time, and their need to strike out in retaliation becomes even more clearly perceptible in the alliterative Arthurian poetry of the north than it was in the Scottish chronicles.[14] Towards the middle of the fourteenth century Robert Mannyng of Brunne somewhat misleadingly asserted that anything known about Arthur in England had come exclusively via prose works in French:

> But ffrensche men wryten hit in prose,
> Right as he dide, hym for to alose;
> in prose al of hym ys writen,
> þe bettere til vnderstande & wyten. (10,975–8)[15]

In fact it was precisely the French Arthurian romances in verse that made it possible to continue the tradition of Arthurian literature in England without any major hiatus, even if eventually in a different language and less refined. The verse ballads *The Weddynge of Sir Gawen and Dame Ragnell*, *Golagros and Gawane*, and *Awntyrs off Arthure at the Terne Wathelyne*, but also the alliterative *Morte Arthur*, take as their theme King Arthur's arrogance and uninhibited lust for power, such as we have already encountered in more than one of the French verse romances. Göller outlines their concern in these terms:

> ...to exemplify the hubris of mankind which derives from an exaggeration of the heroic and leads to a tragic fall... We must not hold it against the writers if they are primarily concerned with practical questions. They are writing against the background of the political situation in northern England and Scotland; the demand for freedom and autonomy is unmistakable.
>
> The admonitions in the texts studied here are directed at Arthur...[16]

In the first three works referred to above the British ruler is presented as someone who has taken possession of Scottish land illegally. His unscrupulous intention to subjugate all the territories not yet doing him homage as their feudal lord was already criticized in the French Arthurian romances (see Chapter 3). In *The Weddynge of Sir Gawen and Dame Ragnell* it is the knight Gromer Somer who has to defend himself against such encroachments. In the *Awntyrs off Arthure at the Terne Wathelyne* another Scottish knight, Sir Galeron, challenges

[13] Translated from Göller, 'König Arthur in den schottischen Chroniken', 390.
[14] As far as factual details of content are concerned, the following section is based on Göller's account in *König Arthur in der englischen Literatur des späten Mittelalters*.
[15] As quoted in Göller, *König Arthur in der englischen Literatur des späten Mittelalters*, p. 28.
[16] Translated from Göller, *König Arthur in der englischen Literatur des späten Mittelalters*, p. 128.

Arthur to release his hereditary territories which the king has meanwhile given to Gawain as a fief. Gawain gives up his 'rights' and Galeron becomes a knight of the Round Table. The illegal appropriation of the property of other nations and of free princes, still a peripheral motif in the French verse romances, now becomes the central theme. Gawain's question as to how a knight is supposed to behave when he has become accustomed to acquiring alien territory 'agaynes the righte'[17] is answered thus by a spirit:

> 'Your king [Arthur] is too greedy for possessions; as long as the wheel of Fortune stands still, no one can do anything about him. Nevertheless, he will eventually be cast down from his lofty seat.' The future fall of Arthur is represented as the just punishment for his greed; the demise of the Round Table and of Arthur's empire are consequences of this key sin.[18]

Golagros, who has inherited Galloway from his ancestors, also defends himself against having any feudal ties to an overlord. This is precisely why Arthur wants to subjugate him. Gawain conquers him, but pretends to have been defeated and thus saves his opponent's life, since the latter wants to die rather than swear fealty to the king. Nevertheless, Golagros is ready to do homage to Arthur after the duel, but on the grounds of this willingness he is rewarded with his freedom as Arthur is moved to make a noble gesture in return. The Scottish poet, who is entirely on the side of the hero, pillories the king's lust for power and possessions, and emphasizes the right of the Scots to self-determination. Here too the warning about presumption and covetousness directed at Arthur is once more central to the work.[19]

[17] Göller, *König Arthur in der englischen Literatur des späten Mittelalters*, p. 125.

[18] Translated from Göller, *König Arthur in der englischen Literatur des späten Mittelalters*, p. 126.

[19] The text of *Lancelot of the Laik* poses a particular problem. Once again the themes are claims to property, disputes over inheritance or the obligations of vassals (Göller, *König Arthur in der englischen Literatur des späten Mittelalters*, p. 137). In this most important example of Scottish Arthurian literature Arthur has become an absolute *exemplum malum* (p. 137ff.). However, we cannot accept the conclusion which Göller draws from that fact, based on the researches of Vogel: see B. Vogel, 'Secular Politics and the Date of *Lancelot of the Laik*', *StPh* 40 (1943), 1–13. Vogel is of the opinion that the author's long digression on the nature and duties of kingship is a 'specific lecture' (p. 4) to James III (1460–88), the Scottish king under whose rule the country had rapidly sunk into a state of decay (Vogel, 'Secular Politics and the Date of *Lancelot of the Laik*, pp. 4–10). Göller takes up this idea and regards the romance as a work in which the more pronounced didactic element gives it more of the character of a Mirror of Princes with a message for the rulers of the time. If it were really the case that the author of *Lancelot of the Laik* identified Arthur with a Scottish ruler he would be breaking with a centuries-old tradition of always equating Arthur with the *English* king; he would thus be breaking through his audience's horizons of expectation in a way that would inevitably meet with total incomprehension. Although this is possible, it does not seem very plausible. Any Scottish king who was directly addressed in this work would have to come to terms not only with being identified with his arch-enemy King Arthur, but also with

As Göller argues in opposition to Köhler,[20] Arthur is not in fact a static entity any more than he is in the French Arthurian romances. As the symbolic figure of an empire and as the vehicle for non-literary thematic purposes his image is constantly transformed according to whichever group the author of the text happens to be representing, and that group may be affected positively or negatively by the aspects of power politics manifested in Arthurian literature. It would therefore seem to be important when interpreting Arthurian works always to begin by enquiring into the nature of the supporting clientele and into the audience for which they were primarily intended. However, even at the level of detail an examination of the ideological changes from one Arthurian romance to the next in the literary sequence can be very revealing. Thus in Chrétien's *Yvain* Arthur is king of 'Bretagne', whereas in the highly derivative Middle English version of around 1350, *Ywayne and Gawayne*[21] as well as in *Arthour and Merlin*, *Le Morte Arthur* and *Sir Gawain and the Green Knight* he is called 'Kyng of Yngland'; in these texts he has won Scotland and Wales in battle as well as many other countries. Malory, the great connoisseur of all things Arthurian but especially of the tradition in French, is still convinced:

> And at that tyme kynge Arthure regned, and he was hole kynge of Ingelonde, Walys, Scotlonde, and of many othir realmys. Howbehit there were many

---

being branded as an *exemplum malum*, two insults so powerful as to exclude any didactic effect. In taking such a direction the work would also be running counter to the very recently established trend against Arthur that was becoming perceptible in the whole of the rest of Scottish Arthurian literature, a trend that always implies criticism of the English ruler. It is not possible in this context to construct a detailed counter-argument; however, it is more probable that towards the end of the fifteenth century, faced with a weak Scottish government and ruled by a king who was anything but exemplary, the Scots' fear of a renewed English attack along the old lines grew, and that for this reason Arthur is presented so thoroughly negatively in this work. The Arthur of the romance, who in the end accepts the admonitions of the author and wins back the love of his people, cannot be used as a counter-argument to this proposal, because even in the other Scottish Arthurian works the king finally shows insight into his failings (and leaves the Scots in peace); it is precisely in this fact, in this tactic of mollification directed at the English ruler, that the didactic intentions of the authors generally lie.

The reign of James III saw the composition of Scotland's only vernacular chronicle, in French in fact, by an anonymous author: *La Vraye Chronique d'Escoce*. The tone is the same as in the Latin chronicles, i.e. predominantly hostile to England. The friendship between Scotland and France is particularly emphasized; see Rickard, *Britain in Medieval French Literature*, pp. 219–20.

20 Compare Göller, *König Arthur in der englischen Literatur des späten Mittelalters*, p. 143, with Köhler, *Ideal und Wirklichkeit*, p. 7.

21 In a formal sense the English poet does modify his source; he dispenses with the hero's double quest, and with his single narrative thread he reverts to the Old French models of the thirteenth century. For more on his alterations to the French original see W. Iser, 'Mittelenglische Literatur und romanische Tradition', in *Grundriß der romanischen Literaturen des Mittelalters*, edited by H. R. Jauss and E. Köhler, Vol. I (Heidelberg, 1972), pp. 314–15.

> kynges that were lordys of many contreyes, but all they helde their londys of kynge Arthure.[22]

In *Libeaus Desconnus*, which derives, though probably only indirectly, from *Le Bel Inconnu*,[23] Arthur no longer rules in Carduel or Carlion, as one would have expected, but in Glastonbury. The balladesque narratives *King Arthur and the King of Cornwall*, *The Boy and the Mantle* and *Syre Corneus* make renewed use of the cuckold motif which is similarly familiar from thirteenth-century Anglo-Norman verse narratives (*Lai du cor*, *Lai du cort mantel*, *Rigomer* and *La Vengeance Raguidel*) as well as the motif of the chastity test conducted by means of a cloak or a drinking-horn; these now become the theme, with pointed emphasis on the negative role of King Arthur. The numerous French romances of the Gawain group in England itself also pave the way for the striking dominance of the figure of Gawain in Middle English Arthurian literature. Several of the earlier romances had already acquired some local colour from northern England and Scotland. The continuity of the Gawain traditions can be seen reflected in the typical characteristics valid in both linguistic areas (see Chapter 4). *Sir Perceval of Gales*, the only Middle English text of the Perceval cycle, resembles the French Arthurian romances of the thirteenth century in completely renouncing any Grail themes, and it is for this reason that Chrétien's influence has always been discounted.[24] *Sir Perceval* is to be regarded merely as a consequence of the reception of thirteenth-century Arthurian romances such as *Fergus*, which acted as filters. In the light of the Anglo-Norman Arthurian romances and their generic history there is scope for re-examination of the common assertion that the Arthurian material in England sank to the level of a naive audience averse to any chivalric or intellectual concepts. In spite of various changes of direction conditioned by the different social and political situations there is still much continuity to be observed on all sides.

ARTHURIAN LITERATURE AS ENGLISH NATIONAL LITERATURE

In terms of form, material and content, but above all in their political and ideological function, the Arthurian verse romances in French, which can emphatically be termed an Anglo-Norman genre, form the link in transmission from Geoffrey of Monmouth's *Historia* to Middle English and Scottish

[22] Quoted from Göller, *König Arthur in der englischen Literatur des späten Mittelalters*, p. 147.

[23] This is the prevailing view. It is contradicted by the fact that even literature that can be proved to be dependent on French sources (such as Laȝamon's *Brut*, which derives from Wace) undergoes a clear transformation; see Iser, 'Mittelenglische Literatur und romanische Tradition', pp. 308–9.

[24] Iser, 'Mittelenglische Literatur und romanische Tradition', p. 315.

Arthurian literature.[25] The knowledge that Arthurian material was English, and that Arthurian literature was English national literature, irrespective of the language in which it was composed, survived until the beginning of the modern age, since when it has been entirely obliterated in France. Ronsard was still fully aware of the fact: in a eulogy of Elizabeth I he ascribes King Arthur and the Round Table exclusively to the English nation:[26]

> ...ta gloire sera telle,
> T'ayant choisy pour *maison éternelle,*
> Qui dois nourrir *tant de vaillans Artus,*
> Grands Roys armez de fer et de vertus...
> De tels guerriers courra par tout le monde
> L'honneur fameux, et de *leur Table Ronde...*

(Your glory will be such, having chosen you as its *eternal home*, who are to nurture *so many valiant Arthurs*, great kings armed with iron and virtues... The famed honour of such warriors and of *their Round Table* will spread throughout the world...)

Another and more pronouncedly Arthurian version of 1584 contains these lines:

> Le vray subject de ceste table ronde,
> Qui de son nom doit couvrir tout le monde,
> Et de laquelle, ô tres-vaillant Artus,
> Seras l'honneur pour tes hautes vertus,
> Et de tous Rois, qui bouillans de jeunesse,
> Voudront un jour *imiter* ta proüesse...

(The true subject matter of this round table, whose name is to spread throughout the world, and of which for your high virtues you shall be the honour, o most valiant Arthur, and the honour of all kings who in the flush of youth shall one day wish to *imitate* your prowess...)

Since the Romantic period the identification of language with nationhood has obscured a great deal in this connection that had remained common knowledge into the sixteenth century even in France. Göller's assembled evidence leads him

[25] This interpretation is opposed to Iser's view ('Mittelenglische Literatur und romanische Tradition', p. 306) that the separation between the languages determined by the social structure in the England of the twelfth and thirteenth centuries stood in the way of the reception of French courtly romances in England.

[26] J. Frappier, 'Les romans de la Table Ronde et les Lettres en France au XVIe siècle', in *Amour Courtois et Table Ronde* (Geneva, 1973): 'This is a lengthy and hyperbolic piece of flattery in honour of Queen Elizabeth, beginning with a hundred and twenty lines in praise of her beauty, her knowledge and her taste in sumptuous jewels. The eulogy of the sovereign is followed by that of her kingdom' (translated from p. 277). The quotations are as cited by Frappier, pp. 278 and 280; the italics are Schmolke-Hasselmann's.

to establish to his own amazement that in Middle English literature Arthur is fundamentally and unproblematically regarded as a native king.[27] However, this is not a case of stylization introduced as an afterthought; it has in fact been the case ever since the beginning of the literary tradition and remains so until this day. Whilst in all other European countries the Arthurian world faded away and became the domain of literary scholarship, it remained part of the national consciousness in England, and not only of those with a literary education.[28]

The Matter of Britain is thus to a large extent a 'Matter of Great Britain'.[29] This is at least true after about 1200, and seen in this light it is perhaps also possible to make an attempt at a new and different interpretation of Jean Bodel's now famous classification of the three *materes* in his *Chanson de Saisnes*:

> Li conte de Bretaigne s'il sont si vain et plaisant
> Et cil de Romme sage et de sens aprendant,
> Cil de France sont voir chascun jour aparant. (9–11)

(If the tales of Britain are so light and entertaining, and those of Rome are wise and instructive, those of France are true for ever.)

Rome and France are two sovereign territories, with which Britain is classed as a third. If the classification is supposed to be identical for all three, then it can only mean *Bretaigne la Grant* inclusive of Brittany which was still annexed to it at the time when *Saisnes* was composed. In addition, one might consider that Jean Bodel as the author of a *chanson de geste* is ideologically on the side of France. With his emphasis on the unique truthfulness in the content of the genre he represents, which itself represents the interests of France, Jean Bodel is obliged of necessity to polemicize against the politically hostile genre of the 'matiere de Bretaigne', and to discount it as *vaine*, given that his definition disputes the historicity of the Arthurian material that was so important to the Anglo-Normans. He asserts: 'Et de ces trois materes tieng la plus voir disant' (12, 'And of these three types of material I shall keep to the most truthful'). An

[27] Göller, *König Arthur in der englischen Literatur des späten Mittelalters*, pp. 61 and 175.

[28] It should be remembered that there are numerous Arthurian poems of the nineteenth century (Tennyson and Morris) and the twentieth century (White), recent films (*Monty Python and the Holy Grail*) and large numbers of visitors to 'Arthurian' sites. The fact that it was even possible for the material to be transferred to other artistic forms such as lyric and film after the loss of its original function, and that a shift to other genres could take place, is likewise proof of the tendency towards continuity inherent in the Arthurian material, although only in England did it find such enduringly fertile soil.

[29] The English term 'Matter of Britain', and not 'Matter of Brittany', expresses this even more clearly. In Chrétien (*Cligés*, lines 16–17) there is clear evidence that 'Bretagne', even without the addition of 'Grande', could be understood as England: '...Engleterre, / Qui lors estoit Bretaigne dite' ('...England, / which at that time was called Britain').

ideological bias and prejudice in his classification cannot be ruled out. The historicity and expressiveness of the material depends on one's perspective in viewing them, which in this case is expressed unmistakably:

> La coronne de France doit estre si avant,
> Que tout autre roi doivent estre à li apendant. (13–14)

(The crown of France should be so dominant that all other kings should be subservient to it.)

Like the *chansons de geste*, the Arthurian compositions also contain frequent assurances of truth, and for the authors of this genre and their public King Arthur is as much a historical ruler from an ideal earlier age and a symbol of their own national history as Charlemagne is for the French of 'France'. The claim to be preserving past deeds, as in *Durmart*: 'Menbre vos des bons ancïens' (15,961, 'Remember the noble men of long ago'), is emphasized just as much as the need to emulate the exemplary ethical behaviour of the particular hero.

Although broadly speaking the public remained clear in their minds about the opposition between the two great narrative genres of *chansons de geste* and Arthurian courtly romance, the distinction is perhaps to be sought more in the literary format, the presentation and the individual generic characteristics than in the classic opposition between *res ficta* and *res gesta* (fiction or real events).[30] Both genres regard themselves as being involved with history and having a part to play in the nation's interpretation of history. The distinctions are probably not as sharply drawn as has previously been supposed. In the course of the thirteenth century the two genres grew closer, and each adopted features from the other. The development of the genres throws up strikingly analogous characteristics: both sequences in the course of their evolution are variations around a single great theme; both are able to make use of a system of internal references; the *Chanson de Roland* and Chrétien's works offer generic prototypes, and the genres undertake the task of playing out their possibilities; both genres tell of historical personalities (at least as they were understood to be at the time), although the fictional adjustments to the narrative vary according to the internal rules of the genre. Their social position is also different: the main point of opposition lies in their contrasting ideologies. In the end, however, the function of all three of the *materes* mentioned by Jean Bodel appears to be identical in terms of their exemplary status, expressed here in *Durmart*:

> Li bons rois Artus est fenis,
> Mais encore dure ses pris,

[30] The categories in this comparison are taken from the structural analysis by Jauss in 'Theorie der Gattungen und Literatur des Mittelalters', pp. 114–18.

Et de Charlemaine ensement
Parolent encore la gent,
Et d'Alixandre, ce savons,
Dure encore li grans renons.
De lor pris et de lor valor
Chantent et content li plusor
Por ce que de haute onor furent;
Puis que lor non encore durent,
Dont vos di je bien sens envie
Qu'il valurent mout en lor vie.
Chascuns hauz hom se doit pener
Qu'il puist en tel guise finer. (15,939–52)

(The good King Arthur is dead, but his fame still survives, and in the same way people still speak of Charlemagne, and as we know the great renown of Alexander lives to this day. So many people tell of their fame and valour in song and story because they were men of high honour. Since their names still survive, I tell you, quite without envy, that they were men of great worth in their lives. Each man of high birth must make an effort to conclude his life in such a state.)

Bibliography

This bibliography reproduces that of the German edition, though all items have been checked against the originals wherever possible. We have added a number of works that are cited by Schmolke-Hasselmann but not included in her bibliography. Works cited only by the translators, and those discussed by Keith Busby in his Foreword, are given separately in a Supplement. Apart from the additions and a few minor adjustments, the list of texts is given in the order established by Schmolke-Hasselmann. For the Arthurian romances, with the notable exception of Chrétien de Troyes, the order is by title rather than author. It is not strictly by the first word of a title, but by the significant word, ignoring such items as definite articles and even 'roman'. For ease of reference we have supplied in small capitals titles that are not immediately apparent from the bibliographical reference itself.

EDITIONS OF TEXTS

Adam le Bossu [Adam de la Halle], *Le Jeu de la Feuillée*, edited by Ernest Langlois, *CFMA* 6, second edition, Paris, 1923.

L'Atre périlleux, edited by Brian Woledge, *CFMA* 76, Paris, 1936.

AUBEREE. *Zwei altfranzösische Fablels (Auberee, Du Vilain mire)*, edited by H. H. Christmann, *SRÜ* 47, Tübingen, 1963.

BEAUDOUS. *Robert von Blois sämmtliche Werke*, Vol. I, *Beaudous*, edited by Jacob Ulrich, Berlin, 1889.

'Le Roman de Biausdous', edited by Gisèle Lamarque, Dissertation, University of North Carolina, 1968, *DA* 29 (1968/9), 4005 A.

BEL INCONNU. Renaut de Beaujeu, *Le Bel Inconnu*, edited by G. Perrie Williams, *CFMA* 38, Paris, 1929.

BERTRAN DE BORN. *Die Lieder Bertrans von Born*, edited by Carl Appel, *SRÜ* 19/20, Halle, 1932.

Bliocadran, edited by Lenora D. Wolfgang, *ZrPh* Beiheft 150, Tübingen, 1976.

Brun de la Montaigne, Roman d'aventure, edited by Paul Meyer, *SATF*, Paris, 1875.

La Chastelaine de Vergi, edited by René E. V. Stuip, The Hague, 1970.

CHEVALIER À L'ÉPÉE. *Two Old French Gauvain Romances*, edited by R. C. Johnston and D. D. R. Owen, Edinburgh and London, 1972 [*Le Chevalier à l'épée* and *La Mule sans frein*].

Li Chevaliers as deus espees, edited by Wendelin Foerster, Halle, 1877, reprinted Amsterdam, 1966.

'Li Chevaliers as Deus Espees', edited by Robert T. Ivey, Dissertation, University of North Carolina, 1973, *DA* 34 (1973/4), 5914 A.

CHRÉTIEN DE TROYES

Kristian von Troyes, *Erec und Enide: Textausgabe mit Variantenauswahl, Einleitung, erklärenden Anmerkungen und vollständigem Glossar*, edited by Wendelin Foerster, second edition, Halle, 1909 (first published 1890).

Chrétien de Troyes, *Erec et Enide*, edited by Mario Roques, *CFMA* 80, Paris, 1953.

Christian von Troyes, *Cliges*, edited by Wendelin Foerster, Halle, 1884.
Christian von Troyes, *Cligés*, edited by Wendelin Foerster, *Romanische Bibliothek* 1, Halle, 1888; fourth edition, Halle, 1921.
Chrétien de Troyes, *Cligés*, edited by A. Micha, *CFMA* 84, Paris, 1957.
Christian von Troyes, *Der Karrenritter (Lancelot)* and *Das Wilhelmsleben (Guillaume d'Angleterre)*, edited by Wendelin Foerster, Halle, 1899.
Chrétien de Troyes, *Le Chevalier de la Charrete*, edited by Mario Roques, *CFMA* 86, Paris, 1958.
Christian von Troyes, *Der Löwenritter (Yvain)*, edited by Wendelin Foerster, Halle, 1887.
Chrétien de Troyes, *Le Chevalier au Lion (Yvain)*, edited by Mario Roques, *CFMA* 89, Paris, 1960.
Christian von Troyes, *Der Percevalroman (Li Contes del Graal)*, edited by Alfons Hilka, Halle, 1932.
Chrétien de Troyes, *Le Roman de Perceval ou Le Conte du Graal*, edited by William Roach, *TLF* 71, second edition, Geneva, 1959.
Li Romans de Claris et Laris, edited by Johann Alton, *BLVS* 169, Tübingen, 1884, reprinted Amsterdam, 1966.
The Continuations of the Old French Perceval *of Chrétien de Troyes*, edited by William Roach, 5 vols, Philadelphia, 1949–83.
COR. *The Anglo-Norman Text of* Le Lai du Cor, edited by C. T. Erickson, *Anglo-Norman Text Society* 24, Oxford, 1973. [See also *Mantel.*]
Cristal und Clarie, edited by Hermann Breuer, *GRL* 36, Dresden, 1915.
DURMART. *Li Romans de Durmart le Galois*, edited by Edmund Stengel, *BLVS* 116, Tübingen, 1873.
Durmart le Galois, edited by Joseph Gildea, 2 vols, Villanova (Pa.), 1965/6.
'Note sur un légendier français conservé dans la Bibliothèque du Chapitre de Carlisle', edited by R. Fawtier and E. C. Fawtier-Jones, *Romania* 50 (1924), 100–10. [*Durmart* fragment on p. 103.]
'*Les Enfances Gauvain*, fragments d'un poème perdu', edited by Paul Meyer, *Romania* 39 (1910), 1–32.
ESCANOR. *Der Roman von Escanor von Gerard von Amiens*, edited by H. Michelant, *BLVS* 178, Tübingen, 1886.
FERGUS. *Le Roman des aventures de Fregus*, edited by Francisque Michel, Edinburgh, 1841.
Fergus, Roman von Guillaume le Clerc, edited by Ernst Martin, Halle, 1872.
[See the Supplement to the Bibliography for the edition used in this translation.]
The Romance of Flamenca, translated by M. J. Hubert and edited by M. E. Porter, Princeton, 1962.
Floriant et Florete, edited by Harry F. Williams, Ann Arbor, 1947.
Gautier d'Arras, *Ille et Galeron*, edited by E. Löseth, Paris, 1890.
Ille et Galeron, edited by F. A. G. Cowper, *SATF*, Paris, 1956.
Gliglois: A French Arthurian Romance of the Thirteenth Century, edited by C. H. Livingston, Cambridge (Mass.), 1932, reprinted New York, 1966.
GOGULOR. 'Fragment d'un roman de chevalerie', edited by C. H. Livingston, *Romania* 66 (1940/1), 85–93.
HEM. Sarrasin, *Le Roman du Hem*, edited by Albert Henry, *Travaux de la Faculté de Philosophie et Lettres de l'Université de Bruxelles* 9, Paris, 1939.
Hunbaut, edited by Jakob Stürzinger and Hermann Breuer, *GRL* 35, Dresden, 1914.
ILAS ET SOLVAS. 'Fragments d'un roman de la Table ronde', edited by Ernest Langlois, in *Mélanges Emile Picot*, edited by H. Omont *et al.*, 2 vols, Paris, 1913, I, 383–9.
Jaufre, edited by Hermann Breuer, *GRL* 46, Göttingen, 1925.
Jaufré, edited by Clovis Brunel, *SATF*, Paris, 1943.
Lancelot. Roman en prose du XIIIe siècle, edited by Alexandre Micha, *TLF* 247, 249, 262, 278, 283, 286, 288, 307 and 315, 9 vols, Geneva, 1978–83.
LANVAL. Marie de France, *Lais*, edited by Alfred Ewert, Oxford, 1944. [*Lanval*, pp. 58–74.]

LAYS. *The Lays of Desiré, Graelent and Melion*, edited with an introduction by Margaret Grimes, New York, 1928.

Les lais anonymes des douzième et treizième siècles: Edition critique de quelques lais bretons, edited by P. M. Tobin, Geneva and Paris, 1976.

Mantel et Cor: deux lais du XIIe siècle, edited by Philip Bennett, Exeter, 1975.

MELIADOR. Jean Froissart, *Méliador*, edited by Auguste Longnon, *SATF*, 3 vols, Paris, 1895–9.

MELIOR. 'Fragment d'un roman en vers du XIIIe siècle', edited by Eugène Vinaver, *Arthuriana* 2 (1929/30), 81.

MERAUGIS. Raoul von Houdenc, *Meraugis von Portlesguez: Altfranzösischer Abenteuerroman*, edited by Mathias Friedwagner, Halle, 1897.

MULE SANS FREIN. 'Paien de Masières, *La Mule sanz frain*', edited by Stephen L. Smith, Dissertation, Pennsylvania, 1968.

Two Old French Gauvain Romances, edited by R. C. Johnston and D. D. R. Owen, Edinburgh and London, 1972 [*Le Chevalier à l'épée* and *La Mule sans frein*].

Les Poésies de Peire Vidal, edited by Joseph Anglade, *CFMA* 11, Paris, 1913; second edition, 1923.

La Queste del Saint Graal, edited by Albert Pauphilet, *CFMA* 33, Paris, 1923.

Renart, Jean, *L'Escoufle*, edited by H. Michelant and P. Meyer, *SATF*, Paris, 1894.

Le Roman de Renart, edited by Ernest Martin, 3 vols, Strasburg and Paris, 1882–7.

Le Roman de Renart, edited by M. Roques, *CFMA* 78, 79, 81, 85, 88 and 90, 6 vols, Paris, 1948–63.

RIGOMER. *Les Mervelles de Rigomer von Jehan: Altfranzösischer Artusroman des XIII. Jahrhunderts*, edited by Wendelin Foerster and Hermann Breuer, *GRL* 19 and 39, 2 vols, Dresden, 1908 and 1915.

Le Roman de la Rose, by Guillaume de Lorris and Jean de Meun, edited by Félix Lecoy, *CFMA* 92, 95 and 98, 3 vols, Paris, 1965–70.

SAISNES. *Jean Bodels Saxenlied*, edited by F. Menzel and E. Stengel, 2 vols, Marburg, 1906–9.

SILENCE. Heldris de Cornuälle, *Le roman de Silence*, edited by Lewis Thorpe, Cambridge, 1972.

Thomas, *Les Fragments du Roman de Tristan*, edited by Bartina H. Wind, Leiden, 1950; second edition, *TLF* 92, Geneva, 1960.

TORNOIMENT ANTECRIST. Huon de Mery, *Li Tornoiemenz Antecrit*, edited by G. Wimmer, *Ausgaben und Abhandlungen* 76, Marburg, 1888.

'Tydorel', edited by Gaston Paris, *Romania* 8 (1879), 66–72.

'Tyolet', edited by Gaston Paris, *Romania* 8 (1879), 40–50.

'Fragment du *Vallet a la cote mal tailliee*', edited by Paul Meyer and Gaston Paris, *Romania* 26 (1897), 276–80.

VENGEANCE RAGUIDEL. Raoul von Houdenc, *La Vengeance Raguidel*, edited by Mathias Friedwagner, Halle, 1909.

'La Vengeance Raguidel', edited by Edward Echoles Wilson, Dissertation, University of North Carolina, 1966, *DA* 27 (1966/7), 3032 A.

WACE. *La Partie Arthurienne du Roman de Brut par Wace*, edited by I. D. O. Arnold and M. M. Pelan, *Bibliothèque Française et Romane*, Series B, Vol. I, Paris, 1962.

William of Malmesbury, *De gesta regum anglorum*, *PL* 179, columns 945–1392.

William of Malmesbury, *De antiquitate glastoniensis ecclesiae*, *PL* 179, columns 1681–1734 (column 1701, 'De illustri Arturo').

Wirnt von Gravenberch, *Wigalois*, edited by G. F. Benecke, Berlin, 1819.

YDER. *Der altfranzösische Yderroman*, edited by Heinrich Gelzer, *GRL* 31, Dresden, 1913.

Adams, A. and Kennedy, A. J., 'Corrections to the Text of *Yder*', in *Beiträge zum romanischen Mittelalter*, edited by Kurt Baldinger, *ZrPh* Sonderband, Tübingen, 1977, pp. 230–6.

Bibliography

CRITICAL STUDIES AND WORKS OF REFERENCE

Adler, A., 'Sur quelques emprunts de l'auteur de la Vengeance Raguidel à Chrétien de Troyes', *Romanistisches Jahrbuch* 11 (1960), 81–6.

Epische Spekulanten, Theorie der Schönen Künste 3, Munich, 1975.

Alexander, F., 'Late Medieval Scottish Attitudes to the Figure of King Arthur: A Reassessment', *Anglia* 93 (1975), 17–34.

Anglade, J., *Les troubadours et les Bretons*, Montpellier, 1928, reprinted Geneva, 1973.

Aselmann, K., 'Der Marschall Keu in den altfranzösischen Artusepen', Dissertation, Jena, 1926.

Ashe, G., *King Arthur's Avalon: The Story of Glastonbury*, London, 1957.

The Quest for Arthur's Britain, second edition, London, 1971 (first published 1968).

Baader, H., *Die Lais: Zur Geschichte einer Gattung der altfranzösischen Kurzerzählungen, Analecta Romanica* 16, Frankfurt, 1966.

Barrow, G. W. S., 'The Anglo-Scottish Border', *Northern History* 1 (1966), 21–43.

Baum, R., 'Eine neue Etymologie von frz. *lai* und apr. *lais*. Zugleich: Ein Plädoyer für die Zusammenarbeit von Sprach- und Literaturwissenschaft', in *Beiträge zum romanischen Mittelalter*, edited by Kurt Baldinger, *ZrPh* Sonderband, Tübingen, 1977, pp. 17–78.

Baumgartner, E., 'A propos du Mantel mautaillé', *Romania* 96 (1975), 315–32.

Becker, P. A., *Von den Erzählern neben und nach Chrétien de Troyes*, Halle, 1936.

Bell, A., 'Comments on the *Lai du Cor*', *Medium Aevum* 45 (1976), 265–8.

Bertoni, G., 'Note varie al romanzo di *Durmart le Galois*', *Archivum romanicum* 3 (1919), 257–9.

Bestman, F. R., *Die lautliche Gestaltung englischer Ortsnamen im altfranzösischen und anglonormannischen*, Paris, 1938.

Bezzola, R. R., *Les origines et la formation de la littérature courtoise en occident 500–1200*, Part III, Vol. I, *La cour d'Angleterre sous les rois Angevins*, Paris, 1967.

Bianchini, S., 'Due brevi romanzi di Chrétien de Troyes?', *Cultura Neolatina* 33 (1973), 55–68.

Blaess, M., 'L'abbaye de Bordesley et les livres de Guy de Beauchamp', *Romania* 78 (1957), 511–18.

Bloch, M., 'Les Rois Thaumaturges', *Publications de la Faculté des Lettres de Strasbourg* 19 (1924), 29–41.

Bloom, H., *The Anxiety of Influence: A Theory of Poetry*, New York, 1973.

A Map of Misreading, New York, 1975.

Bogdanow, F., 'The Character of Gawain in the Thirteenth-Century Prose Romances', *Medium Aevum* 27 (1958), 154–61.

Boiron, F. and Payen, J.-C., 'Structure et sens du Bel Inconnu de Renaut de Beaujeu', *Le Moyen Age* 76 (1970), 15–26.

de Boor, H., *Die deutsche Literatur im späten Mittelalter*, H. de Boor and R. Newald, *Geschichte der deutschen Literatur*, Vol. III.1, Munich, 1962.

Brackert, H., *Rudolf von Ems*, Heidelberg, 1968.

Brand, W., *Chrétien de Troyes*, Munich, 1972.

Brault, G. J., 'A Study of the Works of Girart d'Amiens', Dissertation, Philadelphia, 1958.

'Arthurian Heraldry and the Date of *Escanor*', *BBSIA* 11 (1959), 81–8.

Early Blazon, Oxford, 1972.

Brogsitter, K. O., *Artusepik*, Sammlung Metzler 38, second edition, Stuttgart, 1971 (first published 1965).

Bromwich, R., 'Scotland and the Arthurian Legend', *BBSIA* 15 (1963), 85–95.

Brooke, C., *From Alfred to Henry III 871–1272, A History of England*, Vol. II, Edinburgh, 1961; third impression, London, 1969.

Bruce, J. D., *The Evolution of Arthurian Romance from the Beginnings Down to the Year 1300*,

2 vols, Göttingen and Baltimore, 1923; second edition, Göttingen, 1928, reprinted Gloucester (Mass.), 1958.
Brugger, E., 'Über die Bedeutung von Bretagne, Breton in mittelalterlichen Texten', *ZfSL* 20 (1898), 76–162.
'Huon de Bordeaux et Fergus', *MLR* 20 (1925), 158–75.
'The Hebrides in the French Arthurian Romances', *Arthuriana* 2 (1929/30), 7–19.
'"Pellande", "Galvoie", and "Arragoce" in the Romance of Fergus', in *A Miscellany presented to Leon E. Kastner*, edited by Mary Williams and James A. de Rothschild, Cambridge, 1932, pp. 94–107.
Busby, K., *Gauvain in Old French Literature*, Amsterdam, 1980.
Campbell, D. E., 'Form and meaning in the *Meraugis de Portlesguez*', *Genre* 2 (1969), 9–20.
Chaytor, H. J., *The Troubadours and England*, Cambridge, 1923.
Cohen, G., *Le Roman en vers au XIIIe siècle* (Les cours de Sorbonne), Paris, 1936.
Cormeau, C., 'Rudolf von Ems, *Der Guote Gerhart*: Die Veränderung eines Bauelements in einer gewandelten literarischen Situation', in *Werk–Typ–Situation*, edited by I. Glier, Stuttgart, 1969, pp. 80–98.
'Wigalois' und 'Diu Crône': zwei Kapitel zur Gattungsgeschichte des nachklassischen Aventiureromans, Zurich and Munich, 1977.
Coser, L. A., *Theorie sozialer Konflikte*, Neuwied, 1972.
Critchlow, F. L., 'Arthur in Old French Poetry not of the Breton Cycle', *MPh* 6 (1909), 477–86.
David, C., 'Über den Begriff des Epigonischen', in *Tradition und Ursprünglichkeit: Akten des III. Internationalen Germanistenkongresses 1965 in Amsterdam*, H. Meyer and W. Kohlschmidt, Berne and Munich, 1966, pp. 66–78.
Davis, H. W. C., *A History of Balliol College*, Oxford, 1963.
Delbouille, M., 'Le témoignage de Wace sur la légende arthurienne', *Romania* 74 (1953), 172–99.
'Caërlion et Cardueil sièges de la cour d'Arthur', *Neuphilologische Mitteilungen* 66 (1965), 431–6.
'Des origines du personnage et du nom de Gauvain', in *Mélanges Paul Imbs*, edited by Robert Martin and Georges Straka, Strasburg, 1973, pp. 549–59.
'Le *Draco Normannicus*, source d'*Erec et Enide*', in *Mélanges Pierre Le Gentil*, edited by J. Dufournet and D. Poirion, Paris, 1973, pp. 181–98.
Dictionary of National Biography, edited by Leslie Stephen and Sidney Lee, 63 vols, London, 1885–1900, entry on 'Baliol, John de (1249–1315)', III, 66–70; reissue, 22 vols, 1908–9, I, 986–90.
Diverres, A. H., 'The Geography of Britain in Froissart's *Meliador*', in *Medieval Miscellany presented to Eugène Vinaver*, edited by F. Whitehead, A. H. Diverres and F. E. Sutcliffe, Manchester, 1965, pp. 97–112.
'Froissart's *Meliador* and Edward III's policy towards Scotland', in *Mélanges Rita Lejeune*, edited by F. Dethier, 2 vols, Gembloux, 1969, II, 1399–1409.
'The Irish Adventures in Froissart's *Meliador*', in *Mélanges Jean Frappier*, edited by J.-C. Payen and C. Régnier, 2 vols, Geneva, 1970, I, 235–51.
Düwel, K., 'Werkbezeichnungen in der mhd. Erzählliteratur (1050–1250)', Dissertation, Göttingen [no date given].
Duncan, A. A. M., *Scotland: The Making of the Kingdom*, Edinburgh, 1975.
Emmel, H., 'Formprobleme des Artusromans und der Graaldichtung', Dissertation, Berne, 1951.
Encyclopaedia Britannica, fourteenth edition, Chicago, 1970.
Epro, M. W., 'The Romance of Hunbaut: An Arthurian Poem of The Thirteenth Century', Dissertation, University of Pennsylvania, 1975, *DA* 36 (1975/6), 5274A.
Ertzdorff, X. von, *Rudolf von Ems: Untersuchungen zum höfischen Roman im 13. Jahrhundert*, Munich, 1967.
'Typen des Romans im 13. Jahrhundert', *DU* 20,2 (1968), 81–95.

Fierz-Monnier, A., *Initiation und Wandlung: Zur Geschichte des altfranzösischen Romans im 12. Jahrhundert von Chrétien de Troyes zu Renaut de Beaujeu*, Dissertation, Zurich, 1950, reprinted Geneva, 1973.

Fletcher, R. H., *The Arthurian Material in the Chronicles*, second edition, expanded by R. S. Loomis, New York, 1966 (first published Boston, 1906).

Flutre, L.-F., '*Gogulor*, personnage de romans bretons', *Romania* 66 (1940/1), 530–1.

Table des noms propres...dans les romans du moyen âge, Poitiers, 1962.

Foerster, W., *Kristian von Troyes: Wörterbuch zu seinen sämtlichen Werken*, Romanische Bibliothek 21, Halle, 1914; revised edition by H. Breuer, first published Halle, 1933.

Foulet, L., 'Sire, messire', *Romania* 71 (1950), 1–48 and 180–221, and *Romania* 72 (1951), 31–77, 324–67 and 479–528.

Foulon, C., 'Le rôle de Gauvain dans *Erec et Enide*', *Annales de Bretagne* 65 (1958), 147–58.

Fourrier, A., 'Encore la chronologie des oeuvres de Chrétien de Troyes', *BBSIA* 2 (1950), 70–4.

'Raoul de Hodenc: est-ce lui?', in *Mélanges Maurice Delbouille*, edited by J. Renson (Vol. I) and M. Tyssens (Vol. II), 2 vols, Gembloux, 1964, II, 165–93.

Frappier, J., 'Le personnage de Gauvain dans la *Première Continuation de Perceval (Conte du Graal)*', *Romance Philology* 11 (1958), 331–44.

'Chrétien de Troyes', in *ALMA*, pp. 157–91.

Amour Courtois et Table Ronde, Geneva, 1973.

'Les romans de la Table Ronde et les Lettres en France au XVIe siècle', in *Amour Courtois et Table Ronde*, Geneva, 1973, pp. 265–81.

'A propos du lai de Tydorel et de ses éléments mythiques', in *Mélanges Paul Imbs*, edited by Robert Martin and Georges Straka, Strasburg, 1973, pp. 561–87.

Frescoln, W. L., 'A Study of the Old French Romance of *Fergus*', Dissertation, Pennsylvania, *DA* 22 (1961/2), 259–60.

Gallais, P., 'Gauvain et la Pucelle de Lis', in *Mélanges Maurice Delbouille*, edited by J. Renson (Vol. I) and M. Tyssens (Vol. II), 2 vols, Gembloux, 1964, II, 207–29.

'Bleheri, la cour de Poitiers et la diffusion des récits arthuriens sur le continent', in *Moyen Age et Littérature comparée: Actes du VIIe Congrès National de la Société française de Littérature comparée, Poitiers, 1965*, Paris, 1967, pp. 47–79.

Gerould, G. H., 'King Arthur and Politics', *Speculum* 2 (1927), 33–51.

Glier, I. (ed.), *Werk–Typ–Situation*, Stuttgart, 1969.

Artes Amandi: Untersuchungen zur Geschichte, Überlieferung und Typologie deutscher Minnereden, Munich, 1971.

Göller, K. H., 'Die Wappen König Arthurs in der Hs. Landsdowne 882', *Anglia* 79 (1961), 264–6.

'König Arthur in den schottischen Chroniken', *Anglia* 80 (1962), 390–404.

König Arthur in der englischen Literatur des späten Mittelalters, *Palaestra* 238, Göttingen, 1963.

'Giraldus Cambrensis und der Tod Arthurs', *Anglia* 91 (1973), 170–93.

Greenberg, J., 'Guillaume le Clerc and Alan of Galloway', *PMLA* 66 (1951), 524–33.

Grundriß der romanischen Literaturen des Mittelalters, edited by H. R. Jauss and E. Köhler, Heidelberg, 1968– (Vol. IV, *Roman*, 1978; Vol. VI.1, *La Littérature didactique, allégorique et satirique*, 1968) [*Grundriß*].

Grundriss der romanischen Philologie, edited by G. Gröber, 2 vols in 4, Strasburg, 1888–1902 (Vol. II.1, Strasburg, 1902, especially 'Artusepen und Graaldichtung', pp. 495–510, 'Artus- und Graalependichtung nach Crestien', pp. 511–23, and 'Artusepen', pp. 785–91).

Gürttler, K. R., 'Künec Artus der guote: Das Artusbild der höfischen Epik des 12. und 13. Jahrhunderts', Dissertation, Bonn, 1976.

Habemann, C., 'Die literarische Stellung des *Meraugis de Portlesguez* in der französischen Artusepik', Dissertation, Göttingen, 1908.

Haidu, P., 'Realism, Convention, Fictionality and the Theory of Genres in *Le Bel Inconnu*', *L'Esprit Créateur* 12 (1972), 37–60.

Harms, W. and Johnson, L. P. (eds), *Deutsche Literatur des späten Mittelalters: Hamburger Colloquium 1973*, Berlin, 1975.

Haug, W., 'Rudolfs *Willehalm* und Gottfrieds *Tristan*, Kontrafraktur als Kritik', in *Deutsche Literatur des späten Mittelalters: Hamburger Colloquium 1973*, edited by W. Harms and L. P. Johnson, Berlin, 1975, pp. 83–98.

Haupt, J., *Der Truchsess Keie im Artusroman: Untersuchungen zur Gesellschaftsstruktur im höfischen Roman, Philologische Studien und Quellen* 57, Berlin, 1971.

Heintz, G., 'Epigonendichtung', in *Handlexikon zur Literaturwissenschaft*, edited by Dieter Krywalski, Munich, 1974.

Hempfer, K., *Gattungstheorie, UTB* 133, Munich, 1973.

Henderson, T. F., *Scottish Vernacular Literature*, Edinburgh, 1910.

Herzog, M. B., 'The Development of Gawain as a Literary Figure in Medieval German and English Arthurian Romance', Dissertation, Washington, 1971, *DA* 32 (1971/2), 6377A–6378A.

Hibbard, L., *Medieval Romance in England*, New York, 1924.

Hilka, A., 'Plagiate in altfranzösischen Dichtungen', *ZfSL* 47 (1924), 60–9.

Hoepffner, E., 'Die Anspielungen auf Chrétien de Troyes in *Hunbaut*', *ZrPh* 40 (1919), 235–8.

Holmes, U. T., 'Renaut de Beaujeu', *Romanic Review* 18 (1927), 334–8.

A History of Old French Literature from the Origins to 1300, second edition, New York, 1962 (first published 1937).

Holt, J. C., *Magna Carta*, Cambridge, 1965.

Iser, W., 'Mittelenglische Literatur und romanische Tradition', in *Grundriß*, Vol. I, Heidelberg, 1972, pp. 304–32.

Jauss, H. R., 'Die Defigurierung des Wunderbaren und der Sinn der Aventure im Jaufre', *Romanistisches Jahrbuch* 1953/4, 60–75.

'Chanson de geste et roman courtois: Analyse du Fierabras et du Bel Inconnu', in *Chanson de Geste und höfischer Roman: Heidelberger Kolloquium 1961*, edited by Pierre Le Gentil, Heidelberg, 1963, pp. 61–77.

'Entstehung und Strukturwandel der allegorischen Dichtung', in *Grundriß*, Vol. VI.1, Heidelberg, 1968, pp. 146–244.

'Theorie der Gattungen und Literatur des Mittelalters', in *Grundriß*, Vol. I, Heidelberg, 1972, pp. 107–38.

'Literaturgeschichte als Provokation der Literaturwissenschaft', in *Rezeptionsästhetik*, edited by R. Warning, *UTB* 303, Munich, 1975, pp. 126–62.

Jeanroy, A., review of *Le Roman du Hem*, edited by Albert Henry, *Travaux de la Faculté de Philosophie et Lettres de l'Université de Bruxelles* 9, Paris, 1939, *Romania* 66 (1940/1), 105–9.

'Le roman de Jaufré', *Annales du Midi* 53 (1941), 363–90.

Jones, R. G., 'The Rôle of Gauvain in Mediaeval French Romance', Dissertation, Leeds, 1958/9.

Jordan, L., 'Zum altfranzösischen Fergusroman', *ZrPh* 43 (1923), 154–86.

Kaiser, G., *Textauslegung und gesellschaftliche Selbstdeutung: Aspekte einer sozialgeschichtlichen Interpretation von Hartmanns Artusepen*, Frankfurt, 1973.

Kellermann, W., *Aufbaustil und Weltbild Chrestiens von Troyes im Percevalroman*, *ZrPh* Beiheft 88, Halle, 1936, reprinted Darmstadt, 1967.

'Les types psychologiques de l'amour dans les romans de Chrétien de Troyes', *Marche Romane* 20 (1970), 31–9.

Kelly, D., 'Gauvain and *Fin'Amors* in the Poems of Chrétien de Troyes', *StPh* 67 (1970), 453–60.

Kern, P., 'Rezeption und Genese des Artusromans: Überlegungen zu Strickers *Daniel vom blühenden Tal*', *ZfdPh* 93 (1974), Sonderheft, *Spätmittelalterliche Epik*, 18–42.

Kirchrath, L., *Li romans de Durmart le Galois in seinem Verhältnisse zu Meraugis de Portlesguez und den Werken Chrétiens de Troyes*, *Ausgaben und Abhandlungen* 21, Marburg, 1884.
Klose, M., *Der Roman von Claris et Laris in seinen Beziehungen zur altfranzösischen Artusepik des XII. und XIII. Jahrhunderts*, *ZrPh* Beiheft 63, Halle, 1916.
Köhler, E., 'Zur Diskussion über die Einheit von Chrestiens *Li Contes del Graal*', *ZrPh* 75 (1959), 523–39.
Trobadorlyrik und höfischer Roman, Berlin, 1962.
'Zur Entstehung des altfranzösischen Prosaromans', in E. Köhler, *Trobadorlyrik und höfischer Roman*, Berlin, 1962, pp. 213–23.
Ideal und Wirklichkeit in der höfischen Epik, *ZrPh* Beiheft 97, second edition, Tübingen, 1970.
'Gattungssystem und Gesellschaftssystem', *Romanistische Zeitschrift für Literaturgeschichte* 1 (1977), 7–22.
Kohlschmidt, W., 'Die Problematik der Spätzeitlichkeit', in *Spätzeiten und Spätzeitlichkeit*, edited by W. Kohlschmidt, Berne and Munich, 1962, pp. 16–26.
(ed.), *Spätzeiten und Spätzeitlichkeit* (second international Germanists' congress in Copenhagen), Berne and Munich, 1962.
Koubichkine, M., 'A propos du Lai de Lanval', *Le Moyen Age* 78 (1972), 467–88.
Kuhn, H., *Gattungsprobleme der mittelhochdeutschen Literatur*, Munich, 1956.
Minnesangs Wende, second edition, Tübingen, 1967 (first published 1952).
'Bemerkungen zur Rezeption des Tristan im deutschen Mittelalter: Ein Beitrag zur Rezeptionsdiskussion', in *Festschrift für Herman Meyer*, edited by A. von Bormann *et al.*, Tübingen, 1976, pp. 53–63.
Kuhse, H., 'Der Einfluß Raouls von Houdenc auf den Roman *Les Merveilles de Rigomer*', Dissertation, Göttingen, 1914.
Kundert-Forrer, V., *Raoul de Houdenc, ein französischer Erzähler des XIII. Jahrhunderts*, Berne, 1960.
Långfors, A., review of Wacker, *Dialekt und Schriftsprache* (q.v.), *Romania* 51 (1925), 295–302.
Langlois, C.-V., *La Vie en France au moyen âge de la fin du XIIe au milieu du XIVe siècle d'après des romans mondains du temps*, second edition, Paris, 1926 (first edition 1924).
Lefèvre, Y., 'Bertran de Born et la littérature française de son temps', in *Mélanges Jean Frappier*, edited by J.-C. Payen and C. Régnier, 2 vols, Geneva, 1970, Vol. II, pp. 603–9.
Le Gentil, P., 'The Work of Robert de Boron and the *Didot Perceval*', in *ALMA*, pp. 251–62.
Legge, M. D., 'Some Notes on the *Roman de Fergus*', *Reprint from Transactions of the Dumfriesshire and Galloway Natural History and Antiquarian Society* 27 (1950), 163–72.
Anglo-Norman Literature and its Background, Oxford, 1963.
'Sur la genèse du *Roman de Fergus*', in *Mélanges Maurice Delbouille*, edited by J. Renson (Vol. I) and M. Tyssens (Vol. II), 2 vols, Gembloux, 1964, Vol. II, pp. 399–408.
'The Dedication of *Guillaume d'Angleterre*', in *Medieval Miscellany presented to Eugène Vinaver*, edited by F. Whitehead, A. H. Diverres and F. E. Sutcliffe, Manchester, 1965, pp. 196–205.
'Les chansons de geste et la Grande Bretagne', in *Mélanges Wathelet-Willem*, edited by Jacques de Caluwé, Liège, 1978, pp. 353–5.
Lejeune, R., 'The Troubadours', in *ALMA*, pp. 393–9.
Levy, R., 'La Damoisele a la Mure: étude textuelle', *Medium Aevum* 4 (1935), 194–8.
Chronologie approximative de la littérature française du moyen âge, *ZrPh* Beih. 98, Tübingen, 1957.
Limentani, A., 'Due studi di narrativa provenzale (Flamenca, Jaufré)', *AIV* 121 (1962/3), 51–112.
Locatelli, R., 'L'avventura nei romanzi di Chrétien de Troyes e nei suoi imitatori', *ACME* (*Annali della Facoltà di Lettere dell'Università Statale di Milano*) 4 (1951), 3–22.
Locke, F. W., 'Yvain, "A cele feste qui tant coste qu'an doit clamer la pantecoste"', *Neophilologus* 43 (1959), 288–92.

Loomis, R. S., *Arthurian Tradition and Chrétien de Troyes*, New York, 1949.
'Edward I, Arthurian Enthusiast', *Speculum* 28 (1953), 114–27.
(ed.), *Arthurian Literature in the Middle Ages*, Oxford, 1959 [*ALMA*].
'The Origin of the Grail Legends', in *ALMA*, pp. 274–94.
'Arthurian Influence on Sport and Spectacle', in *ALMA*, pp. 553–9.
The Development of Arthurian Romance, London, 1963.
Loomis, R. S. and Loomis, L. Hibbard, *Arthurian Legends in Medieval Art*, New York, 1938.
Lyons, F., *Les éléments descriptifs dans le roman d'aventure au 13e siècle*, Geneva, 1965.
Mandach, A. de, *Naissance et développement de la Chanson de Geste en Europe*, Vol. III, *Chanson d'Aspremont*, Geneva, 1975.
Marcovescu, N., 'La légende de Gauvain dans les Romans du Graal avant 1200', Dissertation, Pennsylvania, 1963.
Marquardt, W., *Der Einfluss Kristians von Troyes auf den Roman 'Fergus' des Guillaume le Clerc*, Dissertation, Göttingen, 1905; published Göttingen, 1906.
Marx, J., 'La quête manquée de Gauvain', in *Mélanges Etienne Gilson*, Paris, 1959, pp. 415–36.
Mehl, D., *Die mittelenglischen Romanzen des 13. und 14. Jahrhunderts*, *Anglistische Forschungen* 63, Heidelberg, 1967; *The Middle English Romances of The Thirteenth and Fourteenth Centuries*, London, 1968.
Meneghetti, M. L., 'Ideologia cavalleresca e politica culturale nel *Roman de Brut*', *Studi di Letteratura Francese* 3 (1974), 26–48.
'*L'Estoire des Engleis* di Geffrei Gaimar fra cronaca genealogica e romanzo cortese', *Medioevo Romanzo* 2 (1975), 232–46.
Mennung, A., 'Der Bel Inconnu des Renaut de Beaujeu in seinem Verhältnis zu Libeaus Disconus, Carduino und Wigalois: Eine literar-historische Studie', Dissertation, Halle, 1890.
Meyer, H., *Das Zitat in der Erzählkunst*, Stuttgart, 1961; second edition, 1967.
Meyer, H. and Kohlschmidt, W. (eds), *Tradition und Ursprünglichkeit: Akten des III. Internationalen Germanistenkongresses 1965 in Amsterdam*, Berne and Munich, 1966.
Meyer, Paul, 'Notice d'un manuscrit appartenant à M. le comte d'Ashburnham', *Bulletin de la SATF* 1887, 82–103.
Meyer-Lübke, W., 'Crestien von Troyes Erec und Enide', *ZfSL* 44 (1917), 129–88.
Micha, A., 'Raoul de Houdenc est-il l'auteur du Songe de Paradis et de la Vengeance Raguidel?', *Romania* 68 (1944/5), 316–60.
'Miscellaneous French Romances in Verse', in *ALMA*, pp. 358–92.
'Les romans arthuriens', in *Grundriß*, Vol. IV, pp. 380–99.
Mölk, U. (ed.), *Französische Literarästhetik des 12. und 13. Jahrhunderts*, *SRÜ* 54, Tübingen, 1969.
Moelleken, W. W., 'Minne und Ehe in Strickers *Daniel vom blühenden Tal*', *ZfdPh* 93 (1974), Sonderheft, *Spätmittelalterliche Epik*, 43–50.
Monecke, W., *Studien zur epischen Technik Konrads von Würzburg: Das Erzählprinzip der Wildekeit*, Stuttgart, 1968.
Moret, A., 'Un artiste méconnu: Conrad de Wurzbourg', Dissertation, Lille, 1932.
Neilson, G., 'Bruce vs. Balliol, 1291–1292. The Model for Edward I's Tribunal', *Scottish Historical Review* 16 (1918), No. 61, 1–14.
Newell, W. W., 'William of Malmesbury on the Antiquity of Glastonbury, with Especial Reference to the Equation of Glastonbury and Avalon', *PMLA* 18 (1903), 459–512.
Nitze, W. A., 'The Exhumation of King Arthur at Glastonbury', *Speculum* 9 (1934), 353–61.
'The Character of Gauvain in the Romances of Chrétien de Troyes', *Modern Philology* 50 (1952/3), 219–25.
Noble, P., 'Kay the Seneschall in Chrétien de Troyes and his predecessors', *Reading Medieval Studies* 1 (1975), 55–70.

Oehring, R., 'Untersuchungen über Durmart le Galois, insbesondere sein Verhältnis zum Yderroman', Dissertation, Coburg, 1929.
Orr, J., 'La demoiselle a la mure: étude textuelle', *Medium Ævum* 5 (1936), 77–8.
Owen, D. D. R., 'Paien de Maisières—A Joke That Went Wrong', *FMLS* 2 (1966), 192–6.
'Burlesque Tradition and *Sir Gawain and the Green Knight*', *FMLS* 4 (1968), 125–45.
'Two more Romances by Chrétien de Troyes?', *Romania* 92 (1971), 246–60.
Paris, Gaston, 'Lais inédits de *Tyolet*, de *Guingamor*, de *Doan*, du *Lecheor* et de *Tydorel*', *Romania* 8 (1879), 29–72.
'Romans en vers du cycle de la Table ronde', in *Histoire Littéraire de la France*, Vol. XXX, Paris, 1888, pp. 1–270.
PATROLOGIA LATINA. *Patrologiae cursus completus: Series latina*, edited by J.-P. Migne, 221 vols, Paris, 1878–90 [*PL*].
Payen, J.-C., *L'évolution de la courtoisie dans la littérature française aux XIIe et aux XIIIe siècles*, Paris, 1966.
'La destruction des mythes courtois dans le roman arthurien: la femme dans le roman en vers après Chrétien de Troyes', *Revue des Langues Romanes* 78 (1969), 213–28.
Pelan, M., *L'influence du* Brut *de Wace sur les romanciers français de son temps*, Paris, 1931.
Pernoud, R., *Aliénor d'Aquitaine*, Paris, 1965.
Pessen, E., *Die Schlußepisode des Rigomerromanes: Kritischer Text nebst Einleitung und Anmerkungen*, Dissertation, Heidelberg; Berlin, 1907.
Pinkernell, G., 'Zur Datierung des provenzalischen Jaufré-Romans', *ZrPh* 88 (1972), 105–10.
Pollmann, L., *Chrétien de Troyes und der Conte del Graal*, *ZrPh* Beiheft 110, Tübingen, 1965.
Poole, A. L., *From Domesday Book to Magna Carta 1087–1216*, *Oxford History of England*, second edition, Oxford, 1955 (first published 1951).
Powicke, M., *The Thirteenth Century 1216–1307*, *Oxford History of England*, Oxford, 1953.
Ragotzky, H., *Studien zur Wolfram-Rezeption: Die Entstehung und Verwandlung der Wolfram-Rolle in der deutschen Literatur des 13. Jahrhunderts*, *Studien zur Poetik und Geschichte der Literatur* 20, Stuttgart, 1971.
Remy, P., 'A propos de la datation du roman Jaufré', *Revue belge de Philologie et d'Histoire* 29 (1950), 1349–77.
Rickard, P., *Britain in Medieval French Literature 1100–1500*, Cambridge, 1956.
Ringger, K., *Die 'Lais': Zur Struktur der dichterischen Einbildungskraft der Marie de France*, *ZrPh* Beiheft 137, Tübingen, 1973.
Ritchie, R. L. G., *Chrétien de Troyes and Scotland* (Zaharoff Lecture for 1952), Oxford, 1952.
Rohde, R., *La Vengeance de Raguidel: Eine Untersuchung über ihre Beeinflussung durch Christian von Troyes und über ihren Verfasser*, Dissertation, Göttingen, 1903; published Hanover, 1904.
Ruh, K., 'Der *Lanzelet* Ulrichs von Zatzikhofen: Modell oder Kompilation?', in *Deutsche Literatur des späten Mittelalters: Hamburger Colloquium 1973*, edited by W. Harms and L. P. Johnson, Berlin, 1975, pp. 47–55.
Rupp, H., 'Rudolf von Ems und Konrad von Würzburg: Das Problem des Epigonentums', *DU* 17,2 (1965), 5–17.
Rupp, T. H., 'The Influence of Chrétien de Troyes on Jehan's *Les Merveilles de Rigomer*', Dissertation, Pennsylvania, 1954.
Salter, H. E. (ed.), *The Oxford Deeds of Balliol College*, Oxford, 1913.
Savage, H., *Ballio-Fergus*, 1664.
Schelp, H. P., *Exemplarische Romanzen im Mittelenglischen*, *Palaestra* 264, Göttingen, 1967.
Schirmer, W. F., *Die frühen Darstellungen des Arturstoffes*, Cologne and Opladen, 1958.
Schirmer, W. F. and Broich, U., *Studien zum literarischen Patronat im England des 12. Jahrhunderts*, Cologne and Opladen, 1962.

Schlauch, M., 'The Historical Background of *Fergus and Galiene*', *PMLA* 44 (1929), 360–76.
Schmolke-Hasselmann, B., 'Camuse chose: Das Häßliche als ästhetisches und menschliches Problem in der altfranzösischen Literatur', *Miscellanea mediaevalia* 11 (1977), 442–52.
'L'intégration de quelques récits brefs arthuriens (Cor, Mantel, Espee) dans les romans arthuriens du XIIIe siècle', in *Le récit bref: Actes du Colloque 1979 du Centre d'Etudes Médiévales d'Amiens*, Paris, 1980.
'Untersuchungen zur Typik des arthurischen Romananfangs', *GRM* 62, new series 31 (1981), 1–13.
'The Round Table: Ideal, Fiction, Reality', *Arthurian Literature* 2 (1982), 41–75.
Sellar, W. D. H., 'The origins and ancestry of Somerled', *Scottish Historical Review* 45,2 (1966), 123–42.
Slover, C. H., 'The Names of Glastonbury', *Speculum* 11 (1936), 129–32.
Southworth, M. J., *Etude comparée de quatre romans médiévaux: Jaufre, Fergus, Durmart, Blancandin*, Paris, 1973.
Sparnaay, H., 'Hartmann von Aue and His Successors', in *ALMA*, pp. 430–42.
Spensley, R. M., 'The Theme of *Meraugis de Portlesguez*', *French Studies* 27 (1973), 129–33.
Staiger, E., 'Dialektik der Begriffe Nachahmung und Originalität', in *Spätzeiten und Spätzeitlichkeit*, edited by W. Kohlschmidt, Berne and Munich, 1962, pp. 29–38.
Spätzeit: Studien zur deutschen Literatur, Zurich, 1973.
Stefenelli, A., 'Die Autorfrage des *Guillaume d'Angleterre* in lexikalischer Sicht', in *Verba et Vocabula: Festschrift E. Gamillscheg*, edited by H. Stimm and J. Wilhelm, Munich, 1968, pp. 579–91.
Stenton, D. M., *English Society in the Early Middle Ages, The Pelican History of England*, Vol. III, fourth edition, London, 1965 (first published 1951).
Sturm, S., 'The Love-Interest in *Le Bel Inconnu*: Innovation in the roman courtois', *FMLS* 7 (1971), 241–8.
Taylor, R., *The Political Prophecy in England*, New York, 1911.
Thedens, R., 'Li chevalier as Deus Espees in seinem Verhältnis zu seinen Quellen, insbesondere zu den Romanen von Crestien v. Troyes', Dissertation, Göttingen, 1908.
Thorpe, L., 'Notes sur le texte de *La Vengeance Raguidel*', *Romania* 72 (1951), 387–96.
Tyssens, M., 'Les sources de Renaut de Beaujeu', in *Mélanges Jean Frappier*, edited by J.-C. Payen and C. Régnier, 2 vols, Paris, 1970, II, 1043–55.
Vietor, K., 'Die Kunstanschauung der höfischen Epigonen', *PBB* 46 (1922), 85–124.
Vinaver, E., *Form and Meaning in Arthurian Romance*, Leeds, 1966.
Vising, J., *Anglo-Norman Language and Literature*, London, 1923, reprinted Westport, 1970.
Vodička, F. V., 'Die Rezeptionsgeschichte der literarischen Werke', in *Rezeptionsästhetik*, edited by R. Warning, *UTB* 303, Munich, 1975, pp. 71–83.
Vogel, B., 'Secular Politics and the Date of *Lancelot of the Laik*', *Studies in Philology* 40 (1943), 1–13.
Wachinger, B., 'Zur Rezeption Gottfrieds von Straßburg im 13. Jahrhundert', in *Deutsche Literatur des späten Mittelalters: Hamburger Colloquium 1973*, edited by W. Harms and L. P. Johnson, Berlin, 1975, pp. 56–82.
Wacker, G., *Über das Verhältnis von Dialekt und Schriftsprache im Altfranzösischen*, Halle, 1916.
Wagner, A. R., *English Genealogy*, Oxford, 1960.
Wagner, R. L., *L'ancien français, points de vue, programmes*, Paris, 1974.
Waltz, M., 'Zum Problem der Gattungsgeschichte im Mittelalter: Am Beispiel des Mirakels', *ZrPh* 86 (1970), 22–39.
Warning, R., 'Rezeptionsästhetik als literaturwissenschaftliche Pragmatik', in *Rezeptionsästhetik*, edited by R. Warning, *UTB* 303, Munich, 1975, pp. 9–41.
(ed.), *Rezeptionsästhetik*, *UTB* 303, Munich, 1975.
Wehrli, M., 'Wigalois', *DU* 17,2 (1965), 18–35.

West, G. D., *An Index of Proper Names in French Arthurian Verse Romances 1150–1300*, Toronto, 1969.
Weston, J. L., 'Who Was Brian des Illes?', *Modern Philology* 22 (1924/5), 405–11.
'The relation of the *Perlesvaus* to the cyclic romances', *Romania* 51 (1925), 348–62. [Postscript on Brian des Illes p. 362.]
von Wiese, B., *Karl Immermann*, Bad Homburg, 1969.
Wilmotte, M., *L'évolution du sentiment romanesque jusqu'en 1240*, Paris, 1942.
Windfuhr, M., 'Der Epigone: Begriff, Phänomen und Bewußtsein', *Archiv für Begriffsgeschichte* 4 (1959), 182–209.
Woledge, B., *L'Atre Périlleux: Etudes sur les manuscrits, la langue et l'importance littéraire du poème, avec un spécimen du texte*, Paris, 1930.
'Bons vavasseurs et mauvais sénéchaux', in *Mélanges Rita Lejeune*, edited by F. Dethier, 2 vols, Gembloux, 1969, II, 1263–77.
Wolfzettel, F., 'Zur Stellung und Bedeutung der *Enfances* in der altfranzösischen Epik', *ZfSL* 83 (1973), 317–48, and 84 (1974), 1–32.
Wrede, H., 'Die Fortsetzer des Gralromans Chrestiens von Troyes', Dissertation, Göttingen, 1952.
Zumthor, P., *Histoire littéraire de la France médiévale 6.–14. siècles*, Paris, 1954.

Supplement to the bibliography

The first section of this supplement contains the small number of works cited by the translators. The second section contains all works mentioned by Keith Busby in his Foreword. A few of these already appear in the original bibliography or the first part of the supplement, but they are repeated in part two, it being more useful to provide a complete listing than to avoid the occasional duplication.

WORKS CITED BY THE TRANSLATORS

Chrétien de Troyes, *Arthurian Romances*, translated by D. D. R. Owen, *Everyman Classics*, London and Melbourne, 1987.

Guillaume le Clerc, *The Romance of Fergus*, edited by Wilson Frescoln, Philadelphia, 1983.

The Romance of Fergus, introduced and translated by D. D. R. Owen, *Arthurian Literature* 8 (1989), 79-183.

Hartmann von Aue, *Erec*, edited by Albert Leitzmann, fourth edition, revised by Ludwig Wolff, Tübingen, 1967.

The Romance of Hunbaut: An Arthurian Poem of the Thirteenth Century, edited by Margaret Winters, *Davis Medieval Texts and Studies* 4, Leiden, 1984.

[Jehan], *The Marvels of Rigomer (Les Mervelles de Rigomer)*, translated by Thomas E. Vesce, New York and London, 1988.

The Romance of Yder, edited and translated by Alison Adams, *Arthurian Studies* 8, Cambridge, 1983.

WORKS CITED IN THE FOREWORD

EDITIONS OF TEXTS

The Perilous Cemetery (L'Atre Périlleux), edited and translated by Nancy B. Black, New York and London, 1994.

Béroul, *Tristran et Iseut*, edited and translated by Herman Braet and Guy Raynaud de Lage, 2 vols, Leuven, 1989.

The Romance of Tristran, edited and translated by Norris J. Lacy, New York and London, 1989.

The Romance of Tristran by Beroul, edited [and translated] by Stewart Gregory, Amsterdam, 1992.

Chrétien de Troyes, *Œuvres complètes*, under the direction of Daniel Poirion, edited and translated by Anne Berthelot, Peter F. Dembowski, Sylvie Lefèvre, Daniel Poirion, Karl D. Uitti and Philippe Walter, Paris, 1994.

Romans, suivis des *chansons*, avec, en appendice, *Philomena*, under the direction of Michel Zink, edited and translated by Olivier Collet, Jean-Marie Fritz, David F. Hult, Charles Méla and Marie-Claire Zai, Paris, 1994.

Bibliography (Supplement)

Erec and Enide, edited and translated by Carleton W. Carroll, New York and London, 1987.

Erec et Enide, edited and translated by Jean-Marie Fritz, Paris, 1992.

Erec et Enide, [edited by Wendelin Foerster (1934)] with notes and translation by Michel Rousse, Paris, 1994.

Cligés, edited by Stewart Gregory and Claude Luttrell, Cambridge, 1993.

Cligès, edited and translated by Charles Méla and Olivier Collet, Paris, 1994.

Lancelot or, The Knight of the Cart (Le Chevalier de la Charrete), edited and translated by William W. Kibler, New York and London, 1981.

Le Chevalier de la Charrette (Lancelot), edited and translated by Alfred Foulet and Karl D. Uitti, Paris, 1989.

Lancelot ou le chevalier de la charrette, [edited by William W. Kibler (1981)] with notes and translation by Jean-Claude Aubailly, Paris, 1991.

Le Chevalier de la Charrette ou le roman de Lancelot, edited and translated by Charles Méla, Paris, 1992.

The Knight with the Lion, or Yvain (Le Chevalier au Lion), edited and translated by William W. Kibler, New York and London, 1985.

Yvain ou Le Chevalier au Lion, [edited by Wendelin Foerster (1912)] with notes and translation by Michel Rousse, Paris, 1990.

Le Chevalier au Lion ou le roman d'Yvain, edited and translated by David Hult, Paris, 1994.

The Story of the Grail (Li Contes del Graal), or Perceval, edited by Rupert T. Pickens and translated by William W. Kibler, New York and London, 1990.

Le Conte du Graal ou le roman de Perceval, edited and translated by Charles Méla, Paris, 1990.

Le Roman de Perceval ou Le Conte du Graal, edited by Keith Busby, Tübingen, 1993.

The Continuations of the Old French 'Perceval' of Chrétien de Troyes, Volume V: The Third Continuation, by Manessier, edited by William Roach, Philadelphia, 1983.

Première Continuation de Perceval (Continuation Gauvain), edited by William Roach (1952) and translated by Colette-Anne Van Coolput-Storms, Paris, 1993.

Le roman de Floriant et Florete, ou Le chevalier qui la nef maine, edited by Claude M. L. Levy, Ottawa, 1983.

Geoffrey of Monmouth, *The Historia Regum Britannie of Geoffrey of Monmouth, I: A single-manuscript edition from Bern, Burgerbibliothek, MS. 568*, edited by Neil Wright, Cambridge, 1985.

Girart d'Amiens, *Escanor: Roman arthurien en vers de la fin du XIIIe siècle*, edited by Richard Trachsler, 2 vols, Geneva, 1994.

Guillaume le Clerc, *The Romance of Fergus*, edited by Wilson Frescoln, Philadelphia, 1983.

The Romance of Hunbaut: An Arthurian Poem of the Thirteenth Century, edited by Margaret Winters, Leiden, 1984.

Lais féeriques des XIIe et XIIIe siècles, [edited by Prudence M. O'Hara Tobin (1976)] with notes and translation by Alexandre Micha, Paris, 1992.

Lancelot do Lac: The Non-Cyclic Old French Prose Romance, edited by Elspeth Kennedy, 2 vols, Oxford, 1980.

Lancelot du Lac, edited by Elspeth Kennedy (Oxford, 1980), with notes and translation by François Mosès (vol. I) and Marie-Luce Chênerie (vol. II), 2 vols, Paris, 1991.

Lancelot: roman en prose du XIIIe siècle, edited by Alexandre Micha, 9 vols, Geneva, 1978–83.

Marie de France, *Lais de Marie de France*, [edited by Karl Warnke (1925)] with notes and translation by Laurence Harf-Lancner, Paris, 1990.

Lais de Marie de France, edited and translated by Alexandre Micha, Paris, 1994.

Le roman de Perceforest, edited by Jane H. M. Taylor (1ère partie), Geneva, 1979, and Gilles Roussineau (3ème partie), 2 vols, Geneva, 1988–91, (4ème partie), 2 vols, Geneva, 1987.

Les Prophesies de Merlin, edited by Anne Berthelot, Cologny-Geneva, 1992.
La grant Queste del Saint Graal: La grande Ricerca del Santo Graal: Versione inedita della fine del XIII secolo del ms. Udine, Biblioteca Arcivescovile, 177, edited and translated by A. Rosellini *et al.*, Udine, 1990.
La Version Post-Vulgate de la 'Queste del Saint Graal' et de la 'Mort Artu', troisième partie du 'Roman du Graal', edited by Fanni Bogdanow, *SATF*, 4 vols, Paris, 1991.
Renaut de Bâgé, *Le Bel Inconnu (Li Biaus Descouneüs; The Fair Unknown)*, edited by Karen Fresco and translated by Colleen P. Donagher, with music edited by Margaret P. Hasselman, New York and London, 1992.
Robert de Boron, *Le roman du Graal: Manuscrit de Modène*, edited by Bernard Cerquiglini, Paris, 1981.
Joseph d'Arimathie, edited by Richard F. O'Gorman, Toronto, 1995.
Merlin, edited by Alexandre Micha, Geneva, 1979.
Thomas of Britain, *Tristran*, edited and translated by Stewart Gregory, New York and London, 1991.
Le Roman de Tristan, edited by Félix Lecoy, Paris, 1992.
'Un nouveau fragment du *Tristan* de Thomas', edited by Michael Benskin, Tony Hunt and Ian Short, *Romania* 113 (1992–1995), 289–319.
Tristan et Yseut: les Tristan en vers, edited and translated by Jean-Charles Payen, Paris, 1974, revised edition, 1980.
Tristan et Iseut: les poèmes français, la saga norroise, edited and translated by Daniel Lacroix and Philippe Walter, Paris, 1989.
Le roman de Tristan en prose, edited by Renée Curtis, 3 vols, Munich, 1963, Leiden, 1976, Cambridge, 1985.
Le roman de Tristan en prose, edited by Philippe Ménard *et al.*, 9 vols to date, Geneva, 1987– .
[Wace], *La geste du roi Arthur*, [the Arthurian section of *Le Roman de Brut*] edited by Emmanuèle Baumgartner and Ian Short, Paris, 1993.
The Romance of Yder, edited and translated by Alison Adams, Cambridge, 1983.
Ysaÿe le Triste: Roman arthurien du Moyen Age tardif, edited by André Giacchetti, Rouen, 1989.

CRITICAL STUDIES

Andrieu, G. and Piolle, J., *Perceval ou le Conte du Graal de Chrétien de Troyes: concordancier complet des formes graphiques occurrentes d'après l'édition de M. Félix Lecoy*, Aix-en-Provence, 1976.
The Arthurian Yearbook 3 (1993), 171–225, 'The Construction of Manhood in Arthurian Literature'.
Aubailly, J.-C., *La fée et le chevalier*, Paris, 1986.
Baumgartner, E., *L'arbre et le pain: essai sur 'La Queste del Saint Graal'*, Paris, 1981.
Tristan et Iseut: de la légende aux récits en vers, Paris, 1987.
'La *première page* dans les manuscrits du *Tristan en prose*', in *La présentation du livre*, edited by Emmanuèle Baumgartner and Nicole Boulestreau, Paris, 1987, pp. 51–63.
La harpe et l'épée: tradition et renouvellement dans le 'Tristan en prose', Paris, 1990.
Chrétien de Troyes: Yvain, Lancelot, la charrette et le lion, Paris, 1992.
Blakeslee, M. R., *Love's Masks: Identity, Intertextuality, and Meaning in the Old French Tristan Poems*, Cambridge, 1989.
Bromiley, G. N., *Thomas's 'Tristan' and the 'Folie Tristan d'Oxford'*, London, 1986.
Bruckner, M. T., 'Intertextuality', in *The Legacy of Chrétien de Troyes*, edited by Norris J. Lacy, Douglas Kelly and Keith Busby, 2 vols, Amsterdam, 1987–8, I, 223–65.
Shaping Romance: Interpretation, Truth, and Closure in Twelfth-Century French Fictions, Philadelphia, 1993.
'The Poetics of Continuation in Medieval French Romance: From Chrétien's *Conte du Graal* to the *Perceval* Continuations', *French Forum* 18 (1993), 133–49.

Bibliography (Supplement)

Burgess, G. S., *Marie de France: An Analytical Bibliography*, London, 1977; Supplement no. 1, London, 1986.

Chrétien de Troyes: Erec et Enide, London, 1984.

Burns, E. J., *Arthurian Fictions: Rereading the Vulgate Cycle*, Columbus, 1985.

Bodytalk: When Women Speak in Old French Literature, Philadelphia, 1993.

Burns, E. J. and Krueger, R. L. (eds.), *Courtly Ideology and Woman's Place in Medieval French Literature*, special issue of *Romance Notes* 25, 3 (1985).

Busby, K., *Gauvain in Old French Literature*, Amsterdam, 1980.

'Der *Tristan menestrel* des Gerbert de Montreuil und seine Stellung in der altfranzösischen Artustradition', *Vox Romanica* 42 (1983), 144–56.

'William Roach's Continuations of *Perceval*', *Romance Philology* 41,3 (February 1988), 298–309.

'Medieval French Arthurian Literature: Recent Progress and Critical Trends', in *The Vitality of the Arthurian Legend: A Symposium*, edited by Mette Pors, Odense, 1988, pp. 45–70.

Chrétien de Troyes: Perceval, London, 1993.

(ed.), *Towards a Synthesis? Essays on the New Philology*, Amsterdam, 1993.

'The Illustrated Manuscripts of Chrétien's *Perceval*', in *The Manuscripts of Chrétien de Troyes*, edited by Keith Busby, Terry Nixon, Alison Stones and Lori Walters, 2 vols, Amsterdam, 1993, I, 351–63.

'Text, Miniature, and Rubric in the *Continuations* of Chrétien's *Perceval*', in *The Manuscripts of Chrétien de Troyes*, edited by Keith Busby, Terry Nixon, Alison Stones and Lori Walters, 2 vols, Amsterdam, 1993, I, 365–76.

review of Gravdal (q.v.), *Zeitschrift für französische Sprache und Literatur* 103 (1993), 71–3.

Busby, K. and Grossweiner, K. A., 'France' in *Medieval Arthurian Literature: A Guide to Recent Research*, edited by Norris J. Lacy, New York and London, 1996, pp. 121–209.

Busby, K., Nixon, T., Stones, A. and Walters, L., *The Manuscripts of Chrétien de Troyes/Les manuscrits de Chrétien de Troyes*, 2 vols, Amsterdam, 1993.

Cerquiglini, B., *Éloge de la variante: histoire critique de la philologie*, Paris, 1989.

Chênerie, M.-L., *Le chevalier errant dans les romans arthuriens en vers des XIIe et XIIIe siècles*, Geneva, 1986.

Corley, C. F. V., 'Réflexions sur les deux premières continuations de *Perceval*', *Romania* 103 (1982), 235–58.

'Wauchier de Denain et la deuxième continuation de *Perceval*', *Romania* 105 (1984), 351–9.

The Second Continuation of the Old French Perceval: A Critical and Lexicographical Study, London, 1987.

Cormeau, C, *'Wigalois' und 'Diu Crône': zwei Kapitel zur Gattungsgeschichte des nachklassichen Aventiureromans*, Munich, 1977.

Dees, A., 'Analyse par l'ordinateur de la tradition manuscrite du *Cligès* de Chrétien de Troyes', in *Actes du XVIIIe Congrès International de Linguistique et de Philologie Romanes, Université de Trèves (Trier) 1986*, edited by Dieter Kremer, vol. VI, Tübingen, 1988, pp. 62–75.

Dembowski, P. F., *Jean Froissart and His 'Meliador': Context, Craft, and Sense*, Lexington, 1983.

Dubost, F., *Aspects fantastiques de la littérature narrative médiévale (XIIème–XIIIème siècles): l'Autre, l'Ailleurs, l'Autrefois*, 2 vols, Paris, 1991.

Duggan, J. J., 'Oral Performance of Romance in Medieval France', in *Continuations: Essays on Medieval French Literature and Language in Honor of John L. Grigsby*, edited by Norris J. Lacy and Gloria Torrini-Roblin, Birmingham, Ala., 1989, pp. 51–61.

'Performance and Transmission, Aural and Ocular Reception in the Twelfth- and Thirteenth-Century Vernacular Literature of France', *Romance Philology* 43,1 (August 1989), 49–58.

Fleischman, S., *'Jaufre* or Chivalry Askew: Social Overtones of Parody in Arthurian Romance', *Viator* 12 (1981), 101–29.

Bibliography (Supplement)

Frappier, J., *Chrétien de Troyes: The Man and His Work* translated by Raymond J. Cormier, Athens, Ohio, 1982.

Fritz, J.-M., *Le discours du fou au Moyen Age, XIIe–XIIIe siècles*, Paris, 1992.

Gallais, P., *L'imaginaire d'un romancier français de la fin du XIIe siècle: description raisonnée, comparée et commentée de la 'Continuation-Gauvain'*, 4 vols, Amsterdam, 1988–9.

La Fée à la Fontaine et à l'Arbre: un archetype du conte merveilleux et du récit courtois, Amsterdam and Atlanta, 1992.

Gonfroy, G., *Le roman de Tristan en prose: concordancier des formes graphiques occurrentes établi d'après l'édition de Ph. Ménard (t. I)*, Limoges, 1990.

Gouttebroze, J.-G., *Qui perd gagne: le 'Perceval' de Chrétien de Troyes comme représentation de l'Œdipe inversé*, Nice, 1983.

Gravdal, K., *Vilain and Courtois: Transgressive Parody in French Literature of the Twelfth and Thirteenth Centuries*, Lincoln, Nebr., 1989.

Grigsby, J. L., 'Heroes and their Destinies in the Continuations of Chrétien's *Perceval*', in *The Legacy of Chrétien de Troyes*, edited by Norris J. Lacy, Douglas Kelly and Keith Busby, 2 vols, Amsterdam, 1987–8, II, 41–53.

'Remnants of Chrétien's Aesthetics in the Early *Perceval* Continuations and the Incipient Triumph of Writing', *Romance Philology* 41,4 (May 1988), 379–93.

Grimbert, J. T., *'Yvain' dans le miroir*, Amsterdam and Philadelphia, 1988.

Grisward, J., 'Uter Pendragon, Artur et l'idéologie royale des Indo-Européens: structure trifonctionnelle et roman arthurien', *Europe* n° 654 (October 1983), 111–20.

Guerreau[-Jalabert], A., 'Romans de Chrétien de Troyes et contes folkloriques: rapprochements thématiques et observations de méthode', *Romania* 104 (1983), 1–48.

Index des motifs narratifs dans les romans arthuriens français en vers (XIIe–XIIIe siècles) [Motif-Index of French Arthurian Verse Romances (XIIth–XIIIth Cent.)], Geneva, 1992.

Haidu, P., 'The Hermit's Pottage: Deconstruction and History in *Yvain*', *Romanic Review* 74 (1983), 1–15.

Halász, K., *Structures narratives chez Chrétien de Troyes*, Debrecen, 1980.

Harf-Lancner, L., *Les fées dans la littérature française au Moyen Age: Morgane et Mélusine: la naissance des fées*, Paris, 1984.

Hasenohr, G., 'Les romans en vers', in *Mise en page et mise en texte du livre manuscrit*, edited by Henri-Jean Martin and Jean Vezin, Paris, 1990, pp. 245–64.

Hindman, S., *Sealed in Parchment: Rereadings of Knighthood in the Illuminated Manuscripts of Chrétien de Troyes*, Chicago and London, 1994.

Huchet, J.-C., 'Psychanalyse et littérature médiévale: rencontre ou méprise? (A propos de deux ouvrages récents)', *Cahiers de civilisation médiévale* 28 (1985), 223–33.

Tristan et le sang de l'écriture, Paris, 1990.

Hult, D. F., 'Lancelot's Two Steps: A Problem in Textual Criticism', *Speculum* 61 (1986), 836–58.

'Steps Forward and Steps Backward: More on Chrétien's *Lancelot*', *Speculum* 64 (1989), 307–16.

Hunt, T., 'Chrestien de Troyes: The Textual Problem', *French Studies* 33 (1979), 257–71.

Chrétien de Troyes: Yvain, London, 1986.

'The Tristan Illustrations in MS London, BL Add. 11619', in *Rewards and Punishments in the Arthurian Romances and Lyric Poetry of Mediaeval France*, edited by Peter V. Davies and Angus J. Kennedy, Cambridge, 1987, pp. 45–60.

Huot, S., *From Song to Book: The Poetics of Writing in Old French Lyric and Lyrical Narrative Poetry*, Ithaca and London, 1987.

Kellogg, J., *Medieval Artistry and Exchange: Economic Institutions, Society, and Literary Form in Old French Narrative*, New York, 1989.

Kelly, D., *Chrétien de Troyes: An Analytic Bibliography*, London, 1976.

The Art of Medieval French Romance, Madison, 1992.

Kennedy, E., 'The Scribe as Editor', in *Mélanges Jean Frappier*, edited by J.-C. Payen and C. Régnier, 2 vols, Geneva, 1970, I, 523–31.

Lancelot and the Grail: A Study of the Prose 'Lancelot', Oxford, 1986.

Kjær, J., 'L'épisode de "Tristan ménestrel" dans la "Continuation de Perceval" par Gerbert de Montreuil (XIIIe siècle): essai d'interprétation', *Revue Romane* 25 (1990), 356–66.

Köhler, E., *L'aventure chevaleresque: idéal et réalité dans le roman courtois: études sur la forme des plus anciens poèmes d'Arthur et du Graal*, translated by Eliane Kaufholz, Paris, 1974.

Krueger, R. L., *Women Readers and the Ideology of Gender in Old French Verse Romance*, Cambridge, 1993.

Kunstmann, P. and Dubé, M., *Concordance analytique de 'La mort le roi Artu'*, 2 vols, Ottawa, 1982.

Lachet, C., *Sone de Nansay et le roman d'aventures en vers au XIIIe siècle*, Paris, 1992.

Lacy, N. J., *The Craft of Chrétien de Troyes: An Essay on Narrative Art*, Leiden, 1980.

(ed.), *Medieval Arthurian Literature: A Guide to Recent Research*, New York and London, 1996.

Lacy, N. J., Kelly, D. and Busby, K. (eds), *The Legacy of Chrétien de Troyes*, 2 vols, Amsterdam, 1987–8.

Le Menn, G., *La Femme au sein d'or*, St. Brieuc, 1985.

Lozac'hmeur, J.-C., 'Origines celtiques des aventures de Gauvain au pays de Galvoie dans le *Conte du Graal* de Chrétien de Troyes', in *Actes du 14e Congrès International Arthurien*, edited by Charles Foulon *et al.*, 2 vols, Rennes, 1985, I, 406–22.

'Recherches sur les origines indo-européennes et ésotériques de la légende du Graal', *Cahiers de civilisation médiévale* 30 (1987), 44–63.

Lozachmeur, J.-C. and Sasaki, S., 'A propos de deux hypothèses de R. S. Loomis: éléments pour une solution de l'énigme du Graal', *BBSIA* 34 (1982), 207–21.

Macdonald, A. A., *The Figure of Merlin in Thirteenth-Century French Romance*, Lewiston, Queenston and Lampeter, 1990.

Maddox, D., *The Arthurian Romances of Chrétien de Troyes: Once and future fictions*, Cambridge, 1991.

Mathey-Maille, L., 'Traduction et création: de *l'Historia Regum Britanniae* de Geoffroy de Monmouth au *Roman de Brut* de Wace', in *Ecriture et modes de pensée au Moyen Age (VIIIe–XVe siècles)*, edited by Dominique Boutet and Laurence Harf-Lancner, Paris, 1993, pp. 187–93

'De l'*Historia Regum Britanniae* de Geoffroy de Monmouth au *Roman de Brut* de Wace: traduction du texte latin et étude comparative', *Perspectives médiévales* 19 (1993), 92–5.

Méla, C., *La reine et le Graal: la 'conjointure' dans les romans du Graal de Chrétien de Troyes au 'Livre de Lancelot'*, Paris, 1984.

Micha, A., *Essais sur le cycle du Lancelot-Graal*, Geneva, 1987.

Étude sur le 'Merlin' de Robert de Boron, Geneva, 1980.

Middleton, R., 'Coloured Capitals in the Manuscripts of *Erec et Enide*', in *The Manuscripts of Chrétien de Troyes*, edited by Keith Busby, Terry Nixon, Alison Stones and Lori Walters, 2 vols, Amsterdam, 1993, I, 149–93

'Index of Former Owners', in *The Manuscripts of Chrétien de Troyes*, edited by Keith Busby, Terry Nixon, Alison Stones and Lori Walters, 2 vols, Amsterdam, 1993, II, 87–176.

'Additional Notes on the History of Selected Manuscripts', in *The Manuscripts of Chrétien de Troyes*, edited by Keith Busby, Terry Nixon, Alison Stones and Lori Walters, 2 vols, Amsterdam, 1993, II, 177–243.

Milin, G., *Le roi Marc aux oreilles de cheval*, Geneva, 1991.

van Mulken, M., *The Manuscript Tradition of the 'Perceval' of Chrétien de Troyes: A stemmatological and dialectological approach*, Amsterdam, 1993.

Mullally, E., *The Artist at Work: Narrative Technique in Chrétien de Troyes*, *Transactions of the American Philosophical Society* 78,4, Philadelphia, 1988.

Nightingale, J. A., 'Chrétien de Troyes and the Mythographical Tradition: The Couple's Journey in *Erec et Enide* and Martianus' *De Nuptiis*', in *King Arthur Through the Ages*, edited by Valerie M. Lagorio and Mildred Leake Day, New York and London, 1990, I, 56–79.

Nixon, T., 'Catalogue of Manuscripts', in *The Manuscripts of Chrétien de Troyes*, edited by Keith Busby, Terry Nixon, Alison Stones and Lori Walters, 2 vols, Amsterdam, 1993, II, 1–85.

Noble, P. S., *Love and Marriage in Chrétien de Troyes*, Cardiff, 1982.

Beroul's 'Tristan' and the 'Folie de Berne', London, 1982.

Ollier, M.-L., *Lexique et concordance de Chrétien de Troyes d'après la copie Guiot*, Montreal and Paris, 1986.

Poirion, D., *Le merveilleux dans la littérature française du Moyen Age*, Paris, 1981.

Polak, L., *Chrétien de Troyes: Cligés*, London, 1982.

Reid, T. B. W., 'Chrétien de Troyes and the Scribe Guiot', *Medium Ævum* 45 (1976), 1–19.

Rey-Flaud, H., *La névrose courtoise*, Paris, 1983.

Ribard, J., 'Ecriture symbolique et visée allégorique dans *Le Conte du Graal*', *Œuvres & Critiques* 5, 2 (1980–1), 103–9.

Rieger, A., 'Neues über Chrétiens Illustratoren: Bild und Text in der ältesten Überlieferung von *Perceval-le-vieil (T)*', *BBSIA* 41 (1989), 301–11.

'Le programme iconographique du *Perceval* montpelliérain, BI, Sect. Méd, H 249 *(M)*, avec la description détaillée du manuscrit', in *The Manuscripts of Chrétien de Troyes*, edited by Keith Busby, Terry Nixon, Alison Stones and Lori Walters, 2 vols, Amsterdam, 1993, I, 377–435.

Roland, V., 'Folio liminaire et réception du texte: les manuscrits parisiens du *Merlin en prose*', *BBSIA* 43 (1991), 257–69.

Ruck, E. H., *An Index of Themes and Motifs in Twelfth-Century French Arthurian Poetry*, Cambridge, 1991.

Runte, H. R., 'Initial Readers of Chrétien de Troyes', in *Continuations: Essays on Medieval French Literature and Language in Honor of John L. Grigsby*, edited by Norris J. Lacy and Gloria Torrini-Roblin, Birmingham, Ala., 1989, pp. 121–32.

Salmeri, F., *Manessier: modelli, simboli, scrittura*, Catania, 1984.

Schmolke-Hasselmann, B., 'King Arthur as Villain in the Thirteenth-century Romance *Yder*', *Reading Medieval Studies* 6 (1980), 31–43.

'Henri II Plantagenêt, roi d'Angleterre, et la genèse d'*Erec et Enide*', *Cahiers de civilisation médiévale* 24 (1981), 241–6.

'Le roman de *Fergus*: technique narrative et intention politique', in *An Arthurian Tapestry: essays in memory of Lewis Thorpe*, edited by Kenneth Varty, Glasgow, 1981, pp. 342–53.

'The Round Table: Ideal, Fiction, Reality', *Arthurian Literature* 2 (1982), 41–75.

Shirt, D. J., *The Old French Tristan Poems: A Bibliographical Guide*, London, 1980.

Speculum 65, 1 (January 1990), 'The New Philology'.

Stones, A., 'Arthurian Art since Loomis', in *Arturus Rex, II: Acta Conventus Lovanensis 1987*, edited by Willy Van Hoecke, Gilbert Tournoy and Werner Verbeke, Leuven, 1991, pp. 21–78.

Szkilnik, M., *L'Archipel du Graal: Étude de l'Estoire del Saint Graal*, Geneva, 1991.

Taylor, J. H. M., 'The Fourteenth Century: Context, Text, and Intertext', in *The Legacy of Chrétien de Troyes*, edited by Norris J. Lacy, Douglas Kelly and Keith Busby, 2 vols, Amsterdam, 1987–8, I, 267–332.

Topsfield, L. T., *Chrétien de Troyes: A Study of the Arthurian Romances*, Cambridge, 1981.

Uitti, K. D., 'Intertextuality in *Le Chevalier au lion*', *Dalhousie French Studies* 2 (1980), 3–13.

Uitti, K. D. and Foulet, A., 'On Editing Chrétien de Troyes: Lancelot's Two Steps and Their Context', *Speculum* 63 (1988), 271–92.

Van Coolput[-Storms], C.-A., *Aventures querant et le sens du monde: aspects de la réception productive des premiers romans du Graal cycliques dans le 'Tristan en prose'*, Louvain, 1986.

Bibliography (Supplement)

Vance, E., 'Chrétien's *Yvain* and the Ideologies of Change and Exchange', *Yale French Studies* 70 (1986), 42–62.

From Topic to Tale: Logic and Narrativity in The Middle Ages, Minneapolis, 1987.

Vial, G., *Le Conte du Graal: sens et unité. La première continuation: textes et contenu*, Geneva, 1987.

Vitz, E. B., 'Rethinking Old French Literature: The Orality of the Octosyllabic Couplet', *Romanic Review* 77 (1986), 307–21.

'Orality, Literacy and the Early Tristan Material: Béroul, Thomas, Marie de France', *Romanic Review* 78 (1987), 299–310.

'Chrétien de Troyes: clerc ou ménestrel? Problèmes des traditions orale et littéraire dans les Cours de France au XIIe siècle', *Poétique* 21 (1990), 21–42.

Walter, P., *Canicule: essai de mythologie sur 'Yvain' de Chrétien de Troyes*, Paris, 1988.

La mémoire du temps: Fêtes et calendriers de Chrétien de Troyes à 'La Mort Artu', Paris and Geneva, 1989.

Le gant de verre: le mythe de Tristan et Yseut, La Gacilly, 1990.

Walters, L., 'Le rôle du scribe dans l'organisation des manuscrits des romans de Chrétien de Troyes', *Romania* 106 (1985), 303–25.

'The Creation of a "Super-Romance": Paris, Bibliothèque Nationale, fonds français, MS 1433', *The Arthurian Yearbook* 1 (1991), 3–25.

Woledge, B., *Commentaire sur 'Yvain' ('Le chevalier au lion') de Chrétien de Troyes*, 2 vols, Geneva, 1986–8.

Wolfzettel, F., 'Zum Stand und Problem der Intertextualitätsforschung im Mittelalter (aus romanistischer Sicht)', in *Artusroman und Intertextualität*, edited by Friedrich Wolfzettel, Gießen, 1990, pp. 1–17.

Zumthor, P., *Essai de poétique médiévale*, Paris, 1972.

La poésie et la voix dans la civilisation médiévale, Paris, 1984.

Index

The index of the original German edition was divided into three different categories (names, subjects, and titles) with copious referrals between its various sections. The present index has been recast in a single alphabetical sequence, but its contents are those of the original. There are a small number of additional headwords and some further references for existing entries, introduced mainly for the sake of consistency or to remove ambiguities occasioned by the change of language. In the process of translation all the original references were verified in the German edition, and this allowed the correction of the very few typographical errors that came to light. There are no omissions. The only systematic change to the contents (as opposed to the form) is in the cross-referencing between authors and their works, where the relevant information is given as a useful guide regardless of whether there are corresponding entries in the index itself. The names of individuals and the titles of literary works have been standardized to correspond to the forms adopted in the English text.

Index

CAMBRIDGE STUDIES IN MEDIEVAL LITERATURE

1 Robin Kirkpatrick *Dante's Inferno: Difficulty and Dead Poetry*
2 Jeremy Tambling *Dante and Difference: Writing in the 'Commedia'*
3 Simon Gaunt *Troubadours and Irony*
4 Wendy Scrase *'Piers Plowman' and the New Anticlericalism*
5 Joseph Duggan *The 'Cantar De Mio Cid': Poetic Creation in its Economic and Social Contexts*
6 Roderick Beaton *The Medieval Greek Romance*
7 Kathryn Kerby-Fulton *Reformist Apocalypticism and 'Piers Plowman'*
8 Alison Morgan *Dante & the Medieval Other World*
9 Eckehard Simon (ed.) *The Theatre of Medieval Europe: New Research in Early Drama*
10 Mary Carruthers *The Book of Memory: A Study of Memory in Medieval Culture*
11 Rita Copeland *Rhetoric, Hermeneutics and Translation in the Middle Ages: Academic Traditions and Vernacular Texts*
12 Donald Maddox *The Arthurian Romances of Chrétien de Troyes: Once and Future Fictions*
13 Nicholas Watson *Richard Rolle and the Invention of Authority*
14 Steven F. Kruger *Dreaming in the Middle Ages*
15 Barbara Nolan *Chaucer and the Tradition of the 'Roman Antique'*
16 Sylvia Huot *The 'Romance of the Rose' and its Medieval Readers: Interpretations, Reception, Manuscript Transmission*
17 Carol M. Meale (ed.) *Women and Literature in Britain, 1150–1500*
18 Henry Ansgar Kelly *Ideas and Forms of Tragedy from Aristotle to the Middle Ages*
19 Martin Irvine *The Making of Textual Culture: Grammatica and Literary Theory, 350–1100*
20 Larry Scanlon *Narrative, Authority and Power: The Medieval Exemplum and the Chaucerian Tradition*
21 Erik Kooper *Medieval Dutch Literature in its European Context*
22 Steven Botterill *Dante and the Mystical Tradition: Bernard of Clairvaux in the 'Commedia'*
23 Peter Biller and Anne Hudson (ed.) *Heresy and Literacy, 1000–1530*
24 Christopher Baswell *Virgil in Medieval England: Figuring the 'Aeneid' from the Twelfth Century to Chaucer*
25 James Simpson *Sciences and Self in Medieval Poetry: Alan of Lille's Anticlaudianus' and John Gower's 'Confessio Amantis'*
26 Joyce Coleman *Public Reading and the Reading Public in Late Medieval England and France*
27 Suzanne Reynolds *Medieval Reading: Grammar, Rhetoric and the Classical Text*
28 Charlotte Brewer *Editing 'Piers Plowman': The Evolution of the Text*
29 Walter Haug *Vernacular Literary Theory in the Middle Ages: The German Tradition in its European Context*
30 Sarah Spence *Texts and the Self in the Twelfth Century*
31 Edwin Craun *Lies, Slander and Obscenity in Medieval English Literature: Pastoral Rhetoric and the Deviant Speaker*
32 Patricia E. Grieve *'Floire and Blancheflor' and the European Romance*
33 Huw Pryce (ed.) *Literacy in Medieval Celtic Societies*
34 Mary Carruthers *The Craft of Thought: Meditation, Rhetoric, and the Making of Images, 400–1200*
35 Beate Schmolke-Hasselmann *The Evolution of Arthurian Romance: The Verse Tradition from Chrétien to Froissart*

For EU product safety concerns, contact us at Calle de José Abascal, 56–1°, 28003 Madrid, Spain or eugpsr@cambridge.org.

www.ingramcontent.com/pod-product-compliance
Ingram Content Group UK Ltd.
Pitfield, Milton Keynes, MK11 3LW, UK
UKHW042143130625
459647UK00011B/1164
9780521025652